FIRST FOR THE UNION

FIRST FOR THE UNION

*Life and Death in a Civil War Army Corps
from Antietam to Gettysburg*

DARIN WIPPERMAN

STACKPOLE
BOOKS

Guilford, Connecticut

Published by Stackpole Books
An imprint of The Rowman & Littlefield Publishing Group, Inc.
4501 Forbes Blvd., Ste. 200
Lanham, MD 20706
www.rowman.com

Distributed by NATIONAL BOOK NETWORK

British Library Cataloguing in Publication Information available

Library of Congress Control Number: 2020942154

ISBN 978-0-8117-3963-4 (cloth : alk. paper)
ISBN 978-0-8117-6965-5 (electronic)

∞™ The paper used in this publication meets the minimum requirements of American National Standard for Information Sciences—Permanence of Paper for Printed Library Materials, ANSI/ NISO Z39.48-1992.

*Dedicated to those who gave their lives for the United States
while serving in the First Corps, Army of the Potomac, 1862–1864*

No one but a soldier knows what hard times are.
—EDWARD HENDRICK, 6TH WISCONSIN INFANTRY, 1862

CONTENTS

List of Maps

Acknowledgments

Much solitary time awaits those pursuing the truths of the past. Yet, no historian can rightfully work in a vacuum. Many other people made this book possible, and I owe them profuse thanks.

My wife, Jan, was highly supportive of the efforts that resulted in this book, from the very early research stages many years ago to the finished product. With a careful eye for the right word and an ability to keep me motivated, Jan worked very hard to help me. She also served as a highly capable research assistant on several trips. The exhausting task of finishing a book on Civil War history would not have happened in this case without her help.

Governments and libraries have done a tremendous job retaining Civil War records. I found a gold mine on every visit to locations in Maine, Massachusetts, New Hampshire, Vermont, New York, Pennsylvania, and Washington, DC. The staff in all of these institutions were always helpful and highly knowledgeable about their collections. Additionally, public servants have led the way in the internet research revolution, with the continued digitization of old materials. An excellent example is the recent online posting of George McClellan's papers by the Library of Congress (LOC). The LOC also retains many excellent primary sources that were invaluable to me.

Thanks to institutions and individuals, most of the old books I consulted were posted online. Thus, countless hours from people I will never know were central to my project. The amount of labor such hard work saves historians cannot be calculated due to the sheer extent of the help electronic files provide.

I enjoyed several trips to the Rauner Library at Dartmouth College. The Antietam Collection offered an array of insights about the campaign that unfolded in Maryland in September 1862. Each day trip there offered compelling stories, exceeding my high expectations of the collection's merit. No person can truly know the Antietam campaign and the men who fought in Maryland without time studying Dartmouth's collection.

In the early part of my research, Ted Alexander at Antietam National Battlefield talked to me several times about my project. He took an interest in my work from the start, and I benefited from his expertise as I examined letters and other documents at the battlefield library. Ted retired after I concluded my research at Antietam, and I sadly learned of his death as this book was being finalized. I wish to thank him for his long devotion to Civil War history.

The immense profundity in the words of Civil War soldiers themselves made my manuscript real. I was constantly enlightened with the insights the original letters offered. Their service and sacrifice humble and amaze me every day.

Legendary Civil War cartographer Hal Jesperson created seven excellent maps that really help show the movement of troops. Such visuals are vital to books about the conflict. Hal does a terrific job working with authors and making suggestions on how cartographic images can best make an author's words clarify points for readers. Hal cannot be thanked enough for how much he has done across the years to make Civil War history clearer to historians and the public.

Dave Reisch at Stackpole showed immense confidence in me from the very beginning. The company's long appreciation of Civil War history has been exceptional, and Stackpole greatly honored me with the decision to publish this book. Dave's ability to outline the company's process for me was a terrific boost to my labors on the manuscript. Stephanie Otto and Meredith Dias also expertly guided me through the process of turning a manuscript into a book. I also must thank Joshua Rosenberg, who completed an excellent copy edit of the manuscript.

Although I was helped greatly by so many others, any errors in this book are my responsibility alone.

Preface

Change came frequently to the U.S. Army of the Potomac during the Civil War. Soldiers in the ranks likely expected further modifications with the arrival of the nation's new general-in-chief, Ulysses S. Grant, in March 1864. After the losses sustained at the battle of Gettysburg the previous July, the army definitely needed to consolidate. Grant's ascendancy guaranteed new attempts to destroy the Confederacy. Robert E. Lee's weary Army of Northern Virginia remained a determined foe. Union leadership had to consider ways to make their principal Eastern army more efficient. This signaled the end of a superb infantry corps.

The First Corps, Army of the Potomac, originally formed in March 1862. Given different designations twice before Second Bull Run in August, the unit would become the First Corps again after Lee's army invaded Maryland that September. Across blood-soaked fields, the First Corps was called on to spearhead assaults, or sacrifice itself to defend the small town of Gettysburg. This they did, and so much more.

The First Corps included great soldiers, but this book's goal is not to suggest they were the best warriors the country has ever seen. There were incompetent officers in the corps, as well as cowards and those who lacked the desire to fight for their country. At least one of their number was executed for not just desertion, but treason. Evidence existed that he had fought for the Confederacy after running away from the Union army. Nonetheless, First Corps troops were first for the Union in important respects. They were the first infantry to engage at Antietam and Gettysburg, two pivotal battles not just of the country's bloodiest war, but also the history of the world. Men in the First Corps earned a glorious record through tremendous loss. When disbandment came in March 1864, the First Corps included the Union regiment suffering the highest percentage loss at Antietam, the war's bloodiest day, and the regiments ranking first and second in total casualties at Gettysburg, the war's costliest battle.

Maj. Gen. John Newton, the last commander of the First Corps, felt sorrow when orders were issued to end such a hallowed organizational identity. Newton, who assumed command at Gettysburg, honored his men with these words on March 25, 1864.

> *Identified by its services with the history of the war, the First Corps gave at Gettysburg a crowning proof of valor and endurance, in saving from the grasp of the enemy the strong position upon which the battle was fought. The terrible losses suffered by the corps in that conflict attest its supreme devotion to the country. Though the corps has lost its distinctive name by the present changes, history will not be silent upon the magnitude of its services.*[1]

The First Corps has not been forgotten, but Newton's prediction remains unfulfilled. In Ken Burns's *Civil War*, the opening day's fight at Gettysburg, where the First Corps suffered 6,000 casualties, was mislabeled a "skirmish." And an award-winning historian suggests the losses on that day, July 1, 1863, "pale" in comparison to the other two days at Gettysburg, a blatantly unjust and factually untrue statement.[2] When revered historians offer such unsupportable opinions, history has been more silent than the patriotism and sacrifice of the First Corps warranted.

This book, the first concentrating solely on the First Corps, will likely stir up some controversy. John Reynolds, martyr for the Union at Gettysburg, will be shown as an overrated general. These pages reinterpret other

After orders disbanding the First Corps were issued, Maj. Gen. John Newton thanked his command for their dedicated soldiering. LIBRARY OF CONGRESS

events in ways that could leave some students of the war wondering if my analysis has plunged off the deep end. Although historical fact remains constant, historians must continually stoke the coals of the past, especially when the topic is as fundamental as the Civil War.

Components of Union armies were constantly in flux because of casualties and leadership changes. Histories of Civil War infantry corps are rare because detailing these organizational changes can make for difficult researching, writing, and reading. This point was made well in a modern history of the Army of the Potomac's Second Corps.[3]

After an overview of how infantry corps originated, this book's introduction will overview the tumultuous initial months of the First Corps. A primary factor in the early history of the corps was the series of disputes between Gen. George McClellan and the Lincoln Administration during the spring and summer of 1862. The bulk of this book then covers eleven months from September 1862 through July 1863, a period in which 14,000 First Corps soldiers were killed, wounded, captured, or missing. The conclusion surveys the time of relative tranquility after Gettysburg, including the fate of several soldiers. With so much heroism and sorrow, I hope readers earn greater appreciation of the First Corps' vital part in preserving the United States as one nation.

Introduction: March–August 1862

CONTENTIOUS BEGINNINGS

A Civil War infantryman's identity was tied primarily to his regiment, the 88th Pennsylvania, for example. A regiment, with about 1,000 men when first organized (one hundred men in each of ten companies), was the basic unit of army organization. Several regiments were linked to form a brigade, ideally commanded by a brigadier general. Infantry divisions included multiple brigades.

A corps was generally the largest infantry unit below an army. Civil War infantry corps, when first created, would include two or more divisions. There was no absolute rule on how many regiments made a brigade, or how many divisions constituted a corps.

An infantry corps was designed to organize and control a large group of men under the head of one senior general. With infantry, cavalry, and artillery together as an independent mini-army, a corps had capabilities to attack and defend as an isolated actor until supporting elements arrived.[1] Napoleon Bonaparte gave infantry corps their first major trial during his wars across Europe. The French tyrant must have been on to something, because corps remain central to the world's armies. The United States would field forty-three infantry corps over the course of the Civil War.[2]

The Army of the Potomac, led since late July 1861 by Maj. Gen. George McClellan, was the Union's principal field army in the war's Eastern Theater. After major disasters at First Bull Run and Ball's Bluff, President Abraham Lincoln's primary land force started 1862 without great confidence. McClellan did not favor a quick strike at the Confederacy. He spent much time planning, rather than fighting, into the early spring.

McClellan held immense pride in the Army of the Potomac. He also had unrestrained confidence in his own abilities. Not yet thirty-five years old when he became the nation's senior officer, McClellan acted as if he had earned the job through divine right. Distrustful of several officers sometimes decades his senior, McClellan generally possessed the admiration of his soldiers. They felt McClellan knew best how to marshal the army and defeat secession. Nicknamed "Little Mac" or "Young Napoleon," McClellan possessed brilliance and charisma deserving respect. Yet, he, like other high-ranking officers, lacked much experience leading men in battle. McClellan's personal confidence had not been gained through his own extensive service in the field.

McClellan rejected notions that unschooled civilians could teach him how to wield the army.[3] Suspicion of anyone controlling his choices can be gleaned in a letter to Simon Cameron, Lincoln's first secretary of war. This letter outlined McClellan's view that he must make all decisions related to army matters. "In organizing the Army of the Potomac," McClellan wrote, "I have selected General and Staff Officers with distinct reference to their fitness for the important duties that may devolve upon them." The general suggested elected leadership might "fatally impair" the Union cause if changes were made to the army without McClellan's consent.[4] Presidents should not lightly discard a commanding general's views on army organization and selection of officers for promotion. Nonetheless, McClellan's demand for control went too far, especially when considering the limited field experience of all of the players.

McClellan might have earned more faith if he had the pluck of Ulysses S. Grant and others in the West who had achieved measurable success by early 1862. Bold commanders elected to move sooner than orders from Washington required; a general advance of all armies was to begin on February 22. By then, Nashville, Tennessee, was near capture after Grant's victories at Forts Henry and Donelson. Meanwhile, "Young Napoleon" claimed his large army was unprepared to move against Confederate forces in Virginia.[5]

Until March, the division was the largest component in the U.S. Army. McClellan was content to wait to establish corps. He justified the delay because he wanted commanders of such large units to learn from the rigors of field service while excelling at the burdens of division command. In his memoirs, McClellan noted the preference "to postpone the formation of army corps until service in the field had indicated what general officers were best fitted to exercise those important commands." McClellan was not wrong to prefer letting time and experience demonstrate the best candidates for corps leadership. "The mistakes of an incompetent division commander may be rectified, but those of a corps commander are likely to be fatal," he suggested.[6] However, if men who had been soldiers when McClellan was born were incapable of serving as corps commanders, why was McClellan entitled to blind faith from the government as the leader of all armies?

President Lincoln differed with McClellan on when corps should be organized, leading to great controversy. On March 8 Lincoln issued President's General War Orders 2 and 3. The directives created four infantry corps in the Army of the Potomac, while prohibiting McClellan from moving before all four corps commanders believed Washington had sufficient troops to be "entirely secure." Some historians have suggested Lincoln made a mistake. They do not argue against corps organization. Rather, they oppose how McClellan was forced into a specific arrangement while deprived of an opportunity to give advice to the president.[7] Some advantage could have been gained in consulting with McClellan before Lincoln issued the orders. Yet, McClellan mistakenly acted as if he was the ultimate boss.

Lincoln did not bear ill will toward the Army of the Potomac's commander, but an army cannot sit as McClellan's did for several months without the president wondering about his general's intentions. Even some Union officers supportive of McClellan understood how an army cannot be idle indefinitely. George Meade, a brigade commander in the First Corps at the time of its birth, respected McClellan. Nonetheless, Meade said, "something must be done. This condition of quiescence, with such enormous expenses, is ruining the country, and, one way or the other, the attempt will have to be made to come to a conclusion."[8]

With lethargy and mistrust prevailing, misfortune for the First Corps began on the day it was conceived. General War Order Number 2 placed Irvin McDowell at the head of the First Corps. McClellan believed McDowell, commander of the army at First Bull Run, had urged corps formation on Lincoln and Stanton.[9] McClellan's hatred of McDowell grew when the First Corps commander opposed McClellan's first plan to strike at Richmond after a move to Urbanna on the Rappahannock River.[10] McDowell's doubts were a slight McClellan could not forget. The original leader of the First Corps was held in contempt by the army's commander, and McClellan could bear grudges with impunity.

While the bureaucracy was arguing with itself, Confederates vacated their defenses around Manassas. When McClellan's soldiers advanced to examine the position, they found "Quaker guns," logs painted to look like cannon. The deceptive wood was in place to give pause to any Union attack. Rufus Dawes of the 6th Wisconsin, who will play a prominent role in the forthcoming pages, noted how men had prepared for battle by writing wills and farewell letters. Pondering the fake cannons, Dawes concluded, "So much for wooden guns."[11]

The flight of Confederates from Manassas prompted a change in the starting point for the army's campaign against Richmond. McClellan would take his men much farther south of Urbanna, using the peninsula between the York and James Rivers after landing the army at Fort Monroe. A directive specifically related to the First Corps would have a major impact on the general's view of the Lincoln Administration. The reborn First Corps would henceforth garner the disrespect and perhaps even the hatred of the army's leader.

The problem resulted from the administration's fear for the safety of Washington, even after the Confederate retreat from Manassas. McClellan believed all four of the new corps would be shipped to the Peninsula, but the Lincoln Administration retained the First Corps in an effort to bolster Washington's defenses. McClellan complained bitterly in a letter to his wife, Nelly, calling the withholding of the First Corps, "the most infamous thing that history has recorded."[12]

Keeping the First Corps near Washington seemed less like an act of military necessity than a psychological concern for the safety of the capital. No mass of Confederate troops was poised to strike Washington in the spring of 1862. Even so, McClellan likely would have made poor use of the First Corps on the Peninsula. Rather than strike quickly for Richmond, he entrenched around Yorktown, then waited. Siege preparations began before McClellan was informed of the decision to withhold the First Corps, and the men would not have arrived to augment the army for more than a week.[13]

The Army of the Potomac would spend a frustrating and deadly series of weeks on the Peninsula east of the Confederate capital. Despite all the carnage, the grand scheme to take Richmond from the east failed. During a series of bloody engagements known as the Seven Days, McClellan led the Army of the Potomac away from Richmond. With disease, battle, and retreat severely sapping the army's numbers into August, the men would return north via boats. Other federal units, including remnants of the original First Corps, were in dire need of assistance. Robert E. Lee and his Army of Northern Virginia were about to meet Gen. John Pope and the Union's new Army of Virginia in what would become the Battle of Second Bull Run.[14]

Leaders in Washington viewed assistance from McClellan's army as vital to the Army of Virginia's survival. Unfortunately, McClellan dithered. Even Ethan Rafuse, a historian who wrote an excellent defense of McClellan's generalship, agrees McClellan failed to assist Pope as quickly as necessary. With only a small part of McClellan's army on hand, Pope suffered a bitter defeat at Second Bull Run.[15]

One precious commodity the defeated Northern soldiers would not find was extensive rest. Lee used his victory at Second Bull Run to begin a new campaign north of the Potomac. Reluctantly, Lincoln called on McClellan to rally the Union's troops in the East once again. Regardless of the president's doubts about McClellan's willingness to assist Pope or engage the Confederates, Lincoln correctly knew the soldiers would find renewed purpose under McClellan.

While McClellan sorted through the chaos around Washington, Lee's army moved into Maryland. As September continued, the First Corps, reborn for the looming ordeal, would be called on to assist in pushing back the Confederate invasion. Out of the difficulties of their first few months, the men of the First Corps had a bloody rendezvous with destiny.

OVERVIEW OF ORIGINAL REGIMENTS AND LEADERS

While debate about corps organization and control over military strategy swirled around them into the summer of 1862, the men of the First Corps had been soldiers for several months. With fervent patriotism, those in the original First Corps had joined regiments from across the North.

The original organization of the infantry units in the First Corps is shown in Table Intro.1. While McClellan's army was on the Peninsula, the First Corps received two temporary designations. In April, the corps formed most of the new Department of the Rappahannock. Later, McDowell and his men became the Third Corps in Pope's Army of Virginia.

William Franklin's brief tenure with the First Corps was his command of the First Division. He would never live up to the reputation he gained at West Point, where he graduated first in the Class of 1843. Even when Franklin rose to command a corps, and then the Left Grand Division (two corps) at Fredericksburg, his cautious Civil War actions exhibited poor leadership very costly to the army.[16]

Franklin's Division included regiments attached to the First Corps for a short time; the division would go to the Peninsula later in the spring, then become part of the Sixth Corps under Franklin. Nonetheless, the original First Corps could boast of including Gen. Philip Kearny, the esteemed leader of a New Jersey brigade. He would be killed in action at Chantilly, Virginia, at the end of the Second Bull Run campaign. Another original First Division officer, John Newton, started his career with the corps leading the Third Brigade of the First Division.

Table Intro.1: The Original First Corps, March 1862

Corps Commander—Maj. Gen. Irvin McDowell		
1st Division **Brig. Gen. William Franklin**	**2nd Division** **Brig. Gen. George McCall**	**3rd Division** **Brig. Gen. Rufus King**
1st Brigade *Brig. Gen. Philip Kearny* 1st New Jersey 2nd New Jersey 3rd New Jersey 4th New Jersey	*1st Brigade* *Brig. Gen. John Reynolds* 1st Pennsylvania Reserves 2nd Pennsylvania Reserves 5th Pennsylvania Reserves 8th Pennsylvania Reserves	*1st Brigade* *Brig. Gen. Christopher* *Augur* 22nd New York 24th New York 30th New York 14th Brooklyn
2nd Brigade *Brig. Gen. Henry Slocum* 16th New York 27th New York 5th Maine 96th Pennsylvania	*2nd Brigade* *Brig. Gen. George Meade* 3rd Pennsylvania Reserves 4th Pennsylvania Reserves 7th Pennsylvania Reserves 11th Pennsylvania Reserves	*2nd Brigade* *Brig. Gen. James Wads-* *worth* 21st New York 23rd New York 35th New York 80th New York
3rd Brigade *Brig. Gen. John Newton* 18th New York 31st New York 32nd New York 95th Pennsylvania	*3rd Brigade* *Brig. Gen. Edward Ord* 6th Pennsylvania Reserves 9th Pennsylvania Reserves 10th Pennsylvania Reserves 12th Pennsylvania Reserves 13th Pennsylvania Reserves	*3rd Brigade* *Col. Lysander Cutler* 2nd Wisconsin 6th Wisconsin 7th Wisconsin 19th Indiana

Source: Official Records, Vol. 5, I, 21.

In June 1862, the bulk of the Second Division was detached from McDowell to join McClellan on the Peninsula. The unit, known as the Pennsylvania Reserves, would earn one of the best reputations of any division during the war. Recruited from across the Keystone State, the division was known as "Reserves" thanks to the patriotic ardor sweeping Pennsylvania after the Confederate attack on Fort Sumter in April 1861. Nationwide, President Lincoln called for 75,000 volunteers. Thousands of Pennsylvanians came forward in excess of the state's quota. By mid-May, the state organized many of these surplus volunteers into thirteen infantry regiments that could enter state or federal service depending on the needs of a given moment.

John Reynolds led the First Brigade of the Reserves. After graduating in the middle of the 1841 West Point class, Reynolds served in the war with Mexico and in various locations prior to the Civil War. Shortly after Lincoln's election, Reynolds expressed hope for moderation from both North and South to ensure a peaceful resolution of sectional animosity.[17] Reynolds was a warrior who preferred not to shed the blood of his countrymen.

Reynolds was commandant of cadets at West Point when the Civil War started. He became a prisoner on the Peninsula, then was exchanged in time to return to the army at Second Bull Run. As McClellan took the reorganized Army of the Potomac into Maryland, Reynolds would lead the entire division of Pennsylvania Reserves, who would once again be part of the First Corps.[18]

George Meade headed the Second Brigade of the Reserves. Born to American parents in Spain, Meade was a career army officer, graduating near the top third in the West Point Class of 1835.[19] A steady commander and stern disciplinarian, Meade, who would lead the Army of the Potomac from Gettysburg onward, was the kind of general armies need, even if men in the ranks might sometimes lament Meade's brusque demeanor.

Details on the origins of some Reserve units provide examples of how regiments, the backbone of Civil War armies, were formed. An enlistee was recruited into a company, which assembled in camps with large numbers of other men who signed up during the federal government's call for volunteers. North of Philadelphia, in the town of Easton, companies were grouped into what would become the Second, Third, and Fourth Reserves.

In addition to drill and receiving necessary supplies and equipment, the proud new soldiers in Easton were visited by generals and Governor Andrew Curtin. As the military situation in Virginia was beginning to heat up in July, the Fourth, and then the Third Reserves were ordered to Harrisburg, the state capital. Last to depart, the Second Reserves shipped out of Easton on the 24th, three days after the Union defeat at First Bull Run.[20]

Rufus King, not fated for extended war service due to poor health, headed the original Third Division of the First Corps. A native of New York City, King graduated fourth out of forty-three cadets in the West Point Class of 1833. He had a diverse career after leaving the army three years later. Early in his administration, Lincoln appointed King to a diplomatic post in the Papal States. He resigned in August 1861 as the Civil War began in earnest.[21]

Gen. James Wadsworth led King's Second Brigade. A man of immense wealth and compassion, Wadsworth made up for his lack of military training through an intense devotion to the welfare of his men. His first period of service to the corps would be brief, because Wadsworth became military governor of Washington in early 1862. He would be central to Lincoln's decision to retain the First Corps near the capital in early April. Later in the year, the self-taught general lost the governor's race in his home state of New York.[22]

The Third Division's Third Brigade included four regiments King helped organize. Temporarily commanded by Lysander Cutler, the first colonel of one of the brigade's regiments, the hardy men would be the only all-Western (one would say "all-Midwestern" today) brigade in the Army of the Potomac. The 2nd, 6th, and 7th Wisconsin, and the 19th Indiana were destined for some of the hottest spots of the war. Before being known as the Iron Brigade, the Westerners were often referred to as the Black Hats.

Brawner Farm gave the brigade their first major taste of combat. The engagement, which opened the fighting at Second Bull Run on August 28, 1862, was quite a baptism by fire. In a battle with a limited number of men involved, Brawner Farm had devastating consequences, with more than one in three men engaged listed as a casualty.[23]

The First Corps, which would end up sacrificing so much, undoubtedly offered "some exceptionally good material," as the war's most famous casualty counter wrote.[24] A letter one member of the 7th Pennsylvania Reserves penned more than thirty years after his regiment was created provides an example of the intense devotion to country men could exemplify. Before the war, Griffen Lewis Baldwin, a sergeant in Company K, remembered proudly casting votes, including a presidential ballot for Abraham Lincoln in 1860.

Knowing how Lincoln's election led to the war in which he fought, Baldwin connected the North's determination to resist Southern domination of the national government to something much greater than the preservation of the United States.

How sincerely I believe the hosts of Israel never fought the battles of the Lord, nor a cause more sacred than did we. How thankful I am that, when that great struggle for free government came, I was a young man in full vigor, and that, unselfishly, I went to do my little best for the cause of humanity.[25]

To gain independence, the Confederacy had to defeat Griffen Baldwin and hundreds of thousands more like him in the First Corps and all other units of the U.S. Army. Perhaps that was the ultimate reason why the Rebel cause met doom.

PART ONE

Defending Maryland

SEPTEMBER–OCTOBER 1862

Death the Reaper must have mowed them down in swaths.
—CAPT. GEORGE NOYES OF GENERAL DOUBLEDAY'S STAFF

REST AMID MAJOR CHANGE

Historians would have a difficult time overstating the sense of panic gripping Washington, DC, after the Confederate victory against John Pope's Army of Virginia at Second Bull Run. The feeling of despondency did not improve on August 31 when Pope informed Henry Halleck, the U.S. Army's general-in-chief, "I should like to know whether you feel secure about Washington should this army be destroyed." Fear was so rampant, President Lincoln ordered all government employees in the city armed and organized to defend the capital. To the west, retreating as part of Pope's defeated army, Robert Taggart, 9th Pennsylvania Reserves, captured the anguish gripping soldiers in blue, "The battle of yesterday was to us a disaster without a doubt."[1]

On paper, the First Corps would not be reborn until soldiers in the command had already taken many steps in Maryland on the hunt for Lee's army. The men were still officially designated as the Third Corps, Army of Virginia until September 12. The movement of the corps toward intense fighting in Maryland is vital to understanding how a defeated group of men quickly gelled into the solid fighting force that would inflict massive casualties on the Confederates.

Per General Orders Number 12, issued on September 2, the Third Corps, Army of Virginia, marched on several roads to destinations closer to Washington than corps headquarters at Fairfax Court House. Then, as Lee moved north to Maryland and away from Washington's fortifications, the defeated

Union troops settled in for a few days of rest, sorely needed after a summer of intense marching and fighting.[2]

Some rallying remnants of the once and future First Corps found their way to Upton's Hill, Virginia, slightly more than 5 miles west of the White House in Washington. George McClellan, given command of the defenses around the national capital, arrived at Upton's Hill on September 2, where he wrote Halleck. He noted the arrival of men from the divisions of King and Ricketts. McClellan basked in the strong support the fighting men gave him after they were informed of being free from the yoke of Pope's incompetent leadership. McClellan knew—thanks to a note from his best friend in the army, Gen. Fitz John Porter—of Lee's apparent intention not to attack Washington. Lee's forces had yet to head to Maryland as a body, but signs portended a new campaign.[3]

The suffering soldiers used days of relative calm to recuperate from the immense trials earlier in the summer. The Second Bull Run debacle would try the fortitude of the most stalwart patriot. Along a portion of the corps' encampment on September 3, Archibald Penny, 9th New York State Militia (also known as the 83rd New York), wrote his mother, "I have not had a night's rest for 17 days."[4]

Uberto Burnham, in the 76th New York, Doubleday's Brigade, also understood the difficulties war created. In a September 6 letter from Upton's Hill, he recapped the trying summer. His brother was unhurt, and, "We hope to live to see you all again," Burnham wrote. "Things look rather dark now but I trust that the black clouds will soon go away and leave the future bright and clear," he continued. In his immediate future, Burnham merely hoped for bare necessities, "A little soap and water and a little rest will make us all right again."[5]

Basic human needs occupied the mind of another New York soldier. In a letter to a family member, he wrote, "You ought to see me now, you'd swear I was no relation of yours." Listing the dreadful state of his belongings, the writer mentioned "an apology for a coat" and "two very dirty shirts" along with other garments in abysmal condition. He had no other personal effects, because, like hundreds of other men, the soldier lost his knapsack during Second Bull Run.

The determined man continued with a plea for the family not to worry. "I'm happy as a king," the proud soldier informed them, adding, "Supplies are on the way to us. I intend to do my duty, and if I fall it's all right, but I'd like to see the end of it."

The letter concluded with an example of the difficulty soldiers had in finding sufficient food, especially when on the march. Mentioning a comrade, the writer added, "he is now washing out his tin cup; says he had a grand stew for dinner—crackers and water."[6]

Transformation of the army occurred quite rapidly in early September. A key development was the end of Irvin McDowell as corps commander. McDowell's removal from the First Corps was at his own request, as was the convening of a court of inquiry to examine his conduct during Second Bull Run. Although he escaped without censure from the subsequent review of his conduct, McDowell never again held a field command.[7]

Another sign of late summer transition was Special Orders 223, issued on September 5. The order consolidated the Army of Virginia

After a second failure near Bull Run in Virginia, Irvin McDowell, original commander of the First Corps, departed active service at his own request in September 1862. LIBRARY OF CONGRESS

and the Army of the Potomac. McClellan celebrated the news, calling the end of both Pope's command and McDowell's leadership of the First Corps cases of "retributive justice." Clearly, McClellan was on track to command the army that would take the field to counter the Confederate invasion.[8]

In another part of Special Orders 223, Joseph Hooker was slated to become Fifth Corps commander. This order was issued after McClellan began moving elements of the army across its namesake river in response to Lee's northern thrust. For the moment, the men of the once and future First Corps of McClellan's army remained in Virginia.

Halleck did not want the shifts in corps leadership to slow the movement of troops. On September 6, he wrote McClellan, "You need not wait for the change of commanders, but move McDowell's corps at once." Halleck also informed McClellan of Hooker's elevation to the command of the Fifth Corps, with Jesse Reno assigned to McDowell's former command.

McClellan expressed concern that Reno would be taken from the Ninth Corps, which was already heading toward Maryland. He replied, "I would urgently recommend that Hooker be assigned to McDowell's corps. The Secretary [Secretary of War Edwin Stanton] told me he would cheerfully agree to anything of this kind that met your approval." With the consent of his superiors, McClellan made Hooker the commander of the rebuilding First Corps.[9]

Joseph Hooker, a Massachusetts native and grandson of a Revolutionary War officer, graduated in the middle of the 1837 West Point class. He earned accolades in the early part of his army career, including meritorious ser-

Joseph Hooker earned corps command after strong leadership earlier in the war. He took the reborn First Corps into Maryland on the evening of September 6, 1862. LIBRARY OF CONGRESS

vice in Mexico. After heading to California, Hooker resigned from the army in 1853. The years on the West Coast were simply not rewarding for the ambitious man. The war brought Hooker back east, and he quickly gained prominence as an aggressive general officer.[10]

Although there was a basic level of respect between Hooker and McClellan, the two men were not close. McClellan, distrustful and downright disrespectful of many generals not in his inner circle, knew what was good for the army in this case. No one could doubt Hooker's strong offensive mindset, and he certainly knew how to lead men in battle.[11]

Table 1.1: The Reborn First Corps, in the Early Phase of the Maryland Campaign, September 1862

Corps Commander—Maj. Gen. Joseph Hooker		
1st Division *Brig. Gen. Rufus King*	*2nd Division* *Brig. Gen. James Ricketts*	*3rd Division* *Brig. Gen. John Reynolds*
1st Brigade Col. Walter Phelps Jr. 22nd New York 24th New York 30th New York 14th Brooklyn 2nd USSS	*1st Brigade* Brig. Gen. Abram Duryée 97th New York 104th New York 105th New York 107th Pennsylvania	*1st Brigade* Brig. Gen. Truman Seymour 1st Pennsylvania Reserves 2nd Pennsylvania Reserves 5th Pennsylvania Reserves 6th Pennsylvania Reserves 13th Pennsylvania Reserves
2nd Brigade Brig. Gen. Abner Doubleday 7th Indiana 76th New York 95th New York 56th Pennsylvania	*2nd Brigade* Col. William Christian 26th New York 94th New York 88th Pennsylvania 90th Pennsylvania	*2nd Brigade* Brig. Gen. George Meade 3rd Pennsylvania Reserves 4th Pennsylvania Reserves 7th Pennsylvania Reserves 8th Pennsylvania Reserves
3rd Brigade Gen. Marsena Patrick 21st New York 23rd New York 35th New York 80th New York	*3rd Brigade* Brig. Gen. George Hartsuff 12th Massachusetts 13th Massachusetts 83rd New York 11th Pennsylvania 16th Maine	*3rd Brigade* Col. Thomas Gallagher 9th Pennsylvania Reserves 10th Pennsylvania Reserves 11th Pennsylvania Reserves 12th Pennsylvania Reserves
4th Brigade Brig. Gen. John Gibbon 2nd Wisconsin 6th Wisconsin 7th Wisconsin 19th Indiana	*2nd Division Artillery* Battery F, 1st Pennsylvania Light Battery C, 1st Pennsylvania	*3rd Division Artillery* Batteries A and B, 1st Pennsylvania Light Battery C, 5th U.S.
1st Division Artillery 1st New Hampshire Battery Battery D, 1st Rhode Island Light Battery L, 1st New York Light Battery B, 4th U.S.		

Source: Official Records, Vol. 19, I, 170–72.

REBIRTH ON THE MARCH

Thanks to the devotion to the cause held by the rallying soldiers on the Virginia side of the Potomac, the First Corps—for the first time—was about to become central to the military fortunes of the Union. The reborn unit was dramatically different from the initial organization six months before. Several regiments were added and subtracted. Additionally, men returning to the First Corps were often under new leadership when the chase of the Confederate army began. Table 1.1 displays the organization of the corps near the beginning of the Antietam campaign.

Rufus King was the only one of the original First Corps division commanders with the same role at the start of September 1862. King's men were now the First Division, rather than the Third. The division commander would not fill his position for long. Plagued by seizures, King would give up his command on September 14. Health issues did not terminate his military service, but King's assignment to the First Corps was over.[12]

John Hatch took command of King's Division. He had served in the role in an acting capacity in the Second Bull Run campaign during King's previous spells of ill health. Hatch graduated from West Point at a fateful time, immediately before the Mexican-American War. He won multiple brevet promotions, served in a variety of posts across Oregon, California, Kansas, and New Mexico, then rose to the permanent rank of captain shortly before the start of the Civil War. He was a commander of cavalry during Second Bull Run, but conflict with Pope led to a demotion. He would be wounded on August 30.[13]

Still in the division, Hatch's former brigade was given to Col. Walter Phelps, who was not yet thirty years old. Phelps started the war as colonel of the 22nd New York, one of the regiments originally under Hatch. Other regiments in the brigade included the same New York units from the original First Corps outfit, with the addition of the 2nd United States Sharpshooters (USSS). Eight companies constituted the unit. The first three came from Minnesota, Michigan, and Pennsylvania. The remaining five companies hailed from northern New England: one from Maine, and two each from New Hampshire and Vermont. To become a sharpshooter, a soldier was required to place ten consecutive shots no more than 5 inches from the center of a bull's-eye—from a distance of 600 feet.[14]

The sharpshooters were armed with the Sharps Rifle. The outstanding weapon had a great reputation, due to loading at the breech rather than down the muzzle, which gave a soldier a rapid rate of fire. Vermonter Curtis

Abbott noted the sharpshooters were promised a unique role in the army. He explained how he and his comrades worked in "a special line of service with many immunities from the drudgery of the infantry soldier." He accurately deemed the Sharps Rifle as "exceeding any firearm then in use."[15]

The Maine men of the 2nd USSS, who would form Company D, were sought after by Hiram Berdan, the organizer of the army's two sharpshooter regiments. At the end of August 1861, Berdan wrote Governor Israel Washburn about his interest in having some of Maine's boys join the ranks. Three weeks later, Washburn received another letter from one of Berdan's officers at Weehawken, New Jersey, the training camp for the unit. The governor was informed Berdan "shall be greatly obliged to you if you will expedite the organization of your company." The officer concluded, "A post of honor awaits them."

A competent and respected officer, John Hatch led the First Division of the First Corps at the start of the Antietam campaign. LIBRARY OF CONGRESS

Meeting Berdan's strict marksmanship test proved difficult, even in a state like Maine, which included many men familiar with rifles. Washburn received a letter later in September from one officer who did not yet have a single recruit. Jacob McClure, a future commander of Company D, had more luck. By the second half of October, he reported twenty enlistees. McClure predicted his men would be "a better company than ever left New England."[16] On November 13, the Maine marksmen departed the state to join Berdan.

The eight companies of sharpshooters became part of the First Corps a few weeks after McDowell's command was first organized in March 1862. During the campaign in Maryland, Col. Henry Post, a New Yorker, commanded the excellent soldiers.

Brig. Gen. Abner Doubleday led the Second Brigade in King's Division. The native of New York seemed destined for life as a soldier, with several of his ancestors having served in the American Revolution, while his father was a veteran of the War of 1812. Doubleday graduated slightly higher than the middle rank of West Point's Class of 1842. His service included assignment at Fort Sumter in South Carolina during the bombardment starting the Civil War.[17]

The gruff Marsena Patrick led four New York regiments in the division's Third Brigade. Patrick graduated forty-eighth out of fifty-six in the same West Point class as George Meade. He fought in Florida and Mexico in his early career. Resigning from the army in 1850, Patrick worked in railroads and as a farmer, becoming president of the New York State Agriculture College in 1859.

One soldier suggested Patrick was "a brave stern old warrior, who like Stonewall Jackson, could either fight or pray as occasion required." The brigade commander often disrespected other officers, and he was a difficult man to like. Seeing such a strong disciplinarian, McClellan would make Patrick the army's provost marshal in early October. Thus, his stint with the First Corps was brief.[18]

At the rebirth of the First Corps, the Iron Brigade found itself as the Fourth Brigade in King's Division. Brig. Gen. John Gibbon received command of the Western men earlier in the summer. A Pennsylvania native raised in North Carolina, Gibbon had three brothers and other family members in the Confederate army. The author of an artillery tactics manual, Gibbon commanded Battery B, Fourth U.S. Artillery, when the war began. Although the professional soldier had a difficult time winning the respect of the independent Western volunteers, Gibbon was a capable officer.[19]

A brave warrior commanded Hooker's Second Division. Brig. Gen. James Ricketts, born in New York City, a nephew-in-law of former U.S. president Franklin Pierce, stood in the middle of the West Point Class of 1839. With years as a competent soldier behind him, Ricketts was seriously injured while commanding a battery at First Bull Run, where he was also taken prisoner. As a division commander under McDowell, Ricketts performed important service during the summer of 1862.[20]

History offers some strange connections between people and events. A New York mahogany merchant rising to general and leading men in battle is one of those unexpected developments. Abram Duryée may not have had the profession expected of a soldier, but he certainly played the part well.

A photo of the 26th New York infantry early in the war. LIBRARY OF CONGRESS

Starting his military career in the state militia, by 1849 Duryée was a lieutenant colonel in New York's service, where he "evinced much industry, and great military and executive ability."[21] Duryée's First Brigade in Ricketts's Division included the 97th, 104th, and 105th New York and 107th Pennsylvania.

The Second Bull Run campaign was deeply injurious to Union fortunes. One group of soldiers, who would be the Second Brigade, Second Division of the reorganized First Corps, especially suffered due to the loss of a great leader. Brig. Gen. Zealous Tower sustained a serious wound while leading his men in the desperate fight on the afternoon of August 30. The brigade included a duo of regiments from two states: the 26th and 94th New York, along with the 88th and 90th Pennsylvania. Col. William Christian, the brigade's new leader, was the first colonel of the 26th, which organized in Elmira for two years of service. The brigade suffered heavily at Second Bull Run.[22]

The men in the brigade of Brig. Gen. George Hartsuff also endured heavy action in August. Hartsuff graduated from West Point in 1852. After a short time in Texas, he served against Seminoles in Florida, where he suffered multiple wounds. Shortly before the war, he survived a steamer wreck on Lake Michigan, valiantly ensuring passengers found lifeboats.[23]

Hartsuff's regiments were as tough as their leader. Four states were represented by the five units: the 16th Maine, the 12th and 13th Massachusetts, 9th New York State Militia (83rd New York), and 11th Pennsylvania.

Hartsuff's Pennsylvanians were the longest-tenured regiment from the state during the war. Initially a three-month unit, the 11th Pennsylvania trained at Camp Curtin in Harrisburg in the spring of 1861. After some action over the summer, the regiment reenlisted for three years back at Camp Curtin. Richard "Fighting Dick" Coulter served as a senior officer in the regiment throughout the war.[24]

Rejoining McDowell's command after returning from the Peninsula, the Pennsylvania Reserves became the Third Division of the reborn First Corps. The Keystone Staters were smarting from their summer of extensive action. Reynolds took over the command, which had suffered 3,000 casualties on the Peninsula. Many Reserves were captured in action during those dark days.

Even after their travails, the Pennsylvania Reserves had plenty of fight left. Confiding to his wife, Second Brigade commander George Meade correctly said the entire division was "particularly distinguished" on the last day of Second Bull Run. Such valor requires a human cost; Meade suggested the Reserves were "pretty well used up" and in need of reorganization and new recruits.[25]

As the Maryland campaign began, Brig. Gen. Truman Seymour and Col. Thomas Gallagher joined Meade as the division's brigade commanders. Regiments of the Reserves were shuffled a bit across the three brigades, so the grouping of units did not exactly match their original organization.

Seymour's First Brigade now included the 1st, 2nd, 5th, 6th, and 13th Reserves. Their commander finished in the top third of the West Point Class of 1846, perhaps the most famous in the history of the Academy. Seymour won promotions twice in Mexico and also fought Seminoles in Florida. Fatefully, he was assigned to Charleston Harbor in the early 1860s, so, like Doubleday, he witnessed the war's beginning at Fort Sumter. A gifted painter, Seymour taught drawing at his alma mater in the early 1850s.[26]

Four companies of Seymour's 13th Pennsylvania Reserves earned a special gift while resting outside Washington in September. The excellent regiment had been divided earlier in the year, with six companies heading to the Peninsula with McClellan, while the other four remained north with McDowell and the original First Corps. Members of the 13th Reserves with McClellan received Sharps Rifles earlier in the year. The other four companies of the reunited regiment were provided the fine weapon as the Maryland campaign began.[27]

Henry Glasier, a Bucktail in Company D, described the value of the Sharps Rifle in an August letter. "We have the Best gun in the world now," the soldier wrote. Having such a "splendid" weapon, Glasier added, "We can fire ten Rounds a minit now whare we used to fire five times in two minits."[28]

With their great gun and marksmanship skills, the regiment would gain a prominent role in the war as skirmishers, often the first men of the division who would make contact with the enemy. Known as "Bucktails" because of the critter tails attached to the caps of regimental members, the 13th Reserves wanted the rebels to know expert marksmen were on the prowl.

Brig. Gen. Truman Seymour exhibited strong leadership during the Antietam campaign as the commander of the First Brigade of the Pennsylvania Reserves. LIBRARY OF CONGRESS

Meade's Second Brigade grouped the 3rd, 4th, 7th, and 8th Reserves. "We are in a critical position, but I trust will get out of it," Meade wrote his wife on August 31, as Pope's retreating army was trying to reach Washington's fortifications. The general's frustration was evident in other letters written as the disaster at Bull Run turned into the Maryland campaign. On September 4, Meade noted, "I am quite well, notwithstanding we have been for the last ten days without regular food or sleep."[29]

Gallagher's former regiment, the 11th Reserves, joined the 9th, 10th, and 12th, in the Third Brigade. Gallagher himself rose to the rank of brigadier general in the Pennsylvania militia in the years before the Civil War. He had a firm grasp of military tactics and possessed a demeanor fit for a brigade commander.[30] The First Corps would quickly lose Gallagher's commendable leadership.

The First Corps began the hunt for Lee's army with less than half the strength reported at the end of March. The summer's battle casualties account for only a small portion of the total loss of fighting men. Sickness, straggling, and desertion undoubtedly reduced the First Corps. Hooker was about to set out for Maryland with three divisions totaling 15,000 men present for duty, based on numbers reported on the morning of September 6. Including those who were ill, King's Division accounted for 7,357 men, while Ricketts commanded 5,088. The diminished Reserves had only 4,047 men.[31]

"WE WILL WHIP THEM ALL TO PIECES"

Before beginning their march into Maryland, a man in the 11th Pennsylvania, Hartsuff's Brigade, wrote, "Four days of rest and quiet, short as was the time, told wonderfully upon the looks and spirits of officers and men." A member of Doubleday's staff also noted the importance of the days of recovery on Upton's Hill. The officer wrote, "The wardrobes and weapons of our men were thoroughly renovated; fresh arrivals of convalescents from the hospitals and of stragglers from their wanderings swelled their ranks; abundance of food strengthened them; abundance of sleep rested them; all was made ready for the expected move."[32]

A soldier in the 23rd New York, Patrick's Brigade, expanded on the positive sentiment. The men were still very tired from the ordeals of August, but early September brought food, optimism, the return of McClellan, and a chance at revenge for the thrashings received earlier in the summer. The historian of the 23rd expounded by seeing how determined warriors could overcome difficulties. "The condition of the men at this time was pitiful, but cheered by the reinstatement of their idolized commander, and the prospect of driving the invading army from Maryland, hundreds who could but just drag their bodies along mustered all their remaining strength for the march," the determined warrior wrote.[33]

Henry Glasier did not seem concerned about the impact of the Confederates' move into Maryland. Just before beginning the chase of Lee's army, the member of the 13th Reserves expressed a mindset further demonstrating how the First Corps was prepared to meet the enemy. "I guess when they get over the River it will Bee one of the worst things they ever Done," he wrote, "for when they get their armies sepperated again we will whip them all to pieces."[34]

Starting on the evening of September 6, Hooker's men moved from the Virginia fortifications, crossed the Potomac River via the Long Bridge to Washington, then marched to the Maryland town of Leesborough (now

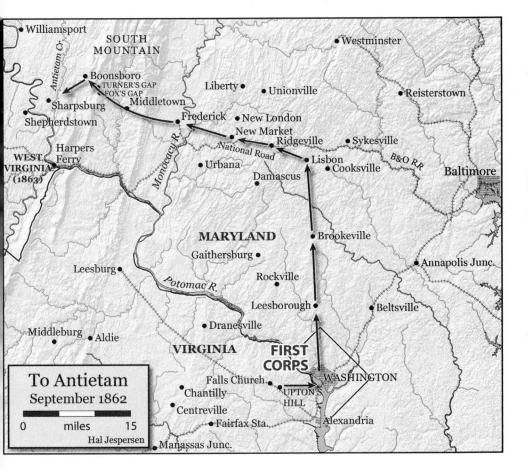

Williamsport

SOUTH
MOUNTAIN

Antietam Cr.

Boonsboro
TURNER'S GAP
FOX'S GAP
Middletown

Sharpsburg

Shepherdstown

Harpers
Ferry

WEST
VIRGINIA
(1863)

Frederick

Monocacy R.

National Road

Urbana

Damascus

Liberty

New London

New Market

Ridgeville

Westminster

Unionville

Reisterstown

Sykesville

Lisbon
Cooksville

B&O R.R.

Baltimore

MARYLAND

Gaithersburg

Rockville

Brookeville

Annapolis Junc.

Leesburg

Potomac R.

Leesborough

Beltsville

Middleburg
Aldie

Dranesville

VIRGINIA

FIRST
CORPS

WASHINGTON

Falls Church

Chantilly

Centreville

Fairfax Sta.

Manassas Junc.

UPTON'S
HILL

Alexandria

To Antietam
September 1862

0   miles   15

Hal Jespersen

known as Wheaton). Pleasant conditions in the overnight period turned oppressive on the 7th. Theodore Gates, commander of the 20th New York State Militia (or 80th New York), in Patrick's Brigade, recalled the difficulty involved in the campaign's first march, a total of about 20 miles. In his regimental history, Gates wrote of "an impenetrable cloud of dust" enveloping the First and Ninth Corps "on that memorable and distressing occasion."[35]

The two corps were the closest Union infantry to Baltimore, a city McClellan and others felt might have been Lee's ultimate target. Regardless of the difficult march, Col. Hugh McNeil and others in the 13th Reserves enjoyed a memorable evening in Leesborough. Roy Stone, a former officer in the regiment now with new troops he raised back home, greeted the Bucktails on the march through Washington. The men were "pretty well worn down" after the difficult trek from Upton's Hill, McNeil wrote. "Although we could ill afford the loss of sleep, in the expectation of a further march at any hour of the night," McNeil noted how Stone spent time conversing with several Bucktails until 11:00 P.M.[36]

After nearly a full day of rest in Leesborough, the march continued. Ambrose Burnside, in command of the army's right wing, reported concerns about the level of straggling in the First Corps. In a 10:00 A.M. dispatch to McClellan on September 8, Burnside declared, "McDowell's old corps is very much demoralized and the road has been filled with its stragglers, but I hope, with Hooker's assistance, to bring them up." Even if notable amounts of straggling plagued the First Corps, the men had a latent energy. They clearly could work hard to put the difficult summer behind them during September's emergency. By early evening on the 8th, even Burnside cheered up. Not long after moving his headquarters to Brookville, about 11 miles north of Leesborough, Burnside wrote, "Our men are in better condition than when they left Washington. Hooker's corps is improving."[37]

The First and Ninth Corps passed through Brookville still heading north. Lisbon, astride the National Road, was reached by the evening of September 11. With three divisions spanning several miles, Hooker was centered a bit west of the halfway point between Baltimore and Frederick. The former city was undoubtedly secure; the latter had just passed four days of rather harmless Confederate occupation. Lee's invaders moved west to continue their aggressive campaign, with the Union garrison at Harpers Ferry ripe for capture. A turn to the west on the National Road would bring the First Corps to Ridgeville (now Mt. Airy) and New Market by September 12.

A modern history of the Maryland campaign correctly suggests McClellan's army did not have widespread morale problems in September 1862.[38] More specifically, in diaries, letters, and regimental histories, soldiers in the First Corps proclaimed their readiness to march and fight to resist Lee's invasion. The words of the soldiers proved Burnside was unkind to report a demoralization problem so early in the march. Men in the corps were not trembling as the Confederate army occupied Union territory. The First Corps had already started their rise to greatness from the ashes of defeat at Second Bull Run.

Curtis Abbott served as a microcosm of his First Corps comrades when he called on an abiding optimism. He suggested Second Bull Run was "far from being disastrous," even though "anything short of victory was appalling." The soldier looked at needed army reorganization as second nature, not the sign of weakness. "The changes went on," he wrote, "while disaster followed disaster. The loyal North bore the test."[39]

Robert Scott, a soldier in Gibbon's Brigade, shared Abbott's sentiment. In a letter published by a Wisconsin newspaper, Scott offered an overview of the Second Bull Run campaign and the prospects for the future. After the retreat to the Washington defenses, circumstances seemed bleak on the surface. Scott even noticed soldiers eating corn laying in the dirt, the slim leftovers after horses had their fill. He remained hopeful, concluding, "though the present seems cloudy, I am firm in the belief that the cause of the Union is yet sound, and has many stout arms to support it."[40]

Edward Barnes, adjutant of the 95th New York, believed the soldiers were ready for another shot at Lee. Acknowledging the reorganization of the army, he suggested it had not "become disorganized or required to be reorganized, so far as the rank and file were concerned, but this department of military science was a specialty of its commander—a faculty to organize soldiers into an army ready to meet the enemy."[41]

During days spent resting or marching through Maryland, several factors promoted the men's renewed faith in the cause of defending the Union. First, Pope was gone and McClellan was back. Colonel McNeil of the 13th Reserves summed up the thinking of many in the First Corps as the Maryland campaign was about to begin. From Upton's Hill, he had written a sister, "We rejoice that we are under McClellan." In his memoir, the observant Rufus Dawes, in the 6th Wisconsin, from Gibbon's Brigade, suggested, "Such a feeling, as that for General McClellan was never aroused for another leader in the war." This sentiment was affirmed by another First Division soldier in the 21st New York. He opined, "No one who saw it can forget the revival of life and hope that stirred our broken ranks" with the announcement of McClellan's continuance as commander.[42]

The lovely countryside and positive reception from the residents of Maryland were additional reasons for growing optimism in the First Corps. A soldier in Duryée's Brigade fondly recalled how the bounty of the land and generous civilians "brought back the memories of home, and the scenes of luxury and comfort appearing on all sides, presented a strange contrast to the barren and wasted fields of Virginia. From many a family group by the wayside, the soldiers were greeted with cheers of welcome and tokens of hospitality, that gave assurance of loyal sympathies and heart-felt prayers for success."[43]

Lyman Holford, in the 6th Wisconsin, was another First Corps man inspired by Maryland's pleasing landscape. In his diary, he wrote, "The appearance of the country here and in Virginia is strikingly different. Instead of weeds as high as a man's head we find corn, potatoes, tobacco, fruit of all kinds and many grain and haystacks."[44]

Even overpriced commodities from sutlers were highly cherished. A man in the 88th Pennsylvania, Christian's Brigade, 2nd Division, wrote, "the hawk-eyed sutler swept down on the bivouac like a bird of prey . . . and the boys esteemed it a privilege to be swindled."

The 13th Massachusetts, in Hartsuff's Brigade, was another regiment receiving the "benefit" of overpriced sutlers' wares. On September 5, a man in the 13th examined the "quantities of canned food, fruits, and other luxuries." He added, "many a belly was fat capon lined" thanks to sutlers. Along with supplies from the army's quartermaster department, the day's goods "succeeded in raising our spirits to a high state of buoyancy."[45]

New recruits buttressed veterans' fortitude. Those joining the ranks were relatively untrained in marching and fighting, but the extra manpower was very necessary after the summer's burdens. While still in Virginia, the 12th Massachusetts, in Hartsuff's Brigade, received twenty-six additional men directly from their home state. The 11th Pennsylvania added fifty new soldiers not long after crossing into Maryland. The 11th's historian noted the recruits served as "a timely addition" to a regiment desperate for more men.[46]

The 16th Maine was an entirely new regiment joining the First Corps on the march. Because the untested unit would be assigned as a railroad guard near Ridgeville, the men of the 16th would miss the battles in Maryland. Recruited in the Pine Tree State over the summer, the 16th Maine arrived in Washington on August 21. They remained in the capital's fortifications through Pope's retreat, then marched north, quickly catching up to Hartsuff's Brigade.[47]

"THE ONLY DOUBTFUL ONES"

Even with important outstanding questions about Lee's numbers and intentions, McClellan oozed confidence on September 12. He knew Lee's army was moving away from Frederick, and he predicted an upcoming battle of epic importance. "I feel sure of one thing now, & that is that my men will fight well," McClellan declared to his wife. He remained uncertain about one element of his army, "The only doubtful ones are McD's old troops, who are in bad condition as to discipline & everything else."

Although the men in the First Corps lacked McClellan's esteem, he had faith in their new commander. McClellan expected Hooker would "bring them out of the kinks, & will make them fight if anyone can."[48]

Regardless of McClellan's dearth of faith in the men McDowell had commanded, circumstances were placing the First Corps in the forefront of Union military planning. Their sacrifice over the five days after being deemed "the only doubtful ones" shows McClellan as a pompous and insolent human being.

Without McClellan's respect, First Corps soldiers kept gaining confidence. Attached to the First Division, a member of the only New Hampshire battery in the army deeply appreciated the kindness of Maryland's citizenry. Houses "looked very inviting," the cannoneer wrote, while each resident "seemed to vie with his neighbor in accommodating us with what food or supplies we wanted and were able to pay for."

Residents of Maryland continued to show their support for the Union troops after the First Corps turned west toward Frederick. The New Hampshire cannoneer was exhilarated because "many of the houses were gaily decked out with flags and streamers, while we were lustily cheered by the people."[49]

Not far north of the celebratory atmosphere, Governor Curtin had no time for patriotic joy. He wired Washington and McClellan several times in early September, pleading for the national army to not forget the fate of Pennsylvania, so close to the action in Maryland. Although he could not persuade Halleck or McClellan to send a detachment of troops from the Army of the Potomac, he requested a senior general to lead Pennsylvania's militia. The First Corps was caught in the middle of this debate.

As leader of the Army of the Potomac, Maj. Gen. George McClellan wrote almost daily to his wife, Nelly. She would be informed that the men in the First Corps were "the only doubtful ones" in McClellan's command. LIBRARY OF CONGRESS

The incident began when Curtin asked for the services of John Reynolds, commander of the Pennsylvania Reserves. The governor had concerns about the effectiveness of the state militia. He knew of the significant number of high-ranking officers from Pennsylvania in national service one state to the south. After informing McClellan of Curtin's request, Halleck at first did not compel Reynolds's sojourn to the Keystone State. He merely asked, on the morning of September 11, if Reynolds could be first sent to Washington prior to heading for Harrisburg.

McClellan lied in his response to the boss, "General Reynolds is now engaged in important service, supporting with his division an attack on New Market." Apparently, he thought informing Halleck of a nonexistent offensive west of Ridgeville was a way to save Reynolds from detached service in Pennsylvania. The army commander showed some surprising respect for the First Corps when he added, Reynolds "has one of the best divisions, and is well acquainted with it. I cannot see how his services can be spared at the present time."

Halleck was unmoved. He quickly ordered Reynolds to Pennsylvania, and McClellan acknowledged compliance with the command. Curtin suggested to McClellan how Reynolds "can do the country great service and of course cooperate fully with you" while in command of Pennsylvania's militia.[50]

Hooker responded with great angst mixed with humor. The First Corps commander illuminated the dark side of his persona after hearing of Halleck's order to send the head of the Pennsylvania Reserves home, even temporarily.

> *I have just been shown an order relieving Brigadier-General Reynolds from the command of a division in my corps. I request that the major-general commanding will not heed this order; a sacred Governor ought not to be permitted to destroy the usefulness of an entire division of the army, on the eve of important operations.*
>
> *General Reynolds commands a division of Pennsylvania troops of not the best character; is well known to them, and I have no officer to fill his place.*
>
> *It is satisfactory to my mind that the rebels have no more intention of going to Harrisburg than they have of going to heaven. It is only in the United States that atrocities like this are entertained.*[51]

Historians often change Hooker's word "sacred" to "scared," assuming he intended to disparage Curtin for his alarm about the safety of Pennsylvania. One wonders, however, if Hooker intended to use "sacred" sarcastically to question Washington's desire to please governors rather than support a field army. Regardless, Hooker was wrong to suggest the usefulness of the division would be destroyed without Reynolds—and in questioning the "character" of the Reserves. More importantly, he ridiculously requested the field commander should reject a direct order from Halleck, the U.S. Army's highest-ranking officer. Hooker used some comedy to question the final destination of the Confederate army and was clearly exaggerating when he called the dispatch of Reynolds to Harrisburg an atrocity.

Meade gained command of the Reserves as a result of Reynolds's reassignment. The grumpy general noted how Reynolds "obeyed the order with alacrity, though very much against his will." Fortified with the satisfaction of division command, Meade concluded, "I am now ready to meet the enemy, for I feel I am in the position I am entitled to. I should have been delighted to have gone to Harrisburg in Reynolds's place, as I have no doubt he will get a large command there."[52]

Promotions continued to fill spaces resulting from Reynolds's departure. Albert Magilton, leading the 4th Reserves, took Meade's place as brigade commander. This gave Maj. John Nyce command of the regiment.

MOVING TOWARD AN UPHILL FIGHT

On September 12, the army's right wing advanced west toward Frederick. The Ninth Corps would have the honor of being the first infantry to enter the city as some elements of the First Corps still had quite a distance to walk on the National Road. Although the Pennsylvania Reserves were close to Frederick, men of Ricketts's Division started the 13th camped around Ridgeville, with tens of thousands of more steps needed to reach the Monocacy River slightly east of town. Of the day's march, Robert Taggart happily wrote, "Passed through New Market. Pleasant looking little town. Display of Union flags and waving of kerchiefs by ladies."

The First Corps would not enter Frederick until the morning of the 14th, while on the way to the campaign's first major infantry battle, along the South Mountain range. The city proved as pleasing to the First Corps as the countryside marched through over the previous week. "Our entry into the city was triumphal," Rufus Dawes wrote, as his 6th Wisconsin led the advance of Gibbon's Brigade. The proud Badger added, "The stars and stripes floated from every building and hung from every window."[53]

Although progress was slow due to the number of troops clogging the city, the reception was simply unforgettable. The 9th New York State Militia's historian noted, "The column passed through amid the plaudits of gaily-dressed women and children, who showered favors upon their country's defenders." The regiment benefited from "substantial creature comforts" residents offered. The support was especially important because, "soldiers are always hungry and thirsty."[54]

In addition to "the wildest enthusiasm" from Frederick's residents, the 23rd New York received a boost when Col. Henry Hoffman returned to command on the 14th. Struggling with sickness for weeks, Hoffman caught up with the 23rd on the march from Washington but was still not feeling well enough to lead until later in the campaign. The determined colonel "was still pale and haggard, and had come out against the advice of his physician."[55]

The strategic picture had become very fascinating. McClellan's possibilities for a grand victory increased when troops of the 12th Corps found a copy of Lee's Special Orders 191 in a field south of Frederick. The document outlined the plan to attack Harpers Ferry with three separate groups of Lee's army, while other troops remained closer to South Mountain west of Frederick. Lee made the choice to invest Harpers Ferry because he wished to continue his campaign. He could not have the thousands of Union troops there manning a major installation along the Confederate supply route.[56]

As the Army of the Potomac moved to seize the three mountain gaps faster than Lee expected, the Confederate army found itself in peril. D. H. Hill commanded Lee's only division in the immediate vicinity, near the area around Turner's Gap and Fox's Gap. Farther south, Franklin's advance could imperil the independent command of Lafayette McLaws, whose brigades were on Maryland Heights as part of the force threatening Harpers Ferry. If pressed by Franklin prior to the capture of the federal garrison, all the troops under McLaws were at risk of capture. As one early historian of the Union army wrote, "This was McClellan's golden opportunity to place his name by the side of Napoleon's."[57]

McClellan celebrated capture of the pieces of paper outlining Confederate planning. He then shrank from the chance to truly hurt Lee's army. Incessant concern about being outnumbered was a constant lament from McClellan. Sticking with his faulty intelligence, McClellan repeated how the Rebels had at least 120,000 men in Maryland. For Scott Hartwig, a historian somewhat supportive of McClellan's progress thus far in the campaign, the pace after discovery of Special Orders 191 was too lethargic for the demands of the moment.[58] McClellan was clearly no Napoleon.

First Corps soldiers had a positive demeanor as they reached the Monocacy. Curtis Abbott noted, "This march had been slow, but on the evening of the 13th . . . rumors of forced marches and approaching battle prevailed." The desire to meet the Rebels again was burning bright for many soldiers. Abbott added, "Our men were in high glee."[59]

Again with the Ninth Corps in the advance, the First Corps marched west early on the 14th in an effort to take Turner's Gap, which the National Road bisected. Troops of the First Corps continued traversing beautiful countryside, this time near Middletown. While heading toward the sound of cannon fire, the First Corps had the sense of impending battle. To cheer on the Union soldiers, residents of Middletown made their appreciation known. Augustus Cross, a twenty-two-year-old adjutant in the Second Pennsylvania Reserves, enjoyed the benefit of some flowers a "pretty young lady" handed him. "She spoke not a word," an officer remembered, "but crimsoned when their eyes met."[60]

Hooker went forward to reconnoiter the targeted mountain ridge. No corps commander, even one as aggressive as Hooker, could have been overjoyed to see the terrain. During the morning, part of the Ninth Corps had engaged Confederates around Fox's Gap, to the left of the National Road. On the right of the pike, north of Turner's Gap itself, stood a steep mountainside destined to be the ground most of the First Corps would attack. Hooker described the slope as "precipitous, rugged, and wooded, and difficult of ascent to an infantry force, even in absence of a foe in front."[61] Confederates north of the pike did not have sufficient numbers to defeat Hooker's attack, but Mother Nature gave the Confederates a wonderful defensive position.

Longstreet's wing of Lee's army was countermarching south from Hagerstown early on the 14th. The move was necessary to support D. H. Hill's five brigades. With the enormous terrain advantage, a small group of Alabamians under the command of Robert Rodes was the primary defensive force north of the National Road by the time Hooker was in position. After some success for the Ninth Corps around Fox's Gap, Lee needed a herculean effort from Rodes and his 1,200 men to hold back the First Corps.

Hill figured McClellan would have sent more men to the south to pressure the Confederate detachments attacking Harpers Ferry. Even while facing an intense concentration of Union forces farther north, Hill felt able to use his terrain advantage long enough for Longstreet's forces to come to his assistance. Looking east, Hill recalled the feeling of seeing four Union corps lining up against the northern gaps. "The sight inspired more satisfaction than discomfort," he wrote, adding, "I felt that General McClellan had made a mistake."[62]

Prior to the first offensive of the reborn First Corps, Burnside, Hooker, and Meade—each a future Army of the Potomac commander—met to discuss the looming battle. Burnside later wrote he was exasperated by Hooker's slow pace of activity that afternoon. He even suggested Hooker had to be ordered four times to attack before the First Corps' assault on South Mountain began. Burnside undoubtedly wanted more support for the Ninth Corps after the morning's battle near Fox's Gap, and Hooker was in a good place to augment the attack. Yet, McClellan seemed unconcerned about the day's pace, perhaps leaning on his inherent apprehension about being outnumbered or making the wrong move. In his own report, Hooker noted McClellan requested the reconnaissance that took the First Corps commander away from his men that afternoon.[63]

Hartwig supports Burnside in his dispute with Hooker about the South Mountain attack. The excellent historian suggests Hooker was negligent in not keeping in touch with Burnside during his reconnaissance.[64] A key fact Hartwig does not mention is the distaste Burnside felt for Hooker by the time the charge was leveled about the supposed failure of the First Corps to attack in a timely manner on September 14. Burnside put forth the allegation four months subsequent to his initial report about South Mountain. Sour grapes undoubtedly governed Burnside's early 1863 condemnation of Hooker. The harsh tone was not in evidence two weeks after the September 14 battle, when Burnside praised Hooker. He reported the First Corps commander "most skillfully and successfully executed" the wing commander's orders during the day.[65]

The charge of Hooker's tardiness was made after Burnside read Hooker's report, in which the First Corps commander wrote of a Ninth Corps division retreating from the area around Fox's Gap. This ruffled Burnside's feathers at a sensitive time for the man who had just lost command of the Army of the Potomac—with Hooker as his replacement. Moreover, Burnside partly blamed Hooker for the disaster at Fredericksburg. Burnside even allegedly suggested Hooker deserved hanging for his performance at Fredericksburg.[66]

One can hardly imagine "Fighting Joe" was willfully apathetic at South Mountain, his first fight as a corps commander. Blame for the dearth of speed on September 14 should fall on McClellan's shoulders, not Hooker's.

By siding with Burnside, Hartwig rendered insufficient justice to Hooker for the very successful attack on South Mountain.

Regardless of where blame should fall for the slow movements on September 14, Meade received orders directly from Burnside to prepare the entire Pennsylvania Reserves for action to seize the high ground to the right of the National Road. The eminence was essentially three separate hills, and the ground offered many advantages to the defending Confederates.[67] But the manpower advantage rested with the Reserves. Meade's Division had three men for each one under the command of Rodes. With a need to watch his right flank, Meade ordered Lt. Col. John Clark and the 3rd Reserves to the north, a bit under a mile from the division's attack.

Closer to the National Road, three of the four brigades in Hatch's Division arrived on Meade's immediate left. The bulk of Ricketts's Division stayed in reserve during the assault. By Burnside's order, Gibbon was detached from Hatch's Division. On the left of the First Corps, the Westerners were slated to charge up the National Road. Gibbon would attack a good friend. The brigade commander and his brother Lardner had been the best men at D. H. Hill's wedding.[68]

"My God, It's the Pennsylvania Reserves"

Despite the terrain, good shots with Sharps Rifles made for an excellent line of skirmishers. Col. Hugh McNeil was ordered to place his 13th Pennsylvania Reserves in the front of Meade's attack. With nearly 290 men, McNeil commenced the assault. The Bucktails had the direct support of Companies A and B of the 1st Reserves.[69]

From left to right, the brigades of Magilton, Gallagher, and Seymour started the difficult work to conquer the heights. Meade hoped the division could advance in a solid line, but the rocks, woods, and incline prohibited symmetry across the three brigades. The vision of a coordinated divisional attack quickly withered. Often, the battle north of the pike was not divisions and brigades fighting in tandem, but individual regiments engaging small parts of the Confederate line.[70]

Although numbers were on the side of Meade's Division, the effort to sweep Rodes off South Mountain encountered early problems. "A terrific fire soon brought the skirmish line to a halt," one army historian wrote. With the advantage of cover, the Alabamians gave pause to the Union advance. Looking uphill and to the left, General Seymour witnessed men from the 5th

Alabama behind a stone wall, firing on his brigade. Showing strong leadership, Seymour directed his troops admirably. The general ordered Col. Biddle Roberts and his 1st Reserves up the slope. Roberts noted how the eight companies with him acted "under the immediate personal direction of General Seymour." The colonel recalled the "particularly destructive" Confederate fire, adding "we suffered severely."

McNeil noticed how the Confederates were making use of good natural cover to thwart the opening of the attack. He implored his men, "Pour your fire upon those rocks!" The Bucktails must have wondered about the wisdom of the order, because rocks were not shooting back at them.[71] Nonetheless, the rapid fire from the regiment undoubtedly provided needed power for Seymour's assault on the right of the First Corps.

Sometimes isolated from support, Seymour's regiments—or portions of regiments—found difficult spots at South Mountain. Strong combat leadership was one way for elements of the First Corps to keep the initiative. One example of a small group achieving excellent results was Companies A and B of the 6th Reserves. Under the command of Captains Wellington Ent and Charles Roush, respectively, the two companies gained ground. With the help of three other companies from the 6th, the men kept up the pressure on the Rebels. The 6th still received "a most galling fire," but with the strong effort of the troops and superb commanders at the point of attack, isolated groups of Pennsylvanians helped the First Corps conquer the slope. One week subsequent to his intrepidity at South Mountain, Ent was promoted to major. After suffering a wound on the 14th, Roush was medically discharged nearly four months later.[72]

Seymour continued to exhibit good leadership on the mountain. He had orders for Col. Joseph Fisher of the 5th Reserves later in the attack, "Colonel, put your regiment into that cornfield and hurt somebody." Happy to obey, Fisher guaranteed some Confederate prisoners for his brigade commander.[73]

Coordinated teamwork between regiments proved difficult in the wooded, rocky ground at South Mountain, but Seymour's clear tactical vision and vital guidance helped the Reserves assail Rodes's determined band. While most of the unwounded Alabamians escaped the wrath of Seymour's Brigade, Fisher proved true to his word. Eleven Confederate prisoners were one of the benefits of Seymour's request for a charge up the slope.[74]

Soldiers in the 10th Reserves, under the command of Col. Adoniram Warner, kept busy. Part of Gallagher's reserve in the opening moments, Meade moved the 10th to the right in support of Seymour when the division

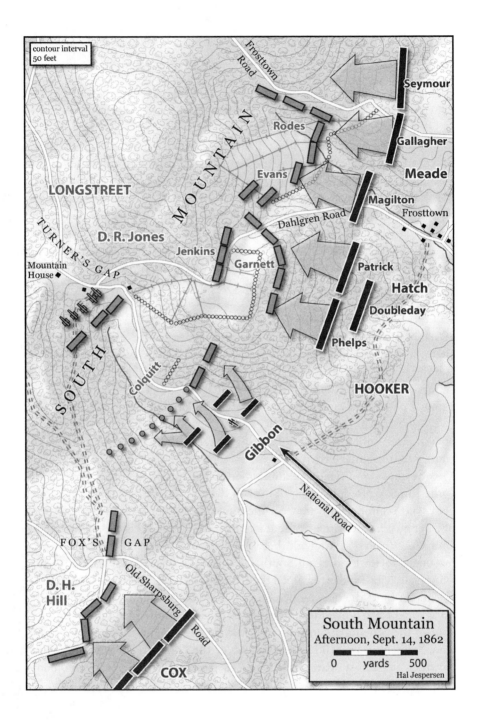

contour interval
50 feet

Frosttown
Road

Seymour

Gallagher

Rodes

MOUNTAIN

Meade

LONGSTREET

Evans

Magilton

Frosttown

Dahlgren Road

D. R. Jones

TURNER'S GAP

Jenkins

Patrick

Mountain
House

Garnett

Hatch

Doubleday

SOUTH

Phelps

Colquitt

HOOKER

Gibbon

National Road

FOX'S GAP

Old Sharpsburg Road

D. H.
Hill

COX

South Mountain
Afternoon, Sept. 14, 1862

0   yards   500

Hal Jespersen

commander grew concerned about the possibility of an attack on his right flank. After that threat did not materialize, Warner's men moved back to the left. Gallagher received a nasty arm wound about this time as further stalemate prevented a rapid advance. In addition to Rebel fire, as the historian of the 12th Reserves wrote, "The ground was of the most difficult character for the movements of troops, the hillside very steep and rocky, and obstructed by stone walls and timber."[75]

After meeting a fierce fire, which killed Warner's horse and several men, teamwork among Reserve regiments was again on display as the attack progressed. The Third Brigade, now under Lt. Col. Robert Anderson, was aligned with the 12th, 11th, and 9th Reserves, from right to left, supported by the return of the 10th Reserves.[76]

As in Seymour's Brigade, good leadership proved critical. Capt. Samuel Dick, twenty-five years old and in command of the 9th Reserves after Anderson's replacement of Gallagher, ordered a charge against Confederates sheltered inside a farmhouse. The action led to an additional haul of about fifteen prisoners. Even with ammunition nearly gone, elements of Anderson's Brigade captured more Rebels as the fight continued. "I halted and endeavored to collect my men, who were much scattered from the broken nature of the ground," Dick reported. He claimed a total of nearly one hundred Confederate prisoners.[77]

Advancing up the hill exacted a price, the loss of dedicated Union men. One of those sacrificing his life was Capt. Nathaniel Nesbit, a company commander in the 11th Reserves. He suffered a serious chest wound while carrying the regiment's flag. Taken to Middletown, the devoted soldier died a week later. Nesbit offered a stellar example of an ardent American fighting man lost to his country forever. The captain was in his mid-twenties.[78]

With both flanks falling back, Rodes received some timely assistance from a South Carolina brigade under Col. Peter Stevens, filling in for Nathan Evans. The 17th, 18th, 22nd, and 23rd Palmetto State regiments, along with the Holcombe Legion, did not add up to more than 600 men. Magilton's three Reserve regiments, including the 8th Reserves on the far left of Meade's Division, gained traction against Stevens.

Maj. Silas Baily, leading the 8th Reserves, was pleased with the "fine style" of his regiment's work. Baily added comments about the cost of victory. First Lt. William M. Carter, from Company B, was "a fine soldier and brave man, who fell while gallantly leading his company in the thickest of the fight." The 8th Reserves sustained fifteen killed and thirty-four wounded.

Baily added, "It gives me great pleasure to state that every officer and man behaved with great gallantry; still, our loss throws a shade of melancholy over the splendor of the action."[79]

Stevens's men suffered horribly for their relatively brief stand to Rodes's right. The South Carolina soldiers sustained more than 200 casualties, almost 40 percent of the men engaged.[80]

As literal and figurative darkness descended on him, Rodes worked hard to rally his brigade. Col. Bristor Gayle, leading the 12th Alabama, tried to discern more about the advancing Federals in the fading light. When asked by Rodes to identify the Union soldiers moving up the mountain, Gayle first said he was not sure. Peering above some rocks before suffering fatal wounds, Gayle declared, "My God, it's the Pennsylvania Reserves!"[81]

With continued persistence in the fading light, Meade's Division completed extraordinary service at South Mountain. Regimental leaders noted the difficulty of keeping units organized as the summit was taken. Capt. Andrew Bolar, 12th Reserves, reported on the battle on behalf of regimental commander Richard Gustin. Of the state of the 12th later in the evening, Bolar noted, "The regiment was somewhat broken when it arrived at the top of the mountain, in consequence of the roughness of the ground and the weariness of the men."[82]

Meade was very satisfied with the performance of his division. He reported the Reserves conduct "was such as to uphold its well-earned reputation for steadiness and gallantry." He added how the Reserves were prepared for a continued struggle on the morning of the 15th after a very necessary visit from the ammunition train. "The command rested on their arms during the night," Meade reported.[83]

A Medal of Honor for General Hatch

Hatch's Division advanced to the south of Meade, still north of the National Road. The Confederates confronted were some of Longstreet's men arriving after a long march from Hagerstown. Like Rodes, the next wave of Confederate defenders had too few men to blunt the First Corps for long. The initial small wave of defensive support came from two Virginia brigades maybe totaling 1,000 men. Later, more South Carolinians arrived.

Hooker rode along Hatch's lines prior to the assault. He conversed with Lt. Col. William Searing, who commanded the 30th New York, perhaps only 110 soldiers due to casualties at Second Bull Run. "You have a small regiment, colonel," Hooker noted. Showing the determination of his band, Searing replied, "Yes, but every musket means a man." To get the soldiers ready for the attack, Searing—inaccurately—informed his regiment that the opposing troops were the same who killed their colonel two weeks before. A soldier later wrote, "The colonel says the yell that the boys gave as they sprang forward to the charge could have been heard a mile away."[84]

Leading the First Division's ascent were the 21st and 35th New York, under the command of colonels William Rogers and Newton Lord, respectively. A gap opened between the two regiments due to the leftward movement of Lord's men. Patrick's other two regiments, also New Yorkers from the 20th State Militia and 23rd Regiment, did not advance when their commander expected, delaying the progress of the entire division.[85]

Problems advancing up South Mountain could be considered inherent to any combat force. Issues with the direction and pace of Lord's men might have resulted from their colonel. Found innocent on a technicality during a court-martial in early 1862, Newton Lord was simply incompetent. Marsena Patrick and other senior leaders had no faith in the abilities of the colonel. Although his absence would not be soon enough to improve the 35th New York in Maryland, Lord would be out of the army in early 1863.[86]

Rogers and his men were on the right of the division's line. The 21st found itself well ahead of the division. With Confederate bullets screaming down the hill, the regiment's historian made special note of the contrast between "our present fearful business" and the unforgettable beauty of the valley below. The men quickly got to work in support of the Reserves, with the New Yorkers helping to force the retreat of a Confederate battery firing on the Pennsylvanians.[87]

Curtis Abbott's company history explained how Vermont sharpshooters could never forget the pleasing vista in such a deadly place. The 2nd USSS, attempting to create a connection between Meade and Hatch, were moving up the hill to the right of Rogers. Abbott remembered, "This skirmish was especially interesting to the Vermonters from the nature of the ground. The advance was up the heights from rock to rock and amidst the trees. The very difficulties of the ascent brought back memories of their native hills and lent an inspiration to their efforts."[88]

After receiving an update on the imminent arrival of support from the rest of the division, the 21st New York continued moving up South Mountain. In the distance, enemy infantry could be seen along a fence bordering a cornfield. The regiment's historian recalled the assistance Phelps's Brigade provided at a key moment.

A fierce volley welcomes our friends in gray, and they are driven back with terrible loss to the fence on the other side, where they rally and return the fire. Rapid and continuous is the fusillade that follows; the mountain top reeks with the sulphurous veil, out of which rise a horrid turmoil, and the echoes fly to hide in every nook and valley, so peacefully slumbering an hour ago.[89]

As warriors from both sides fell, Hatch's vital presence was noted by several men. More than thirty years later, Capt. Henry Cranford of the 14th Brooklyn, acting adjutant in Phelps's Brigade, praised Hatch for ensuring the attack made progress. Cranford wrote, "It is due to the intelligent foresight, valor and magnetism of General Hatch that this gallant veteran brigade seized and held this most important point of the battle field, and held it like a solid wall."[90]

The laudatory words from officers were a reason Hatch won the Medal of Honor for his work on South Mountain. Unfortunately, the brave general was experiencing his last day in the First Corps. Even after a bullet caused a serious leg wound prompting the division commander to head downhill, Hatch's example was electric. In his report, Phelps thanked the wounded brigadier by noting how soldiers were "encouraged by his valor and inspiriting orders," which ensured the attack did not lose momentum.[91]

The brigades of Phelps and Patrick eventually formed a strong line, with Patrick's men divided by Phelps's men in the middle. Col. Theodore Gates, commander of the 20th New York State Militia, later wondered if the high ground actually worked against the small number of Confederate defenders. As the two brigades kept marching up the hill, Gates noticed a circumstance he deemed common during the war. Gates recalled how the Virginians' fire was often too high. On the left of Rogers and his 21st New York, Gates recalled, "the Confederates still fired too high, and at least 80 per cent of their shot flew harmlessly over the heads of the Federals." Even excellently drilled Civil War troops on "the most favorable ground" tended to fire high, Gates added.[92]

With Hatch out of action, Doubleday was elevated to command of the First Division. His brigade, now under the leadership of Col. William

Wainwright, ascended the mountain about 200 yards behind Phelps. These men offered important support that convinced many remaining Confederates of the hopelessness of their defense. Strong leadership was still necessary for victory against the holdouts, with tragic results for some First Corps soldiers.

One of those men was Charles Stamp, of the 76th New York. Proudly carrying the colors, a privilege he earned for bravery earlier in 1862, Stamp became concerned when the 76th did not advance as quickly as needed against the Virginians. Charging several feet beyond the regiment's line, as bullets buzzed around him, Stamp firmly planted the flag in the ground, then yelled back at the regiment, "There, come up to that." He was soon killed by a shot to the head. The regiment had lost "one of the truest and best men," according to the 76th's historian.[93]

The strength of Wainwright's attack pressed Confederates higher up the hill. A soldier in the 95th New York suggested his brigade was so eager to knock the Confederates back a charge did not even need to be ordered. With reinforcements, the division suppressed a counterattack as darkness settled in.[94]

Sometimes supporting troops might cause more harm than good in war. A situation along Hatch's line after dark seems almost comical. In his report, Col. Henry Hoffman, of Patrick's 23rd New York, expressed scorn for some Union troops arriving amidst the muddle created by darkness and the occasional need to respond to fire from Confederates. Hoffman recalled the moment "when a brigade came up in the darkness hooting and yelling, running over everybody and throwing everything into even worse confusion than before."[95]

These men were likely from Christian's Brigade. The additional firepower helped beat back efforts from the Confederate counterattack. Hundreds of fresh muskets also allowed Phelps and Patrick to move their troops down the hill a bit to their bivouac as late summer coolness settled in. A member of the 14th Brooklyn was certainly ready for a cool break. He referred to the limited supply of ammunition in the regiment.[96]

"FOR THE LOVE OF GOD, 'WILD IRISHMAN' IS HIT"

The First Corps' attack on South Mountain had proven costly to the Pennsylvania Reserves and Hatch's brigades assaulting the Virginians closer to the National Road. The troops suffering the most that afternoon and evening were farther to the south, along the road itself. John Gibbon's "Black Hats," the four regiments of Westerners, were charged with taking on Colquitt's Brigade, Georgians posted in a superb defensive position.

Gibbon's attack played out as essentially two separate actions on either side of the National Road. The brigade's alignment and the topographical layout dictated such an outcome. The 19th Indiana was on the left front of the assault, with the 7th Wisconsin on the right front. The 2nd Wisconsin served as the 19th's support, with Edward Bragg and his 6th Wisconsin advancing behind Capt. John Callis and the 7th. In total, Gibbon had about 1,300 men for the attack, which started a bit after 5:00 P.M.

Alfred Colquitt's defenders possessed several advantages. Near numerical parity with the Unionists was certainly important, since no attacking force wanted to be confronting equal numbers at a higher elevation. Additionally, Colquitt's two left regiments, the 23rd and 28th Georgia, had fantastic cover due to the forested ground and a stone wall. The position would prove a costly one to attack for the two Badger regiments. Thirdly, the looming darkness shrouded the generally hidden defenders, making the Iron Brigade's battle even more enervating.

At least the location was the best spot along Hooker's line for artillery support. A section of Battery B, 4th U.S. Artillery, under the command of Lt. James Stewart, had a good position behind Gibbon's two left regiments. Col. Solomon Meredith, leading the 19th Indiana, received assistance from the battery early in the attack. Stewart's two guns placed a shot in the upper story of a house. The structure had allowed Colquitt to harass the advance. Stewart stayed busy during the fight, with counterbattery fire and shots aimed at Colquitt's men.[97]

Meredith's side of the attack quickly lost the services of an excellent officer. A company commander in the 2nd Wisconsin, Capt. Wilson Colwell had been elected the mayor of La Crosse in the same month the war started. Now, well over a year later, he continued to dodge a life of safety and ease back home while leading the skirmish line on the left side of the pike. Colwell was a true soldier. Early in 1862, one man noted to a newspaper back home, "Capt. Colwell has endeared himself to his men and proven that he means business."[98]

Colwell's bravery was unquestionable, but not so his interest in surviving the fight. A detractor had written the state's governor earlier in the war, essentially calling the captain a coward. Another soldier thought Colwell went into the fight with a desire to die, rather than live with such a false condemnation of his character.

As he marched up toward Turner's Gap, Colwell fell after being shot in the abdomen, a dreadful wound to anyone, but especially destructive to Colwell's body. He stayed on the field as a mortally wounded spearhead, fearlessly giving orders to screen the brigade's advance. Colwell lived only a short time after being taken back down the National Road. Regimental commander Lucius Fairchild felt the hurt of Colwell's death. "His place can hardly be filled," Fairchild reported. "He was a fine officer and beloved by the whole regiment."[99]

Persistence from the 19th Indiana proved vital. Meredith reported how the fire forced the Confederates "to retreat precipitously, which gave us an opportunity of pouring upon them a raking fire as they retreated." He added that Captain Clark's Company G took eleven prisoners (including three of Colquitt's officers). After adding praise for the important assistance the 2nd Wisconsin provided his regiment, Meredith happily, although prematurely, noted how the two cooperating regiments gave "three hearty cheers as the fate of the day was thus decided."[100]

On the right of the pike, the 7th Wisconsin was moving toward the most difficult position any First Corps troops attacked on South Mountain. The unit would suffer nearly half of Gibbon's casualties, although the 7th made steady progress during the initial part of the attack. Callis kept the main line of the regiment 100 yards behind his skirmishers. When reaching an open field, musketry from the Confederates became very heavy. With his regiment's left on the road, Callis noted, "The enemy opened a destructive enfilading fire from a stone fence on our left, at a short range." Advancing farther, the 7th was caught in a whirlwind, with Colquitt's men opening a severe fire against the right of the regiment. Proudly finding his men returning fire "with great vigor," Callis still knew he needed help. Thanks to another example of bold First Corps leadership, assistance was on the way.[101]

Col. Edward Bragg made an interesting tactical decision to support his fellow Wisconsin men up ahead. Having Maj. Rufus Dawes take command of the right wing, Bragg led the 6th's left. After Dawes and his half of the regiment fired into the woods to support Callis, Bragg had Dawes order the right of the regiment to lie down. Bragg then swung the 6th Wisconsin's left to the right, over the prone members of the regiment. The regiment's halves alternated firing at the obstinate Confederates. One man in Bragg's regiment said the tactics on the right of the Iron Brigade's attack allowed the Badgers to fire "volley after volley into the enemy."[102]

Receiving an order from Gibbon to keep the focus on flanking the enemy in the woods, Bragg continued to lead the 6th Wisconsin ahead. He formed a semicircle around the left side of Colquitt's command, delivering a solid sheet of lead. Bragg wrote, "The fire of the enemy, who fought us from behind rocks and trees, and entirely under cover was terrific, but steadily the regiment dislodged him."[103]

Callis also had important friends on his left. The 2nd Wisconsin supplied timely fire to support the 7th. The action of the 2nd, "relieved us from further annoyance," Callis concluded. The uneasy feeling of firing against a generally hidden enemy as darkness descended continued for Gibbon's men, but they defiantly continued the engagement. The brigade did not rout Colquitt's men, but it was able to hold the ground gained.[104]

Among the list of casualties for the 7th Wisconsin were men like Sgt. Linus Bascom of Company A. Wounded on South Mountain, he would die on the last day of 1862 in Middletown. Pope Briggs, from Company B, became a prisoner at South Mountain. Corp. William Durley of Company C suffered a wound earlier at Second Manassas, so South Mountain was his second injury of the summer. He was discharged due to wounds in March 1863. James Clark, Company F, was one of the eleven men of the regiment killed outright during the battle.[105]

James Whitty provided an example of how tough a soldier can be. In Company A of the 6th Wisconsin, he used a rock as a platform to shoot at Colquitt's line. A Rebel ball found Whitty at his battle perch, prompting him to exclaim, "For the love of God, 'Wild Irishman' is hit." This was one of several wounds Whitty suffered during the war. Whitty lived for more than forty years after the war. The bullet he received at South Mountain was never removed.[106]

At least one brigade of the "doubtful ones" elicited positive comments from their army commander. McClellan was pleased with the boldness of the Westerners. At South Mountain, the Army of the Potomac commander wrote that Gibbon "handled his brigade with as much precision and coolness as if upon parade, and the bravery of his troops could not be excelled."[107]

Gaining McClellan's respect was not worth the price. Suffering more than 300 casualties, the Iron Brigade's attack accomplished the least of any brigade at South Mountain. With a firm hold on Fox's Gap, and the inevitable success farther north due to Meade and Hatch's overwhelming numbers, there was no reason to assault the National Road itself. Colquitt's position would have been untenable with other Union successes on South

Mountain.[108] The 317 men in Gibbon's command knocked out of the ranks on the 14th, including 37 killed in action, might have made a much bigger difference three days later along Antietam Creek.

"NOTHING BUT UNDAUNTED COURAGE"

The men referred to as "the only doubtful ones" two days earlier certainly proved their worth to McClellan at South Mountain, suffering 923 casualties. The total loss in the Ninth Corps, attacking Fox's Gap, was 889.

With their assault up the National Road, Gibbon's Brigade recorded more than one third of Hooker's entire loss, 16 percent of which were the 147 casualties, including 30 captured and missing, in the 7th Wisconsin. The 6th Wisconsin sustained 92 casualties, second in the corps, including 11 killed in action, the same number as the 7th Wisconsin.

Seymour's five regiments reported 171 casualties, the second highest brigade total for the corps at South Mountain. The 6th Reserves led the division's loss, with 54 casualties. Both the 6th and 13th Reserves suffered 11 killed in action. The 13th matched the 8th Reserves in the Second Brigade with 50 total casualties.

Due to the reserve position of the Second Division, the total loss in Ricketts's command was only thirty-five. The 107th Pennsylvania, under Capt. James MacThompson, recorded twelve casualties, the most of any in the division.[109]

The conduct of the corps at South Mountain should give pause to any historian wishing to continue the myth of a defeated, demoralized army incapable of matching Lee's men in battle. The First Corps' day began east of the Monocacy River. After a march of more than a dozen miles, the troops pushed D. H. Hill and his reinforcements off of South Mountain, a truly wicked place to attack, even with the great manpower advantage Hooker enjoyed.

A Wisconsin man, showing a healthy dose of Western common sense, summed up the struggle for South Mountain by praising the heroism both armies displayed. In a long letter about the battle, he noted the Confederates "had a formidable ground of defense, and nothing but undaunted courage wrested it from him."[110] Plenty of battle remained in the campaign. South Mountain would seem like a small engagement compared to what was in store three days later outside the town of Sharpsburg.

Advance to the Antietam

Darkness quickly ruled South Mountain. In a 9:00 P.M. note to Hooker, McClellan requested, "Please hold your present position at all hazards." Israel Richardson's Division of the Second Corps was sent up as support. Hooker later reported, "all were directed to sleep on their arms." Hartsuff's Brigade climbed the hill to ensure a connection in the dark between Meade and Doubleday.[111]

Some men, like soldiers in the 6th Wisconsin, remained at the last point of their advance, not far from Confederates. "The night was chilly," Rufus Dawes remembered, "and in the woods intensely dark." The diligent major recalled the difficulty of reaching some injured men. Hearing piteous cries for help, Dawes was relieved to see stretcher bearers taking men to nearby makeshift hospitals.[112]

Tense moments remained along the line of the First Corps, but no doubt existed as to the result of the carnage. Lee grew greatly concerned about the viability of his bloodied and exhausted army after the Unionist success. Unfortunately for the Union cause, McClellan had been too slow to rescue 12,000 troops at Harpers Ferry. Lee now had to find a way to reunite his army before McClellan could strike a fatal blow.[113]

Ready to expand on the victory, the First Corps was disappointed on the morning of September 15. The heavily outnumbered Rebels had retreated to the west, heading through the towns of Boonsboro and Keedysville toward the defensive position at Sharpsburg on the west side of Antietam Creek. The stand in Maryland was an utterly audacious move, with Jackson's command not yet on the field. Lee simply did not wish to abandon his campaign without another fight, regardless of the odds against him.

First Corps regiments were pushed forward by about 8:00 A.M. on September 15. As part of Hartsuff's Brigade, the 13th Massachusetts sent two companies of skirmishers forward to the Mountain House at the top of Turner's Gap.[114] Richardson's Division, still under Hooker's orders, was sent down the mountain to the west as the lead element of the army's pursuit.

McClellan made an easy decision regarding army organization as the renewed advance began. Burnside was informed of the dissolution of the wing structure originally placing Hooker under his command. Without control over the First Corps, Burnside was to lead only the 9th Corps while linking up with Franklin, who was advancing from Crampton's Gap.[115] Some historians, including Hartwig and Carman, have criticized the wing structure's elimination, but the First and Ninth Corps fought at different gaps on

South Mountain, then would advance to Sharpsburg on different roads. No pressing military necessity called for Burnside's control over the First Corps on the 15th. The two corps would fight at Sharpsburg on opposite ends of the army.

Brig. Gen. Jacob Cox in the Ninth Corps was friendly to Burnside. He suggested Burnside grew "disturbed and grieved" after he lost control over the First Corps. Yet, linking the two commands on the 15th prior to the pursuit of Lee—simply to assuage Burnside's ego—would have wasted time.

Hooker wanted the First Corps' soldiers to have a meal. As he reported, "My corps were ordered to make a little coffee and eat their breakfasts, which they had not been able to do since the beginning of their march from the Monocacy, the morning previous." The corps started out after this break, following cavalry regiments and Richardson.[116] After Burnside failed to move the Ninth Corps by early afternoon, Fitz John Porter received approval from headquarters to move elements of the Fifth Corps ahead of the brooding Ninth Corps leader.

Prior to the First Corps' advance, one soldier looked west to see enemy troops already nearing Boonsboro. "It is not without some truth they were called the 'Fleet-footed Virginians,'" he recalled. In the afternoon, residents of Boonsboro and Keedysville were happy to see the progressing protectors of the Union. The historian of the 13th Massachusetts remembered seeing "Uncle Sam's bunting displayed" while hearing "encouraging words from friends" in town.[117]

A Vermonter in the 2nd USSS recalled the 15th as a day "we were engaged in skirmishing" and "picking up stragglers from Lee's army," perfect roles for sharpshooters. Nonetheless, steady progress against a defeated enemy held dangers. Near Boonsboro, Charles Kay, a New Hampshire man in the sharpshooter outfit, was wounded. Born in the state's northern community of Lisbon, Kay was discharged for disability ten weeks later.[118]

Corp. Benjamin Van Valkenberg, in the 76th New York, had a better day than Kay, even though scared out of his wits. Assigned as an orderly at division headquarters, Van Valkenberg was gathering provisions near a stream fed from South Mountain. The surprised First Corps man encountered five Confederates filling canteens. Although horribly frightened, Van Valkenberg drew his revolver and threatened to shoot, leading to the capture of the enemy soldiers.[119]

In dispatches to Washington, McClellan was full of fight. At 8:30 A.M., he informed Halleck of Lee's army being "in a perfect panic." The army commander added, "I am hurrying everything forward to endeavor to press their retreat to the utmost." To his wife an hour later, McClellan noted, "If I can believe one tenth of what is reported, God has seldom given an army a greater victory than this."[120]

Audacious commanders follow up a day of victory with bold movements. All McClellan said he would do was press Lee's retreat. Some men in the First Corps wondered about the dilatory army on the 15th. Colonel Gates of the 20th New York State Militia suggested, "The army would have cordially seconded any bold and dashing tactics of its leader, but he was hampered by his cautious policy and his apprehensions of Lee's 'overwhelming numbers.'" Gates chided McClellan for bragging to Franklin on the 13th of the plan to divide the Confederates in two and defeat Lee's smaller forces. "But when the enemy himself had presented the first condition to him voluntarily," McClellan "would not avail himself of the opportunity."[121]

Battle was certainly on the mind of President Lincoln. Giving a short message of encouragement during the afternoon of the 15th, the commander-in-chief issued a specific request to McClellan: "Destroy the rebel army, if possible."[122]

No doubt should have existed in any First Corps heart about whether another battle was imminent. As the sounds of cannon and the persistent tramp of soldiers' feet filled the countryside, the historian of the 88th Pennsylvania, Christian's Brigade, kept the idea of another fight in his mind. He figured thousands of men in the Army of the Potomac "perhaps somewhat nervously speculated upon their chances of filling a soldiers' grave in the coming battle."[123]

Fear of combat can be eased when warriors receive overdue rations. Alexander Murdock, of the 9th Pennsylvania Reserves, recounted the happiness he felt after arriving at Keedysville. The regiment received "rations of newly killed, warm beef which was immediately cooked and eaten." Not all members of the First Corps were treated to a bovine dinner. A soldier in the 9th New York State Militia remembered the regiment camped for the night with "nothing to eat."[124]

Richardson's Division and another from the Fifth Corps arrived east of Antietam Creek before Hooker's men. Most of McClellan's troops were massing around Keedysville, on the east side of the creek, by the late afternoon. The chance to strike an even more decisive blow against the still-divided Army of Northern Virginia remained. Lee decided to arrange the small part of the army he had with him on good ground west of Antietam Creek. Jackson was nearly a full day from arriving to bolster Lee's force.

The tangled state of McClellan's units was one factor decreasing the chance of an attack against Lee's roughly 15,000 men, which Hooker estimated amounted to 30,000 Confederates. "Fully conscious of my weakness in number and *morale*, I did not feel strong enough to attack him in front," Hooker reported. This was far different from Fighting Joe's views earlier in the day. Before departing South Mountain, a staff officer wrote army headquarters of Hooker's belief "that we can capture the entire rebel army." Surveying the scene along Antietam Creek later in the day, Hooker penned a 2:15 P.M. note to McClellan, briefly explaining how Lee's army was arrayed on "open ground" west of the creek. Of the Confederates on the afternoon of the 15th, Hooker concluded, "Their position is not a formidable one."[125]

But Hooker would not endorse an attack after pondering the situation, due to the lack of Union troops on hand. If Fighting Joe felt restraint from a battle, no one could expect McClellan to find the willpower to launch an afternoon offensive. The army's leader took his time joining the advance. He commendably visited wounded men in the vicinity of South Mountain. "From McClellan's tardiness in reaching the front and other surrounding circumstances, we are led to the conclusion that he had no serious intention of giving Lee battle on the fifteenth," Carman suggested. McClellan may have figured the campaign already won.[126] Like so many conclusions Carman drew from his decades of studying the Maryland campaign, this particular insight is irrefutable.

The likelihood of an assault withered as quickly as the sun was sinking to the west. Any chance Lee had to place doubts in McClellan's mind made the Union army equivocate. September 14 was a disaster for Lee, but the following day was a clear tactical victory, because he understood his opponent all too well. Lee knew McClellan was not going to attack.[127]

At least Hooker was active that afternoon. After arriving east of the Antietam, Hooker decided to have engineers examine the creek for crossing points. A flank attack was on the mind of Hooker, and determining the best place to cross Antietam Creek was necessary. The First Corps bivouacked west of Keedysville, close to the juncture of Antietam Creek and the Little Antietam. The spot was near North Bridge and Pry Ford, locations the corps would use to cross the creek the next day.[128]

Hooker's command was obviously being positioned to play a major role in the army's next attack. When would the attack occur? Even if McClellan could be justified in not attacking on the 15th, surely the following day was the chance he would seize to push Lee into the Potomac. But this was George McClellan after all. In his self-serving memoirs, McClellan marveled at the strong position Lee had selected at Sharpsburg. With well-posted artillery, the army commander noted Lee's arrangement "was one of the strongest to be found in this region of the country, which is well adapted to defensive warfare."[129]

Still, one does not need to be second in his class at West Point to see the possibilities of an assault on the 15th. The First Corps attacked the day before subsequent to a long march from the Monocacy to South Mountain. They would launch a massive attack against Lee's left flank at Sharpsburg early on September 17 without senior leaders having studied the ground much. Why not embrace Lincoln's order to destroy the Rebel army on the same day of the president's missive? Crushing Lee was far more likely on the afternoon of the 15th than at any time two days hence.

Early on the 16th, fog took the blame for McClellan's hesitancy. In a 7:00 A.M. telegram to Halleck, McClellan noted the inability to do anything except "ascertain that some of the enemy are still there." He promised to attack "as soon as situation of the enemy is developed."[130]

The day's promised attack never happened. One reason for McClellan's procrastination was his view that Jackson's men had arrived from Harpers Ferry by early morning to reinforce Lee. Stonewall's troops actually did not begin to appear at Sharpsburg until almost midday, with many of the vaunted Southern fighters still miles away due to intense straggling. After Stonewall's arrival, three of Lee's nine divisions were still absent. By early afternoon on the 16th, better planning and placement of forces could have given McClellan a great opportunity.[131] Yet, he was still busy with preliminaries, while the First Corps stood idle east of Antietam Creek.

Some soldiers were taking action to get out of harm's way before fighting erupted. Benjamin Oliver and Michael Mahoney were listed in the roster of the 26th New York as deserting on September 16. Perhaps they hatched a plan to slip away together. The 14th Brooklyn also had men deserting, with three running away on the 16th.[132] Not everyone who volunteered to fight was able to stand the rigors of field service or the obvious signs of a large battle.

When McClellan finally prepared for the army's opening foray across Antietam Creek, he placed Hooker in charge of the movement on the army's right. The First Corps was ordered to move west with an early afternoon message from McClellan. Already close to crossing points, the First Corps claimed the army's lead position. Unfortunately, McClellan did not call Hooker to cross hours earlier. Why the delay? Not fog or a disorganized army this time, but McClellan's need to babysit Burnside's placement of the Ninth Corps. With fog lifting by mid-morning,[133] no reason existed to keep the First Corps idle until the afternoon. But that is exactly what McClellan did.

McClellan envisioned Brigadier General Mansfield's 12th Corps as Hooker's eventual support for the planned attack. The two corps should have been across Antietam Creek together much earlier in the day. If hours were not wasted, Hooker could have reconnoitered the ground to be attacked, an item of vital importance McClellan overlooked in his planning. Instead, the First Corps would cross Antietam Creek alone, except for a small cavalry escort. Well after dark, the 12th Corps would bivouac west of the creek, but a mile or more in the rear. Of McClellan's prep work at Sharpsburg, Carman skillfully mused, "The plan was a good one, but its execution, from beginning to end, was miserable."[134]

DOUBTS ABOUT MCCLELLAN'S ATTACK PLAN

Even when finding ways to support some of McClellan's decisions, historians are generally very critical of how McClellan planned and executed the opening of the attack at Antietam.[135] The battle was a Union victory, but McClellan's lackadaisical communication and incomplete orders were inexcusable. Under any circumstance, destruction of Lee's army would have been far easier said than done, but McClellan's effort did not get close to Lincoln's request to destroy the Confederate army, if possible, which the president made on September 15.

Not long after crossing the Antietam, Hooker felt misgivings about the army's plan, or lack thereof. He only had the First Corps immediately with him; both Mansfield's 12th and Sumner's 2nd Corps were still on the other side of Antietam Creek. With McClellan's unexpected arrival west of the Antietam shortly after Hooker crossed, the First Corps commander requested help. Even after a plea for more men, McClellan, wishing to maintain a reserve far larger than the First Corps, did not advance either the Second or 12th Corps immediately. Mansfield's corps, the smallest in the army, would not settle down west of the Antietam until after midnight. Orders to Sumner kept the Second Corps east of the creek until the following morning.

On the question of the plan for Hooker's opening attack, McClellan changed his story between his initial and final campaign reports. The difference is both slight and exceedingly important. McClellan's preliminary analysis of the Maryland campaign was completed four weeks after the battle of Antietam.

The design was to make the main attack upon the enemy's left—at least to create a diversion in favor of the main attack, with the hope of something more by assailing the enemy's right—and, as soon as one or both of the flank movements were fully successful, to attack their center with any reserve I might then have on hand.

Was the First Corps the main attack or a diversion in favor of the main attack? A month after the battle, McClellan's literal words do not provide an answer. In his final campaign report, completed in August 1863, McClellan added more detail.

My plan for the impending general engagement was to attack the enemy's left with the corps of Hooker and Mansfield, supported by Sumner's and, if necessary, by Franklin's, and, as soon as matters looked favorably there, to move the corps of Burnside against the enemy's extreme right, upon the ridge running to the south and rear of Sharpsburg, and having carried their position, to press along the crest toward our right, and whenever either of these flank movements should be successful, to advance our center with all the forces then disposable.[136]

One wonders if McClellan listed Mansfield as part of the initial attack and two other corps as support in his later report to make Hooker accountable for the morning's confused feeding of troops into the meat grinder. A man as self-righteous as McClellan was certainly capable of such an act.

Rafuse suggests McClellan's ambiguity was a sign of the general's ability to improvise and craft adaptable plans.[137] Those traits may be important, but not at the cost of insufficient support to the vanguard of an attack.

Since the First Corps was the only infantry in position at dawn on September 17, the army commander should not have had doubts about where his main attack was to fall. Also, if the 12th Corps was to be part of the opening attack, McClellan should have ordered so. He did not. Granting McClellan the benefit of the doubt is not justified in this case. His order for Hooker to advance across the creek came way too late in the day to do any good. This, coupled with the slowness in ordering up Mansfield's support, made for a strong sense of confusion about what units would be attacking when. Responsibility for a clear, written attack plan rested with McClellan. He failed.

Mansfield's men marched north after crossing Antietam Creek. Darkness certainly did not help them find Hooker's men, who were to the west. As reality played out, the 12th Corps should have simply stayed east of the creek overnight. An incredibly cogent analysis of the 2nd Corps at Antietam concluded the 12th Corps' final overnight position was nearly as distant to Hooker as Mansfield's men were before their crossing.[138]

There was also no credible reason why the Second Corps, the army's largest, stayed east of the Antietam until the morning of the 17th. McClellan was content with simply ordering Sumner to prepare for marching an hour before dawn.[139] With the inevitable chaos a large attack involved, coordinating the arrival of Sumner as battle raged was not a recipe for defeating Lee.

Some historians criticize the lack of surprise in the attack because Hooker moved troops across the Antietam a day early. This is an overrated point. The creek had few crossing points, none of which were wide enough to quickly move an overwhelming force to the west side. The only way to attack was to post corps across the creek hours before an attack could occur. Lee, a highly competent military engineer, could not have been shocked that he would eventually be attacked if he continued to stand at Sharpsburg. Even a timid general like McClellan was compelled to at least try to throw the enemy out of Maryland. Lee knew his left was McClellan's best option for opening the assault.

Surprise was as impossible at Sharpsburg as it was unnecessary. The Army of the Potomac did not need to surprise Lee at Antietam. They needed to overwhelm Confederate troops. The movement across the creek on the 16th lacked manpower. If the First and 12th Corps had been posted on high ground north of Miller's Cornfield by late afternoon on the 16th, failing to surprise Lee would not have mattered. Due to the slow nature of the movement and the lack of the 12th Corps in a front-line position, the attack on the morning of the 17th had limited potential to devastate Lee's army.

Could a vile reason have existed for McClellan's lack of direct orders of support for the First Corps? History should not lose sight of who the men were in the army's vanguard. Less than a week before the battle of Antietam, McClellan viewed the First Corps as "the only doubtful ones" in his army. The nearly 1,000 casualties they suffered at South Mountain likely did not totally diminish McClellan's qualms about the First Corps. Did he want to give Hooker's soldiers another chance to prove themselves? Or did McClellan hope the First Corps would suffer a thrashing west of Antietam Creek while his favorite troops—Porter's 5th Corps and Franklin's 6th—barely fired a shot? Keeping the Second and 12th Corps out of Hooker's dawn attack may not have been malice on McClellan's part. Yet, one may wonder why McClellan, so afraid of being outnumbered throughout his career, initially planned sending only the First Corps into the opening slaughter at Sharpsburg.

One can hardly imagine any general, even one as opinionated and arrogant as McClellan, wishing undue harm on any of his troops. Did the pettiness of McClellan and his lack of faith in the First Corps lead to their unsupported attack at Antietam? Perhaps questioning McClellan on this point is unfair. Nonetheless, the issue deserves to be pondered more by students of the campaign.

Fighting aplenty was the unalterable fate of the First Corps. As the men marched west from Antietam Creek, their first thoughts likely did not dwell on what the morning would bring. They faced more imminent danger. The late afternoon of September 16 began twelve hours of intense unknowns for the entire First Corps, from Hooker down to the humblest private. Some brave men would not live to see the next sunrise.[140]

A VERY DIFFICULT EVENING

Ricketts and Meade led the 2nd and 3rd Divisions across the North Bridge. Doubleday's 1st Division used Pry Ford downstream from the bridge. Hooker, accompanied by elements of the 3rd Pennsylvania Cavalry, crossed at the ford. With the Reserves in the lead, the First Corps initially moved northwest from the crossing points, generally following the path of the road linking Keedysville and Williamsport. Four companies of the 13th Reserves, again under the skillful leadership of Colonel McNeil, initially served as skirmishers. Eventually moving south on the Smoketown Road, the entire ten companies of McNeil's "Bucktails" lined up in the advance of the brigade. Rounds of Confederate fire echoed through the sublime Maryland landscape near the farm of the Line Family.[141] The mysterious, darkening ground and a lurking enemy of unknown force illustrated McClellan's folly of moving across Antietam Creek so late in the afternoon, rather than hours earlier.

Bold as was his style, Colonel McNeil offered to assist a company of the 3rd Pennsylvania Cavalry as sunset neared. Exchanging shots with the

Rebels for about fifteen minutes, the 13th Reserves started moving closer to the Confederates. Then, McNeil ordered his men to charge. They were the last words the respected private-turned-colonel would utter. The fatal shot entered below McNeil's right arm, passing through his lungs.

At least revenge belonged to the Reserves. As the Bucktails' historian wrote, "A mad fury seized his men. . . . With their breech-loading rifles and ample cover they were prepared to make the enemy pay dearly." Good support from other regiments in Seymour's Brigade proved important to the seizure of the East Woods during this opening brawl of the battle.[142]

Gaining part of the East Woods came at a stiff price, even if McNeil had been the only casualty. He was not. Seymour's Brigade lost "our most estimable and gallant adjutant," Augustus Cross, the young fellow who received flowers from the kind young lady in Middletown two days before. Seymour himself had requested Cross's services on the brigade staff. Only twenty-two years old, Cross would be buried at Laurel Hill Cemetery in Philadelphia.[143]

Battery B, 1st Pennsylvania Light Artillery, commanded by Capt. James Cooper, was part of the engagement, along with additional batteries from both sides. Cannoneer officer Jason Gardner remembered the fight as "the fiercest beginning of a battle that we ever saw." With combatants "full of energy," Gardner added, "We aimed our guns by the blaze from the enemy's guns."[144]

The opposing lines along Seymour's front settled into uneasy positions close to each other. A mission Colonel Fisher of the Fifth Reserves ordered during the evening cost the Reserves more men, including another officer. Concerned about the possibility of Confederates around the East Woods, Fisher, with his regiment on the left of Seymour's line, sent Lt. Hardman Petrikin and twenty-four men out to see what they could learn about the enemy. The mission was of questionable merit in the dark.

Petrikin and his band soon ran into trouble. South of the East Woods, they noticed some campfires. These brave Confederates decided to illuminate their surroundings, even in close proximity to enemy units. Although they would be surprised by Petrikin's band, the men of the 4th Alabama, on the right of Law's Brigade, were fully capable of defending themselves.

When some of the Alabamians fired, as Milton Laird of the 5th Reserves noted, "the flash of their guns" was "showing the enemy quite plain." William Rogers, major in the 4th Alabama, "was suddenly roused and startled by a volley fired by the two or three left companies of the regiment." Later, Rogers helped Petrikin, who suffered a bullet in the upper chest. Knowing his wound was mortal, Petrikin asked Rogers to return a valuable watch to his family. "I died like a soldier should, doing my duty," was what Petrikin requested be passed along to Union troops Rogers might meet. Petrikin's body was found in the Dunker Church on September 18.

Laird suggested Petrikin disobeyed Fisher's orders on the night of the 16th. Petrikin was only supposed to go "out in the field to the left of the regiment." Instead, the Pennsylvanians kept advancing south. By the time the men ran into the 4th Alabama, they were nearing the Mumma Farm, almost 2,000 feet from Fisher's line in the East Woods.[145]

Darkness certainly created havoc in the further deployment of the First Corps. Traffic jams, confused positions, and concerns from men about being separated from comrades pervaded the evening along Hooker's disjointed line.

The Reserve divisions of Anderson and Magilton moved west during Seymour's fight. The men of the 3rd Reserves, Magilton's Brigade, had known confusion for the last few days. After being separated from the division to guard the army's right flank at South Mountain, darkness on the 14th prevented Lieutenant Colonel Clark from finding the rest of Meade's command. "We were unable to rejoin the division until sunrise on the 16th," Clark wrote. Then, with many in the regiment on skirmish duty west of Antietam Creek, the impenetrable night kept several men from finding the regiment even by dawn on the 17th.[146]

Doubleday's four brigades ended up in a poor position north of Magilton and Anderson. The advance of the First Division was slowed when other elements of the corps marched across Doubleday's path, separating Patrick's Brigade from the rest of the division. After what Doubleday called "a long delay," the brigades of Phelps, Hofmann, and Gibbon joined Patrick on the Joseph Poffenberger farm.[147]

Scattered shots echoed across Doubleday's front, with some periods of more intense action prevailing. One Virginian wrote of the "very heavy fire" during the evening. The night proved deadly to Arthur Tucker, Company D, 2nd USSS. He was killed in action, undoubtedly as darkness hindered operations. An expert marksman in his early twenties, Tucker hailed from Cherryfield, in southeastern Maine near Bar Harbor.[148]

Ricketts placed his men along the Smoketown Road, due east of Magilton. Hartsuff lined up in front, with Duryée and Christian in reserve. A 13th Massachusetts man recalled how good training allowed Hartsuff's soldiers to maneuver into place under fire. The proud Bay Stater said the men "performed with as much precision and coolness as though the regiment was on a battalion drill." After the initial stress of finding their bivouac, the evening passed "quietly away" near Sam Poffenberger's farm.[149]

Charles Sloat, of the 94th New York, in Christian's Brigade, remembered the trying nature of the evening. "At intervals, the quick report of picket guns, and occasional volleys on our front kept us reminded of our business there," he wrote. Some elements of Christian's command, apparently part of the 26th New York, bivouacked farther to the east, in Poffenberger's woods.[150]

Another of Christian's soldiers, John Vautier, 88th Pennsylvania, understood how the morning portended an epic fight. In his regimental history, he philosophically wrote of what a soldier near a great battle can feel. Vautier suggested, "there was no trifling or jesting, a deeply solemn feeling entering the soul of every man as he thought of the chances for entering eternity on the morrow."[151]

About a half-mile due west, Uberto Burnham ignored the evening's intensity. He recalled sleeping soundly. "I dreamed of home," while catching some shut-eye along the Hagerstown Pike on the right wing of the First Corps. "Everything in my mind was as quiet and peaceful as if no dangers threatened me," he concluded.[152]

There were major problems with Hooker's position as dawn approached. No one had adequate knowledge of the ground. The small amount of cavalry was of limited use on unknown fields in the dark. With more time on September 16 and the 12th Corps by his side, Hooker undoubtedly would have done something about Nicodemus Hill, to the west of his position. The high ground was an excellent place to set up artillery. Enemy batteries on the hill would cause much trouble for the First Corps in the morning.

Due to a major bend in the river, the Potomac was less than a mile from the westernmost point of Hooker's line. With several hours of daylight and at least one other full corps, Hooker could have swept Confederates out of the area west of the Hagerstown Pike, dominated Nicodemus Hill, and forced Jackson out of his position by sundown on the 16th. Many of Hooker's men were posted along the high ridge along the Hagerstown Pike. But Hooker did not know enough about the countryside to see the value of attacking from a position closer to the Potomac, perhaps from the tiny towns of New Industry or Mercersville. As Hooker reportedly lamented during the evening, "If they let us start earlier, we might have finished tonight."[153]

Ignorance induced by darkness dictated another reality. An additional limitation of Hooker's line was Seymour's unsupported position. From their line in the East Woods, the isolated regiments had no friendly troops on their immediate right or left. Meade's other two brigades were positioned nearly 2,000 feet away in what history calls the North Woods. Ricketts's Division was to the north of Seymour by about the same distance.[154] Confederate pickets were literally a few yards in front of Seymour.

Near the center of Seymour's line in the East Woods, Pvt. George Palmer, who would win promotion to corporal on the following day, noted the isolated nature of the brigade's line. The soldier had "no recollection of *sleeping anywhere*, as we were so close that all their (rebel) conversation was plainly audible." During the night, seven unlucky Confederates, including a lieutenant "came into our lines, and were captured," Palmer added.[155]

Evidence suggests Meade was not aware Seymour was so far in advance of the division's other two brigades. John Burnett of the 4th Reserves suggested Meade admitted this to Hooker. If Meade's entire division had been arrayed in a single imposing line to launch a dawn attack, Burnett suggested, "the reading of history of that awful day would have been very different."[156]

Isolated regiments and mysterious topography were not the biggest problem for the First Corps west of the Antietam. Robert E. Lee certainly did not plan to grant any favors to the Army of the Potomac. McClellan's force outnumbered the Confederates by about 20,000 men at dawn on September 17, but Lee's soldiers were utterly devoted to their leader. An Alabamian wrote a letter home on the 16th. He illustrated the sheer sense of will driving Lee's men. He proudly declared, "I have had many chances to desert since we have been in Maryland but my pride will not permit me, although I was always opposed to this war and think it was begun without good cause, and only to gratify the ambition of broken politicians, yet I cannot bear the disgrace of being called a deserter."[157] This member of the 5th Alabama, his comrades, and opponents in blue were about to show the great cost of civil war. The looming morning began what remains the bloodiest day in the history of the country.

DEVIL'S DAWN

Unfamiliar with the ground around them, ignorant of enemy troop strength, and lacking support, the First Corps launched a major attack at dawn on September 17 north of Sharpsburg. The tragedy ended in a tactical stalemate, as if the gods of war wished to taunt both sides with the 8,000 casualties inflicted in Hooker's sector of the field. Due to the rate of carnage in and around Miller's Cornfield, many veterans of the battle would remember the morning as the most difficult hours of their war experience. One officer in the Pennsylvania Reserves noted a comment from Hooker late in life, when asked where the toughest combat occurred in the war. "My corps at Antietam," was Fighting Joe's immediate reply.[158]

Unsurprisingly, combat commenced with the brigade of Truman Seymour. After staying close enough to Confederate troops to hear the enemy's conversations overnight, Seymour's men found targets prior to daylight, with some sources noting 3:00 A.M. as the start of heavier firing in the East Woods. Just like the evening before, the 13th Reserves were the tip of the brigade's spear.

Now under the command of senior captain Dennis McGee, the Bucktails started firing at elements of two Confederate brigades southwest of the East Woods. With the same devotion to supporting each other shown earlier in the campaign, the four other regiments in Seymour's command were also active in the renewal of heavier fighting in the East Woods. The persistence of the brigade's regiments was "driving my pickets in," according to Confederate brigade commander James Walker. Nonetheless, Seymour's command could not push much farther than the southern boundary of the East Woods.[159]

The brigade's stellar participation in the campaign essentially stopped as other elements of the First Corps entered the fray. Sparse information exists about Seymour's five regiments as the battle intensified, and they suffered considerably fewer casualties than the average brigade under Hooker at Antietam.

Not all officers in Seymour's command earned praise. In Colonel Fisher's report, two men in the Fifth Reserves were called out for cowardice. Fisher noted how Capt. Arnodt Collins, of Company K, "by some strange fatality finds his health to fail about the commencement of every battle." The captain, who remained in the army for more than a year, was absent without leave days after the battle. Fisher also criticized Lt. A. Percival Shaw of Company F. Shaw "disgracefully fled when the regiment was fired upon during the night." Fisher continued, "My only regret is that his cowardly legs were not equal to the task of carrying him out of reach of the regiment."[160]

Two unreliable officers leading troops in direct contact with the enemy were certainly problems for an army. The misfortunes for the Union cause would grow much larger during the deployment of Ricketts's men, who had been called in to support Seymour. The losses in both armies were about to grow to horrifying proportions.

Although not the first of Ricketts's three brigades in the fight, Hart-suff's troops were likely intended as the initial wave of the division's attack toward Miller's Cornfield. Not only were Hartsuff's warriors posted farthest south, but the general was examining the area of attack prior to the assault. A serious hip wound knocked Hartsuff out of the fight, a difficult blow to Union fortunes. Headquarters erroneously received a report calling Hart-suff's wound mortal. He survived, but Hartsuff would never serve with the First Corps again. "Fighting Dick" Coulter of the 11th Pennsylvania took over as temporary brigade commander.[161]

In the confusion occurring after Hartsuff's wounding, Duryée's Brigade, originally moving south on Hartsuff's right, became the sole infantry leading the attack. In support, the division's two artillery batteries, under Ezra Mat-thews and James Thompson, wheeled south.[162] The infantry halted for a short time as cannons fired toward the waiting six Georgia regiments under the command of Marcellus Douglass, posted in a clover field south of Miller's tall cornstalks.

Although Douglass had two more regiments than Duryée, the two brigades fated to shoot each other to pieces were of nearly equal strength, about 1,100 muskets. Duryée's alignment placed the 107th Pennsylvania on the right, followed by the three New York regiments, the 97th and 104th in the middle, with the 105th extending toward the East Woods. Some members of the 105th were detailed to support Matthews's guns, which had moved even farther forward to assist the infantry.

Confederate cannons proved dangerous even before Duryée's men passed through the corn. Rufus Barnhardt of the 105th New York "was mocking the shells as they were passing over our heads, calling them little Tea-pots," according to another member of the regiment. Then, a Confederate cannon firing from the plateau east of the Dunker Church—near the battlefield's current visitors center—ended Barnhardt's life. The youngster "had the top of his head blown off by a shell or solid shot," his comrade continued. The fatal wound left "only the point of his nose and the lower part of his chin."[163] Barnhardt was one of ten men in the 105th killed outright on the 17th.

Dangers multiplied after Duryée's men reached the southern end of the cornfield. At a distance of about 200 yards, lethal range for the rifled muskets of the day, the two opposing brigades saw each other clearly for the first time. According to the historian of the 97th New York, the beloved Duryée bel-lowed to his brigade, "There they are boys, give it to them!" This was likely after some of Douglass's men fired the first shots.

Every second suddenly turned the surrounding acres into an infernal ground of horrible injuries and death. A member of the 104th New York recalled seeing the intensity of the fight to his left, where his comrades in the 105th "were being terribly slaughtered, yet dealing hard blows." These words describe how the two sides fought each other. The chance for Duryée's two left regiments to advance, then strike the side of Douglass's right allowed the Union troops to inflict their share of carnage.

One surprise to the New Yorkers was fire from the East Woods. Multiple First Corps veterans recalled being shot at from the timber after some Confederates managed to find Duryée's left flank. Artillery fire also continued to add to Duryée's casualty list.

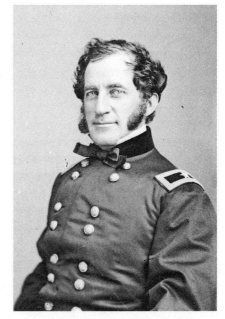

Brig. Gen. Abram Duryée led his brigade into the Cornfield at the battle of Antietam shortly after dawn. LIBRARY OF CONGRESS

The trying moments for the solitary four regiments earned Duryée even greater appreciation from his troops. The 97th's historian made the point well to Franklin Hough, who authored a history of Duryée's command. He noted, "A general that can march men into such a fight and hold them during such a carnage as was witnessed on that battlefield has acquired a moral force over them surpassed by no General in the field."[164]

A kid on the firing line could claim his share of moral force. Only fourteen years old, John Delaney, wounded in the Cornfield, was deeply admired by his superiors. The captain who recruited Company I said the underage warrior "importuned so strongly to go," Delaney was added to the muster roll. Of Delaney, Captain Sheafer added, "Such men are the real heroes of our late war, and I do think our country owes them a debt of gratitude that can never be repaid."

Without the benefit of much cover, Duryée and Douglass tore into each other for what must have seemed like an eternity to those involved.

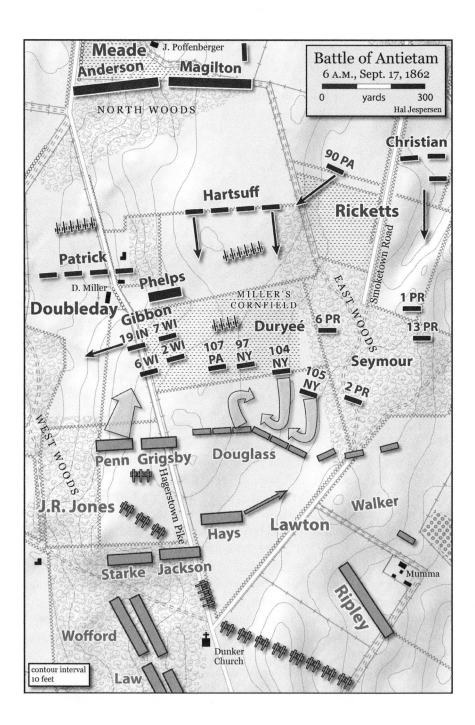

Battle of Antietam
6 A.M., Sept. 17, 1862

0   yards   300

Hal Jespersen

Meade
Anderson

J. Poffenberger

Magilton

NORTH WOODS

90 PA

Christian

Hartsuff

Ricketts

Patrick

D. Miller

Phelps

Doubleday

Gibbon

19 IN 7 WI

6 WI 2 WI

MILLER'S
CORNFIELD

Duryeé

6 PR

EAST WOODS

Smoketown Road

1 PR

13 PR

107 97
PA NY

104
NY

105
NY

Seymour

2 PR

WEST WOODS

Penn Grigsby

Douglass

Walker

J.R. Jones

Hays

Lawton

Mumma

Starke Jackson

Ripley

Wofford

Dunker
Church

Law

Hagerstown Pike

contour interval
10 feet

"They fought like devils," one New Yorker said to compliment his opponents. Douglass himself was killed in action. The Confederates wounded Lt. Col. Howard Carroll, commander of the 105th New York. As he was carried off the field, Carroll declared, "Give them another charge, boys." The native of Ireland would die on September 29.[165]

More brave men fell as the early morning progressed. James Adsit, 97th New York, received a nasty wound. He would lose most of his lower right leg at Smoketown Hospital, north of the battlefield.[166]

By 6:15 A.M., a stalemate prevailed between Duryée and the stubborn Georgians. Eventually, Duryée decided his men had endured enough. With questions about the stability of his line, low ammunition, and the imminent arrival of support, Ricketts's initial line of battle started to fall back. The retrograde was "not a retreat," one of Duryée's men wrote, "as the enemy had made no attempt to charge. We could have no occasion under the sun to retreat."

Duryée reported casualties of nearly 30 percent. The 97th New York bore the brunt, with more than half of its soldiers becoming a casualty. Staying in line longer and facing additional federal troops, Georgians suffered more; nearly 550 casualties were reported, half of the men Douglass took into action. Because of the generally static nature of the Confederate line, Union men found a haunting symmetry after seeing the remnants of the Georgians on the following day. As Isaac Hall of the 97th New York noted, "In all the battles in which I participated, I never saw a more uniform and perfect line of dead, and in no other so numerous in line." Even after dealing out so much damage, Hall felt, "Our brigade seemed but a corporal's guard" after the fight in the Cornfield.[167]

Developments along the Hagerstown Pike to the west of Duryée's position were destined to devastate more regiments. Doubleday had his men moving south, with Gibbon's Iron Brigade receiving support from Phelps and Patrick. Lt. Col. J. William Hofmann of the 56th Pennsylvania and his three other regiments would spend the battle supporting batteries to the north. The start of Doubleday's initial contribution to the Cornfield bloodletting was occurring as Duryée's fight was already underway. One can only imagine how overwhelming the First Corps could have been if all three of Ricketts's brigades hit the Cornfield and East Woods at the same time Doubleday's units struck.

The unchecked Rebel guns on Nicodemus Hill had perfect range and a protected position to be merciless. Although Phelps's regiments did not lose a man to the fire, the brigade commander reported, "The direct and cross artillery fire from the enemy's batteries playing upon this field was very heavy." Rufus Dawes, major of the 6th Wisconsin, recalled how the shells bursting overhead hurt his regiment. Capt. David Noyes lost a foot to one blast, while twelve other casualties were suffered from the same shot, including one soldier who lost both arms.

More deaths and wounds followed. A captain who was Dawes's best friend lost his life on the ground of D. R. Miller's farmhouse and orchard. Then, before the 6th Wisconsin had moved beyond the Cornfield, regimental commander Edward Bragg, a gifted and respected officer, suffered an elbow wound serious enough for him to leave the field. Dawes now found himself in command of his regiment, divided into two sections by the amount of Confederate fire near the Hagerstown Pike. The only choice was to advance through the leaden storm. Immediately after the battle, Lyman Holford wrote how the 6th Wisconsin was "badly cut up," with some companies having only six men present for duty.[168]

Assistance from Phelps's men caused the area on both sides of the Hagerstown Pike to roar with an intensity the men could never forget. Like the struggle Duryée faced, men fell rapidly on both sides, with First Corps troops greatly bothered by additional elements of Jackson's command in the West Woods. Gibbon's tactical skill showed during this part of the fight, as he had the 19th Indiana and 7th Wisconsin swing to the right, with Patrick in support.

Phelps ordered Col. Henry Post and his Second United States Sharpshooters forward and to the right to protect the brigade from enfilading fire. The Unionist marksmen found many targets. But great shots can themselves become the hunted. As Phelps reported, "The loss of the Second U.S. Sharpshooters at this point was severe." Lt. John Whitman, known as "Jack," fell with a mortal wound "while leading and cheering on his men," Michigan troops from Company B. A Vermont sharpshooter, Silas Howard, was hit multiple times, with his death expected quickly from the devastation his body endured just one month before his twenty-first birthday. Discharged in March 1863 for his Antietam wounds, Howard had plenty of life left. He died one week shy of his eighty-seventh birthday in 1928.

Post would miss six weeks recovering from a wound sustained south of the Cornfield. "The fire from both sides seemed to blacken out all at once," reported William Humphrey, a Vermonter. Lewis Parmelee, adjutant in the 2nd USSS, would die during the battle. While only in his early 20s, Parmelee was considered "the beau ideal of a soldier, of charming manners and beloved by the men."

According to New Hampshire sharpshooter Edwin Chadwick, "Lt. John W. Thompson of Nashua was shot through the head while advancing with or near the Adjutant." Like Humphrey, Chadwick found the engagement to be disorienting as well as frightening. He added, "The smoke was so dense that we could hardly tell friend from foe." Overall, the 2nd USSS suffered thirteen killed in action and more than sixty total casualties, a loss well exceeding 25 percent.[169]

As minutes passed, Union troops pressed resolutely against Stonewall Jackson. Pressure from Doubleday proved too much for Confederates defending the area west of the Hagerstown Pike and south of the Cornfield. The concentrated slaughter of Rebel brigades under the commands of William Starke and James Jack-

Lt. Lewis Parmelee, adjutant of the 2nd United States Sharpshooters, was a young officer killed in action at Antietam. LIBRARY OF CONGRESS

son was notable. These men from Stonewall's command faced withering fire along a fence bordering the west side of the Hagerstown Pike. A Virginia officer described the fight as "terrible" and "very hotly contested."[170]

To the east, Ricketts's sector of the Cornfield, Coulter was leading his brigade toward their Maryland destiny. The 9th New York State Militia was on the brigade's left, entirely within the East Woods. Originally, the formation also had the 13th Massachusetts under arborous cover, but Seymour recommended Coulter shift to the right to avoid the Reserves. Thus, half of the 13th Massachusetts were in the corn. With the 11th Pennsylvania on the 13th's right, the 12th Massachusetts covered the brigade's western flank.[171]

The four regiments "Fighting Dick" led faced what the First Corps endured all morning: tenacious Southern warriors.

"Never did I see more rebs to fire at then that moment," George Kimball, 12th Massachusetts, noted. The combat was exceedingly bloody. After progress beyond the southern edge of the corn, Kimball recalled the damage both sides sustained. He wrote, "We literally wiped out the rebs in our front," while the cost to the 12th Massachusetts was the highest as a percentage of engaged men for any Union regiment at Antietam. "We closed upon the colors till there were not even enough in our regiment for a decent company," Kimball recalled.

Table 1.2: Casualties by Company in the 12th Massachusetts at Antietam

Company	Killed	Wounded	Total
A	4	16	20
B	9	22	31
C	2	22	24
D	4	9	13
E	9	21	30
F	2	11	13
G	4	25	29
H	0	1	1
I	7	24	31
K	5	15	20
Total	46	166	212

Note: To the total of casualties by company must be added staff officers Burbank and Kimball. The data in the table was gleaned from a letter located in the casualty folder of the 12th Massachusetts' box at the Office of Adjutant General Archives Museum in Concord. Sources differ regarding the number of casualties suffered at Antietam for the 12th Massachusetts, but numbers gained from analysis of this document are used here. The single casualty recorded for Company H suggests the regiment likely only had nine companies engaged, which would raise the casualty percentage to about 75 percent, rather than the 67 percent if all ten companies were in action.

The 214 casualties in the 12th Massachusetts were inflicted over just about thirty hellish minutes. The list included a mortally wounded commanding officer, Maj. Elisha Burbank. Another officer who would die was assistant surgeon Albert Kendall. Kimball was impressed by the surgeon's courage. Kendall was "a good, brave man, and was hit while attending to wounded men in the line of battle, or near it. I saw him well out to the front." Table 1.2 lists the casualties in the regiment for each company under Burbank.

"Men falling very fast" was a memory for Sgt. Lewis Reed of the 12th Massachusetts. He recollected the sheer horror the brigade experienced in and near the Cornfield. He saw his tentmate Benjamin Curtis fall, then Reed suffered his own wound to the neck. Recalling the ordeal, he wrote, "My right arm was useless. With my left hand I found my shirt and blouse filled with blood, and I supposed it was my last day on earth. I had the usual feelings of home and friends. And thousands of thoughts ran through my mind at once."

Reed dropped some equipment and his canteen to decrease the load he carried as he moved to the rear. He certainly regretted the loss of a water source, but "I hope it helped some poor fellow out of suffering." He fainted several times before finding a hospital. After getting his wound dressed, Reed concluded, "I was so weak I could not stand."[172]

In battle line next to the 12th Massachusetts, men of the 11th Pennsylvania, under the command of Capt. David Cook due to Coulter's elevation to brigade command, experienced its own set of problems. Robert Shearer nearly had a deadly encounter with a Keystone State man close to him on the firing line.

> *The man in rear of me was very excitable, and every time he fired he would get back a step or two. I pulled him up into the line a few times but he got back again. [F]inally he fired his gun so close to my ear that I staggered. As soon as I recovered, I grabbed him and kicked him into the line. He swore he would shoot me. I said, "Now is the time." I levelled my gun on him and that cured that notion and we were soon both busy shooting at the Rebs.*[173]

A 13th Massachusetts soldier recalled how control of the eastern Cornfield switched a few times during the fight. One side would gain the upper hand, fall back, then retake lost ground as more dead and wounded fell.

Artillery fire played havoc, as well.[174] History can never know how many men were hit by cannon shots from artillerists on their own side.

William Prince of the 9th New York State Militia, wounded in the fight, remarked how the battle turned men into machines. "I was *mad*," he noted, "I loaded and fired and loaded and fired." The color company—with twenty-four men as the action began—dwindled to twelve, "all in a bunch around the colors." With the fight swirling around in a fiendish intensity, Prince "took deliberate aim at someone every time," firing about twenty rounds "when we were being so cut up." Although sustaining the least loss of the brigade's four regiments, Prince and his comrades suffered more than a hundred wounded and six killed in action.[175]

The 11th Pennsylvania endured casualties in excess of 50 percent. The brigade suffered nearly 600 casualties, half of the division's total, and the most by far of any First Corps brigade at Antietam.[176]

A COLONEL'S COWARDICE

Christian's Brigade lined up on the southern edge of the East Woods, essentially serving as the far left of the First Corps. Like Hartsuff's men, the movement forward of Christian's Brigade was delayed. The reason for the postponement was not the wounding of a gallant commanding officer. Instead, the men found themselves abandoned by Christian as the fight commenced.

John Vautier wrote of the enemy's cannon fire "shrieking and flying all around, striking the ground in a wicked manner and throwing up dirt and dust in great clouds as high as the trees." Falling limbs became a danger to the confused regiments.[177]

Lt. William Halstead of the 26th New York, Christian's former command, described the brigade commander's reaction to the tumult. "A soldier of the Mexican War and a man of many noble qualities," Christian still "could not stand shells." As the deadly barrage rained down, the colonel dismounted and led his horse away from the action. William Gifford, another officer in the 26th, said Christian "almost created a stampede among some troops in the rear."

The loss of another brigade commander brought the chance of coordinated effort to a halt at a vitally important moment. Gifford believed the time called for a charge from the woods toward generally unseen Confederates to the south, "but for lack of concerted action on the part of our line officers, it was not undertaken."[178]

Enlisted men who fled the field of battle could be subjected to death, a fate Christian deserved for running away from battle on September 17. Instead, he was allowed to resign.[179] Peter Lyle, far more courageous and competent than the buffoon he replaced, assumed brigade command.

In the northern section of the trees, Enoch Jones of the 26th New York recalled, "I was unable to see clearly what was in front of us. I saw no troops other than our regiment." Then, a strong leader appeared. Truman Seymour apparently decided the regiments from another command needed nudging. The Pennsylvanian demanded, "Why do you halt, who commands this brigade?" Seymour then ordered, "Forward, brigade."

Christian's men would prove far worthier of the title of American soldier than their failed colonel. Forming a front in the southern edge of the East Woods, albeit late, the brigade aligned well with Hartsuff. With Lyle's 90th Pennsylvania, now under the control of Lt. Col. William Leech, detached for a time to support artillery, the 88th Pennsylvania was close to the left flank of the 9th New York State Militia. To the 88th's left were the 94th New York and the 26th New York in the southeastern corner of the woods.

Maj. Gilbert Jennings of the 26th was thankful to see a man-made obstruction offering protection along the southern line of the woods. He wrote, "Thanks to the Maryland fashion of building fences, our men were saved from many casualties." One mysterious aspect of the fight was the difficulty in seeing the enemy, even though their fire was a great danger to Lyle's troops. "They gave it to us in a little better shape than we were able to return it," Lieutenant Halstead remembered. Initially, opposing troops were from Trimble's Brigade, under the command of James Walker, who would be wounded in the fight.

Halstead also noticed the possibility of a flank attack from the Confederates. The 26th New York's left flank lacked support. Actually, Walker saw more of an opportunity to wheel his right regiments toward the 9th New York State Militia. This effort failed, as Walker noted in his report. Clearly, Lyle's three regiments farther to the east assisted with the repulse of this attack.[180]

At about this time, the 90th Pennsylvania began to move south toward its three sister regiments. Another key reason for the success against Walker's attempted flank attack was the presence of General Ricketts, according to Lt. George Watson of the 90th. The division commander "encouraged us by his presence and had his horse killed near me," Watson remembered.

After assisting in the repulse of Confederates to the south, the brigades under Coulter and Lyle were not in the greatest of shape to advance as far south as Doubleday's Division to the west. Vautier argued the brigade should have stayed in line longer, perhaps to attack as a means to end the stalemate prevailing at the southern end of the East Woods. However, "much to our surprise and against our protests, we were ordered to fall back."[181]

When the moment seemed propitious for an advance to rout Confederate defenders, one of the most spectacular yet doomed counter charges of the war was unleashed. John Bell Hood's two brigades responded to the call for Confederate reinforcements. As the First Corps was about to learn, Hood never advanced without an impetuousness propelled by the immortality of his command.

James Ricketts, leading the Second Division of the First Corps, had two horses shot from under him at the battle of Antietam. LIBRARY OF CONGRESS

TEENAGERS WIN THE MEDAL OF HONOR

Always ready for a brawl, Hood's two brigades numbered about 2,200 men. Under the command of William Wofford and Evander Law, strong leadership blessed the two brigades. Famished from days without rations and the fight against Seymour's Brigade the night before, Hood ordered the charge in an attempt to stabilize Jackson's wavering line. The division commander wrote, "With the trusty Law on my right, in the edge of the wood, and the gallant Colonel Wofford in command of the Texas brigade on the left, near the pike, we moved forward."[182] The Cornfield, already soaked in Northern and Southern blood, was about to have gallons of redness added to the soil.

The sight of so many tenacious Confederates running at them inspired dread and fear among the men of Doubleday's Division. After about ninety minutes of hard-won advances, the men knew they could not hold out against Hood's charge. Soldiers of various commands, together in the clover field south of the corn, made the best decision they could to retreat northward.

Times such as this displayed the reason why an infantry regiment was often held in reserve to guard artillery and serve as a backup to advancing troops. Following time in the corn, the 20th New York State Militia, part of Patrick's Brigade, moved west near the two guns of Lt. James Stewart. In this supporting role, the 20th assisted in the withdrawal of Wisconsin men and others falling back. With pride in his memoirs, Col. Theodore Gates noted Maj. Jacob Hardenbergh gave valuable service at this time covering the retreat. Additionally, Gates wrote, "he also captured and brought off a Confederate battle-flag, the bearer of it having been shot down by private Isaac Thomas."

Two of Patrick's other regiments deserve credit for helping blunt Hood's charge. Advancing earlier in the morning on the right, the 21st and 35th New York had a position in the northern part of the West Woods. The 19th Indiana and 7th Wisconsin from Gibbon's Brigade were in the same area, a spectacular spot to hit Wofford's left. First Corps men "sent a hail of lead into the flank and rear," of Wofford's men, one historian suggested.[183]

Active friendly infantry did not guarantee the safety of Stewart's guns. Under a stunning amount of fire from Wofford, Stewart was rapidly losing gunners and horses. General Gibbon dismounted to aid his old command as a cannoneer. "Seeing the gunner of the left piece fall," an appreciative Stewart recalled, General Gibbon "dismounted from his horse and acted as gunner of the piece."

The moment was truly desperate. Concerned his guns would fall into Rebel hands, Stewart wrote, "The General's valuable service on that occasion was possibly the means

Brig. Gen. John Gibbon provided direct assistance to Battery B, 4th U.S. Artillery, during the terrible minutes the guns fought against Confederates near the Cornfield on the west side of the Hagerstown Pike. LIBRARY OF CONGRESS of saving glorious old Battery B from capture." Of the fight, which would cost the battery forty casualties and dozens of horses, Stewart remarked how the Confederate attackers were "at, possibly, as close a range as ever troops reached a battery without capturing it."[184]

Commendable service was being performed by a determined boy. Johnny Cook, only fifteen years old, was the battery's bugler. With fire from the enemy less than 50 feet way, Cook became a cannoneer, just like Gibbon. Blasting the Rebels with shots of canister, Stewart's smoothbore cannons served as giant shotguns, wiping out the Confederates who had the audacity but not the numbers to seize the battery's pieces.

For his work with Stewart's guns, Cook would be one of four First Corps soldiers under the age of twenty to win the Medal of Honor at Antietam. His citation denoted, "Volunteered at the age of 15 years to act as a cannoneer, and as such volunteer served a gun

During the hellfire at Antietam, Lt. Hillary Beyer's efforts to assist wounded comrades in the 90th Pennsylvania won him a Medal of Honor, the nation's highest military award. LIBRARY OF CONGRESS

under a terrific fire of the enemy." William Hogarty, 23rd New York, and John Johnson of the 2nd Wisconsin, two infantrymen detached to help the battery, also won the Medal of Honor while working Stewart's guns.[185]

To the east, the timing of the 90th Pennsylvania's advance made them victims of the whirlwind. Hartsuff's command was about spent, and the time for support was at hand. "It was a hot place where we were," wrote officer A. J. Sellers of the 90th. During the regiment's time supporting artillery, Sellers recalled Coulter's plea to Lyle for assistance. "For God's sake, come help us out," one new brigade commander said to another.[186]

Spared the initial part of the fight on the firing line, the 90th Pennsylvania's battle was still very costly. Nearly 100 casualties were reported, including 13 dead. Lyle's four regiments combined for 254 casualties, more than 10 percent of which were men listed as missing.[187]

The right to be referred to as a great battle leader does not belong solely to generals. A humble seventeen-year-old private can inspire through bold action. William Paul of the 90th experienced vicious combat during his regiment's advance. Seeing the color-bearer and other members of his company hit, Paul, "under the most withering and concentrated fire," picked up the regimental standard to help rally the regiment. He would win the Medal of Honor for the deed, as would one of the regiment's officers. Lt. Hillary Beyer remained on the field for a time after the 90th fell back. He assisted some wounded comrades, "carrying one of them to a place of safety." Beyer, less than two weeks away from turning twenty-five, was the oldest of seven First Corps Medal of Honor winners at Antietam.[188]

MOWED DOWN BY THE PENNSYLVANIA RESERVES

Staggered by massive casualties, Hood's men still had fight left. They pressed Northern soldiers out of the corn. Two brigades of the Pennsylvania Reserves now had the chance to shine. Anderson and Magilton's troops were in an excellent spot to serve as an additional check on Hood.

Men in the two brigades had an interesting start to their day, thanks to actions by General Meade, who had been in a foul mood at the start of the battle. His regular level of low patience with imperfection hit rock bottom as he led two brigades out of the North Woods. On three different occasions, Meade railed into those of questionable judgment.

First, during a conversation with Hooker, Meade was interrupted by an officer who was having second thoughts about the previous evening. Recalling a Confederate battery in the distance as darkness came on, the major regretted the lack of a charge against the cannons.

"We could have taken that battery last night," the major said, per a man in the 4th Reserves. The soldier added, "Meade was annoyed at the interruption, and said in his *usual courteous style*, 'Well, why the hell didn't you?'"

Artillery fire was landing in the vicinity of the two Reserve brigades during these tense minutes. One man of the 7th Reserves cracked. Rushing out of line, the shirker attempted "to dig his way into the root of a large tree." Agitated by the scared soldier, Meade charged on his horse, then "gave that poor fellow a stinging taste of the flat side of his old saber." Perhaps sensing more of a threat from his division commander than Confederate shells and bullets, the soldier rejoined the ranks.

Meade's cantankerous ways were again on display after he saw a dismounted Colonel Magilton. Although friends for an extended period, Meade did not like to see the brigade commander dismounted. "Wild with anger," Meade gave Magilton "such a sulphorous bath ...I have never heard equaled."[189]

Desperate work called, so the brigades went forward, offering a stabilizing presence to those units along the First Corps front falling back from Hood's charge. In his report, Meade wrote the brigades had the role "of covering the withdrawal of our people and resisting the further advance of the enemy." With the 10th Reserves sent to the right across the Hagerstown Pike, the line of men from west to east included the 9th, 11th, 12th, 7th, 4th, 3rd, and 8th Reserves.[190]

George Meade, who would command the Army of the Potomac at Gettysburg and beyond, led the Pennsylvania Reserves at Antietam. His notorious temper was on display prior to the movement of two of his brigades to assist other First Corps units. LIBRARY OF CONGRESS

An order from Hooker to send a brigade to solidify the line in the East Woods arrived as Hood's Division approached. Law's attack on the left side of Meade's line at nearly the same moment Magilton's regiments were moving left caused havoc, threatening the ability of his two brigades to fulfill the role Meade envisioned north of the Cornfield. Three regiments of Law's command and supporting Confederate artillery delivered "a severe fire" as Magilton's troops tried to execute Hooker's order to support the East Woods. Dozens of Pennsylvanians fell.[191]

Some of Law's men jumped the fence to engage Magilton's Brigade in close quarters. A member of the 8th Reserves recalled the intensity of the combat. George Harlan, a corporal in Company I who suffered a broken leg, was "sitting upon the ground" as "he called to us to rally around the flag and not to desert it." As Confederates were "piling over that fence, I lost all interest in that flag." The brave Harlan was then the victim of a head shot from one determined Southerner. Enough troops from the 8th Reserves remained to retaliate; a barrage of lead brought down the Confederate who killed Harlan.[192]

With Colonel Bolinger wounded at South Mountain, Maj. Chauncey Lyman commanded the 7th Reserves. The regiment stood near the middle of the two-brigade line Meade had advanced. Lyman reported his men were under "a galling fire of musketry for some time." Even with losses mounting, Lyman's soldiers "firmly remained on the ground until their ammunition was nearly expended." Remembering the intensity of the battle, Griffen Baldwin of the 7th Reserves wrote, "We made history fast that day."[193]

To the immediate west of Lyman and his brave regiment, Anderson's men made sure Hood's attack foundered. The smoky ground to the south obscured the Cornfield, so the charging Confederates remained hidden from view. "The first notice they got of us was a volley at point blank range, which brought them to a halt," a member of the 11th Reserves wrote. Such close firing was especially devastating, because the regiment used high-caliber smoothbore muskets shooting "buck and ball," making each weapon a very powerful shotgun.

As if this was not punishment enough, Captain Dick of the 9th Reserves reported his men "delivered the entire volley of the regiment." Visions of the awful morning were still fresh for one veteran of Dick's regiment in the early twentieth century. He wrote how the fight with part of Hood's Division began. The soldier stated, "We held our fire until we could see their knees, and then let them have it." Wofford's advance ground to a halt.[194]

Victims of walls of lead from Anderson's Brigade included the 1st Texas. Nearly 90 percent of that regiment's engaged troops were casualties at Antietam. Samuel Johnson of the 9th Reserves would be wounded capturing two flags from the overwhelmed Texans, an act for which he would win the Medal of Honor. Johnson was only seventeen years old. The following day, Meade informed McClellan of the flag capture. The proud division commander suggested the 1st Texas was "completely annihilated" by the determined Reserves.[195]

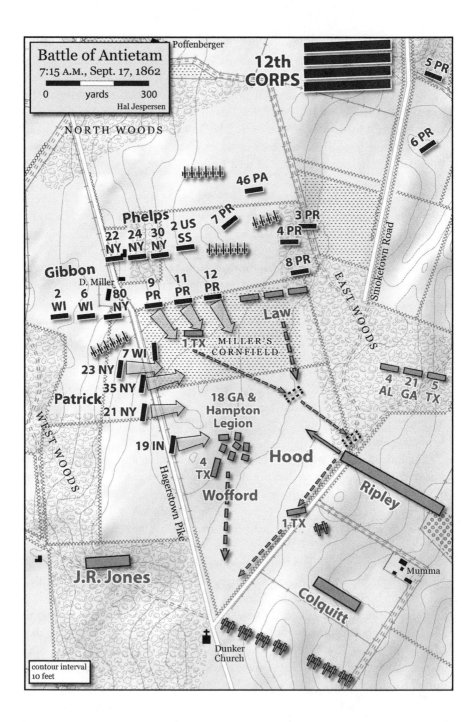

Battle of Antietam
7:15 A.M., Sept. 17, 1862

0   yards   300
Hal Jespersen

12th
CORPS

Poffenberger

5 PR

6 PR

NORTH WOODS

46 PA

Phelps   7 PR   3 PR
22 24 30 2 US   4 PR
NY NY NY SS

Gibbon   8 PR
D. Miller   9   11   12
2   6   80   PR   PR   PR   Law
WI WI NY

EAST WOODS

Smoketown Road

1 TX   MILLER'S
        CORNFIELD

7 WI

23 NY   4   21   5
                                   AL GA TX
35 NY

Patrick   21 NY   18 GA &
                       Hampton
                       Legion

          19 IN   Hood

               4
               TX   Ripley
          Wofford
                              1 TX

J.R. Jones   Mumma

                    Colquitt

                    Dunker
                    Church

WEST WOODS

Hagerstown Pike

contour interval
10 feet

Seeing the retreat, regiments that had delivered flank fire against Hood's left on the Confederates' way north saw the opportunity to charge. While assisting in the final repulse of Hood's attack, the 19th Indiana suffered notably. The action cost the regiment its leader, Lt. Col. Alois Bachman, hit multiple times. Capt. William Dudley, barely twenty years old, took command of the battered regiment.[196]

Hood lacked sufficient troops to press the advantage his surprise counterattack offered. As the pugnacious Confederate general noted in his memoirs, "whole ranks of brave men, whose deeds were unrecorded save in the hearts of loved ones at home, were mowed down in heaps to the right and left."[197]

THE WHAT IFS OF UNINJURED JOE HOOKER

At about the time Hood's attack reached its denouement, the First Corps was finally receiving infantry support. Joseph Mansfield and the 12th Corps approached from the north. After surviving the Cornfield fight, Robert Shearer of the 11th Pennsylvania was overjoyed as fresh troops arrived: "I remember we cheered Mansfield as he came marching to help us." The appreciative Keystone Stater added, "We happened to need someone just about then to hold up our end of the line."[198] It was only 7:30 a.m.

Mansfield's time as a corps commander on the field was exceedingly brief. He suffered a mortal wound near where the 13th Reserves had met the enemy the evening before, a bit north of the East Woods. The new 12th Corps commander, Alpheus Williams, a diligent volunteer officer, quickly sought out Hooker to gain insights into the best deployment for the arriving troops. Elements of Williams's command would stretch out along the First Corps' original battlefront, with one brigade augmenting Gibbon and other units on the right flank. Additionally, the 12th Corps placed a division well south of the Cornfield within ninety minutes.

Besides the obvious need for more men, another necessary element during this part of the battle was strong leadership. First Corps units were tired and running low on ammunition when a period of relative stability prevailed following Hood's retreat. Hooker had a chance to bring order to the chaos and put the First Corps in better position with the infusion of morale that a fighting corps commander could provide. Mansfield and Williams were inexperienced in field command, and Sumner—whenever he would finally arrive with the 2nd Corps—knew nothing of the morning's action and lacked McClellan's trust. Hooker was the man to bolster fortunes on the Union right. Perhaps Fighting Joe could turn the limited progress of the morning into greater success in conjunction with fresh supporting troops.

The chance existed to throw retreating Confederate units back even farther, perhaps placing Lee's entire army at McClellan's mercy. Scanning the ground to the south, Hooker undoubtedly developed some ideas to press the issue to a satisfactory conclusion. Then, one Confederate bullet changed the picture.

On a slight rise of ground south of the Cornfield, perhaps around 8:00 A.M., Hooker and his already wounded white horse made an obvious target. A shot hit Hooker in the middle of his right foot without damaging any bones. Although far from the most serious wound inflicted on September 17, Hooker began to lose a good deal of blood, especially problematic because the First Corps commander did not immediately know of his wound. While heading north on a stretcher, the general—his fighting proclivities intact—ordered forward regiments of the 12th Corps.[199]

No student of the Maryland campaign would conclude McClellan might grow suddenly aggressive with Edwin Sumner as the senior field officer north of Sharpsburg. The loss of Hooker guaranteed a defensive mindset would overtake Union tactical thinking. This became even more likely after Sumner's first major move at Antietam. John Sedgwick's Second Corps division was about to be seriously chopped up.[200]

Potential existed for Sumner to plan a better attack than the disaster Sedgwick encountered in the West Woods. According to Doubleday, General Patrick—the officer on the field who knew the most about the ground in the northern part of the West Woods—suggested the position for the renewed attack. With better analysis of the situation, the Second Corps division could "enfilade the enemy's line and drive him from his strong position, near the Dunker Church, which seemed to be the key of the battlefield."[201] Instead, Sedgwick's brigades charged nearly due west with unprotected flanks. One of three men in the division's attack became a casualty.

A portion of Sedgwick's fleeing division ran north, into a line of three regiments under Patrick. "Partly to rally the retiring troops and partly to hold with our remaining cartridges until order could be restored," Patrick kept his men in line near the northern terminus of the West Woods. Few rallied around the New Yorkers, so Patrick fell back to a point where the 20th New York State Militia rejoined the brigade.[202]

Two officers at Antietam wrote about the readiness of the weary First Corps to continue the fight. Even with perhaps no more than 6,500 men after Hooker's wounding, Jacob Cox suggested the First Corps' "organization was preserved," and "the story that it was utterly dispersed was a mistake." Ezra Carman, who devoted much of his later life to studying the battle, added the First Corps "had suffered loss, but was not dispersed or routed. There was fight in the men yet, and they would have proven it had they been called upon."[203]

As the only major general in the army with experience observing battle in the area around and south of the Cornfield, Joe Hooker gave the army the best opportunity for late morning success north of Sharpsburg. He might have found the right combination of forces to renew the attack with elements of three corps. Simply placing the First and 12th Corps out of the fight seems ridiculous, but McClellan's lack of topographical knowledge and offensive planning dictated the end of the battle around the bloody acres so many men had fought over.

McClellan agreed with the idea of Hooker being his only hope in the battle's northern sector. Perhaps his words were merely meant to make Hooker feel better, but McClellan expressed deep appreciation to the First Corps commander on September 20. Thanking Hooker and expressing "intense regret" of his subordinate's wound, McClellan suggested,

> *Had you not been wounded when you were, I believe the result of the battle would have been the entire destruction of the rebel army, for I know that, with you at its head, your corps would have kept on until it gained the main road. As a slight expression of what I think you merit, I have requested that the brigadier-general's commission rendered vacant by Mansfield's death may be given to you. I will this evening write a private note to the President on the subject, and I am glad to assure you that, so far as I can learn, it is the universal feeling of the army that you are most deserving in it. With the sincere hope that your health may soon be restored, so that you may again be with us in the field, I am, my dear general, your sincere friend.*[204]

McClellan undoubtedly exaggerated. By itself, the First Corps could not completely crush Confederate resistance north of town. But three Unionist corps attacking from the north had potential for dramatic results. Hooker's wound qualifies as a fascinating What If in a battle filled with such items for historians to ponder.

Aftermath of Armageddon

As the battle continued on September 17, McClellan came close to a major victory. With progress at the Sunken Road—south of the East Woods but still north of town—as well as Burnside's eventual crossing of Antietam Creek to the south, the Army of the Potomac seriously pressed Lee's men. Timely arrival of A. P. Hill's division from Harpers Ferry forced Burnside back, although the Ninth Corps held the west side of the creek as the battle closed.

Suffering 11 percent of the battle's total casualties, the First Corps' opening attack proved very costly. Nearly 2,600 killed, wounded, and missing were reported by Hooker's command, almost three of every ten men of the corps who were engaged. On the Union side, only the Second Corps suffered more at Antietam. Ricketts lost slightly more than one in three men, almost 10 percent of the Army of the Potomac's loss.

Like all other parts of the army, the First Corps did not strike a decisive blow, but immense casualties were inflicted on Jackson's men. The great Stonewall despaired of his ability to hold the Cornfield sector. Might have beens do not create military victory. The vision of a unified attack at dawn with the First and 12th Corps are now just for armchair generals and historians. Lee's ultimate retreat across the Potomac during the night of September 18–19 ended his invasion of Maryland, at least. Three days later, President Lincoln felt Lee's flight from Sharpsburg justified issuing the preliminary Emancipation Proclamation, which announced, at least on paper, the intent to free slaves in those states still in rebellion.

On September 18, only 6,337 men in the First Corps answered roll call. This includes 353 infantry officers and 5,327 enlisted men. Artillery units added 21 officers and 663 cannoneers. In addition to killed and wounded, stragglers and sick men grievously hindered the corps' effectiveness. Ricketts's Division was in the worst shape. The command listed only 890 infantrymen present, plus 74 officers.[205]

No one in the First Corps had previously endured a three-week period as difficult as the close of the summer. Several regiments engaged at Second Bull Run also suffered greatly during the Maryland campaign. Gibbon's Brigade sustained more than 1,500 casualties from August 28 through September 17. The First Corps' mid-September amounted to 3,600 casualties, leaving several commands terribly weakened. The return of hundreds of stragglers could not compensate for the deaths and wounds of those strong and brave enough to face destiny in the Cornfield and East Woods.

South Mountain and Antietam shook the foundations of the First Corps' stability: competent officers. The two engagements inflicted eighteen casualties on corps, division, brigade, regiment, or battery leadership in Hooker's command. Several excellent men, such as Hatch, Hartsuff, and O'Neil, were lost to future service. At least the wounds to Wisconsin regimental leaders Fairchild and Bragg did not end their service to the Iron Brigade.

Acting corps commander George Meade's slight wound did not merit mention on the casualty list. He let his wife know of the minor bruise from a shell. His favorite horse, Old Baldy, was seriously injured, but the fighting equine was going to be just fine. "Baldy was shot through the neck, but will get over it," Meade wrote. Five days later, the mount was showing signs of the fortitude of a legendary combat horse. Meade added, "Old Baldy is doing well and is good for lots of fights yet."[206] Meade was not always right, but he knew Old Baldy well.

Truman Seymour certainly knew the Pennsylvania Reserves. On September 27, while acting as commander of the Third Division, he wrote Governor Curtin to discuss the battered condition of the command. Noting how the Reserves had "justly won every title to esteem," Seymour pressed for more recruits; the command was only at half strength. If faced with more fighting,

the "Reserve Corps" must become entirely dissolved, and cease to exist, except in name or on paper—unless its ranks are promptly filled. Recruiting has thus far proved a failure, and cannot be relied upon. It is respectfully suggested that, if the requisite number of men cannot be added by draft, or otherwise, to these skeleton companies (which is the best possible course to pursue) that new companies should be sent out with organization complete—and that those now in the field be consolidated in the proper standard.[207]

For the second time in seventy-two hours, men of the First Corps awoke to the cost of a battle. Possessing a field of victory at Antietam like they had at South Mountain, few aspects of a First Corps soldier's life left more indelible memories than the carnage north of Sharpsburg.

George Noyes of Doubleday's staff discovered many ghastly sights. "Passing through this cornfield," he lamented, "with the dead lying all through its aisles, out into an uncultivated field beyond, I saw bodies, attired mainly in rebel gray, lying in ranks so regular, that Death the Reaper must have mowed them down in swaths."[208]

George Ely, 2nd Wisconsin company commander wounded at Antietam, noted the macabre post-battle scene.

Our late battlefield is an awful spectacle—only our own troops have been buried. The Wisconsin boys were nicely interred and a fence built around their graves. If you should pass over that field, you would never go over another. The dead so disfigured—swollen and black as ebony.[209]

Near the ground where so many men of different states fell, the corpse of Capt. Werner Von Bachelle of the 6th Wisconsin was covered by his beloved Newfoundland dog. The devoted canine perished while protecting his dying master from the furious shot and shell. Von Bachelle fell along the Hagerstown Pike, near the southwest corner of the cornfield.[210]

Men of the First Corps witnessed horrible sights like this after the battle of Antietam. These dead Confederates fell near a fence line on the west side of the Hagerstown Pike on September 17, 1862. LIBRARY OF CONGRESS

"Oh! What a horrid site," Uberto Burnham of the relatively unscathed 76th New York wrote home. He had seen "hundreds of bodies, mutilated, blackened, bloody, and bloated." As the month nearly ended, he continued, "So late as yesterday all the Rebel dead had not been buried." Sharpshooter Edwin Chadwick took the time to pinpoint the number of dead in a small area. "I counted fifty-three dead rebels lying close to the fence within sixteen lengths of rails and there were twenty five or thirty more in the field beyond," he reported.[211]

The line immediately south of the Cornfield showed the effectiveness of First Corps musketry. Isaac Hall's fellow members of the 97th New York certainly inflicted their share of damage. On the 18th, he discovered "the destruction of the Confederate line in our front." Prince Dunton of the 13th Massachusetts reviewed similar ground, writing, "I was on the battlefield the next day and such a sight I never saw before. The Rebels lay dead in windrows just as they stood in line of battle."

Nearby, one of Seymour's men inspected the area around the East Woods to see the cost Confederate troops incurred attempting to defend the ground. The member of the 5th Reserves "counted twenty-seven dead—some of whom were in the act of drawing ram-rods or loading their muskets." Spending time at a hospital close to the battlefield, William Prince wrote, "The men who have been burying the dead say that it is beyond description."[212]

Wounded men from the First Corps suffered long after the battle. James Adsit, a member of the 97th New York, dictated a letter to his wife, Mary, on October 13. He was still confined to Smoketown Hospital, north of the battlefield. "I have as good care as I could expect in an army hospital," Adsit noted. With many helpful volunteers, life was not horrible. Adsit added, "we are as well provided for as anyone can be except as to my leg." Due to his combat wound, Adsit's right leg had been "taken off about 4 inches below the knee." With the stump doing well, Adsit was optimistic about his recovery. "How long I shall have to suffer longer God only knows," Mary read. "But I hope for the best. If my strength holds out I shall get over it all and as I feel today that I am somewhat stronger, I have hope I shall weather the storm."

Unfortunately, Adsit's goal was not fulfilled. Six days later, another letter to Mary departed the hospital. The opening sentence must have broken the young wife's heart. "May God comfort you in this time of trial," Mrs. John Harris, of Philadelphia Ladies Aid, began. "He had no fears for himself," Harris said of Adsit, "but his anxiety for you and his two children was hard to be overcome." She added, "His message to you and to them was to live near to Christ and meet him in heaven. Your brave husband never expressed a regret at having come to defend his country from foes within." Harris concluded, "Your husband slept in Jesus, and was buried with his comrades who had stood shoulder to shoulder with him on the bloody field of Antietam." Adsit, who was twenty-six years old, was reinterred in his state's section of Antietam National Cemetery.[213]

Anne Colwell, a worried wife who did not yet know of her widowhood, wrote husband James of the 7th Reserves on the day after the battle. "I am so dispirited in not having heard from you for so long a time. Two weeks! That I cannot write neither can I do anything till I hear from you." Grasping at hope, Anne added, "If the road between Hagerstown & Frederick was fixed I could go to see you. . . . Won't you give me some encouragement to go? . . . Oh! This terrible war how much bitterness & misery it is creating."

During the intense shelling of the day before, James Colwell had been killed leading his company. Twenty years her husband's junior, Anne lived for another forty-five years. She was buried next to her husband in Carlisle, Pennsylvania.[214]

Capt. Daniel Porter, commanding Company B of the 11th Pennsylvania Reserves, fulfilled a sad duty on September 23. He wrote the father of Thomas Moore, a soldier who had died from a severe wound suffered on the 17th. He recalled the "wild, generous nature" of the departed son, adding how heroically the young man fought. Porter concluded, "I miss him much. . . . But, thank God, we were victorious."[215]

The sacrifice registered at the top. McClellan never referred to the First Corps as doubtful again. He did not even wait until the resolution of the campaign before extolling the Pennsylvania Reserves. To Governor Curtin on September 15, McClellan provided words of victory at South Mountain. "I congratulate you on the gallant behavior of the Pennsylvania Reserves, who, as well as all the troops, both old and new, acted with the greatest steadiness and gallantry," McClellan wrote. The army commander finally started seeing his entire army as worthy of respect, rather than divided into groups, with men like those in the First Corps seen as second class.

After Lee's retreat to Virginia, using words fitting for the entire First Corps, McClellan showed appreciation to the governors of Wisconsin and Indiana for the boundless mettle in the Iron Brigade. Governor Edward Salomon of Wisconsin was informed of McClellan's

*. . . great admiration of the conduct of the three Wisconsin regiments
in General Gibbon's Brigade. I have seen them under fire acting in a
manner that reflects the greatest possible credit and honor upon themselves and their State. They are equal to the best troops of any army in
the world.*[216]

BUCKTAIL BLOOD

The body of Hugh McNeil arrived home in Auburn, near his birthplace in
Cayuga County, New York, on September 22. Prior to burial in Fort Hill
Cemetery, a funeral procession moved through town. Due to McNeil's
respected status in the community, "the hilltops were thronged with our citizens," a newspaper reported, "amid the profoundest respect, the deepest gratitude of a grateful people" was evident. Of McNeil, the account continued,
"Although he died early in manhood, he had lived long enough to achieve
enduring honors, and gain a name that shall be identified with the illustrious
band of heroes who have fallen gloriously in defending Free Institutions and
a Free Government."

Another article about the loss of McNeil added to the laudatory remembrance, calling the colonel "a daring & intrepid officer, a generous friend and
kinsman and was cordially esteemed wherever he was known. He was the
idol of his family and regiment, and his loss cannot be replaced."[217]

Regimental records demonstrate how three days of fighting in Maryland impacted the 13th Reserves. Lt. William Allison, leading Company B,
lost his life on the evening of September 16. In the same company, Conrad
Jumper had been killed at South Mountain, while hostile fire took the lives
of four Company K men during the campaign: Thomas Riley, William Cum-
mings, Joseph Broomall, and Charles Hall. Jeremiah Brechbill would be one
of the Bucktails wounded during the campaign who recovered and continued
serving in the army. In total, more than eighty men were killed or wounded
in the 13th Reserves at South Mountain or Antietam.

Early autumn proved fatal to Bucktails who missed the Maryland campaign. Company K lost two men away from action. George Knapp died on
a transport on September 23. After being paroled while a prisoner of war,
Knapp was returning from Richmond, with his death recorded from an
unknown cause. Burton Granger died from lockjaw in Washington. Only
nineteen years old, Granger had been hospitalized since being wounded at
Second Bull Run.[218]

On September 22, Frank Williams of Company D informed Marcellus Glasier of the death of his brother Henry.

Dear Friend: I had rather it were some [one']s task than mine to write to you in the present occasion for it is a sad task to write to a Brother the news of a Brother['s] death. Yes, Henry is dead. He was shot while we was on a charge against a rebel force that lay behind a stone fence, our Colonel was shot at the same time. He did not speak or stir after being shot. Henry was shot through the neck and killed instantly. We buried him in nice grove along side of another young man of our Co[mpany] that got killed in the same place.[219]

MARYLAND POSTLUDE
As men settled into new camps surrounding Sharpsburg, a mistake made in the 88th Pennsylvania almost led to tragedy the day after the battle.

On the 18th rations were issued, the first for several days, including some green coffee, which the men roasted in their tins, crushing the berries as best they could. One group of grinders had improvised a cracker-box and a huge elongated shell for duty as a coffee-mill, and were doing a brisk business in ground coffee, when a red-edged artilleryman passing by examined the shell, and informed the astonished grinders that it was primed with a perfect percussion-cap, which needed but a slight blow to explode it. Business in that shop was suspended without further ceremony.[220]

A member of the 23rd New York appreciated the corps' first new camp after the battle, essentially the western flank of the army near the Potomac. "An abundant supply of fresh water," the New Yorker wrote, was for the taking at the new camp. The return of some wounded men in addition to new recruits also lifted the mood along the river.[221]

"Those were glorious autumn days that followed the battle of Antietam," recalled the historian of the 11th Pennsylvania. The veterans enjoyed a great view of the Potomac from a walnut grove on a beautiful farm. Deserving what was termed "masterly inactivity," rest and time away from the scarred battlefield revitalized the experienced fighters. Drill became part of life's routine again. The exercises, termed "dull monotony," at least reminded the men how soldiering did not constantly mean fighting.[222]

As recovery was beginning from the shock of such an intense battle, Marsena Patrick and John Gibbon, brigade commanders in Doubleday's Division, debated their conduct on September 17. Patrick took umbrage when Gibbon expressed some doubts about Patrick's decisions. The charge, whatever the specifics, appears unfair; Patrick's men were engaged throughout the morning, occupied important ground on the north side of the West Woods or in battery support, and suffered more than 250 casualties. A staff member at division headquarters noted the resentment Patrick felt. "General Gibbon," Patrick retorted, "I want no straw stack general to tell me my duty on the field of battle."[223] Perhaps Patrick's name-calling related to hay bales used around Gibbon's Battery B on September 17.

With shattered bodies, lingering pain, and death still haunting the region, the First Corps would see major changes in the days after Antietam, although the army would not move into Virginia for nearly six weeks. The rest was deeply appreciated, but many men who sacrificed so much in the Maryland campaign began to wonder if the effort was wasted. McClellan's reputation suffered measurably, and not just in the eyes of President Lincoln and other Washington officials. Before pondering the fitness of the army commander, officers and soldiers in the First Corps had a variety of problems to sort out as autumn began.

Hooker passed the time in Washington, convalescing from his wound and intriguing for higher command. Treasury Secretary Salmon Chase was one man who favored replacing McClellan with Hooker. The wounded general tried too hard to win the job. He clearly did not see impropriety in tooting his own horn, questioning other generals' conduct during the Maryland campaign, or making himself visible to Washington's power players. Praise of Hooker from the disgraced John Pope likely hurt his quest to climb the army's ladder as the foot wound healed. During the latest leadership shuffle, Hooker was stuck with corps command, taking over Porter's Fifth Corps as another campaign beckoned.[224]

Much to his satisfaction, John Reynolds did not remain a veritable prisoner in his own state as the leader of the Pennsylvania militia. He returned to the army as First Corps commander on September 29. Meade went back to the Third Division and Seymour again served as First Brigade commander. Three days before his return, Reynolds's contempt for the militia's lack of grit and discipline was evident. Reynolds humorously wrote of the militia's desire to protect their homes, but "they preferred to wait until the enemy actually reached their own doorsteps" prior to engaging the Confederates.[225]

Hooker's battlefield decision on the 17th gave corps command to Meade over the senior Ricketts. Orders from McClellan during the afternoon of September 17 affirmed Hooker's preference. Ricketts had protested the order, "because he considered it a matter of principle," Meade wrote his wife. "In this I think he was right," Meade said, "and I should have done the same thing myself, for I do not believe McClellan had the right to do what he did."[226]

Ricketts ended his service with the First Corps after Antietam, where he was injured when his second horse of the day was killed. In an order dated October 4, his slot leading the Second Division was given to Nelson Taylor. One month later, the division belonged to John Gibbon, with Taylor leading a brigade under Gibbon, replacing Hartsuff, with Coulter reverting to command of the 11th Pennsylvania.

Taylor, a native of Connecticut born in 1821, had served as a captain of the 1st New York in Mexico. Stationed in California before the state joined the Union in 1850, Taylor served in various public positions on the West Coast, then returned east, graduating from Harvard Law School in 1860. He was an unsuccessful candidate for the U.S. House of Representatives that year. His first assignment in the Civil War was colonel of the 72nd New York. He gained a brigadier's star early in the Maryland campaign.[227]

General Duryée departed the First Corps on October 5, erroneously thinking the break would end after thirty days of leave. Col. Thomas McCoy of the 107th Pennsylvania received temporary brigade command, followed by Adrian Root of the 94th New York, who would lead the brigade for six months.

In the First Division, the promotion of Marsena Patrick to the army's provost marshal gave brigade command to Gabriel Paul. Born in St. Louis in 1813, Paul graduated from West Point in 1834. Frontier service was his fate prior to the Mexican War, where his gallantry earned a brevet promotion to major. The competent Paul commanded the 8th U.S. Infantry at the start of the Civil War. He was part of the effort successfully denying the New Mexico Territory to the Confederates early in the war.[228]

A September 22 order augmented the ranks of decimated Battery B, 4th U.S. Artillery. Suffering more than half of First Corps artillery losses on September 17, Battery B, like most infantry regiments, needed an infusion of men. The order detailed five infantrymen from each of Gibbon's four regiments to the battery.[229]

The 16th Maine returned to the Hartsuff/Taylor Brigade three days after the battle. Although the 16th missed South Mountain and Antietam, conditions were not bright for the new regiment. As an officer wrote, "I think that the Regt was put into hard service rather too soon." The warmer climate and marching, "has tended to thin the ranks."[230] The regiment's brigade, which endured horrendous casualties in Maryland, may have found the Maine soldiers' "hard service" of guarding railroads a bit comedic.

Entirely new regiments boosted the number of soldiers in the ranks. In Special Orders 267, dated September 30, four outfits from the defenses of Washington were added to the First Corps. The units included three from Pennsylvania: the 121st, 136th, and 142nd. The 121st and 142nd went to separate brigades in the Pennsylvania Reserves, with the 136th assigned to Ricketts's command. The 24th Michigan was destined to join Gibbon's Brigade.

The four new regiments, all raised during the summer of 1862, added 3,400 men to the corps' ranks. By the end of September, the First Corps listed 14,102 present for duty, an increase of 7,765 effectives since the battle of Antietam.[231]

Reynolds appreciated the extra firepower the duo of new regiments offered the Reserves. On October 25, Reynolds informed his sisters of a very pleasant conversation with Col. Chapman Biddle of the 121st. The corps commander praised the "very fine" regiment and noted Biddle's solid instruction of his soldiers.[232]

The 24th Michigan had a more difficult time being accepted. Bloodied boys in the Iron Brigade did not accept the Wolverines at first. With fresh uniforms and nearly as many men as the four veteran regiments combined, the Michigan soldiers were treated as outcasts.[233] Fated for disrespect early on, the 24th would prove its worth to the brigade, First Corps, and the country in the coming months.

The addition of manpower did not end senior leaders' concerns about the inability of some men to fulfill their duties. Shortly after the battle, Meade suggested the vexing issue of absent men required infliction of the death penalty. He poured out his scorn in a letter to his wife. The "serious evil" of absent men, Meade explained, sprang from "the character and constitution of our volunteer force, and from the absence of that control over the men, which is the consequence of the inefficiency of the officers commanding them." Any army has such problems, Meade added, "but never in so great a ratio as in this volunteer force of ours." The Confederates must have the same level of straggling and cowards, Meade concluded.[234]

Meade lacked an understanding of why men may choose to become lazy in camp—or disregard their duties completely prior to battle. Well into October, conditions in some regiments tried the fortitude of many. In the 30th New York, the poor quality and quantity of clothing was simply deplorable. As a visitor to camp found on October 17, "I don't think that one man in the regiment had a full suit of clothes, and many had scarcely sufficient to save them from complaints of indecent exposure."[235]

The same situation prevailed in the 107th Pennsylvania. Lack of shoes, garments, blankets, and proper shelter prevailed. Some men even went without trousers, "obliged to do duty even in their under clothes." The main difference between a shirker and hero was the ability to face such problems with the stout resilience only possible in a devoted soldier. The 107th's observer added, "the men knowing that they were engaged in a most righteous cause willingly submitted to these privations and hardships and performed their duties cheerfully."[236]

Other reasons explained why soldiers could become neglectful of duty. Uberto Burnham, a great chronicler of life in the 76th New York, was quite distressed in an October 1 letter. "There is five months pay due us," he declared, adding, "*I have no money, am ragged and lousy.*"

Describing the revolting experience combatting lice, Burnham added, "Everybody else in the Regt is in the same uncomfortable fix." The miserable soldier continued, "No one can with good grace call another a lousy dirty fellow. It would be like the donkey jeering at the mule for having long ears. I have no lice on my head for I have a fine comb, but I in common with every body else have what they call 'body lice.'"

Picking the tiny vermin out of clothes proved very difficult. Burnham termed the "battle" waged against lice as "skirmishing with Ashby's Cavalry," a reference to a deceased Confederate officer. At least lice had considerably more men to target. Burnham said the 76th only fielded 80 men immediately after Antietam, but the ranks now totaled 200.[237]

Fresh troops could not eliminate the serious emotional burden hanging over shattered lives. Vermont sharpshooter Curtis Abbott mourned, "One sad result of a battle is to deprive the survivors of their tentmates." The ardent marksman added, "These autumn days were among the saddest ever experienced by the survivors of this army."[238]

Lyman Holford of the 6th Wisconsin waged an unexpected battle across two days. In an effort to slumber off the ground, he used some cedar wood for a bed, but some spiders did not like his idea. The pests "tried to get possession of my plate" during dinner. He proved able to remove the spiders without eating any accidently. Sleep was interrupted due to his uninvited guests, prompting Holford—"with relentless fury"—to wage a "war of extermination" during the whole day.[239]

A visit from President Lincoln served to brighten days for some men. Lincoln arrived at army headquarters on October 2, the day after a quick tour of Harpers Ferry with McClellan. Given an overview of the battle by the army commander, Lincoln must have annoyed McClellan when he asked to see the part of the field where Hooker went in.[240]

Although the army was in considerably better shape in early October, Lincoln was able to see the immense cost of war. Curtis Abbott recorded only seventy-two sharpshooters in the ranks of the 2nd USSS on October 4, the day Lincoln reviewed the First Corps. The president asked about the 8th Pennsylvania Reserves, seeing the limited number of men present and the mangled state of the devoted soldiers' battle flag. Meade confirmed for Lincoln the intense losses of the regiment he was inspecting. The sacrifice made "Uncle Abe" appear "careworn," especially when compared to "the gay and dashing officers who accompanied him," according to Lyman Holford.[241]

Rufus Dawes observed the president's respect for the sacrifice of his soldiers.

> *Lincoln was manifestly touched at the worn appearance of our men, and he, himself, looked serious and careworn. He bowed low in re[s] ponse to the salute of our tattered flags. As I sat upon my horse in front of the regiment, I caught a glimpse of Mr. Lincoln's face, which has remained photographed upon my memory. Compared with the small figure of General McClellan, who, with jaunty air and somewhat gaudy appearance, cantered along beside him, Mr. Lincoln seemed to tower as a giant.*[242]

DOUBTS ABOUT MCCLELLAN

The difference in physical size between Lincoln and McClellan metaphorically displayed how the First Corps was starting to see the world. The army's lack of boldness after September 17 was on the mind of many soldiers. Their thoughts provide a microcosm explaining the growing lack of patience Lincoln felt regarding McClellan.

John Delaney of the 107th Pennsylvania wondered why McClellan kept so many troops out of action on the 17th. The army had "20,000 men who did not fire a shot at Antietam," the veteran wrote after the war. This led to engagements during the battle, such as the opening clash between Duryée and Douglass, where each side had about the same number on the firing line. Uberto Burnham was curious about the lack of a stronger follow-up on the morning of the 18th. With the infusion of fresh troops against the Confederates, McClellan could have pushed Lee across the Potomac. "It seems to me that it might have been done," Burnham wrote on October 6.[243]

After their difficult fight in the East Woods, members of the 9th New York State Militia wondered about the reasons for not continuing the battle on the 18th. Acknowledging issues with tired troops and limited supplies,

Many in the Union Army thought then—and time has not changed the impression—that, after having been successful in two battles, and the defeated enemy hemmed in between a victorious army on the one side and a river difficult to cross on the other, the victors had, at least, a very reasonable prospect of success in the renewal of the contest on the 18th.[244]

The regimental historian of the 13th Massachusetts suggested several men were hoping for a transformational victory at Antietam. Granting McClellan's arguments about supply problems and exhaustion in the ranks, the Bay State veteran wrote:

When men are stimulated by success in battle they forget everything but pushing their good fortune to a complete triumph.... A prominent public man who knew McClellan as an engineer, before the war, once remarked that if he had a million of men it would take a million years for him voluntarily to move, which number is probably an exaggeration by several years.[245]

McClellan wrote his wife the morning after the battle, contemplating a renewal of fighting on the 18th. Nonetheless, all remained quiet along the Antietam. McClellan later justified the inactivity by referring to his most persistent enemy: risk.

Success of an attack on the 18th was not certain. I am aware of the fact that, under ordinary circumstances, a general is expected to risk a battle if he has a reasonable prospect of success; but at this critical juncture I should have had a narrow view of the condition of the country had I been willing to hazard another battle with less than an absolute assurance of success.[246]

Like the afternoon of the 17th north of Sharpsburg, McClellan was not going to attack along his whole line on the 18th. He was psychologically incapable of such a move.

One then wonders why McClellan ordered an attack by just the First Corps twenty-four hours earlier against an enemy he thought had 120,000 men west of Antietam Creek. Some of McClellan's friends in the army questioned the lack of initiative after the battle. John Gibbon, who had known McClellan as a friend for two decades, respected "Little Mac" as a leader and understood the army's need for more supplies. Gibbon still witnessed a pervading desire to get moving. After returning to his command following a visit with family in Baltimore, Gibbon reported the strong feelings of uneasiness among his Westerners. Even after a cataclysmic three weeks for the command, the Iron Brigade seemed ready to brawl again with Lee's minions. As the historian of the 88th Pennsylvania added, "if McClellan had possessed the military intuition to gauge the condition of his opponent, he would have checkmated him in one move—forward."[247]

Meade, another officer respectful of McClellan—and knowledgeable of the army's prevailing logistical challenges—expressed concern with the slow pace of operations. Meade was especially bothered by another of Jeb Stuart's cavalry raids, where the feared Southern general took 2,000 horsemen around McClellan's army, a feat the dashing cavalier had accomplished on the Peninsula. The post-Antietam raid destroyed clothing and other materials in Chambersburg, Pennsylvania. The important supplies were meant for McClellan's army. To his wife on October 12, Meade suggested,

> *McClellan does not seem to have made as much out of his operations in Maryland as I had hoped he would, and as I think he is entitled to. His failure to immediately pursue Lee (which Hooker would have done), and now this raid of Stuart's in our rear (for permitting which the public will hold McClellan accountable), will go far towards taking away from him the prestige of his recent victories. I don't wish you to mention it, but I think myself he errs on the side of prudence and caution, and that a little more rashness on his part would improve his generalship.*[248]

Supporters like Gibbon and Meade were not powerful enough to get McClellan to move. On October 6, immediately after his Sharpsburg visit, Lincoln had Halleck order McClellan forward. The general-in-chief declared, "The President directs that you cross the Potomac and give battle to the enemy or drive him south. Your army must move now while the roads are good."[249]

On October 20, as the movement of the whole army was nearing, the First Corps reported 17,810 men present for duty, with 3,554 either on special duty, sick, or under arrest. Reynolds's command had added 11,000 men to its ranks since September 18, perhaps 2,000 more men than Hooker took into action at the Battle of Antietam.[250]

Reynolds focused on ensuring his men had sufficient supplies for the expected march into Virginia. In an October 22 circular, he listed the wide range of clothing available at either Harpers Ferry or Hagerstown. "The general commanding directs that division commanders send their trains for the clothing required, to-night, that all may be supplied by to-morrow evening," Reynolds declared.[251]

Rufus Dawes understood why Reynolds focused on clothing. "It is true that the army is in a suffering condition for clothing and shoes," Dawes wrote as the movement south was beginning. "Our regiment was never before nearly so destitute," and he reported Reynolds's efforts were bearing fruit.[252]

Fifteen days after receiving the president's order to march, McClellan was still finding reasons to delay. He had the audacity to ask General-in-Chief Halleck on October 21 if Lincoln still wished him to move right away.

The boss man responded for Lincoln, "He directs me to say that he has no change to make in his order of the 6th instant. If you have not been and are not now in condition to obey it, you will be able to show such want of ability." McClellan acknowledged by confirming the army's orders to head south.[253]

Like any action McClellan initiated, his boldest stroke could seem tediously sluggish to others. On the 21st, Archibald Penny saw signs of activity several days before the men actually marched. As a member of the 13th Massachusetts suggested, "At the rate we moved, the youngest amongst us would be grey before we could reach Richmond." The First Corps was finally at the Potomac on October 28, with the crossing completed on the 30th.[254]

The belated pursuit of Lee's army was not enough to save McClellan. He would be relieved of command in early November, a day after elections across the North gave Lincoln's Republican Party a severe thrashing. With the move back to Confederate territory, the First Corps did not need to worry for now about Maryland. They would return to the state in June, after eight months of distress and immense sacrifice on the sacred soil of Old Virginia.

PART TWO

Virginia Blues

November 1862–May 1863

There is blundering imbecility somewhere.
Uberto Burnham, 76th New York Infantry

Heading to Warrenton

The land traversed by the First Corps early in the new campaign reminded some of Maryland's delights. Although in the Confederacy, there was evidence of residents supportive of the Union cause. Col. Charles Wainwright, appointed head of the First Corps artillery in September, enjoyed the wonders of nature and a pleasant greeting from northern Virginia Unionists. On October 30, he wrote, "The day was superb," with "the air soft and balmy, the smoky mist hanging on the mountains." Several officers spent an evening at a delightful farm with a family more than happy to provide a meal for men in blue.[1]

In Waterford on November 1, the First Corps benefited from a town "Union to the core," as a man in the 12th Massachusetts wrote. "The inhabitants turned out," he added, "and, to the best of their ability, fed the regiment." Later in the day, the troops were in Hamilton, another town not happy with the Confederacy, about 3 miles west of Leesburg. Some sporadic firing in the distance did not bother the men, who enjoyed generally easy marches in cool weather.[2]

Natural beauty filled the eyes of each member of the corps in this part of Virginia. John Gibbon remembered, "I shall never forget the magnificent appearance presented by the vast columns of troops moving along the foot of the mountain." After the march through Hamilton and Purcellville, the corps pressed onward. One member of Doubleday's Division recalled, "A thousand

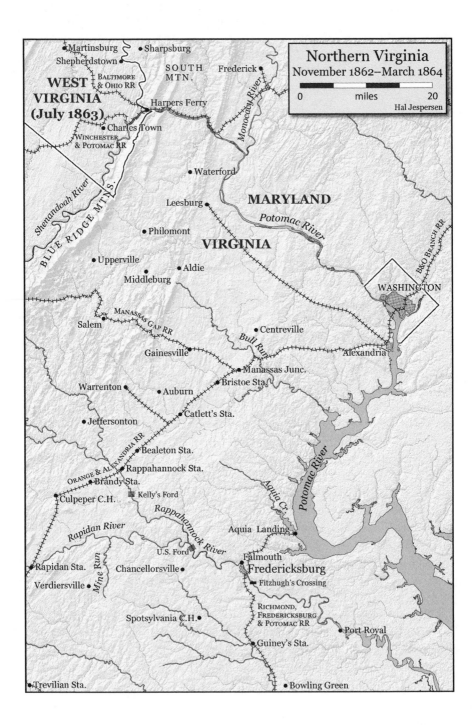

Northern Virginia
November 1862–March 1864

0   miles   20

Hal Jespersen

Martinsburg   Sharpsburg
Shepherdstown   SOUTH   Frederick
                      MTN.
BALTIMORE
& OHIO RR
WEST
VIRGINIA   Harpers Ferry
(July 1863)
          Charles Town
WINCHESTER
& POTOMAC RR

Waterford

MARYLAND

Leesburg   Potomac River

Philomont   VIRGINIA

Upperville   Aldie
Middleburg

MANASSAS GAP RR
Salem   Centreville
Gainesville   Bull Run   Alexandria
                    Manassas Junc.
Warrenton   Auburn   Bristoe Sta.

Jeffersonton

Catlett's Sta.

ORANGE & ALEXANDRIA RR
          Bealeton Sta.
          Rappahannock Sta.
Brandy Sta.
Culpeper C.H.   Kelly's Ford

Rapidan River   Rappahannock River

Aquia Cr.   Potomac River
          Aquia Landing
U.S. Ford
Rapidan Sta.   Falmouth
Verdiersville   Chancellorsville   Fredericksburg
Mine Run   Fitzhugh's Crossing

RICHMOND,
FREDERICKSBURG
& POTOMAC RR
Spotsylvania C.H.
          Port Royal
          Guiney's Sta.

Trevilian Sta.   Bowling Green

WASHINGTON

B&O BRANCH RR

Shenandoah River
BLUE RIDGE MTNS.

Monocacy River

glories are added to these forests of autumn, and with foliage of every hue of the rainbow covering the hills and glades and climbing up the steep sides of these mountains, they present a scene that thrills the beholder."[3]

Around Upperville, men in the 1st New Hampshire Battery began to see more Confederate proclivities from civilians. A sweet distraction led the artillerists to forget the unfriendly locals. One cannoneer recalled, "Here we found secession and honey in abundance." The treat did present some inconveniences for the soldiers, with the historian writing "horses, harnesses, carriages and men, were alike sticky. It was honey everywhere."[4]

Hofmann's Brigade was on detached service from Doubleday's command, assisting some cavalry and artillery. Shortly after crossing the Potomac, the regiments were near Ashby's Gap, in the Blue Ridge Mountains. While the 76th New York supported a battery, the rest of the brigade helped expel Confederate troops from Uniontown. The Rebels were driven west of the gap, "and thus ended the running fire which had been kept up for three days, and extended over from twelve to fifteen miles."[5]

On November 3, the Pennsylvania Reserves were a bit farther north, around Philomont, ending their day about 2 miles outside of the town, near Snicker's Gap. The First Corps reunited by November 6, in the vicinity of Warrenton, 15 miles west of Manassas. Reynolds's men arrived in the town a day ahead of schedule, and no corps was lagging behind expected progress.[6]

Then, the weather was turning less cooperative. As a member of the 14th Brooklyn, Phelps's Brigade, said, camp was made on the Sulphur Springs road "in the midst of a raging snow storm."[7]

Some men in the corps had remained in Maryland due to wounds suffered in September. Surgeons were necessary to care for the fallen warriors. Still in Frederick on November 2, Horace Hanks, of the 30th New York, wrote to "My ever dear Mattie." The dutiful healer informed her, "I should die with the blues if I had nothing to busy my hands and mind with." He lamented the dreadful sights of the concluded campaign, still so visible in the number of men needing medical attention.

"I have seen enough of the dark side of war to satisfy me—and I have seen but very very little as yet." Hanks added, "What an awful thing is war! How cruel!—how monstrous, how everything that is hateful!" He fervently informed Mattie of a hope the blood is not in vain "so that good may come out of this barbarous evil."[8]

The 24th Michigan's commander, Col. Henry Morrow, had a homecoming during the army's autumn march. Born in Warrenton in 1829, Morrow entered the town with his regiment on a chilly November day. Morrow's mother was buried nearby, and the residents seemed "bitterly disloyal." Other towns in the area, where "desolation reigns supreme," did not inspire the Wolverine troops.[9]

Robert Taggart, an officer in the 9th Reserves, thought battle might have been necessary to claim Warrenton. A fight was avoided, but his expectations of unfriendly residents was met. He recorded, "We have had a brisk march today and contrary to expectations entered the little Secession town of Warrenton without a fight. We are now encamped on the same place we occupied last August before the battle of Bull Run. And I find the people stronger Secessionists than they were two months ago."[10]

Charles Wainwright was another man to comment on the transition from Unionist residents to avid secessionists over a relatively short distance. He experienced the scorn a pro-Confederacy town could show to the U.S. Army. Nonetheless, Wainwright commented on the virtues of the region, including how beautiful the surrounding area must have looked before the war. About 150 Confederate wounded were housed in Warrenton, with the benefit of rations supplied by the U.S. Army.[11]

Assignments detaching units from the rest of the corps provided distractions for some men. On November 8, Taylor's Brigade joined up with cavalry to patrol the area from Beverly's Ford to Kelly's Mill, with the 11th Pennsylvania establishing regimental headquarters near Rappahannock Station. With the rest of the corps moving southeast, Taylor's men would reunite with Reynolds's command around Stafford Court House.[12]

THOUGHTS ON MCCLELLAN'S FIRING

The most momentous event for the men while they rested around Warrenton was the dismissal of McClellan. Ambrose Burnside was given command of the army, much to his own disappointment. He had rejected such a high command before. Perhaps the threat of Hooker becoming his boss was the reason Burnside accepted. The army's new leader had a very modest persona, the polar opposite of McClellan.

The outcome of the Maryland campaign led some members of the First Corps to question McClellan's philosophy of war. Nonetheless, many men held McClellan in high regard. The change in command was not greeted warmly by Reynolds's soldiers. Curtis Abbott wrote of his comrades having diminished yet enduring respect for their dismissed general. The sharpshooter noted how the men reacted when seeing McClellan near the time of his removal: "His reception was not like that in Maryland but there was still much cheering."[13]

Corp. Lewis Benedict, 24th New York, tried to be optimistic about McClellan's ouster. From a hospital in Washington, Benedict wrote his mother on November 13, "I hope that the change will be for the best, but I am afraid that it will not." Benedict extolled McClellan as "the soldiers' man, and he is the only man that can take a disorganized army and drive the rebels from Maryland." After the "great victory" at Antietam, Benedict wondered why "the damn fools can't be satisfied."

The dismissal of McClellan likely meant disaster, Benedict continued, "The Union is gone up now I'm afraid, but I hope not." After seeing how well Confederates fought, "I don't expect that the war will be ended as long as the rebels can muster 10 men." He added, "They can fight like tigers, and they do," then signed off, "I remain as ever your son and true to the old flag and Union."[14]

"There is little doubt that a mistake was made in the removal of McClellan at this time," the historian of the 9th New York State Militia wrote. The chronicler of the 12th Massachusetts declared McClellan's firing "one of the political moves of the war, unwise and inexplicable." He added, "The universal testimony of history is, that at this time McClellan was doing better than ever before."[15] McClellan's clear lack of initiative in October cost him much respect with his bosses. He was now moving well enough, but a month late.

Meade echoed the thought about politics governing the timing of McClellan's removal. On the first morning under the new army commander, Meade lamented, "If he had been relieved immediately after the battle of Antietam, or at any period before he moved, I could have seen some show of reason on *military* grounds." Instead, the day after a disastrous election for Lincoln's party, "This removal now proves conclusively that the cause is political." The next day, Meade noted McClellan's visit with senior officers of the First Corps, where men were close to tears. "The army is greatly depressed," Meade wrote.[16]

Robert Taggart witnessed McClellan's departure from the troops, a deeply emotional moment. "As the General rode off with 'good by lads' he turned around and kept those piercing eyes fixed on the men," Taggart recorded. "The eyes of the men followed him and their hearts went with him. No other man can so gain the affections of the soldiers of The Army of The Potomac."[17]

Rumors were heard of mass resignations to protest Lincoln's action. Rufus Dawes witnessed "considerable expression of feeling" against McClellan's removal, but any officers with the idea of resigning quickly changed their minds. Col. Lysander Cutler, former commander of the 6th Wisconsin, reminded the men of the army's subordination to civilian authority. Dawes wrote of Cutler's "excellent restraining influence" on malcontents in the brigade. Cutler "declared that he would recommend for dismissal, for tendering a resignation while in the presence of the enemy, any officer who offered to resign for such a reason" as the firing of McClellan. Unsurprisingly, no resignations were requested.[18]

Scorn for McClellan did exist. George Darby, 8th Pennsylvania Reserves, suggested McClellan was a Southern sympathizer and "the chief traitor of the nineteenth century." The witty historian of the 13th Massachusetts mocked the army's idolatry of McClellan.

A good many people have been puzzled to account for McClellan's popularity with the army. It is just as difficult to understand why sheep follow sheep to destruction, or ducks are decoyed on to a pond by a wooden likeness of themselves,—lack of reasoning power.[19]

The historian of the 11th Pennsylvania said Burnside possessed the ability to lead. The removal of McClellan, "in a record of the lights and shadows of army life . . . must be seen as one of the shadows." Yet, Burnside held the confidence of the men, all things considered. As a member of the 26th New York suggested, "amid all the regrets consequent upon the removal or withdrawal of McClellan . . . there was no objection raised to Gen. Burnside."[20]

General disappointment with the leadership change was far less important to the First Corps than finding something to eat around Warrenton. A 6th Wisconsin man remembered, "While making so many changes the powers that be seemed to forget that the men could not live without rations. We reached the point of starvation before rations were furnished us." An enterprising member of the outfit captured some sheep, so Company A's motto for a few days was "mutton or nothing."[21]

Getting lost along the way was an exasperating trial for the new troops of the 121st Pennsylvania. On the march to Warrenton, near the town of White Plains, the regiment endured darkness and thick woods in an attempt to find the evening's bivouac. Their brigade comrades, experienced veterans in

Table 2.1: The First Corps, December 1862

Corps Commander—Maj. Gen. John F. Reynolds		
1st Division **Brig. Gen. Abner Doubleday**	**2nd Division** **Brig. Gen. John Gibbon**	**3rd Division** **Brig. Gen. George Meade**
1st Brigade Col. Walter Phelps 22nd New York 24th New York 30th New York 14th Brooklyn 2nd USSS	*1st Brigade* Col. Adrian Root 16th Maine 94th New York 104th New York 105th New York 107th Pennsylvania	*1st Brigade* Col. William Sinclair 1st Pennsylvania Reserves 2nd Pennsylvania Reserves 6th Pennsylvania Reserves 13th Pennsylvania Res. 121st Pennsylvania
2nd Brigade Col. James Gavin 7th Indiana 76th New York 95th New York 56th Pennsylvania	*2nd Brigade* Col. Peter Lyle 12th MA 26th New York 90th Pennsylvania 136th Pennsylvania	*2nd Brigade* Col. Albert Magilton 3rd Pennsylvania Reserves 4th Pennsylvania Reserves 7th Pennsylvania Reserves 8th Pennsylvania Reserves 142nd Pennsylvania
3rd Brigade Col. William Rogers 21st New York 23rd New York 35th New York 80th New York	*3rd Brigade* Brig. Gen. Nelson Taylor 13th Massachusetts 83rd New York 97th New York 11th Pennsylvania 88th Pennsylvania	*3rd Brigade* Brig. Gen. C. Jackson 5th Pennsylvania Reserves 9th Pennsylvania Reserves 10th Pennsylvania Reserves 11th Pennsylvania Reserves 12th Pennsylvania Reserves
4th Brigade Brig. Gen. Solomon Meredith 19th Indiana 24th Michigan 2nd Wisconsin 6th Wisconsin 7th Wisconsin	*2nd Division Artillery* 2nd and 5th Batteries Maine Light Batt. F, 1st Pennsylvania Light Batt. C, 1st Pennsylvania	*3rd Division Artillery* Batteries A, B, and G, 1st Pennsylvania Light Battery C, 5th U.S.
1st Division Artillery 1st New Hampshire Battery Batt. D, 1st Rhode Island Light Batt. L, 1st New York Light Battery B, 4th U.S.		

Source: *Official Records*, Vol. 21, I, 57–59.

the 1st, 2nd, 6th, and 13th Reserves, expressed disappointment in Meade as the regiments walked blindly in the cold darkness. The historian of the 121st heard "such adjectives in the expression of their indignation as would scarcely bear repetition."[22]

Reorganization Before Winter

As shown in Table 2.1, the First Corps looked much different in late 1862 than the command departing Washington for Maryland in September. Of the ten brigades under John Reynolds, only Walter Phelps commanded a unit unchanged in either brigade commander or regimental composition. Colonels James Gavin and William Rogers officered the 2nd and 3rd Brigades in Doubleday's Division, with Lysander Cutler, then Brig. Gen. Solomon Meredith, taking over the five regiments in the Iron Brigade.

Regiments were shuffled in the Second Division, commanded by John Gibbon as of early December. Each of Gibbon's three brigades had a new commander. Adrian Root's First Brigade included the 94th New York and 16th Maine, moved from the Second and Third Brigades, respectively. Three regiments from Duryée's days remained in Root's unit: the 104th and 105th New York and the 107th Pennsylvania.

Root, only thirty years old, had served from the early stages of the war. He took a leading role in raising the 21st New York in his hometown of Buffalo. A promotion to colonel in May 1862 gave Root command of the 94th New York. Leading his men at Second Bull Run, Root sustained a wound on August 30. His first return to action, as brigade commander, was effective November 15.[23]

Peter Lyle retained command of Gibbon's Second Brigade. The 26th New York and 90th Pennsylvania, holdovers from Christian's days, remained, joined by the 12th Massachusetts and 136th Pennsylvania. The Third Brigade, under Nelson Taylor, had five regiments: the 13th Massachusetts, 9th New York State Militia, 97th New York, 11th Pennsylvania, and 88th Pennsylvania.

The two rookie regiments and some shuffling of old units gave a new look to the Pennsylvania Reserves, which Meade still commanded. The determined leader of the First Brigade was gone, as Truman Seymour returned to a previous command, Charleston, South Carolina. Col. William Sinclair, 6th Reserves, took command of the 1st, 2nd, 6th, and 13th Reserves, plus the 121st Pennsylvania.

Sinclair was a worthy heir to the leadership example Seymour had set for the First Brigade. A native of Ohio, Sinclair graduated slightly above the middle of the West Point Class of 1857. He was part of the contingent, under the command of Col. Robert E. Lee, sent to Harpers Ferry in 1859 after John Brown's famous attack on the arsenal. Subsequently on the West Coast, Sinclair was promoted to first lieutenant of the 3rd U.S. Artillery shortly after Fort Sumter was bombarded. Sinclair earned an eagle on each shoulder during the Peninsula campaign as the leader of the 6th Reserves, with prominent battle experience prior to his elevation to brigade command. At Fredericksburg, he was two months shy of his twenty-eighth birthday.[24]

Except for the addition of the 142nd Pennsylvania, Albert Magilton's Second Brigade retained the same regimental lineup. For the Third Brigade, Brig. Gen. Conrad Jackson led the 5th, 9th, 10th, 11th, and 12th Reserves. Jackson, a native of Pennsylvania, was forty-nine years old in late 1862, with experience in the War with Mexico and the state militia. He took the lead in organizing the 9th Pennsylvania Reserves at the start of the war, proving himself to be a highly capable commander.[25]

The early part of the new campaign provided soldiers a chance to see certain officers back in the ranks, having recovered from wounds sufficiently to retake the field. William Wainwright of the 76th New York returned to the regiment after convalescence from his South Mountain wound. The 2nd USSS enjoyed the appearance of Col. Henry Post, as well. One of the regiment's casualties at Antietam, Post received a warm greeting. "The men gathered to welcome him with cheers that were manifestly heartfelt, but the Colonel seemed embarrassed," recalled Curtis Abbott.

Unfortunately, the revered leader of the marksmen was not well enough to remain. Resigning due to continued medical problems, Post was discharged on November 16. His stellar example remained with the men. Abbott wrote, "The respect which he won is immortal."[26]

The early days of Burnside's command saw the army remain around Warrenton. On November 10, the First Corps reported a present strength of 20,518, with the five other corps in the army adding just over 100,000 more troops. Burnside had a manpower advantage over Lee of about 50,000 soldiers. An additional 80,000 men manned the defenses of Washington.

Commanding such a large number of men spread across six infantry corps, Burnside resorted to an organization of grand divisions, with orders promulgated on November 14. Alongside the Sixth Corps, Reynolds's men were part of the Left Grand Division, under the command of William Franklin. Sumner and Hooker commanded the Right and Center grand divisions, respectively.[27]

Burnside crafted a plan to advance toward Richmond from Fredericksburg, a town due north of the Confederate capital, and 35 miles southeast of Burnside's camps around Warrenton. By early November, Lee's divided army included Longstreet's command in Culpepper, while Stonewall Jackson's troops were on the other side of the Blue Ridge Mountains. Burnside did not waste much time moving to the southeast. Like the strategic magician, Lee anticipated his opponent's moves.

Alacrity from the Army of the Potomac likely surprised Washington authorities. Burnside had parts of the Union army near Falmouth, just north of Fredericksburg, by November 18. He moved so quickly, pontoon boats needed to cross the Rappahannock River did not arrive on time, an oversight most historians see as the fault of General-in-Chief Halleck.[28]

"COLD AND HUNGRY"

The First Corps had a generally uneventful advance to the area north of Fredericksburg. Familiar problems cropped up for the men on the move. Uberto Burnham and many of his comrades continued to suffer from unserviceable clothing and footgear. "Our army shoes do not last long," Burnham complained, adding, "They don't keep our feet very dry. My feet are now as wet as can be."

Mud became the inveterate foe of the army during the early part of the campaign. "The amount of muscular energy required to lift your feet with ten pounds or more of mud clinging to each foot, can hardly be appreciated except by persons who have a knowledge of the 'sacred soil' of Virginia," wrote the historian of the 13th Massachusetts. The battle against rain and mud did not halt the men completely, as camps began to rise near Stafford Court House, 8 miles north of Fredericksburg, by the evening of the 20th.[29]

Rufus Dawes wrote a letter the same day, reporting his location as "Ten miles from anywhere." Due to the inclement weather and mud, the First Division needed all day to move 2 miles on the 19th. He also noted the return of Lieutenant Colonel Bragg. The brave commander had recuperated from his Antietam wound and lost a race for Congress. Bragg had run as a "War Democrat," in favor of fighting the Confederacy as a member of the opposition party. Dawes suggested, "They are for peace at any price in his district."[30]

Resilient men continued their weary lives. In the same letter he despaired about shoes, Burnham noted, "What there is left of this Regt are tough fellows." A Maine man in the state's 5th Battery, recently added to the corps' Second Division, felt the strong pull of a mission to prevail. Lt. A. B. Twitchell informed the state's adjutant general, "Our Battery is in a most prosperous condition." Devoted to the cause, the battery strives "to answer the just expectations of our state, and we will serve with continued zeal, if politicians will let our Generals alone."[31]

Still near Stafford Court House on the 22nd, Meade wrote of the difficulties moving supplies and troops.

> *We have to haul all our supplies from the landing at Aquia Creek, ten miles distant, over roads which are barely passable with half-loaded wagons, and which in a short time, from the great number of trains passing over them, will become impassable. Hence we have out, since we have been here, the greater portion of our command, trying to make the roads passable by corduroying them—a work of labor and time.*[32]

Lyman Holford of the 6th Wisconsin echoed Meade's observation. Soldiers knew the difficulty of a quick end to the war, and they understood the impossibility of an advance due to weather. Holford wrote, "I wish to God that those editors who are preaching so hard and long about a winter campaign had been out in the last storm as we were. I guess they would change their tune."[33]

The question of who was to command the Iron Brigade after Gibbon's promotion was resolved during the November drudgery. The outcome did not make all happy. Special Orders 62, issued on November 25, had Solomon Meredith, a new brigadier general, report to Doubleday for assignment. On leaving for divisional command, Gibbon suggested either Cutler or Fairchild, two capable men with extensive experience in the brigade. Neither wore a general's star, so Meredith won out. Gibbon despised volunteer officers who apparently pulled political strings to garner a promotion. Meredith had spent time back home healing up from wounds and seeking higher command.[34]

Regardless of what others might have thought of Meredith's abilities, he showed great willingness to sacrifice for the Union cause. No one could doubt his personal courage. Wounded in action at Second Bull Run and providing good judgment while leading the 19th Indiana at South Mountain, Meredith—like Gibbon—was a Southerner who rejected the Confederacy. Born in North Carolina, Meredith made his way to Indiana in the late 1820s.

He served in law enforcement, as a legislator, and as a railroad executive prior to the war. His most notable physical characteristic was stature. Known as "Long Sol," Meredith's 6'7" made him the tallest general to serve in the war.[35]

Cold, wet camps with scanty supplies led First Corps soldiers to find little joy over the next several days, including Thanksgiving. Even a bit of adventure, such as guarding railroad tracks bringing supplies to the army, did not enliven the mood. The 24th Michigan was a regiment drawing duty protecting rail transportation. Each company under Morrow's command was in a semi-isolated portion of track, an arrangement prevailing for eleven days. The regiment's historian reported "usual camp duties" on Thanksgiving, with "none of the good things the day brings at home." Similar sentiment prevailed in the 9th New York State Militia, where the "feast" of the day included "salt-junk" and "mess-pork." The 12th Massachusetts historian remembered the day with only three words, "cold and hungry."[36]

Robert Taggart sat listless in the camp of the 9th Pennsylvania Reserves.

Perhaps the desolation of the country incident to the war may cause a more sacred observance of the day. There is no heart and less inducement in camp to make it an occasion of feasting. My thoughts were "homeward bound" and if left to my own choice my body would have been "homeward bound" too.[37]

Gloom was not the lot of every soldier on November 27. General Patrick visited his former brigade to provide a "Thanksgiving sermon." The gruff old warrior had detractors who disliked his personality, but Patrick's former regiments enjoyed the visit. "He was enthusiastically welcomed, and listened to with deep interest," the historian of the 23rd New York noted. "Very few generals have that firm hold upon the hearts of the men that General Patrick has upon this brigade," the historian added. Two days later, good moods prevailed in the brigade again, when six months of back pay was provided. Families back home and soldiers in Virginia benefited from the largess.[38]

As the new month began, some signs existed of the army's improving the supply situation. In the 3rd Pennsylvania Reserves, winter clothing and better access to food was reported. In addition to the warmth thicker coats, new shoes, and blankets provided, the regiment found, "Our rations were made full and liberal, and the men appeared in excellent spirits."[39]

Men began to wonder if the army was about to go into winter quarters. After an aborted move on December 3, thinking prevailed that the army might remain stationary for months above Fredericksburg. Two days later, additional orders came for an advance, but 4 inches of snow fell on the 5th. Reynolds had issued General Orders 61, which called for all three First Corps divisions to advance at three-hour intervals starting at 6:00 A.M. The same day, the move was countermanded, "but all preparations for the march will be made so as to move as soon as the road permits."

Soldiers suffered amid the indecision and bad weather. On December 6, the 12th Massachusetts chronicler recorded, "Intensely cold. Many cases of frost-bite. Absolutely nothing to eat, as usual, and very little to wear." Contradictory rumors filled camps. Was there going to be imminent aggressive movements, enemy attacks, or the possibility of giving up campaigning for the winter?[40]

Burnside's ability to cross the river and reach Fredericksburg without stiff resistance had been diminishing for days. As December continued, the corps of James Longstreet and Stonewall Jackson presented a formidable line from the town itself well to the south. Jackson's position was on excellent ground around Prospect Hill, while Longstreet enjoyed superb terrain and man-made obstacles immediately to the rear of Fredericksburg.

With the chance of a bloodless crossing into town gone, Burnside continued to ponder his options. On the 9th, orders for a move along the lines of General Orders 61 arrived. Two divisions of the First Corps were to head for the area of Belle Plain Road, around the camp of the Pennsylvania Reserves. "As the ground was frozen hard, the traveling was good," wrote Charles Davis of the 13th Massachusetts, adding, "This was so much preferable to mud, that no complaints were heard, though our 'winter quarters' scheme was completely 'busted.'"[41]

PREPARING FOR BATTLE

The Left Grand Division was moving out to live up to its name, to serve as the left flank of the army, about 2 miles south of Fredericksburg. As at Antietam, the alignment would place Stonewall Jackson in the path of the First Corps. General Orders 64 commanded twenty extra rounds of ammunition (sixty total) be supplied to every man on the evening of December 10. The divisions were told to begin moving at 3:00 A.M. on the 11th.[42]

When considering an enhanced supply situation by December 10, the First Corps looked strong. With ten artillery batteries and forty-seven infantry regiments, Reynolds had 18,667 men present for duty. Perhaps 16,000 would cross the river.[43]

Signs of battle mounted. A member of the 9th New York State Militia recorded, "Heavy cannonading was heard, which was ascertained to proceed from the rebels" attempting to prevent Burnside's minions upstream from bridging the river directly into Fredericksburg. Although a movement to cross the First Corps was planned for the night, another countermanding order was delivered, so bivouacs were made in woods near the river. "Suffering neither from want of rations or the fatigue of a long march," Reynolds's men seemed energized for the expected fording of the Rappahannock.[44]

Surgeon Horace Hanks had made his way to Fredericksburg from Maryland in time for the battle. Departing Frederick in the third week of November, Hanks stopped at Armory Square Hospital in Washington. He was with the army before Thanksgiving. On December 11, he wrote again to "My ever dear Mattie," wondering about the nature of man. Tired of seeing the waste of war, Hanks wrote, "Peace is an improvement." On the 11th, he added, "There are men enough here to do something, and I guess twill be done."[45]

The rookies in the 121st Pennsylvania included men in awe of the sights witnessed during preparations to cross the Rappahannock.

The manoeuvring of immense bodies of troops in the immediate vicinity, the shifting of numerous batteries of artillery and the great roar of the heavy guns used during the day in the bombardment of Fredericksburg, were certainly very assuring to men who had never before beheld the handling of troops on the eve of a great battle, and naturally, their belief in the impossibility of a successful opposition to such an army was considerably strengthened.[46]

Veterans too familiar with scenes of death and devastating injuries were far less optimistic. On December 10, Rufus Dawes sent a letter to his sister. He was concerned how so many in the country wanted Burnside "to drive his army to butchery." Thinking no general would order an attack against miles of prepared Confederate defenses, Dawes warned, "if General Burnside allows himself to be pushed into a battle here, against the enemy's works, the country will mourn thousands slain, and the Rappahannock will run red with blood expended in fruitless slaughter."[47]

Robert Taggart, a cagey veteran in the 9th Reserves, shared Dawes's stark view. The Pennsylvanian wrote, "The sight of the strong fortifications in front of us, the huge cannon glistening in the sunlight and the reflection that they are to be used upon, and against us, are not calculated to enliven the spirits."[48]

Most members of the 2nd USSS likely had a vision more in line with Dawes and Taggart than the rookie warriors in new regiments. Joel Ellis, one new recruit in the marksman outfit, showed a brave face before the Rappahannock was crossed. Climbing one of the many trees near the river, Ellis "threw forth a loud challenge toward the lines of the enemy," according to Curtis Abbott. Seeing the obvious signs of approaching battle and the lack of danger Confederates faced from Ellis's words, his comrades "promised him a better opportunity if he would be patient." Interestingly, Ellis would leave the picket line on the army's southern flank during the battle, apparently making an escape to Canada.[49] Brave words are meaningless from cowards.

Franklin's two corps started moving closer to the bridges, still under construction, on the morning of December 11. The grand division commander reported completion of both spans by 11:00 A.M. Due to the nature of the ground and the impressive line of Union cannon on the east side of the river on Stafford Heights, "The enemy made but feeble efforts to prevent the construction of the bridges," Franklin reported. This was the opposite of the story upstream, where some in Sumner's grand division had to fight through the streets of Fredericksburg.

Like the tactical situation along Antietam Creek, an attack a day earlier offered tantalizing chances for Union fortunes. The delay in getting the entire army across the river led Burnside to keep Franklin's men inactive for the rest of the 11th. After filing across the bridges, starting at daylight on the 12th, the First Corps guarded the far left of the army, with Smith's 6th Corps farther to the right, spread out across the west side of the Rappahannock.[50] Elements of Jackson's command were returning to the Confederate right flank after guarding portions of the river several miles farther south of Franklin's grand division. Much to his army's misfortune, Burnside simply had no idea of the state of the Confederate defenses and wanted all portions of his army ready before making an attack anywhere along the line.[51]

A lack of shared understanding between Unionist generals at Fredericksburg echoed the miasma of confused expectations McClellan and Hooker had created on September 16. Much ink was spilled in the years after the battle on the question of whether Burnside or Franklin was more to blame for the Fredericksburg disaster. Based on a conference between the two prior to the attack, the grand division commander was expecting orders for a massive effort of his whole command against Jackson's position. After hours of delay and a tense overnight period with no written orders from headquarters, Franklin began to wonder about Burnside's goals.

When orders finally came, Franklin grew very confused.[52] The part in question read,

> *The general commanding directs that you keep your whole command in position for a rapid movement down the old Richmond road; and you will send out at once a division at least to pass below Smithfield, to seize, if possible, the heights near Captain Hamilton's on this side of the Massaponax, taking care to keep it well supported and its line of retreat open. He has ordered another column of a division or more to be moved from General Sumner's command up the plank road to its intersection with the Telegraph Road, where they will divide with a view to seizing the heights on both of those roads. Holding these heights with the heights near Captain Hamilton's, will, he hopes, compel the enemy to evacuate the whole ridge between these points. He makes these moves by columns, distant from each other, with the view of avoiding the possibility of a collision of our two forces, which might occur in a general movement during the fog. Two of General Hooker's divisions are in your rear, at the bridges, and will remain there as supports. Copies of instructions given to Generals Sumner and Hooker will be forwarded to you by an orderly very soon. You will keep your whole command in readiness to move at once as soon as the fog lifts.[53]*

Franklin's two corps had 40,000 men, but Franklin ordered an attack of one division, as if Burnside limited the attack to the bare minimum number of troops in his order. Meade's Pennsylvania Reserves were selected for the task, although Meade had the fewest men of any division under Reynolds. Smith's entire 24,000 men did not participate in the attack, while Doubleday protected the army's left flank. Only Gibbon's Division moved to Meade's support.

Stonewall Jackson's command was in unknown strength and possessed obvious terrain advantages. A West Point flunky should have been able to discern how one First Corps division could not meet Burnside's goal, clearly stated in the order: pushing Lee's army off the ridge south of Fredericksburg. Burnside gave Franklin discretion in this area, much to the detriment of the Union war effort.

Without doubt, Burnside's order to Franklin was not completely clear. With fewer words, Burnside should have directed a much larger attack against Jackson. More imagination from Franklin obviously was necessary. William Marvel, as great a student of the question as any across the generations, rightly states how Burnside's order granted Franklin the ability to launch a major attack.[54] Only a weak field leader would have missed the message.

The ever-cautious Franklin, a disciple of McClellan, gave an incredibly feeble defense for not adding the Sixth Corps to attack.

As Smith's corps was in position when the order for attack was received, and as a change in the line would have been attended with great risk at that time, and would have caused much delay, I considered it impractical to add his force to that about to make the attack.

Instead of an overwhelming force charging Jackson's lines, the First Corps was about to launch its second unsupported assault of the latter half of 1862.[55]

ATTACK OF THE RESERVES

George Meade doubted the viability of Franklin's plan. He raised concerns about using just his division for the main assault, but the grand division commander merely referred to Burnside's order. Writing his wife as the bridge crossings neared, Meade stressed the fate soldiers must face. "Keep up your spirits," he requested, adding, "Of course, no man can go into action without running risks, but our heavenly Father has shown us so much mercy and loving kindness hitherto, that we may pray for its continuance and hope for the best."[56] Stonewall Jackson was undoubtedly calling on the same God to provide his men with not just protection, but the fortitude and power to crush Meade and his troops.

Full of fight and seeing divine favor blessing the Confederate cause, Jackson previously argued for the order to attack Franklin's men as the river crossings progressed. Lee, his well-trained engineer eyes appreciating Jackson's defenses, balked. Scant evidence of the Confederate works was visible to the First Corps near the river. When an aide asked Jackson if he was concerned about the large numbers of men poised to attack, Stonewall declared his soldiers had never been pushed off a strong defensive position.[57] The First Corps alone tried to beat Jackson at Antietam. Three months later, the men were about to be given another chance.

Due to the relatively warm temperatures, "a deep impenetrable fog" shrouded the field on the morning of December 13. Visibility improved by 9:00 A.M. Then, troops began to organize for the attack, with men advancing to the Bowling Green Road, roughly parallel to and about 2,000 feet beyond the Rappahannock.

Near the position of the 121st Pennsylvania, an incident occurred giving the new troops a humorous respite from the stress of what would be their baptism of battle. "A rabbit was sufficiently indiscreet to make its appearance," the regimental historian wrote, "and the consequent scrambling and tumbling and hooting among the soldiers in their efforts to capture the spry little fellow were enough to drive away all serious thoughts of the coming conflict." The Iron Brigade, on the left flank facing south, apparently did not find a distraction. Not destined for the attack, Meredith's men still had to worry about whether random Confederate shells would maim anyone in the five Western regiments.[58]

For a time, all Jackson needed was two artillery pieces to frustrate Franklin's plan. First, John Pelham, an intrepid young major serving under Jeb Stuart, rode down the hill to cause much consternation with a single cannon on Franklin's left. Closer to Jackson's main line, another cannon started to annoy Reynolds's men.

Pelham had picked an excellent position to create havoc with one gun. Four First Corps batteries were detailed to counter Pelham's lone cannon, with perhaps an hour passing before the nuisance was silenced. When able to turn their attention to Prospect Hill, the superior Union cannon had a chance to shine. Confederate general A. P. Hill said the First Corps artillery and supporting guns "opened a terrific fire upon the positions occupied by my batteries and shelled the woods promiscuously."[59]

Meade's Division remained under threat from Confederate artillery as time approached for the assault. Capt. William Stewart, Company C, 11th Reserves, was hit by cannon fire. Considered a great leader and inspiring the men by his bravery, Stewart appeared to move as if to dodge the incoming ball. Unfortunately, "a solid shot struck him in the breast and he fell to his right and rear over my feet," an enlisted man recalled. Of the doomed captain, another wrote, "as a last request he asked them to go into the impending struggle as bravely as if he were with them." Stewart lived only a short time. Command of the company fell to a corporal, whose gallantry would soon earn him a lieutenancy.[60]

The corps' guns were supported by the 13th Reserves, which normally would have been ahead of Meade's initial battle line. Instead, the 6th Reserves of Sinclair's Brigade served as skirmishers.[61]

Charles Wainwright supervised the guns sending regular barrages of lead into Jackson's position. Riding to the left flank, he assisted some of Doubleday's guns sparring with several Confederate cannon. Doubleday also reported concerns about Confederate cavalry to the south. Initially, two divisional batteries formed with the 1st New Hampshire Light on the right and Lieutenant Stewart's Battery B, 4th U.S. on the left. While engaged during the day, the cannoneers suffered several casualties. One of the Granite State fatalities was Thomas Morrill; a shell passed clearly through his body.[62]

Some shells found marks among Doubleday's command with the end result being humor. While the 30th New York was prone, observing potential threats to the army's left flank,

> *A soldier lying on his face had his knapsack struck with round shot cutting it open, it sent a cloud of underwear into the air and high above them floated a pack of cards. The boys called out, "Give us a deal," and the soldier finding himself unhurt joined in the laugh occasioned at his expense.*[63]

The time for frivolity quickly waned. Lined up near the Bowling Green Road by early afternoon, Meade's brigades, totaling fewer than 4,000 men, had Conrad Jackson on the left with Sinclair to his right. Magilton was positioned in reserve behind Sinclair. A gap of several hundred feet existed between Meade's right and Root's Brigade, the left of Gibbon's Division. Skirmishers from the 9th Reserves, 6th Reserves, and 13th Massachusetts were about halfway between the road and a railroad track, which ran parallel to the road before curving west. Stonewall's command was positioned behind the tracks.[64]

The defensive position was quite strong, but the Reserves found a good spot to hit. Three Confederate brigades were in Meade's bull's-eye. Gaps existed in the line, with Archer on Meade's left and Lane on the right. Maxcy Gregg's South Carolinians were behind and between the first two brigades. None of the three Confederate brigades had protected flanks, a necessity to defend a battle line properly.

The historian of Gregg's Brigade recalled the opening of Meade's attack. After Confederate artillery started firing, "the scene," the South Carolinian recalled, "grand before, now became terrible. All air and earth in the surrounding terrain seemed filled with smoke and the messengers of death."[65]

The field Meade's soldiers advanced over was quite undulating, with some dips and trenches several feet deep. Such obstacles made precise lines impossible to maintain. Conrad Jackson's men became nothing close to unified, with the 9th Reserves staying on the left flank.[66]

Sinclair's main line only included three regiments. With the 6th Reserves as skirmishers and the 13th supporting artillery, the 2nd Reserves, 121st Pennsylvania, and 1st Reserves moved forward. As Conrad Jackson engaged Archer's men, Sinclair's command found a surprise: an unprepared enemy. Gregg seemed always in the mood to kill Yankees, but when Sinclair's line hit, muskets were still stacked, the men apparently thinking the advancing troops were Confederates. Gregg suffered a mortal wound while his brigade was exposed to withering fire from the Reserves.[67]

Tremendous musketry erupted as the opposing forces fought in close quarters. The assault was assisted by the arrival of the 13th Reserves, which Meade had ordered forward. The regiment actually fought in Jackson's line, adding firepower to the attack against Archer. At first, the Confederates seemed comfortable with their ability to hold the position. An officer under Archer reported the fire "had great effect upon the Federal lines, killing and wounding a large number of men and officers and confusing others." A member of the 8th Reserves, who would die less than a month later from a wound, wrote a week after the battle of the "engulfing fire," which "fearfully thinned" the Pennsylvanians.[68]

Two officers were lost as Meade sent an order for Jackson's Brigade to move to the right in response to Confederate artillery fire. Lt. Arthur Dehon, an aide to Meade from the 12th Massachusetts, was killed when communicating the order to Jackson. A Harvard graduate, Dehon was only twenty-one years old. The brigade commander also fell, killed by a shot to the head.[69]

The commander of the 13th Reserves, Charles Taylor—only twenty-two years old—lost his horse early in the fight, then fell wounded himself. Color corporal John Looney was killed. "As he dropped with his death wound," a veteran wrote, "his blood spurted over the tattered flag."[70]

Magilton's men found impossible the maintenance of a single battle line. The brigade commander noted the 142nd Pennsylvania and 8th Reserves were stopped near the railroad track. His 3rd, 4th, and 7th Regiments were able to penetrate farther into the woods. The balance of the engagement soon turned against Archer.

Regiments from multiple Pennsylvania brigades assisted each other to roll up Archer's left flank. Adjutant Evan Woodward earned a Medal of Honor while leading men and capturing elements of Archer's command. A Philadelphia native born in 1838, Woodward's citation declares the lieutenant, "Advanced between the lines, demanded and received the surrender of the 19th Georgia Infantry and captured their battle flag."[71]

With chaos everywhere and men on both sides falling with alarming frequency, the Reserves lacked support. Penetrating several hundred feet into the woods and forcing back the first lines of Confederates would not be enough to win against Stonewall Jackson. As Magilton reported, his regiments drove the enemy until the Second Brigade "reached a new line of the enemy, concealed just beyond the summit of the hills, when they opened a dreadful fire upon the line, at a few yards distant."[72]

More desperate fighting occurred within the forest, but pressed on both flanks, Meade's men were compelled to retreat. As Woodward noted, "The Reserves had done all that mortal men could do, and they felt if they stood they would be simply wiped-out by the fire of an overwhelming foe, without achieving any good." With the strength of their unsupported charge fading, a Pennsylvanian declared, "the Reserves had found themselves into a death-trap, and a terrible slaughter ensued."

Meade was in a highly excited state in an effort to rally his regiments. The general "broke the point of his sword upon a retreating lieutenant's shoulder blade," one regimental historian recorded. Receiving fire from three directions, the Reserves "fought valiantly until their ammunition, as well as their hope, was exhausted." Another soldier suggested, "There comes a time with every attacking column when its strength is spent by its own impetus—when the force is disorganized by its own energy."[73]

O'Reilly's contention of subpar brigade leadership negatively impacting the attack seems questionable.[74] Jackson was killed, Sinclair was wounded.

Magilton's support was certainly positive. The most important component of a successful attack, as outlined in Franklin's orders, was timely support from Gibbon, something corps commander John Reynolds should have spent his early afternoon ensuring. One weakness of the grand division structure was a decrease in the impact corps leaders could provide at pivotal moments. Little is known of Reynolds's activities on the afternoon of December 13, but he clearly failed to coordinate sufficiently to ensure his two divisions hit the Confederate line at the same time. O'Reilly would have been closer to the chief reason for an unsuccessful effort along the railroad if he pointed the finger at Reynolds, not Meade's three competent brigade commanders.

Faint praise was the best Meade could say of Gibbon's assistance. "Gibbon's division advanced into the wood on our right in time to assist materially in the safe withdrawal of my broken line," Meade reported. The commander of the Reserves expressed "deep regret" in his inability to hold the ground gained. Still, "I deem their withdrawal a matter of necessity." The retreat, occurring to a division suffering 40 percent casualties, was compelled by confusion in the woods, fire on both flanks from charging Confederate reinforcements, and the loss of two brigade commanders. Under the circumstances, "the best troops would be justified in withdrawing without loss of honor," Meade correctly suggested.[75]

Men in the bloodied Reserves certainly did not lack the will to succeed. But the most devoted patriot could begin to doubt the entire war effort after the debacle at Prospect Hill. Robert Taggart stewed with anger. Shortly after the attack, he lamented, then wondered, "I am sick of this *butchery* and there seems to be so little gained. When will it end?" The next day, he added more fatalism, "The undertaking seemed like madness, but was tried bravely. I am sick at heart of this."[76]

"It Was Impossible to Advance"

Gibbon's three brigades were lined up in one column, with Taylor in front, Lyle behind, and Root in the rear. During the start of the morning's artillery barrage, James Hall and his Second Maine Battery occupied dangerous ground between Meade and Gibbon. Providing important support to Meade's advance, Hall lost men and a limber chest, which was blown up by a very accurate Confederate cannoneer. Then, "When General Gibbon's line went forward, he ordered the battery to advance, posting it within 200 yards of the woods," Hall reported. The battery fired 1,100 rounds during the battle.[77]

The 13th Massachusetts performed skirmish duties in front of the entire division. Charles Davis penned a vivid recollection of the regiment's efforts to screen Gibbon's brigades. The work of skirmishers focused on keeping an eye on the enemy's line while several hundred feet in front of friendly troops. At Fredericksburg, the 13th Massachusetts also had to focus on protecting Hall's Battery. The regiment sent messages back to Hall reminding the battery commander to raise his guns a bit to avoid wiping out the skirmish line.

Skirmishers operated "between two fires," Davis continued. Because of the friendly cannon shots from behind, the Bay Staters spent much of the day prone, rolling over onto their backs to reload. The tedious process made for dozens of mud-covered Bay Staters. Danger increased when Taylor's Brigade advanced; the men of the 13th were needed to screen the attack, but at least no more mud would drench the advancing skirmishers. The duty "is no place for skulkers, as every man is in plain sight, where his every movement is watched with the closest scrutiny," Davis wrote.[78]

The 13th Massachusetts did not participate in the main part of Gibbon's attack due to lack of ammunition. This limited the regiment's casualties to only sixteen, barely 5 percent of the total in Taylor's command. Davis credited drill in the art of skirmishing as conducive to the regiment's excellent service at Fredericksburg, as well as the low loss.

An incident during the morning rattled the 88th Pennsylvania. General Taylor grew concerned about the threat Confederate battery fire posed to the right of his line. He ordered Maj. David Griffith and the 88th "forward under the cover of a slight elevation of ground, with directions to fire a volley at the battery." At first pleased with the effects of the regiment's fire, Taylor sarcastically observed how the Pennsylvanians, "apparently frightened at the noise they had made themselves," began to withdraw from the advanced position without orders. Calling on an aide to help, Taylor added, "I succeeded in stopping this disgraceful and causeless retrograde movement."

The Confederate battery proved "particularly annoying" to the division prior to the 88th's volleys against the guns. The regimental historian suggested canister from the enemy was "knocking over many of the men and sweeping part of the regiment back in some confusion."

Griffith reported "very severe" fire from the Confederates. He took part of the blame for the regiment's withdrawal. "I gave the command 'march on retreat,'" Griffith wrote, "which was unfortunately misunderstood by my men." The "partially disorganized" Pennsylvanians scrambled to a ditch east of the brigade's line, where rallying officers proved decisive to restoring regimental cohesion.[79]

Unprepared to advance when Meade's attack began, Gibbon's men moved forward on the right of the Reserves after the Pennsylvanians' assault of the position had started. Because of the glaring oversight by John Reynolds, there was never a direct connection between the two divisions. Both Franklin and Reynolds suggested the dense woods prohibited the attacking columns from linking up,[80] but this is not the whole story. Poor planning from the corps commander must be part of the reason for the failure to connect the two divisions.

Taylor's line included the 11th and 88th Pennsylvania on the left and right flanks, respectively, with the 9th New York State Militia and 97th New York in the middle. In his report, Col. Charles Wheelock, the leader of the 97th, said 213 men and 17 officers were part of his regiment. Of the enlisted men, only 181 had muskets. "My object in taking in men without guns," Wheelock continued, "was to take the arms of those that fell and to help the wounded, which they did to my entire satisfaction."[81]

Capt. James Thompson's Pennsylvania Light Artillery, Battery C, advanced on the right of the division, with the goal of inflicting damage on the North Carolinians under Lane who prepared to face Taylor's men. Thompson reported being the target of Confederate batteries on the right, but infantry support was his focus. The Keystone State cannoneers did not fire back at the enemy artillery until after Gibbon's men fell back. Thompson likely dished out more than he received; the battery only reported two casualties.[82]

Lane skillfully commanded his Tar Heels. He had to worry about a flank attack from elements of the Reserves as Gibbon's line moved toward the railroad tracks. Turning part of his right-most regiment failed to stem the oncoming Reserves, but Lane was determined to do or die. As the Confederate general noted, "Our position was deemed too important to be given up without a blow, and nobly did both officers and men await the approach" of Gibbon's three brigades.[83]

The two regiments on Taylor's left experienced severe punishment from the resolute Confederates. In Gibbon's words, the 11th Pennsylvania and 9th New York State Militia were "thrown into confusion." Early on, the 11th had three flag bearers hit. Maj. John Hendrickson, commanding the 9th, was just one of several officers shot during the few moments when the left regiments essentially served as target practice for Lane's men.

"It was impossible to advance, as our boys fell as fast as they attempted it," one New Yorker wrote in his diary. Confederate artillery seemed to be in a contest with Lane's infantry to see who could decimate Taylor's two left regiments faster. The heroic diarist continued, "About six feet to the right of where I lay, two men were killed by a shell which took the head off one and passed through the body of another, while between them and me a Lieutenant was shot through the head."[84]

Hendrickson's replacement, Capt. Joseph Moesch, was wounded, but he remained on the field. The 9th New York State Militia quickly lost dozens of soldiers, men like Patrick and William Kelly, both in their early twenties. Patrick would die of wounds in February, while the older William would be discharged eighteen months later. John Knife, Andrew Lewis, David Morgan, and Jeremiah Osbourne were four of the men in the 9th killed in action at Fredericksburg. Osbourne had been wounded at Antietam.

A man in Company D recalled, "we received a destructive fire of musketry," prompting men to use their knapsacks as protection after laying down. Confederate musketry and artillery still found men of the 9th New York State Militia. Moesch reported the regiment staying in line for about thirty minutes, which seems generous. Other reports suggest the two left regiments were in flight soon after being engaged, but their combined casualties well exceeded 200, and one soldier wrote of a charge, albeit unsuccessful, of the brigade's left regiments. After retiring from the main line, Moesch turned command over to Capt. Isaac Hoagland.[85]

The 88th Pennsylvania possessed the chance to earn back the confidence of its brigade commander, and they were worthy of Taylor's hopes. As the 11th Pennsylvania and 9th New York State Militia fell back, the right regiments in the brigade's line provided strong support to the regiments under Lyle. The 88th Pennsylvania and the 97th New York moved right near the railroad tracks to make room for Lyle's regiments.

As Lyle arrived on the firing line, his men were aligned with the rookie 136th Pennsylvania on the left, followed by the 90th and 26th New York, with the 12th Massachusetts on the right. The brigade commander reported being about 50 yards from the woods at this point, with his men greeted by "a most galling fire."

During their movement forward, Col. William Leech and his 90th Pennsylvania were ordered to advance to a rise of ground, estimated to be 40 yards from the woods. "We continued our fire upon the enemy until all available ammunition was expended," the commander reported. Taylor requested more from the 90th, but Leech referred the general to Lyle. Seeing no support at the time, Leech thought, "It would have been worse than madness" to make the charge Taylor sought.[86]

While on the left flank, Col. Thomas Bayne wrote of his rookies firing while advancing in battle line. "None faltered," the proud colonel added, "all stood at their post of duty, and were loth to quit their position, even when they knew it was impossible to hold it longer." A member of the new regiment proved especially brave. Philip Petty, a native of England, knew the importance of visibility for the regimental colors. He "took up the colors as they fell out of the hands of the wounded color bearer and carried them forward in the charge," according to Petty's Medal of Honor citation.[87]

The 12th Massachusetts fought somewhat isolated from the rest of the brigade. Taylor's withdrawing regiments created a gap between the 12th and the rest of Lyle's command. After other elements of the brigade started falling back, Col. James Bates wrote of his regiment, "We were alone until the third line came forward."

About thirty minutes elapsed with Lyle exposed to the whirlwind of shot and shell. At first doubtful of support, he ordered his regiments to stay in position, even as ammunition was running low. With Root's regiments closing in, Lyle figured the time had come for his men to replenish ammunition. A captain from Gibbon's staff assumed the worst when he saw two regiments, the 26th New York and 90th Pennsylvania, well behind the battle line. As Leech noted, "in a most insulting manner," the staff officer "drew his pistol" on the New Yorkers. Leech's men returned to the action without much ammunition.[88]

A man from the other Massachusetts regiment in the First Corps proved especially heroic that afternoon. George Maynard, while on the skirmish line of the 13th Regiment, applied a tourniquet to the leg of George Armstrong, an injured comrade. With so much on his mind, Maynard later fell back with the regiment to the Bowling Green Road. Shortly thereafter, he envisioned his wounded comrade, then went to retrieve Armstrong. This type of action was what the Medal of Honor was meant to recognize. Maynard, "voluntarily returned to the front under a severe fire and carried the wounded man to a place of safety." Unfortunately, Armstrong died later in the day.[89]

"Every Man's Heart and Soul"

Adrian Root recorded 1:45 p.m. as the time Gibbon ordered the advance of the brigade. Initially deemed a reserve, Root's five units had not moved forward with Gibbon's other two brigades. Left to right, Root placed the 107th Pennsylvania, 105th New York, and the rookies of the 16th Maine in his first line. The 94th New York was immediately behind the Maine men, with the 104th New York to the rear.

With the attack happening a bit later in the afternoon, the unseasonable warmth further hindered Root's men by turning the ground into a muddy mess. Then there was the enemy. The brigade commander knew the difficulty of his task with a quick review of the field in front. One of the first problems Root faced was sorting out how to advance through retreating elements of Taylor's and Lyle's regiments. He noted only the 12th Massachusetts, 88th Pennsylvania, and 97th New York in any organized state along the division's advanced line.

Root scanned the area beyond the railroad tracks. "On approaching the wood the enemy's position was first fully developed to my brigade," he reported. Root noted "the embankment and ditches of the Richmond railway," with "approaches being rendered extremely difficult by several parallel ditches, or rifle-pits, and its rear protected by thick wood, sheltering infantry supports."

The brigade commander from Buffalo called the subsequent Confederate hellfire "incessant and galling," during the move forward. He continued, "so many of my men fell killed or wounded, that the front line of the brigade slackened its pace." This led to men firing without orders, something Root did not approve of or expect. He knew a charge was the best opportunity to stun Lane's diminished line.

Considering the enemy's musketry "very disastrous," with his men's return fire having limited effect, Col. Charles Tilden of the 16th Maine was another officer who saw the limits of the status quo. John Kress of the 94th New York echoed the sentiment. He witnessed the "close and telling fire" from Lane's line.[90]

The 107th Pennsylvania, on the left of Root's front, also encountered difficulties in the initial stages of the engagement. "We were under a most destructive fire," Col. Thomas McCoy reported, "and our brave fellows were falling fast." As units from earlier in the afternoon rallied to the rear, McCoy received a timely visitor, John Gibbon. The division commander "ordered that the wood should be taken at the point of the bayonet," McCoy recalled.[91]

Gibbon was shortly thereafter wounded in the wrist seriously enough to leave the field. Command of the division devolved to General Taylor.

With the limited number of units from other brigades still organized, this last attacking line of the First Corps at Fredericksburg included regiments from all three of Gibbon's brigades. Due to the lack of ammunition, Colonel Bates had been preparing to withdraw the isolated 12th Massachusetts. Root requested the continued presence of the Bay Staters, prompting Bates to report, "I at once gave the command to fix bayonets and filed to the right," then the 12th Massachusetts prepared to move forward. "Not once did the regiment falter," Bates wrote, adding, "Every order was obeyed promptly and not a man fell from the ranks after the advance began."[92]

"The power of numbers forced them entirely across the railroad," Lane wrote of the wave attacking his Confederates. Then, with hand-to-hand fighting, as one historian recorded, "the awful carnage of death began." The fighting grew vicious, with Gibbon's order to use the bayonet being implemented. Bates was reported to have told his men to club the back of Confederate heads with the butt of the musket in an effort to decapitate. Lane's innovative Confederates made use of a spear by throwing their muskets tipped by a bayonet, with some wounds to First Corps troops inflicted in this fashion.[93]

As with previous efforts along the railroad tracks, signs of progress were promising. Lane's men were compelled to fall back after the brief yet gruesome melee. The lack of support, recorded by commanders on the field, letter writers, and regimental historians, limited the attack's power. Across the entire First Corps front, the position proved far too deep for two divisions to devastate. The day was lost, even with some ground won and hundreds of Confederate prisoners going to the rear under guard.

As the Confederates massed reinforcements to sweep the remnants of two First Corps divisions out of the woods, another valiant soldier from the 90th Pennsylvania added luster to the regiment's strong reputation. John Shiel grabbed a wounded man before departing the field. His Medal of Honor citation praised the corporal, who, "Carried a dangerously wounded comrade into the Union lines, thereby preventing his capture by the enemy."[94]

Defiance was shown before the retreat along Root's disorganized line. Tilden noted the men responded to the order to fall back, "but not without giving the rebels two volleys as a parting salute." A cannoneer from the 5th Maine Battery was happy to extol the brave infantry from his state. Observing the action of the 16th Maine, John Varney wrote of how "they so gallantly immortalized their names" during the hopelessness of Fredericksburg.

Sustaining 231 casualties, more than half his command, Tilden expressed great pride in the conduct of the 16th Maine at their first battle. He informed Governor Washburn of "the disastrous engagement near Fredericksburg" in a letter two days before Christmas. Tilden added his warriors were "the first regiment to make the charge and the last to leave the field." The state's chief executive could be proud because, "The Regt has certainly done credit to itself and the Old Pine Tree State altho' at a great sacrifice."

Washburn was provided a casualty list showing the immense loss. With such evidence, Tilden concluded, "Every man's heart and soul seemed bent upon having a chance at the enemy."[95]

"IF IT HAD COST EVERY MAN IN THE REGIMENT"

Losses mounted for the troops forced out of the woods by Confederate reinforcements. Lt. William Bacon, adjutant of the 26th New York, was a brilliant student who had left college to fight for his country. Wounded at Second Bull Run, he recovered at home before returning to the regiment at Fredericksburg. He was seen using a musket to fire at the Confederate counterattack at around 2:30 P.M. Bacon then suffered a wound in the left leg, the same limb hit earlier in the year.

Men of the regiment truly admired Bacon. They were deeply hurt to know he was shot again, but also heartbroken when their commander, Maj. Ezra Wetmore, noted the order not to leave the ranks to help the wounded. The drive to help their cherished adjutant made orders seem irrelevant. As a member of the 26th wrote, "The men say some of their wounded were left on the field, but they say that if it had cost every man in the regiment to take Willie off, they would not have left him." Wetmore decided not to interfere as soldiers gave Bacon assistance.

A memorial book to Bacon recounted his rescue and the rest of the tragic story.

From the time the amputation was performed on the evening of Saturday, the thirteenth of December, the sufferer lingered, mostly in a state of unconsciousness, and probably with very little pain, until about five o'clock on the morning of the sixteenth, when he quietly breathed his last.

Even with a privileged upbringing and intelligence enough to read Latin and Greek by his twentieth birthday, Bacon was not a haughty Yankee. He respected enlisted men and viewed them as comrades. William Cleminger, a musician in the 26th New York, recalled, "We shall miss him very much, he was so kind and social, and was not too proud to come into our tents, and talk and joke with a private soldier."[96]

Bacon's classmates at Hamilton College recorded highly positive recollections of the deceased patriot. During a service on campus, each member of the Class of 1863 received a copy of the memorial Bacon's father had published. A newspaper described Bacon's qualities, "Perhaps his most striking trait was his fearlessness. It adorned his countenance, and beamed in his bold, dauntless eye. . . . He was the soul of honor. No one can accuse him of ever having consciously done a mean or ungenerous thing."[97]

"A Sacred Relic"

Although pushed out of the woods, the First Corps remained on the west side of the Rappahannock the night of the battle. Orders to recross the river were not issued until more than two full days later. After supporting troops waylaid Jackson's counterattack, Lee was content to hold the heights commanding the area.

In case of unexpected boldness from the troops on Prospect Hill, lines of the First Corps were reorganized later in the day. Hall's overworked battery was moved to the left flank to assist Doubleday, as was Gibbon's Division. Doubleday said only about 2,000 men from the division were present in the three brigades recently thrown out of the woods.

Doubleday responded to what he deemed a leadership failure on his relatively unengaged part of the field. Still charged with protecting the flank of the army, Doubleday grew concerned about the exposed nature of a part of his line, the brigades of Rogers and Meredith. Doubleday wanted pickets left out as darkness descended, but he ordered the two brigades to fall back to a safer position. "There was unusual, and, as I deemed, unnecessary, delay in obeying this order on the part of General Meredith," the division commander reported. After two hours, "I felt it my duty to relieve him of command," Doubleday added, giving the Iron Brigade to Lysander Cutler. Evidence showed a staff mix-up could have prevented Meredith from receiving Doubleday's order. Thus, Meredith was not yet done as leader of the Westerners.[98]

"There was a great deal of heavy picket firing during the night, but toward morning, all became quiet," Doubleday reported. His goal for the morning of the 14th was to reoccupy the ground taken the previous day along the left flank. The First Division "formed as before in two lines, obliquely from the angle of the road to the river."

Late in the morning, a cannon known for screeching noises capable of terrifying the bravest went into action against the left flank. Doubleday reported the Whitworth cannon, which the Confederacy imported from England, was countered by Hall's Battery. A member of the First Division staff remarked, "It is agreed by all that the yell of this projectile was the most ear-piercing we had ever listened to." The grooved, oblong ordnance created "a rapid spin or rotation in the air, which adds to the music of its flight." An attack from the Confederate right was then expected, but the loud, frightening shells were the worst part of the day for many men.[99]

Enemy pickets were a hidden and dangerous part of the period after the battle. In the 1st New Hampshire battery, Sgt. Sam Piper, a gun chief, was wounded by a Southern marksman.[100]

Colonel Phelps recorded 8:00 P.M. on the 15th as the time Doubleday informed him of the expected retreat. "At 9:45," Phelps added, "I received orders to put my column in motion, and recrossed the river without loss." A man in the Iron Brigade wrote, "Not a word was uttered above the lowest kind of whisper and in silence broken only by the cracking of dry weeds, we took our departure from the most dangerous part of Dixie." About a mile beyond the Rappahannock, Phelps and his men camped, "on the ground occupied by the brigade on the night of Thursday, the 11th."[101] So much was witnessed in those five days without anything for the First Corps besides the butcher's bill.

Cavalry patrols delivered the retreat order to some elements of the First Corps. Those soldiers still on the west side early on December 16 needed to hustle, as the pontoon bridges were slated for dismantling. Lt. Clayton Rogers, a 6th Wisconsin man serving on Doubleday's staff, received praise for his work getting the word out to pickets, some a few miles downriver. Doubleday thanked Lt. Col. Sam Williams of the 19th Indiana and his picket group. "A portion of his men were compelled to pass in boats, the pontoon bridges having been cut away," the general wrote.[102]

Other soldiers in the First Corps had similarly close calls in the wee hours of December 16. The night before, 250 men were detailed from the 11th Pennsylvania and 13th Massachusetts to picket down the Rappahannock.

At around 2:00 A.M., "we were awakened by a cavalryman who notified us that the rest of the army had crossed the river." This was the first notice the startled men had of the potential for being trapped. They had a few miles to cover before reaching the last bridge still in place. "The knowledge that we were in a very dangerous position lent an activity to our muscles they rarely felt on approaching an enemy," Charles Davis reported.[103]

Four Minnesota sharpshooters from Company A, 2nd USSS, were on a picket patrol during the overnight period. An officer wrote of the inability to find them early on the 16th. Across the eight companies in the marksman regiment, only 121 men were present late in December.[104]

Fredericksburg was very costly to the First Corps. With nearly 800 more casualties suffered compared to the hell along Antietam Creek, the carnage was truly horrendous. Meade's Division suffered the most, with 1,846 casualties. Gibbon's strong but late attack caused another 1,266 men to fall, while Doubleday's relatively unengaged command suffered only 214 casualties. The other two grand divisions were roughly handled on the Union right. Burnside's defeated army suffered more than 13,000 casualties.

The First Corps lost many leaders at Fredericksburg. Twelve officers in Meade's Division were killed outright, with five more mortally wounded. Five of these seventeen men were from the 5th Reserves, the regiment still under the command of Col. Joseph Fisher. His five lost officers were: Capt. Charles Wells and Lt. David Zentmyer (both killed in action), and Maj. Franklin Zentmyer, Capt. Charles Schaffle, and Lt. Israel Kinch each mortally wounded.

The Zentmyers were brothers. Franklin's leg wound led to his capture, where a Confederate amputation table awaited him. He died in late December. David, adjutant of the regiment, was twenty-seven years old, sixteen months senior to Franklin. John and Margaret Zentmyer, parents of the deceased officers, long outlived their brave sons.[105]

The four new regiments in the First Corps proved their worth in their initial battle. The most casualties for a First Corps regiment at Fredericksburg were suffered by the 142nd Pennsylvania, part of Magilton's Brigade. With 16 killed, 182 wounded, and 45 missing, the 142nd experienced a vicious baptism. The 231 casualties from the 16th Maine ranked second in the list of corps' losses for a single regiment. Tilden recorded 27 dead in his command. The 121st Pennsylvania's 138 casualties added to the loss in the new regiments.

Although the 24th Michigan was relatively unscathed on the left flank, its thirty-two casualties, including seven killed, amounted to almost half of the loss in Meredith's Brigade. Of the Michigan men, one member of the 7th Wisconsin wrote, "They are a new regiment, but done credit to themselves and the State from whence they hail."[106]

Based on official returns, the four rookie units suffered nearly one in five First Corps casualties at Fredericksburg. Meade might have been quick to find fault, but he also wished to recognize a solid effort by a new regiment. The historian of the 121st proudly noted how Meade praised the new troops "in the presence of the division," by declaring, "Well done, 121st; good enough for one day." Reynolds also extolled the four rookie regiments. In his report, the corps commander wrote "the new regiments" were "vieing with the veterans in steadiness and coolness."[107]

Reynolds also wrote of the strong leadership First Corps batteries showed at Fredericksburg. The cannoneers across the battle line had difficult work on December 13 due to the excellent positioning and natural defenses protecting Confederate artillery. Cross fire created havoc during the day, with ten First Corps batteries recording sixty-seven casualties, a relatively small sum not indicative of the intense pressure the artillery endured. Of his batteries, Reynolds reported how "great credit is due for the intrepidity with which they maintained their positions, and the coolness and judgment with which they managed their commands under the severe fire of the enemy's batteries."[108]

William Hogarty once again shined as an infantryman turned cannoneer. In addition to Antietam, Fredericksburg was listed on his Medal of Honor citation. Assisting Stewart's Battery B, 4th U.S., Hogarty lost an arm along the Rappahannock. Speaking of the day at Fredericksburg, Hogarty gave credit to his comrades. "Each and every man of the battery present and participating in the battle of Fredericksburg shares equally with me in the glory the medal commerates," Hogarty said.[109]

Horses also suffered as a result of the batteries' tough assignment. They were prime targets of enemy infantry; fewer animals to move guns increased the chances of capturing cannons with charging troops. Sixteen of the New Hampshire battery's equines were killed, with as many wounded.[110]

Under a flag of truce, the body of Lieutenant Dehon was found shortly after the battle. Meade reported the death "is greatly to be deplored, as he was a young officer of high promise." The lieutenant earned respect "for his manly virtues and amiable character." In a letter to his wife, Meade expounded, "I had become very much attached to Dehon for his many excellent qualities, and it does seem as if the good luck that attends me is to be made up in the misfortunes of my staff." Meade was riding a government-issued horse during the battle; the equine sustained an injury. The general informed his wife of Old Baldy's safety.[111]

The area fought over south of Fredericksburg on December 13 would become known as the Slaughter Pen Farm. A First Corps surgeon tended to the injured for days. In a letter on December 18, the exhausted healer recorded that nearly 900 men received care at his location.

Not long after the battle opened, our day's work began, and during the day, the trains of wounded brought frequent additions to our numbers, until every room and outhouse, and place for laying wounded men in the yards was filled, and every surgeon was active in his painful business of mending up the bleeding and shattered forms of our unfortunate men.[112]

Death stalked the army around Fredericksburg for months after the battle. On January 2, 1863, William Broughton, commander of Company D, 16th Maine, informed the state's adjutant general of the death of Corp. Edwin Farrar. Broughton was new to company command; the lieutenant previously in charge had been killed in action on December 13. Later in the month, Lieutenant Atwood of the 16th received an honorable discharge for wounds suffered at Fredericksburg. Dozens of First Corps men who survived wounds on December 13 were never able to serve again.[113]

In addition to men and horses, battle flags took a beating. To the adjutant general of Massachusetts, Colonel Bates described the status of the colors in the 12th Massachusetts. He wrote, "Our State Flag, which is riddled and torn to tatters, I propose to send to you as a sacred relic, should you approve of me doing so. It can be carried no longer except it be furled."[114]

POST-BATTLE RECKONING

Senior commanders were deeply upset with the decision to attack without the whole Left Grand Division. In his memoirs, Gibbon recalled departing rearward after his wound, knowing how two divisions of the First Corps went in without support. "As I left the field, I could not help noticing the great number of unemployed troops in sight, and reflected how useful they *might* have been to us in the fight."[115]

Meade rode back during the height of the Reserves' struggle to beg for help from men in Birney's Division, Third Corps. Very active on the field, Meade's attempt to gain support was another role Reynolds should have assumed. Reynolds did laud the assistance from Birney's brigades, which "materially aided in saving Hall's battery." Hall had to leave one gun for want of horses; the cannon was subsequently withdrawn with help from infantrymen.[116]

Reynolds blamed his infantry, rather than a lack of support, for the inability to hold positions Meade and Gibbon gained. In a letter to his sisters on December 17, the corps commander suggested his infantry "let it slip" at Fredericksburg. They "faltered and failed," Reynolds added, thinking the army fortunate the rout had not been worse.[117]

Meade articulated a different and more accurate perspective. "My men went in *beautifully*," Mrs. Meade was informed, then "carried everything before them, and drove the enemy for nearly half a mile." Due to lack of support, the letter continued, "they were checked and finally driven back." In addition to the killed and wounded, Meade estimated 400 men in the Pennsylvania Reserves were missing. "All the men agree it was the warmest work the Reserves had ever encountered," which was certainly saying a lot.

Frustration about the lack of support was vented to Congress when senior leaders testified before the Joint Committee on the Conduct of the War. Meade discussed the initial success of the Reserves against Jackson's line. He had expected simultaneous assistance from Gibbon, but, as Meade said, the Second Division was not ready. He informed Congress, "That delay enabled the enemy to concentrate their forces and attack me on my front and both flanks." Meade was not so disturbed by Gibbon, but by Franklin. The Reserves' leader suggested, "I think if we had been supported by an advance of the whole line, there is every reason to believe that we could have held the ground."[118]

Union officer and historian Francis Palfrey provided a reasonable defense of Franklin's conduct. Yet,

> *Franklin might have done something more than he did, with the large force under his command, if he had been impelled by the energy of the strongest natures. . . . He was not a man of active temperament, and he was certainly wanting in audacity. . . . One remark must be added, and that is that it excites both surprise and regret to find such a total want of evidence that Franklin communicated to Burnside during the whole day of the battle anything in the way of suggestions, requests for instructions, or remonstrance.*[119]

The First Corps suffered the most from Burnside's indistinct orders and the painfully methodical and insipid Franklin. As at Antietam, the corps ferociously attacked Jackson, seized ground, and inflicted large numbers of casualties. Yet, one corps makes not an army, and heroism alone could not conquer the Confederacy.

DEJECTION AND HOPE AS WINTER SETS IN

Distress prevailed after the First Corps moved away from the river. Zero ground held and unbearable suffering were the price tag for Burnside's failed offensive. "It is needless to say that the men were very much discouraged by the miserable failure," the historian of the 9th New York State Militia lamented. "When soldiers have been defeated in battle," he added, "are hungry and cold withal, it is an easy matter for them to find fault with every one in authority."[120]

"About one half of our division is gone," Captain Porter of the 11th Reserves informed his mother on December 14. His own Company B took forty-five men into the fight, with twenty becoming casualties. Full of despair as he was after Antietam, Porter wrote, "I have little heart left. My brave comrades have fallen without gain."[121]

Burnside, showing a modesty widely unknown in the Army of the Potomac's senior officers, took responsibility for his army's inability to achieve victory. Several in the First Corps developed doubts about the army's commander. "If Burnside had been selected to destroy this army, a better executioner could not have been found," a member of the 97th New York wrote. Depressed later in December, Rufus Dawes suggested the army was "overburdened with second rate men in high positions, from General Burnside down."[122]

Just like the previous months of the bleak year, some men remained positive. Horace Hanks pointed to some good news in letters to his wife and parents on the 26th. "I could have been easily homesick, but somehow did not allow myself to be," Mrs. Hanks was informed about her husband's Christmas Day. The entire 30th New York, Hanks said, had "a really merry" day on the 25th. Although suffering from a cold, Hanks "was abundantly able to assist in eating an apple dumpling and some stewed beans which our hospital steward had furnished us."

To his parents, Hanks wrote of the army's "good spirits" and "confidence in Burnside," less than two weeks after the disaster across the Rappahannock.

"Officers and soldiers are in good condition," the Empire State surgeon added. "Ready for another fight" was how Hanks described the army's status. During this period, several senior members of the army were also saying Burnside's troops were not suffering from demoralization.

Hanks even found a positive way to express his view of outdoor living in winter. "There is so much romance in sleeping in the woods," he continued. Mattie must have smiled when she read a question from Hanks, "How would you enjoy that provided you could have a large oak tree for a pillow?"[123]

Uberto Burnham could recall the last three major battles to see how his 76th New York was spared, relatively speaking. Near Aquia Creek north of Fredericksburg, Burnham looked back on the previous six months, the last time he had been at the location. He had marched 700 miles since June. "Now the 76's a tried body of disciplined soldiers that has *done* something *worthy of note*," he suggested. Burnham credited his regimental commander William Wainwright for the tone in the regiment. "His standard of military excellence is very high," Burnham wrote, adding, "He never seems discouraged."

A positive outlook did not make Burnham a Pollyanna. He mentioned some of the supply problems plaguing the army. Footwear was again one of his concerns. "I want a good looking durable pair of boots—and don't care what they cost," Burnham concluded.

By New Year's Day, Burnham looked for meaning in the unending contest with the Confederacy. He wavered between finding reasons to maintain hope and seeing nothing but darkness. As he documented close calls for himself and the regiment at Fredericksburg, Burnham was somewhat happy to stay busy as an acting captain. Still, he wrote, "Oh what a horrid game is war! How hardened is man. He will *do* what he will not *dare* look upon." Some measure of inner strength impelled him forward, as Burnham added, "We can get used to anything. Nothing bares my nerves now."

Peace, Burnham wrote,

Is now covered with a black cloud, entirely hidden from view. The dark demon of war has unlimited license to work ruin through the land. Unchecked he promises to have a funeral in every family, every household in mourning, every heart bereaved, every head bowed in sorrow. We must conquer a head. For one I devote myself to the work.

On the first day of the new year, Burnham found comfort in a warm fire. At camp near Pratt's Point, he may be seen as a spokesman for the army. "Often does the soldier think of home," he wrote. Burnham's comrades "attribute our late reverse to the removal of McClellan, and are clamorous for his restoration to the command of the army." Burnham was enjoying flames from "a fire as warm and bright as any our grandparents used to sit by. The blaze seems to shine right into the heart and warm up the better feelings of man's nature."

Quickly returning to his avocation as military strategist, Burnham declared, "If the 'Powers that be' at Washington will give us a general that is a match for Gen. Robert Lee then the shameful disasters in Virginia will cease." No regiments faltered at Fredericksburg, he asserted, so leadership must take the blame. Burnham concluded, "There is blundering imbecility somewhere."[124]

THE CONSTANCY OF CHANGE

From a few days after the battle through most of January, the First Corps was camped around White Oak Church and Fletcher's Chapel, about 6 miles southeast of Fredericksburg. In this location, the corps remained as the left flank of the army, with the rest of Burnside's command toward Falmouth. Burnside began planning a late December offensive to cross the Rappahannock using fords upstream from Fredericksburg, then circling around to attack Lee's left flank. Lincoln called off the maneuver on December 30. Once and future First Corps officer John Newton's complaints to Lincoln about the army's lack of confidence in Burnside made the president reticent.[125]

Another reshuffling of officers grew inevitable after December's extensive damage to the First Corps. In the area of senior leadership, Meade's time in the corps was ending. With his promotion to major general dated November 29, Meade finally received a new command on Christmas Day: leader of the Fifth Corps. He would retain this role until promoted to head the Army of the Potomac seven months later.[126]

On the same day Meade's reassignment was ordered, he penned a letter to Franklin. The noble sentiments Meade expressed were his last act as a senior commander in the First Corps. The subject was near to Meade's heart. The "statement showing the present condition of the thirteen regiments of infantry constituting the Pennsylvania Reserve Corps" used numbers to illustrate the need for the division's overhaul. Meade estimated the

James Wadsworth, seated and the third person from the right, spent a great deal of his own money improving the lives of the soldiers in his division. The general earned great respect even from the enemy for his bravery. LIBRARY OF CONGRESS

Reserves required 200 new officers and 7,000 men to reach the necessary state of efficiency.

Although a common practice throughout the army during the war, Meade called the return of officers to their home states for recruiting "a signal failure" in the effort to stock the Reserves with men. The option to parcel out the regiments to other commands would be too detrimental to morale of the veteran regiments, Meade suggested. He hoped the Reserves could receive months back home to fill up the ranks, while "pruning" the regiments "of all useless members."

Data on each of the thirteen regiments was attached to the request for time away for the Reserves. On average, a regiment had 326 enlisted men and 15 officers present for duty. With only 9 officers and 235 men, the 2nd Reserves were in the worst quantitative shape.

Reynolds added a short note to Meade's analysis. The First Corps commander "most heartily" agreed with Meade's ideas. To Franklin, Reynolds opined of the "uselessness" of the division "in its present state." Franklin referred the matter to army headquarters, where he endorsed Meade and Reynolds's ideas. The Pennsylvania Reserves were "in great need of reorganization and recruiting," Burnside was informed.[127] The division was not immediately taken from the field army, although their days with the First Corps were numbered.

Changes to the high command in the First Corps were quickly evident. On December 16, orders were issued to bring "Old Waddy" back. James Wadsworth had spent most of the last year in Washington. Defeated in the race for governor in New York in 1862, Wadsworth began his return to the corps with Special Orders 352.[128] He would first take Doubleday's Division, then serve in an acting capacity as corps commander during the winter for short periods. Although doubted by some due to his lack of military training, Wadsworth was more than ready to use his philanthropy, dedication to the Union, and concern for his men to serve the First Corps and nation yet again.

John Robinson was another general unafraid to serve in battle along with his infantrymen. He would lead the Second Division of the First Corps from shortly after Fredericksburg to the dissolution of the command. LIBRARY OF CONGRESS

Later in the month, another new division commander who would serve for the rest of the First Corps' existence gained his new assignment. In Special Orders 366, dated December 29, John Robinson was appointed to lead the Second Division, marking the permanent departure of John Gibbon from the First Corps. Robinson, born in Binghamton, New York, in 1817, did not have an auspicious beginning to his military career. Enrolled at West Point in the summer of 1837, he was court-martialed for insubordination in March 1838. Near the end of October of the following year, he was nonetheless an army officer. Quartermaster department experience in Mexico aided

Robinson's rise to the rank of captain in 1850. Like many men who would be Civil War generals, Robinson had diverse army assignments in the 1850s, often in isolated frontier posts. When the Civil War arrived, Robinson was at Fort McHenry in Baltimore.

The West Point expellee earned plaudits and promotions for service in the early part of the war. By September 1861, Robinson was a colonel commanding a Michigan regiment. Wearing a brigadier's star by April 1862, Robinson saw a great deal of action in the Third Corps, suffering an injury in Virginia that summer. His brigade was central to the defeat of the last Confederate counterattack against the Left Grand Division at Fredericksburg, the general's fitting introduction to the First Corps.[129]

Some brigade and regimental changes were in store during the last part of December. The most notable subtraction was the move of the 2nd USSS out of the First Corps. They were transferred to the Third Corps in a brigade with the 1st USSS. The sharpshooters had performed quite well since the start of the Maryland campaign. Curtis Abbott noted a speech Colonel Phelps gave on December 31 thanking the sharpshooters from six different states for their devoted duty to the First Brigade, First Division.[130]

Other than the loss of the sharpshooters, the regimental makeup of Doubleday's First Division did not change in the wake of Fredericksburg. George Biddle, originally the colonel of the 95th New York, ascended to command of Doubleday's Second Brigade. A New York City native and Mexican War veteran, Biddle joined Phelps, Paul, and Meredith as Doubleday's brigade leaders.[131]

For their last weeks in the First Corps, the Pennsylvania Reserves had a new division commander and three new brigade commanders due to the large numbers of casualties at Fredericksburg. By early February, the convalescence Meade requested and the men very much deserved was ordered. The Reserves then departed the First Corps forever. They would return to service in the Army of the Potomac's Fifth Corps later in the year, destined for more arduous months of excellent soldiering.[132]

MUD RULES THE WINTER

Around First Corps campsites, men benefited from bearable weather early in the year. Lewis Benedict of the 24th New York described the area as "warm and pleasant" on January 4. The possibility of a long stay gave men hope of winter meaning rest. Even if eventually called into action, "we are going to make ourselves as comfortable as we can while we do stay," Benedict concluded. Sadness was still the lot of many. William Woodruff, 104th New York, Root's Brigade, attended the funeral of a young soldier in the regiment's Company E on January 2.[133]

A common complaint about inadequate footwear was evident in various regiments. Wesley Shaw, 35th New York, Paul's Brigade, penned such a letter on January 5: "I have not got any boots yet. I am almost bear foot fore the want of something to wear on my feet." After five requisitions, Shaw decided he needed to try again. The lack of boots was made worse by the cost requested for a new pair, as high as $12.[134]

The historian of the 24th Michigan grew distressed by the poor quality of garments and shoes, especially when "shoddy material" failed to protect sick and hospitalized men from exposure. The Wolverine offered a solution to the problem of contractors swindling the government and harming fighting men. "Had one of these rascals been occasionally hanged or shot," perhaps the quality of material soldiers wore would dramatically improve.[135]

Frederick Ranger, 22nd New York, wondered why the army had such trouble getting men serviceable boots. In the second week of January, he wrote about the need to protect his feet. Old boots "are whole but are run over, so I can't march in them." Ranger had the pride of knowing his men respected him. As an acting captain, Ranger wrote, "Little did I think when I joined Co. F I should ever be its Captain, and as the boys say the only officer who has stuck by them."

Memories of home gave Ranger the ability to enjoy mental images of happier times. To "My Darling Aggie," Ranger wrote, "I am missing the skating parties this winter. I presume I should be thar if I were home."[136]

An enlisted man in Ranger's regiment was writing the same week about his inability to be a great soldier. A volunteer from early in the war, and later promoted to sergeant, Newton Church could not get away from gloomy feelings as winter continued. From Belle Plain, Church informed a friend, "As far as my own bodily health is concerned I am well but my mind is not easy. The fact is I am not content enough under all circumstances to make a good soldier."

Disappointments of the last few weeks worsened Church's morose mindset. He suggested, "inaction, failures, and reverses are death to a soldier." His friend Charley then read, "I am almost sick of the war. The fact is I do not mind the fighting so much although this is rough enough." The worst aspect of his life was "marching with heavy loads." In an attempt to better his frame of mind,

Church imagined being home planting seeds and potatoes. He was not long for the army. A discharge for disability was granted on February 22.[137]

As the first two weeks of 1863 played out, a variety of activities, events, and camp routines occupied time for the First Corps. Through January 12, William Woodruff listed several generally mundane aspects of his life. Playing cards, building and maintaining fires, picket duty, and a review by General Robinson were part of the soldier's life. He was especially happy to record the completion of a fireplace on January 6. "We got along very well that day," he wrote.

Spirituality did not leave Woodruff among all the death and despair. On the 11th, he noted, "We had religious services for the first time in good while."[138]

Pleasant weather gave men hope in the new year. On January 10, Hiram Hodgkins, 13th Massachusetts, Taylor's Brigade, informed his sister, "We have had splendid weather for the last few weeks. I am enjoying good health as I ever did in my life this winter." A lack of money due to inefficient and slow paymasters was one criticism Hodgkins—and many other soldiers—had for the army. "I don't think *Uncle Sam* is very good to pay his help," he wrote.[139]

Death exerted power over the army, even without notable military engagements. Losing men to wounds, disease, or a variety of ailments may not have seemed like a glamorous end for a soldier. To the historian of the 11th Pennsylvania, Pvt. Charles Adams's death from a fever on the 14th did not dull the appreciation of sacrifice. Wanting to remember his comrade, the historian penned deeply emotional words.

Almost every part of Virginia has become sacred to us as the burial place of our companions; and each new grave is as another reason why the Old Dominion must not be given up. Not only her battle-fields, but her grave-yards and highways belong to the North as the endeared depositories of its noblest and bravest sons.[140]

Some comedy enlivened winter camps. In many cases, officers were highly respected men who assisted and motivated their soldiers. This did not mean practical jokes could not be played on company commanders for the good of a regiment's mood. On January 16, William Woodruff wrote of Hiram Passage, who "stole the captain's shirt," then "sold it for 50 cents."[141]

Larger strategic questions occupied army headquarters in January. Burnside struggled to devise a plan capable of bringing progress to his cause. His ability to lead an army of 125,000 during winter was inherently suspect. On New Year's Day, the army commander reminded President Lincoln of his offer to resign. He also suggested neither Secretary of War Stanton nor General-in-Chief Halleck had the army's confidence.

Later in the first week of the year, Burnside sent another letter to Washington, saying none of his senior leaders had faith in a plan to re-cross the Rappahannock and give battle to Lee. Burnside wished to do so, but he doubted the army's ability to transcend defeatism.

Halleck could not accept a decision to go into winter quarters yet. The general-in-chief told Burnside to "occupy the enemy" and prevent "large detachments or distant raids," perhaps for no other reason than the political embarrassment such relatively harmless enemy movements caused. Halleck then laid down the law: "It will not do to keep your large army inactive."[142]

A repeat of direct assaults against heavily fortified Confederates was absolutely out of the question. Thus, Burnside continued to consider the possibility of flanking Lee out of Fredericksburg, as he had planned in late December prior to Lincoln's cancellation of the move. Specifics of a new flanking movement were soon on Burnside's drawing board.[143]

Respected officers returning to service after a long absence boosted morale in some First Corps units. Col. Edward Fowler's successful convalescence from serious wounds at Second Bull Run put smiles on many faces in the 14th Brooklyn. On January 20, the same day men started to march according to Burnside's new plan, Fowler "was enthusiastically welcomed" back. The 14th was a regiment in federal service directly descended from the New York State Militia; Fowler had first joined the outfit as a lieutenant in 1847. "There was a general feeling of happiness over his resumption of command," the regimental historian said of Fowler.[144]

Unfortunately, the good weather First Corps men wrote of earlier in the month began to change. Harsh days in Virginia might not have felt as bad as Wisconsin, New York, or Massachusetts men were used to, but Old Man Winter could halt Union progress easier than Lee could.

Weather had not been a problem through mid-January. On the 13th, Horace Hanks had written of mild days and "perfectly lovable moonlight evenings." Strong gales were starting, with the doctor continuing, "You can't imagine how the wind is blowing, Mattie—it seems almost as though the tent would blow away—and we have a large, nice, new one."[145]

As he stayed busy with officer chores and overseeing the First Corps artillery, Charles Wainwright had time to make observations about the weather. On the morning after the fierce gale Hanks reported, Wainwright said the weather was so "wonderfully fine" tents stayed open and no fires had to be lit during the day. He wondered if the winds would bring rain, with the unpleasant implications such changes foretold. Thinking a general movement of Burnside's force was imminent, Wainwright continued to worry about how Mother Nature could impact operations. Although he reported good weather on the 19th, by the time troops began moving, Wainwright grew as gloomy as the sky.[146]

Signs of a new advance multiplied. "The boys *hate to move now*," Hanks wrote on the 19th. "To leave comfortable quarters to be obliged to camp out—perhaps even without time to pitch their tents. I am very sorry for them," he added. With dreariness on the rise, Hanks did not want his wife to think he gave in to discouragement. "I have faith in our cause," the surgeon concluded.[147]

A less optimistic member of the 9th New York State Militia was defeated before the troops began to move. "We looked at the clouds and guessed that all the enemy we should meet would be mud," the fatalistic warrior lamented.[148]

Burnside's plan offered hope if the weather was better. He ordered the Left Grand Division to proceed 10 miles north of Fredericksburg. The destination was United States Ford. Franklin's command would become the right flank of the army on what was an errand to deceive Lee. Hooker's Center Grand Division would cross the Rappahannock nearly 5 miles south of Franklin at Banks Ford. After a few miles march from there, Hooker would be only 1 mile from Lee's left flank. Sumner's two corps were to stay put directly opposite of Fredericksburg on the east side of the river. If implemented well, Franklin's men would back up Hooker's Center Grand Division to make Lee either retreat south or engage 80,000 Unionists menacing the Confederate left flank.[149]

First Corps troops marched behind the Sixth Corps starting about midday on January 20. Rain began after dark, with the weather seeming "strangely cruel," a veteran recalled. With rain falling and good roads quickly turning into goopy, heavy mud, "the men had no heart to continue their disagreeable labors," a 9th New York State Militia soldier wrote. "The men staggered and reeled as they endeavored to maintain their footing," he added. Persistence kept regiments moving toward the river, but the rain continued. One man recalled seeing sixteen horses working to pull a single cannon out of the mire. "A tempest of wind" was another aspect of the marching misery.[150]

In what history dubs "The Mud March," Burnside struggled under the diffidence that led him to turn down army command before. He seemed never able to defeat his doubts, especially as he worried about leading an army with so many senior officers more his rival than partner.[151]

"At daylight, everything was a sea of mud," a 12th Massachusetts man recorded on January 21. As the army tried to keep moving, the Bay Stater continued, "It is useless to try to add anything to the picture, for the wildest narrative would fail to do full justice to the subject." Soldiers had to persevere when "hard roads of yesterday had sunk two feet below, and the army waded through a sea of mud."[152]

A 24th Michigan man was another who found words inadequate to describe the fiasco of the Mud March. He might have seen the record number of horses attempting to free one cannon. Twenty-six poor equines were engaged in the task. Struggling so hard against the mud and elements, many mules and horses lost their lives during the few days of Burnside's doomed advance. Corduroying roads—using logs in an attempt to solidify the ground—was a labor many men commenced.[153]

Charles Wainwright helped the 5th Maine Battery move a stuck wagon to keep from needlessly exhausting some horses. The haughty colonel had limited faith in the volunteers he commanded, writing about "the ignorance of drivers and officers" being the primary cause of the delay in getting the army moving. Wainwright's diary singled out Lt. Edward Whittier as one of the incompetents. On the contrary, Whitter, who was only twenty-two years old, was a highly respected cannoneer who would win the Medal of Honor in September 1864.[154]

No such awards were in the offing for the Army of the Potomac during the Mud March. Abandoning the movement became necessary. Nothing could be accomplished, especially as pontoons for bridges and cannons to protect Union positions east of the Rappahannock were not timely or in sufficient quantities to implement Burnside's plan. With orders to return south issued, getting back to camp became imperative and seemingly impossible. Instead of finding a dry place to rest, men encountered "nothing but mud, mud on every hand," a Pennsylvanian recalled. In describing the Mud March, an early chronicler of the army waxed biblical. He suggested the rain and mud "showed such a spectacle as might be presented by the elemental wrecks of another Deluge."[155]

Rufus Dawes reported men dying from the ordeal. With only one regimental ambulance, surgeons had to determine the men least likely to survive the muddy return to camp. Dawes said some men were unburdened of knapsacks and equipment in an effort to improve their odds of survival. One fellow, not known for being a sick soldier, received that relief only to die from exhaustion before reaching camp. Dawes lamented, "It was only another form of the casualties which in a thousand ways destroyed human life in the war."[156]

With the doomed Mud March now part of the war's history, Burnside decided the time had arrived to take drastic action against those generals he deemed unreliable, or worse. Burnside gave Lincoln a choice: purge the army of Hooker and several other officers or accept his resignation. The president chose the latter. Burnside undoubtedly regretted news of his replacement. Joe Hooker was the new commander of the army.[157]

NEW LIFE WITH FIGHTING JOE

Hooker could not warm up the days and nights, make mud disappear, or force Lee's army back by sheer will, but, unlike Burnside, he had great confidence in himself. No general can succeed without the willpower to craft strong plans and earn the respect of his men. Hooker possessed an inflated ego, but the vanity that would contribute to his ruin did not seem troubling during the first months of his control over the army.

Change for the First Corps continued. An order of battle on January 31 showed the move of the four regiments previously under Marsena Patrick and Gabriel Paul to the provost marshal brigade. Paul remained Third Brigade commander, but with different regiments he would command through the battle of Chancellorsville. At the end of January, Paul had six regiments: the 22nd, 29th, 30th, and 31st New Jersey; the 147th New York; and the 137th Pennsylvania. All but the 147th would muster out of the army soon after Chancellorsville.

The 147th New York was destined for glory in the First Corps. Another of the many regiments raised over the summer of 1862, the companies came from Oswego County, on the east side of Lake Ontario. Like other parts of Paul's new organization, the 147th served under the provost marshal prior to joining the First Corps.

In early February, the Pennsylvania Reserves departed. With Special Orders 36, the Reserves were "to embark at Belle Plain without unnecessary delay for Alexandria," reporting to Maj. Gen. Sam Heintzelman, who commanded Washington's defenses.[158]

Replacing the fighting grit of the Reserves was likely impossible, but cogs in the army bureaucracy worked to put a new division in place quickly. The departure of the Reserves did not mean a change in the state represented in the division. Halleck corresponded with Heintzelman about the possibility of trading the Reserves for Pennsylvania troops assigned to the Washington defenses. Heintzelman was not in favor of the swap, suggesting his command would be diminished if he lost several regiments for the worn-out Reserves. In data he provided Halleck, Heintzelman listed five regiments and two companies totaling nearly 4,200 men. These soldiers were the only regiments from Pennsylvania in and around the capital.[159]

Neither Reynolds nor Hooker liked the deal. Reynolds took umbrage at Heintzelman implying the Reserves were somehow too weak to be useful. "The Reserves are worth more to him than their numbers indicate," Reynolds opined. Hooker's reply to Heintzelman echoed Reynolds's perspective.[160]

With all impacted generals upset with the switch, Halleck acted as a general-in-chief could: He ordered the trade of Pennsylvania units. Then, Reynolds issued Special Orders 39, organizing the new Third Division, which Doubleday would command until immediately prior to the battle of Gettysburg.

The new First Brigade was under the temporary command of a reassigned colonel. The regiments included, per Reynolds's order, the 121st, 135th, 142nd, and 143rd Pennsylvania. After arriving, the 143rd moved to the Second Brigade, with the 151st Pennsylvania transferred to the First Brigade.

In late March, Brig. Gen. Thomas Rowley took command of the First Brigade. Born in Pittsburgh, Pennsylvania, the cabinetmaker gained experience leading volunteer troops in the Mexican War. He was also civically engaged in his hometown. During the early part of the Civil War, Rowley led a nine-month regiment from Pennsylvania, then took the reins of the same group when the regiment reenlisted later in 1861. Receiving a slight wound on the Peninsula, Rowley had a general's star in November 1862, as a Sixth Corps brigade commander.[161]

Roy Stone, a native of New York and 1856 graduate of Union College, would lead the Second Brigade. Moving to Pennsylvania, Stone was the original captain of Company D, 13th Reserves, known as the Raftsman Guards. An energetic recruiter of the lumbermen and mountaineers in his company,

Stone gained promotion to major before the 13th Reserves departed Pennsylvania for Washington in 1861. He then led the companies of Bucktails sent to McClellan on the Peninsula.[162]

After the decision to swap regiments, Stone, only twenty-six years old, commanded the 143rd, 149th, and 150th Pennsylvania. Hugh McNeil had praised Stone's conduct in the field, suggesting the New York native was an "accomplished officer" exhibiting "distinguished gallantry." During the summer, Stone went home to recruit troops worthy of the fine tradition of the 13th Reserves, a development leading to the organization of the 149th and 150th Pennsylvania. Honoring the custom of the Bucktails, the two new regiments adorned their caps with the tails of critters as a sign of their experienced marksmanship.

Reaching Washington during the crisis after Second Bull Run, Stone was the colonel of the 149th at the time of elevation to brigade command in February 1863. The bulk of the new brigade's service had been in the defenses of Washington.[163]

Across the army, Hooker worked to instill more efficiency, morale, and discipline. With General Orders No. 6, issued on February 5, the grand divisions were abolished. First Corps commander John Reynolds, as well as the other six corps leaders, now reported directly to Hooker. Rightfully pointing out the weakness of Burnside's organization, the order noted how the abandoned grand divisions were "impeding rather than facilitating" the army's operations.[164]

In an early message to his troops, Hooker, writing of himself in the third person, declared, "Since the formation of this army he has been identified with its history." An exceedingly important missive was General Orders No. 9, issued on February 7. "Flour or soft bread will be issued at the depots to commissaries for at least four issues per week to the troops," the order began. Two issues of fresh potatoes or onions, if possible, were ordered per week, with weekly disbursement of desiccated mixed vegetables or potatoes also required. Corps, division, or other officers were empowered to demand answers if the required food was not provided. The health and spirits of the army received a boost as the order was implemented.

Also on the 7th, General Orders 10 established policies on furloughs or leaves of absence. The rules were highly supportive of enhanced morale across the army, certainly a way to decrease desertion. Later, Hooker ordered the wearing of badges on the top center of each soldier's cap. Designed to enhance the ability to identify units during and after battle, the badges became a source of great pride for individual soldiers. Men in the First Corps would wear a sphere as their badge, with the color being red, white, or blue depending on a soldier's division. Historians have credited Hooker's varied reforms as good for the army, while showing him to be "an able administrative officer."[165]

Patrick Walker, 104th New York, was one soldier in need of whatever motivation came his way. Near Falmouth on January 27, he had written of the horrible six weeks since the battle of Fredericksburg. He was especially concerned about the continued want of strong leaders. Of many officers, "it would be better to have them home than be a disservice to the north" while in the field. Wounded at Antietam and erroneously put on the list of killed at Fredericksburg, at least Walker could report, "I am living yet."[166]

First Corps soldiers were a resilient lot, for sure. Men likely would never think of themselves as lucky to get wounded, but William Ray, 7th Wisconsin, missed action since late August after a wound at Brawner Farm. He returned to the First Corps nearly five months later. His extensive surviving diary points toward his effort to be optimistic, even during the dreariness of winter camp.[167]

Knowing a cold-weather campaign was off the table, the men spent the early part of the year performing a variety of duties. They also looked to improvise as a way to pursue whatever happiness they could find, with food being high on the list. Brigade bakeries were a way to supplement the bread Hooker viewed as vital to the army's sustenance. The 12th Massachusetts historian said some men were disappointed in the results at first, with bakeries making bread "not half kneaded." Practice made perfect, as the men grew to appreciate the luxury. Bakeries were a memorable part of the winter for men across the First Corps.[168]

Uberto Burnham noted but transcended the depressing status quo after the Mud March. "The rebs were exultant" after Burnside's final advance, Burnham wrote in late January. The "sticky sacred soil of Virginia" was both physically and emotionally fatiguing for Burnham. In February, he complained, "The mud is so deep that it is now impossible for the army to move in any force." Expressing the latent optimism so much a part of his nature, Burnham requested his mother not worry. "Man has a faculty of adapting himself to circumstances," he wrote. Two days later, Burnham found good news with the near completion of his brigade's bakery. He praised Reynolds for his attention to improving the lives and nutrition of First Corps men.

The weather and a strong leader made for a growing sense of purpose in the First Corps. "The army begins to have more confidence in itself and Gen. Hooker," Burnham suggested, adding, "He has succeeded admirably." At the beginning of spring, Burnham's parents were informed, "Everything is being put in its most efficient state," and the prospects of a new campaign seemed as pleasing as the warming air.[169]

Better attention to soldiers' welfare and improved weather helped Charles Tyrel. Wounded at Second Bull Run, Tyrel, Company E, 22nd New York, spent extended time in several hospitals. By mid-January, Tyrel was much closer to home, writing his wife from a Philadelphia hospital. He could finally report, on February 20, "I am here again doing duty as of old although I have no gun yet." Being a soldier in camp again "makes me stronger," he continued, so "don't worry on my account. I am getting tough again."

Lt. Col. George McFarland and his 151st Pennsylvania tried to make the most of late February's miserable weather. "We are all engaged in trying to keep ourselves warm and supplied with food," his wife was informed from near Belle Plain on February 22. Accounting for the hard times, McFarland still possessed great faith in his men, most of whom "are contented and show themselves worthy of the name of soldiers. We feel great confidence in our regiment."[170] Time would prove his confidence was not misplaced.

The processing of firewood allowed some First Corps soldiers exercise to stay in shape while defeating the cold. On March 13, Lyman Holford, "went out to the woods and chopped pretty lively until about 3 o'clock PM." The next day was not as agreeable. "Today has been clear, cold and windy," the Badger jotted in his diary, "making it anything but pleasant to stand guard but a soldier can't back out of these pleasantries."[171]

Some men could not defeat winter. Corp. William Hittle, 151st Pennsylvania, had a very difficult season. In his diary for February 22, he recorded morning snow falling quite intensely. "Had to cover myself with blankets or freeze," Hittle added, then he noted some work helping cooks with their firewood supply. Three days later, Hittle wrote of a "very damp and disagreeable day." The conditions had tragic effects on Hittle's health. He died near Belle Plain on March 24.[172]

On the last day of March, Charles Tyrel informed his wife, "I am well and tough and so you need not be concerned about me." Tyrel felt very confident in the future and held fast to his duty, which included the possibility of death. Although the regiment's service was due to end in May, another battle would likely occur before then.

I am willing to go and I shall do the best I can, if I get killed I die in a good cause, the cause of right and justice. Our government with all its faults is still the best Government on earth, and it must and shall be preserved. I for one am willing to shed my last drop of blood for it if need be.[173]

The four original regiments of the Iron Brigade had proven their willingness to sacrifice for the United States. Men in the units also grew to respect and appreciate the 24th Michigan by spring. After a reconnaissance near Port Royal, south of Fredericksburg, a member of the 6th Wisconsin applauded the Wolverine unit. "Their soldierly qualities" and "sturdy loyalty to the old brigade" called out for respect from the Wisconsin and Indiana regiments under Meredith, the Badger man recorded. Rufus Dawes added how Colonel Morrow proved a very capable commander of the Michigan unit.[174]

The camp of the 150th Pennsylvania, Stone's Brigade, at Belle Plain, Virginia, in the spring of 1863. LIBRARY OF CONGRESS

"A good deal of confidence was restored by the appointment of General Hooker," the 13th Massachusetts historian wrote. As spring arrived the First Corps continued with routine duties: drills, inspections, days on picket, visits from generals, processing firewood, and finding water. Hooker's popularity and the improved supply situation were of the utmost importance to the army's confidence.[175]

Regiments and batteries could only be as strong as the brave men constituting their commands. John Varney, Fifth Maine Battery, wrote of the excellent health he had enjoyed over the winter, which gave him optimism for the inevitable marching and fighting. "I have not been off duty a single day," Varney continued, making him "better prepared for the summer's campaign than I was last year."[176]

As weather improved, a member of the 2nd Wisconsin wrote to a newspaper in response to a story about antiwar sentiment back home, including possible resistance to conscription. The nation's first ever military draft became law earlier in the year. As with the letter from Charles Tyrel, the Wisconsin soldier showed a clear dedication to continue the struggle, regardless of the lingering scars from Fredericksburg and a tough winter.

There will be a sad day of reckoning for those who are opposed to the government, when the army returns home—it will hardly favor disloyal men. I feel more than I can express on this subject. I cannot imagine how any sane man, who is not a traitor at heart, can stand up and advocate such principles. Should resistance be offered to the conscription, I hope the guilty ones will be hung on the first tree.[177]

Venting to newspapers was one way to get the patriotic juices flowing again. Music was another positive distraction soldiers enjoyed. By April, the 16th Maine had several amateurs bringing delight through their tunes. One Pine Tree State diarist proudly wrote of the instruments officers donated in April. "Fifteen beginners" would soon rise to the point where "we blessed the Lord, every one of us, for the inspiring music of the best band in the division."[178]

EMANCIPATION'S FIRST WINTER

Blood the First Corps shed in 1862 helped lead to the Emancipation Proclamation, officially announced to the army as General Orders No. 1 on January 2. The patriotic drive propelling men to fight the Confederacy undoubtedly included some strong antislavery sentiments. Others questioned, sometimes in scathing terms, the validity of using military power to free slaves. Winter gave men additional time to ponder the important subject.

Horace Hanks wrote his dear Mattie on the first day of the year to expound on the idea of ending slavery. He viewed slavery as "the cause of all the trouble." The war offered a chance for all human beings in the nation to enjoy "God's sacred birthright—freedom." Maybe some in the 30th New York doubted the Proclamation, or even opposed the idea of fighting to free slaves. Hanks felt pride while serving to "purge the nation of its greatest sin," because the United States "must look to the good of future ages."[179]

Charles Wainwright held the opposite view. The artillery commander felt liberating slaves would motivate the South. He wrote of Lincoln seeming to "turn into rebels those who have heretofore been Union men, and to still further embitter the feelings of all." Wainwright added how emancipation could turn Maryland and Kentucky into Confederate states, while dividing the people of the North. Showing great scorn for Lincoln, the colonel asked, "What is to become of us with such a weak man at the head of our government?"[180]

Regardless of what some men in the ranks wanted, the Army of the Potomac was in the business of freeing slaves. Some officers of the First Corps used part of March to express either their pride or revulsion toward abolition.

Old Man Winter began to give way as warmer winds dried out the muddy fate Northern soldiers had endured for months. A major benefit of the drier ground was the improved efficiency of foraging parties. A detachment from the First Brigade, First Division boarded barges at Belle Plain in the first week of March, with Colonel Phelps in command. The band (with the 14th Brooklyn contributing seventy-five men) landed at Cowe's Point on the 4th. After a march to Heath's Point, groups fanned out "in every direction, returning with corn, cattle, horses and mules."

As dozens of Union troops in Phelps's foraging party passed through a part of Virginia undefended by Confederates, "contrabands," as escaped slaves were often called, flocked to the men in blue.[181] The troops found the barges and time to transport the freed slaves back to First Corps lines. The level of disgust one member of Phelps's Brigade felt over the incident led him to pick up his pen.

Henry Bates, a native of Vermont born in 1809, was the chaplain of the 22nd New York, the regiment Phelps commanded early in the war. From Pratt's Landing, Bates wrote to Reuben Abel later in March. Bates suggested eight of ten men would consider him an abolitionist, but the war put slavery on display to the point where the chaplain doubted emancipation. Bates now wanted to "place the slave and slaveholder in a proper light, before those not familiar with the indolent habits of one and the indulgence of the other."

Bates classified Virginia's slaves as "robust—yet one white laborer at the north is worth 3 of them." Mentioning some residents of New Jersey who came to Virginia to work plantations under Union control, Bates said the Garden State visitors "wanted to get more work out of them than they had been in the habit of doing for their masters."

In the most startling portion of the letter, Bates mentioned the case of a teenager whipped by a Confederate officer. "On her arms and shoulders," he wrote, "were welts large enough to lay the thickness of your fingers in. Yet were she a slave of mine for the same offense I would have cut her in 2 pieces."

Bates wondered if slaves truly wanted freedom. He cited the example of freed individuals flocking behind the foraging party Phelps led. General Wadsworth, a "strong abolitionist," as Bates wrote, gave orders to bring more "contrabands" into Union lines. Bates assumed, "there is not one out of 100 of that load of negroes" who would not prefer "himself back on the ole plantation this day."

Soldiers should envy the slaves, Bates suggested, because the latter can consistently find "a good dry warm shelter," with a plentiful variety of food. "These negroes had ought to be satisfied with their lot," the man of God informed Abel. Bates concluded by hoping those in the North opposed to slavery would visit Virginia. "Yes, indeed, he will be surprised beyond measure," the chaplain added, "those poor negroes are fools for leaving such a good home."[182]

The evening before Bates scrawled such a pompous letter, Rufus Dawes gave a speech of a radically different tone. Happy to gain a fifteen-day leave of absence under Hooker's furlough policy, Dawes headed to Ohio on March 10. With a home in Marietta, Dawes was invited to speak at the town's courthouse. He fielded a variety of questions about the army, as well as the soldiers' views on the Emancipation Proclamation.

"If there remains any one in the army, who does not like the Proclamation, he is careful to keep quiet about it," Dawes began, "We are hailed everywhere by the negroes as their deliverers." As the command of the president and as a matter of justice, Dawes concluded, emancipation was simply right.

Slavery is the chief source of wealth in the South, and the basis of their aristocracy, and my observation is that a blow at slavery hurts more than battalion volleys. It strikes at the vital. It is foolish to talk about embittering the rebels any more than they are already embittered. We like the Proclamation because it hurts the rebels. We like the Proclamation because it lets the world know what the real issue is.[183]

A reconnaissance in the spring gave Lt. Col. George McFarland an appreciation for the necessity of emancipation. Taking out a squad of his 151st Pennsylvania, McFarland arrived at plantations near the Rappahannock. After one trip, he wrote his wife, "I left the place half sad and half jealous of the comfort these Southerners enjoy while we guard their property and are hundreds of miles from home." In a letter later in April, McFarland continued, "The slaves are hired to the Confederacy to dig entrenchments for us to storm."

I wish those who are opposed to depriving our enemies of this aid could see what I have seen, and were compelled to help drive the rebels from entrenchments made and kept in repair in this manner. If the missiles of the Rebels did not sweep them off, they would at least change their minds very materially.[184]

Fortunately, history played out in a way proving Hanks, Dawes, and McFarland right, with Wainwright and Bates wrong. But in the spring of 1863, the ultimate triumph of freedom was not inevitable. A better army commander, more food, and additional confidence could not win the war. "Early in April," the 11th Pennsylvania historian recorded, "throughout every department of the troops, there was the usual hurry attendant on an important movement."[185] Hooker's options were not much different from repeating the same route as the Mud March. Mother Nature can cooperate in April and May, but Robert E. Lee was in no mood to oblige.

FITZHUGH'S CROSSING
The positive impact of Hooker's administration can be detected in studying data about Fighting Joe's minions. On February 10, the First Corps listed 14,018 enlisted men and officers present for duty. The entire army had 124,552 across seven infantry corps and the newly organized cavalry corps.

Counting those present *and* equipped (men "actually available for the line of battle"), only 12,467 were in the First Corps and 105,270 in the entire army. By comparison, on April 30, as a new campaign was underway, Reynolds had 17,130 present for duty, with 15,783 equipped. The command boasted more than 3,000 additional men at the end of April compared to February 10, but 204 fewer were unequipped. Hooker commanded more than 110,000 fully equipped soldiers, more than twice the force under Lee.[186]

Of the Army of the Potomac at the end of April, First Corps division commander Abner Doubleday wrote, "it would have been hard to find a finer body of men, or better fighting material than that assembled on this occasion, in readiness to open the spring campaign." John Varney of the Fifth Maine Battery wrote, "This army is in excellent condition, all seem cheerful and confident of success." Finding comfort from Hooker's leadership, Varney predicted the Unionist can "flog the rebs sweetly and show them that the Army of the Potomac is a good army."[187]

What to do with his army became the primary question for Hooker as spring advanced. Although formally abolished, the Left Grand Division was indirectly retained in late April. John Sedgwick's Sixth Corps, the largest in the army, was teamed up with Reynolds. With most of the army heading north of Fredericksburg, Sedgwick and Reynolds occupied an area south of town, near where the First Corps attacked on December 13. The Sixth Corps massed close to December's crossing site, while Reynolds's position is usually referred to as Fitzhugh's Crossing, near the site of Pollock's Mill, a mile south of Sedgwick.

Moving out about midday on April 28, the First Corps once again headed toward the Rappahannock. Phelps and his brigade were given an important task on the evening of the 28th. The brigade commander detailed the 22nd, 24th, and 30th New York to carry the heavy pontoons to the crossing site, as the 14th Brooklyn served as skirmishers. With the difficulty of the work, Phelps gave the 30th a break for a time, which brought the Brooklyn men off the skirmish line to assist getting the boats to the river.[188]

With the benefit of excellent natural positions for cannon east of the river, First Corps artillery chief Wainwright concentrated his guns. By dawn on the 29th, four batteries with twenty rifled guns were above Pollock's Mill with three batteries (fourteen guns) below the mill. Ransom's six-gun Regular army battery was also in the vicinity.[189]

Fog once again shrouded a planned attack of the First Corps along the Rappahannock. Even with reduced visibility, Capt. James Thompson ordered his Pennsylvania battery to fire about a dozen shots at enemy troops he could discern to the west. When visibility improved, a line of soldiers from the 13th Georgia attempted to keep Union infantry from crossing. Reynolds found his batteries insufficient to push the enemy troops away. Wadsworth was ordered to send First Division soldiers across the river in pontoon boats, with the 6th Wisconsin and 24th Michigan leading the charge.[190]

Although numbers certainly favored Wadsworth's Division, the Confederates had a higher position on the west side of the river. The lack of cover for the Brooklyn boys added to the danger of skirmishing. Lt. James Bloomfield was mortally wounded as he led the 14th Brooklyn's "short but deadly" work.[191]

The Georgians received needed support from a Louisiana regiment, but the Iron Brigade seized the day. The advance was relatively easy, even with the dangers of friendly fire from across the river. The 6th Wisconsin apparently won the informal race with the 24th Michigan to see which regiment could cross the Rappahannock first.[192]

"The Rebels were completely surprised," Uberto Burnham wrote of the attack. He witnessed one unfortunate Confederate refuse to surrender after the two attacking regiments crossed the river. "He was immediately shot dead," Burnham coldly reported.[193]

Colonel Bragg thanked the three other Iron Brigade regiments and the 14th Brooklyn for their covering fire. The 6th Wisconsin was able to capture dozens of Confederate prisoners, then moved to the right of the original crossing point. Cutler's Brigade came up to allow the 6th Wisconsin to return to Meredith's other regiments. "The conduct of every officer and man in my command was splendid," Bragg concluded.[194]

Wadsworth crossed the river in gallant style, after he assisted men with pontoon boats. Some historical debate exists about how involved the general was in the advance, but Wadsworth's active participation would be in line with his reputation. One early chronicler of the army offered evidence of the enemy's respect for Wadsworth as he crossed the river in a boat as his horse swam alongside. The historian wrote, "I have been told since the war by Confederates that they so admired that gallant act in General Wadsworth that they refrained from firing on him."[195]

After the successful crossing of the river, the 22nd and 24th New York assisted engineers in the construction of a pontoon bridge spanning the Rappahannock. With little other resistance, more of Wadsworth's men were soon across. The following day, Confederate cannon fire started falling among the

First Corps. One shot struck within the position of the 13th Massachusetts, killing two officers, Capt. George Bush and Lt. William Cordwall. Additionally, a sergeant in the regiment lost a leg and arm to this single shot.[196]

Wadsworth's Division proved very effective in the battle of Fitzhugh's Crossing. The command sustained only 167 casualties from the start of the operation on the 29th through the first hours of May 2. The 24th Michigan's 24 casualties (4 killed and 20 wounded) topped the entire division, with the 14th Brooklyn logging 23 losses. The 6th Wisconsin sustained 16 casualties.[197]

The nine casualties for the 7th Wisconsin included two officers, Capt. Alexander Gordon and Lt. William Topping. Both men were praised in the report of Col. William Robinson. "The regiment has met with a heavy loss, which cannot be replaced," Robinson lamented. The last original captain still remaining in the 7th, Gordon served as "one of my most efficient officers," while being "remarkably brave under fire." Of Topping, Robinson added, "his fine soldierly qualifications and gentlemanly bearing had won him the esteem of the entire command."[198]

THE COST OF SLOW ARMY BUREAUCRACY

As the force south of Fredericksburg, the First and Sixth Corps were a diversion, attempting to keep Lee's army in the Fredericksburg defenses while the bulk of Hooker's army moved toward the Confederate left flank. The rest of the Army of the Potomac was not aggressive enough against Lee after Hooker crossed the Rappahannock and Rapidan north of Fredericksburg. Leading a whole army, Hooker simply did not operate with the "Fighting Joe" mentality he had earned in 1862. As a soldier in the 30th New York suggested, "Lee was not easily deceived. Great things were expected of the new commander, General Hooker, but the new movement though brilliantly conceived, was badly executed."[199]

With the dense thickets and forests around Chancellorsville, Hooker's mind filled with an array of doubts belying his reputation as an aggressive combat leader. At the end of April 1863, after three days of troop movements and excellent progress, Hooker lost his nerve. On the morning of May 1, he remained concerned about whether Lee had moved north to counter the Union flanking force. Both Reynolds and Sedgwick were asked to provide "frequent and full information of any movements of the enemy in your front." Later in the day, Reynolds informed Sedgwick, "The enemy appear to remain in their position, and, as far as we can learn, have not changed." At the same time, Reynolds wrote, "The fog is so thick that we can do little but be ready to meet an attack."[200] Lee had no interest in being aggressive south of Fredericksburg, especially when he could seize the initiative against Hooker's halted advance.

A May 1 order reflected Hooker's interest in having the First Corps keep Confederates occupied around Fitzhugh's Crossing and the ground near Slaughter Pen Farm. The order's delivery was delayed several hours. By mid-afternoon, not knowing of Hooker's order, Reynolds noticed Confederate defensive preparations along Bowling Green Road. At 3:00 P.M., the First Corps commander informed Sedgwick, "I could not move without bringing on an engagement." By mid-evening, learning of the late delivery of his order seeking more information from Reynolds, Hooker canceled any aggressive move from the First and Sixth Corps.[201]

The worst step a general could take in the war was giving Robert E. Lee the initiative in Virginia. McClellan learned as much on the Peninsula, Pope found out the same at Second Bull Run, and Burnside's delays caused by tardy pontoon boats brought a bitter harvest at Fredericksburg. Joe Hooker was about to be the latest army commander at the mercy of Lee's risky yet brilliant aggressiveness.

With five corps north of Fredericksburg, Hooker still possessed a strong defensive position, for the most part. The weak link in the army's line was the 11th Corps, which Oliver Howard commanded. As four corps formed a U-shaped position around Chancellorsville, Howard's men were to the right with inadequate support, and, due to Howard's incompetence, poor defensive positioning. After being informed of Howard's position, Hooker attempted to remedy the unfortunate alignment, but Lee was already on to the matter. Separating his small army, Stonewall Jackson was heading to assail Howard.[202]

Knowing of Lee's withdrawal from the Fredericksburg defenses, Hooker ordered, at 1:55 A.M. on May 2, the First Corps to join the main army. Reynolds was required to "march at once" for Chancellorsville. Due to the courier getting lost between Hooker and the telegraph station at United States Ford, the order did not reach Chief of Staff Dan Butterfield near Falmouth for three hours. Then, the First Corps' marching orders were sent initially to Sedgwick, not Reynolds, an unnecessary delay with the abandonment of grand divisions earlier in the year.[203]

Reynolds received Hooker's order at 7:00 A.M., five hours after the command was sent from Chancellorsville. The corps commander put the divisions of Robinson and Doubleday in motion to join Hooker. Doubleday and Stone reported the Third Division was required to cover 22.5 miles to reach U.S. Ford, with the corps' final position near the army, about 2 miles beyond the ford. Wadsworth had the longest march, about 26 miles. Based on a corps itinerary attached to Reynolds's campaign report, Wadsworth's men started moving at 9:00 A.M., with Butterfield informed all First Corps troops, except skirmishers, were east of the Rappahannock at 9:53 A.M.[204]

Questions about when orders were issued and received, and the timing of the start of the First Corps' march north on May 2, became fodder for debate. A modern history of the 11th Corps specifies five reasons for the rout of Howard's men. One deficiency was the inability of the First Corps to reach the area swiftly enough.[205] Although quicker receipt of Hooker's marching orders for the First Corps and a faster pace could not guarantee salvation for the beleaguered Howard, the 11th Corps historian has a point.

Confederate artillery did delay the First Division's return to the east side of the Rappahannock, but one wonders why two hours elapsed between Reynolds's receipt of Hooker's order and Wadsworth's initial move. Was Reynolds discussing matters with cannoneers again, as at the battle of Fredericksburg, and neglecting his infantry?

Regarding Reynolds's journey north, Sedgwick had informed Butterfield at 8:55 A.M., "The whole movement will be pushed." This does not seem to be the case, with Reynolds deserving the blame, in addition to Mother Nature.

Another reason for the delay was Hooker's order assigning Reynolds to oversee removal of the Fitzhugh's Crossing pontoon bridges. "The troops are all across and moving up the road," Reynolds reported at 11:05 A.M., six hours after Butterfield informed Hooker that the "march at once" command was sent to Sedgwick. "I report that pontoon bridge will be piled on this side and left. There are no trains to haul them off," Reynolds added. Sedgwick and army engineers, not the First Corps commander, should have worried about when and how the pontoon span would be removed.[206]

The timing of movements reported in the *Official Records* may not be a fully reliable measure of exact moments when troops started a march. Only five days after the period in question, however, Walter Phelps recorded 9:00 A.M. as the time he received the order to move to the east side of the Rappahannock. The pickets of the First Brigade, First Division rejoined Phelps by 10:00 A.M., with a move north starting at 10:30 A.M. Less than a week later, Phelps would not have reported ninety minutes between the order to cross and the start of the whole brigade's march toward Chancellorsville if the troops moved rapidly.[207] A significant amount of time passed before Wadsworth's Division followed the rest of the First Corps.

Men from various parts of Reynolds's command recalled the difficulty of the May 2 march. "Excessively wearied" was how Col. Thomas McCoy of the 107th Pennsylvania described his troops after reaching the vicinity of U.S. Ford in the evening. Abner Small of the 16th Maine called the day "most exhausting," because "the heat of the sun was intense." The comment was echoed by the historian of the 14th Brooklyn, who recorded "a long hard march under a hot sun." Rufus Dawes was another veteran to recall feeling the heat during the march north.[208]

Doubleday wrote of the heavy nature of the soldiers' equipment and provisions as part of the trouble on May 2. Although in "excellent order," the division's soldiers were "loaded down with eight day's provisions, blankets, shelter-tents, and 60 rounds of ammunition." One soldier added, "Some of the knapsacks assumed the proportions of a pedlar's outfit," something the rookies of the 150th Pennsylvania dealt with by dropping much of their gear.[209]

Nonetheless, one wonders why the march to United States Ford and beyond took so long. If the Second Division began marching around 9:00 A.M., as Adrian Root reported, they needed about eight-and-a-half hours to reach U.S. Ford, a distance of roughly 20 miles. After some rest, Root's men continued to their line of defense, completing a 22.5-mile march early on May 3. Doubleday noted the Third Division's sundown arrival at the ford. This was decent progress for the hot day, but far from a record pace for Civil War troops.[210]

Meredith reported the Iron Brigade's arrival 2 miles from U.S. Ford at 10:00 P.M. Even assuming a late morning departure, the Third Division did not make fast progress during the day. To assist Howard, the men still had miles to go. Meredith noted his brigade gained some rest early on May 3, with the arrival along the corps' defensive line south of the Rapidan at 6:00 A.M. Twenty-three hours after Reynolds received his order to march, Wadsworth's Division was finally in position on Hooker's northern flank.[211] Barely a mile an hour for his corps does no credit to John Reynolds.

Although much safer work than being on a firing line against charging Confederate hordes, the First Corps had to struggle to find their assigned position after crossing the ford. The 11th Pennsylvania's historian described the march after the ford as, "Filing down a narrow and tortuous road." Marching through part of what was known as The Wilderness, the Pennsylvanian continued, "Never was a dreary and desolate belt of country more properly named."[212]

Col. Robert Cummins, 142nd Pennsylvania, reported his regiment "marched with life through the forest under circumstances of no ordinary difficulty." The men were discouraged due to reports of the 11th Corps' rout by Jackson, Cummins added. Adrian Root recalled, "The movement to the front in the darkness through a heavy forest was quite difficult, the woods having been set on fire by the enemy's shells, and being thronged with fugitives from the disorganized Eleventh Corps."

Civil War troops were not in their best combat condition after a hot, difficult march of well over 20 miles. But that is what the army commander expected. The march was wicked and packs were heavy. Reynolds had to believe Hooker's order for his men to augment the main army meant the First Corps was desperately needed.

Wounded four times throughout the war, Brig. Gen. Henry Baxter faced his foe with intense determination, leading his brigade from the barren plains of Virginia to destiny in the summer of 1863. LIBRARY OF CONGRESS

Reynolds should take the blame for the First Corps' slow start and unimpressive marching time from Fitzhugh's Crossing to the right flank at Chancellorsville. He seemed to lack imagination on May 2, as he did on the Slaughter Pen Farm the previous December. Maybe Hooker should have ordered the First Corps' march a day earlier. Also, slow message delivery can take some of the blame, but John Reynolds failed when celerity was needed.

Whether tardy or not, the First Corps bolstered the Army of the Potomac on the evening of May 2 and the next morning. A new general in the First Corps was there. Henry Baxter had received command of the Second Brigade, Second Division in late April. A New York native, Baxter spent time in Michigan, followed by a quest for gold in California in the late 1840s. Three years later, Baxter was back in Michigan. He earned captain's bars in the 7th Michigan early in the war, then suffered three wounds in 1862: a serious abdominal hit on the Peninsula, a leg wound at Antietam, and then a third injury while leading troops crossing the Rappahannock at Fredericksburg on December 11. Earning a brigadier's star in March, Baxter's ascension to brigade command returned the competent Col. Peter Lyle to his regiment, the 90th Pennsylvania.[213]

"The Flower of the Army"

For the First Corps, the costliest part of the battle of Chancellorsville was the distinguished work of the Fifth Maine Battery, on detached service near the conflagration's epicenter. Close to the troops of Winfield Scott Hancock, Second Corps division commander, the battery suffered greatly. During the short action on May 3, the battery would sustain nearly 10 percent of the First Corps' total casualties across the eleven days of the campaign, including Fitzhugh's Crossing.

The men had experienced very stressful and hazardous battle before. During Longstreet's unyielding flank attack on August 30, 1862, the Mainers lost four guns during the final afternoon of Second Bull Run. From the beginning, the battery was commanded by Capt. George Leppien, a native of Philadelphia born in 1836. A loving and affluent father sent the young Leppien to Europe for more than a decade, where the future battery commander learned military tactics and leadership. Knowing the respect Leppien had earned in the war, the state's adjutant general summed up the battery and its commander, "Whatever it accomplished for itself and for the honor of the state, may be considered as a direct result of his constant care, labor, and study."[214]

With the intense chaos of battle roaring to the south at about 9:00 A.M., the battery was diverted—by Hooker's order—from the First Corps line to near the Chancellor House. With five guns, Leppien and his men were placed to the right of the house central to the defensive position of the entire army.

The whirlwind of battle began with Confederate batteries firing from several positions only about a third of a mile away. Advancing enemy infantry were another threat. "Having our exact range," Lt. Greenleaf Stevens reported, the Confederate guns, "opened a most galling fire." The brave Leppien suffered a serious leg wound in the fight, which would kill the officer later in the month. Leppien earned posthumous brevet promotions to major and lieutenant colonel for his service during the war.[215]

After the loss of Leppien, an officer from a Second Corps battery was given the unenviable task of countering the raging inferno. The substitute commander soon fell, mortally wounded, with the battery's leadership devolving to Lieutenant Stevens, an original member of the outfit. Without any cover, Stevens recalled, "the right half of the battery engaged the enemy's artillery, the left half holding in check a large body of infantry massing on our left."[216] The dwindling number of men and horses able to serve the guns made Stevens's task impossible.

One cannoneer under such horrible fire might have wished he was not so eager to serve. Only seventeen years old in 1861, Napoleon Perkins had to travel to multiple states to enlist as a minor in the State of Maine. The underage warrior "expected to get hit in every battle we were engaged in, but after passing through Cedar Mountain, Bull Run, and Fredericksburg," he decided he "was going to pull through all right till the close of the war." Working furiously like his comrades at the four other cannons near the Chancellor House, Perkins recalled, "I saw the boys falling at the guns, and the Schrieks & groans of the wounded men and horses was heartrending . . . I saw Corporal Grove[r] fall, he was struck in the breast with a shell, just as he had sighted the gun. Poor Fellow, he never knew what hurt him, he was badly torn."

Shortly after the loss of the corporal, Perkins's prediction of his own safety was shattered. As he saw one of his horses hit, the wounded equine

commenced to struggle and was bleeding bad. Seeing Sergeant Loomis passing near me, I called to him and said, "my horse is hit bad." He said, "Unhitch him and get a spare horse." Just at this time I was struck in my right leg just above the knee. I again called to Loomis and told him I was hit. He said, "Go to the rear." I did not then realize that I was wounded bad, for the shot did not knock me down. I was holding my near horse with my right hand, Sergeant Loomis' horse with my left hand. When I attempted to walk, I found I could not use my leg.[217]

After a plea for help from Corp. J. H. Lebroke, Hancock issued orders to save the battery with infantry support. Men from three Pennsylvania regiments were called forth to retire the battery with prolonge ropes, an arduous task under perfect conditions. All five of the guns were saved as the brave Union infantry pulled the cannons away.[218]

The cost to the battery was immense. Six men were killed outright, with twenty-two wounded. Forty-three horses were killed or disabled. "Notwithstanding the disadvantages under which we labored, our men behaved in the most gallant manner," Stevens, who was wounded slightly in the side, reported.

> *It is with the deepest regret that I mention the names of Sergt William F. Locke and Corpl. Benjamin F. Grover among the killed, as they were the best of soldiers, and showed themselves at the battles of Bull Run, Fredericksburg, and Chancellorsville as the bravest of men.*[219]

John Chase was one of the heroic gunners to survive the battle. He provided a magnificent example of the fearless and undaunted American soldier. His Medal of Honor citation reads, "Nearly all the officers and men of the battery having been killed or wounded, this soldier with a comrade continued to fire his gun after the guns had ceased. The piece was then dragged off by the two, the horses having been shot, and its capture by the enemy was prevented."[220]

Perkins received a canteen from the generous Sergeant Loomis, but he was still in danger on the field. An exploding ammunition chest killed six battery horses, with Perkins gaining a shower of dust over his body. His wounded leg grew very painful. A tourniquet from Loomis and another man "hurt me very bad," Perkins recalled, because "they drew it so tight, but it probably saved my life." Eventually, Loomis, Horace Harris, David H. Benton, and Bennett Morse carried Perkins away. "These men stood by me like brothers, and I have always felt grateful to them," the appreciative boy warrior recalled. Somehow, the New Hampshire kid in a Maine battery survived the firestorm and loss of a leg. Perkins probably thought May 3, 1863, was his last day on Earth. Five decades later, he still lived.[221]

In addition to Locke and Grover, four privates were killed in action: William Ripley, Timothy Sullivan, James Nason, and James Holt. Several gruesome wounds were recorded during the battery's short period near the Chancellor House. Disfigured men resulted from head, facial, and other injuries. Based on the list Stevens provided Maine's adjutant general, privates Charles Kimball lost an arm, Edward Stuart a leg, and William Nason a hand.[222]

The battery's soldiers earned the praise of their fastidious corps artillery commander. Colonel Wainwright, who did not see the action, said the men "suffered severely," while they "behaved excellently." The colonel gave "especial approbation" to Lt. A. B. Twitchell, "who, though twice wounded and his clothing badly burned at the commencement of the engagement at Chancellorsville, continued to command his section until struck a third time." Twitchell lost two fingers on May 3.[223]

The sacrifice and action of the Fifth Maine Battery at Chancellorsville qualifies as a case of history being silent. Two books on the campaign were published in the 1990s. Both have excellent features and deserve careful study as solid contributions to Civil War history. Yet, Furgurson's work does not mention the battery at all, with the book by Stephen Sears giving the battery only three paragraphs. John Chase is mentioned in the book, but Sears neglected to note the Medal of Honor the twenty-year-old cannoneer won.

Perhaps Leppien was biased, but he knew the special qualities of his men long before May 3. During the battery's Washington refit after Second Bull Run, more than half a year before the hell near the Chancellor House, the battery commander wrote, "Our Maine Artillery can be called among the flower of the army."[224]

PROTECTING A SAFE FLANK

In what would be the second bloodiest day of the Civil War, First Corps infantry were generally idle on May 3. The corps was never called to attack Lee's left flank, although their position was excellent for such a move. A charge from Reynolds's troops and others nearby could have hindered if not eliminated the Confederate army's ability to keep pushing against Hooker's men south of the First Corps' position. Doubleday was upset about the wasted opportunity. Soldiers on the Army of the Potomac's right flank were "spectators," although "their mere advance would have swept everything before it," Doubleday wrote. Distressed about how a large chunk of the army remained unengaged, Doubleday pointed out how those 37,000 men "made a new army" capable of noble service.[225]

Hooker suffered an injury during the day's fighting. A Confederate cannon ball splintered a pillar at Union headquarters, with pieces hitting Hooker in the head. His biographer suggested the wound rendered Fighting Joe immediately incapable of army leadership, but he did not cede command.[226] How Hooker could have used the First Corps later in the day becomes conjecture, just like the tactical impact of his foot injury at Antietam. But the possibilities at Chancellorsville seem less conducive to success than Antietam; Hooker had not been aggressive for three days, and the First Corps may never have been called to attack anyway. Fighting Joe had not been himself since halting the army's advance well short of the enemy.

In a limited role, men in Reynolds's command performed good work as battle raged nearby. Patrols and picket duty kept a watchful eye to the southwest and west. The First Corps could prevent penetration into the Union line of retreat from their position. Visionary leadership would have realized Confederate troops were too engaged with other elements of the Army of the Potomac to try for such a move, so Doubleday's idea of the First Corps launching a flank attack had merit. Like so many other times during the war, the Union army failed to attempt a clearly available knockout punch.

First Corps troops received a great deal of experience building and improving entrenchments at Chancellorsville. The men created a right angle toward the Rapidan with the Fifth Corps to the left and rear. Root wrote, "The entire brigade passed the night in throwing up breastworks, which by daylight acquired considerable strength." Based on words from captured Confederates, Root expected an attack on the position on May 3, but examining the defensive works of the First Corps, he felt "justified in my belief in a successful defense."[227]

Colonel McCoy was another officer who saw the benefit of improving the ground. An attack was "momentarily expected," McCoy reported on the morning of May 3. "We continued to strengthen our works," while often being "directed personally" by General Robinson or Colonel Root. In another part of the line, Col. Edmund Dana, 143rd Pennsylvania, said the men built breastworks and other protective structures "capable of being held against greatly superior numbers."[228]

Regardless of their reserve role, regiments earned plaudits for the capture of Confederate prisoners with very small losses to the First Corps. Stone's three regiments captured 132 Confederates during their time probing the woods, in addition to inflicting ten battle wounds on Lee's soldiers. Stone's entire command suffered just three wounded men during the battle.[229]

The 12th Massachusetts was another unit taking dozens of Confederates captive. Colonel Bates said his men advanced through the thick woods for more than a mile. The 12th approached "so near the lines of the enemy that we could hear them talk, and could hear the groans of their wounded of the past day's fight." The Bay Staters grabbed 101 prisoners, including

2 officers, Bates reported. The Confederates "fell into the beautiful trap set for them."

Danger lurked in the dark woods, including the possibility of friendly fire. Bates recalled how William Wood in Company F was shot by one of Stone's men "who mistook him for a rebel."[230]

First Corps men could also be taken prisoner. Over the night of May 5–6, Lt. Henry Reinhold and twenty-seven men from the 135th Pennsylvania were captured. They had been serving as pickets but could not be found as the army retreated. The loss in Reinhold's command was nearly 10 percent of the First Corps' casualties since the fight at Fitzhugh's Crossing.[231]

Along the Iron Brigade's portion of the line, the 24th Michigan was withdrawn, then sent to the far right of the corps to ensure the Rapidan was fully covered. The position "was dangerous, but honorable," according to the regiment's historian.[232]

Being placed in a position of little use to the rest of the army frustrated many First Corps soldiers. In his report, Colonel Bragg of the 6th Wisconsin was itching for a chance to contribute more. Of his regiment, Bragg wrote, "A disposition to engage and beat the enemy so occupied their minds that no other feeling had an opportunity to obtain a foothold."[233]

ANOTHER SEASON OF DEFEAT AND REORGANIZATION

An early historian of the Army of the Potomac summed up the Chancellorsville campaign by accurately declaring, "Hooker made no attempt to destroy his adversary." Potential to do so existed for days. Instead, Hooker called for a retreat. Ordered to march in the evening of May 5, the directive was countermanded due to high water, prompting a return to the defensive works that served as the First Corps' home for three days. Charles Davis of the 13th Massachusetts remembered, "In the three years' service of the regiment it would be difficult to recall a night that seemed longer or where there was more physical discomfort. Wearied and dejected, drenched with cold rain, in expectation to move at any moment, we still stayed and stayed and stayed."

"Not a foe followed our retreat," a Keystone Stater added, obviously curious and disappointed about the move back to the other side of the Rappahannock.[234]

Returning to camps south of Fredericksburg presented men of the First Corps with familiar surroundings. Memoirs and regimental histories note the performance of normal camp duties for the rest of May, but the feeling of despondency prevailed. "The affairs of the country and the situation in the Army of the Potomac at this period were probably the darkest in the history of the war," veteran John Vautier wrote. The Union troops were "defeated, baffled, and thwarted time and again." At least some good weather was a major improvement.[235]

Reynolds's command sustained only 300 casualties from Fitzhugh's Crossing to the Chancellorsville retreat. Returns for May 10 showed the First Corps with 16,289 men present for duty, with more than 2,000 additional troops present but not fit for duty. The number present for duty had been nearly 800 men higher on April 30.[236]

The "green fields, fine groves and stately oak forests" around campsites gave some solace and pleasure to members of the 24th Michigan. The innovative Wolverines called into duty two oxen found nearby. The beasts of burden proved very useful, "as they saved the men some hard lugging" of wood and water. The oxen were not destined for long life as a reward for their labor. They were slaughtered for the nourishment of the regiment.[237]

Changes to the First Corps began in May, as two-year regiments headed home. Hooker listed thirty-six regiments set to leave the army in a May 28 letter to Washington. Eight of these were First Corps units with service expiring by June 22, a drop of 4,700 men, more than 25 percent of Reynolds's manpower. The departing regiments included long-timers in the First Corps, such as the 22nd and 30th New York in Phelps's Brigade. The gallant colonel and leader of the First Brigade would depart the corps with his 22nd New York. Several nine-month regiments were also slated to leave, including all five under Gabriel Paul.[238]

Inevitably, regiments and commanders in the corps would see a shuffle before the next campaign began. Adrian Root reverted to command of the 94th New York due to the seniority of Col. Samuel Leonard. From White Oak Chapel on May 21, Root issued General Order 36 "to express my earnest gratitude" to the brigade's men "for the manner in which they have discharged their duties." He admired the First Brigade's "patience, fortitude, courage, and obedience." He concluded by wishing the brigade's men, "a safe return to the happy firesides and loving friends of home, and finally an unending reunion in the happier life of a better world."[239]

A preliminary new look for the First Corps was evident by the end of May, when 13,522 men were present for duty. Edward Fowler commanded the two-regiment First Brigade, First Division. Paul had his New Jersey regiments for just a few days, so further reorganization of Wadsworth's Division was still needed. Robinson's Second Division was down to two brigades commanded by Colonel Leonard and Gen. Henry Baxter. The First Brigade under Leonard included the 16th Maine, 13th Massachusetts, 94th and 104th New York, and 107th Pennsylvania. Baxter controlled the 12th Massachusetts, 9th New York State Militia, 97th New York, and the 11th, 88th, and 90th Pennsylvania. Even with only two brigades, Robinson commanded eleven excellent veteran regiments. Rowley and Stone were both down to three regiments each in the Third Division.

Further change resulted from consolidation of the army's artillery and the creation of an Artillery Reserve. Charles Wainwright commanded a five-battery brigade at the end of May. Twenty-eight guns were part of the arrangement, with other First Corps batteries transferred to the reserve.[240]

Reynolds held a review of the First Corps on May 30. The 7:00 a.m. event provided an opportunity for the command to make a good showing in front of their leader. Stephen Weld, a new aide to Reynolds, wrote, "Considering the wind and dust and rain, I think the review passed off well." Weld said about 8,000 men participated.[241]

Uberto Burnham used much of the last several months to ponder with pen and paper. His level of disappointment after the latest defeat was obvious on May 8. "The retreat is a mystery to all," he wrote. Later in the month, he thanked his "Remembered Parents" for $10 sent in the mail. Burnham then spilled out his frustration about Chancellorsville. "We *need* not and *ought* not to have retreated. No one can tell *why* we recrossed the river," he declared. Noting the progress armies in the Western Theater were making, Burnham wrote, "I hope that the day will some time come when it will prove itself the peer of those noble armies of the west." The army deserved "results worthy of itself."[242]

Robert E. Lee was not a general to rest on his laurels, so Burnham and the First Corps were in for an intense summer. Knowing aggression was the best bet for the Confederacy, Lee's eyes turned north again. In mid-May, Lee began discussing with civilian authorities the need for concentration of Confederate forces, with another move north clearly Lee's hope.[243] The next great battle would not be in Virginia, but rather two states away. Gettysburg unknowingly beckoned.

PART THREE

Gettysburg, Death of a Corps

JUNE–JULY 1863

I know not how men could have fought more desperately.
GEORGE MCFARLAND, 151ST PENNSYLVANIA

HEADING NORTH AGAIN

General Reynolds started June on a trip to Washington. Doubleday had been placed in temporary command of the First Corps on May 31. Evidence suggests Reynolds was ordered to the capital as part of a plan to make him commander of the army. Subsequent correspondence from Meade and Charles Wainwright details how Reynolds turned down command because Lincoln would not yield ultimate control over military operations. Reynolds proved to be another general who balked at the civilian control the U.S. Constitution placed over the military. Hooker's command of the army remained unchanged, at least for now, with Reynolds still in charge of the First Corps and possessing the confidence of his superiors.[1]

A new month brought familiar duties to men across the First Corps. On June 2, Henry Matrau, a teenage warrior in Meredith's Brigade, informed his mother about the friendly exchanges between soldiers on picket duty in the opposing armies. The practice was quite common, although contrary to orders. Matrau wrote of the Rappahannock being a poor barrier against enemy troops sharing items.[2]

By June 3, Lee was moving his men out of Fredericksburg, toward Culpepper and beyond. The uncertain target of the latest Confederate campaign led to several Unionist marching orders, followed by countermanding instructions leaving soldiers in camp. On June 4, the First Corps was expecting to move early in the day. "When everything was all nicely packed," the 12th Massachusetts historian wrote, the stand down order was issued.[3]

Rumors flew through campsites, with much anticipation for orders that would actually lead to marching. Soldiers liked to gossip and ponder when the new campaign would start. Nonetheless, a First Corps man suggested, "the wisest prophet was at a loss, and the knowing ones were as ignorant about the future as the dullest man in camp."[4]

Rufus Dawes continued to pen letters to M.B.G. (future wife Mary Beman Gates, also known as "My Best Girl"), while hoping she did not worry if less frequent contact prevailed for a time. "I am a poor soldier campaigning, and make due allowance for short and unsatisfactory letters," he wrote on the 4th, still near White Oak Church. Whenever the 6th Wisconsin was called to move, Dawes said he would be in command. Of the devoted Colonel Bragg, Dawes suggested, "He is wholly unfit for duty in the field" due to declining health.[5]

Bragg and other wounded leaders tried remaining with their men. Members of the 9th New York State Militia recalled: "Colonel Hendrickson, supplied with a wooden leg in place of the member lost at the Battle of Fredericksburg" visited the regiment in early June. "His advent was hailed with delight," as the men "loudly welcomed" their commander. The prosthetic proved too painful for either walking or riding, so Hendrickson could not remain with the regiment. Command still belonged to well-liked Lt. Col. Joseph Moesch, who had gained his silver oak leaf cluster early in 1863.[6]

With only six infantry brigades and the twenty-eight guns in Wainwright's artillery, the First Corps reported 14,608 total men present on June 10. Of the aggregate number of soldiers, 12,112 were present for duty, with only 11,263 equipped. Only the Sixth Corps had more equipped men than Reynolds's command.[7]

In early June, the First Corps reorganized, a necessity after the loss of regiments with expiring service. The alignment of brigades and regiments would stay constant through the battle of Gettysburg. Meredith's men were now the First Brigade, First Division. With six regiments, Lysander Cutler led an excellent command in Wadsworth's other brigade: 7th Indiana; 14th Brooklyn; 76th, 95th, and 147th New York; and 56th Pennsylvania. Robinson's two brigades remained under Paul and Baxter. The Third Division would add a brigade later in the month. Vermonters formed Rowley's Third Brigade under the command of Brig. Gen. George Stannard.

Table 3.1: The First Corps Before the Battle of Gettysburg

Corps Commander—Maj. Gen. John F. Reynolds		
1st Division *Brig. Gen. James S. Wadsworth*	*2nd Division* *Brig. Gen. John Robinson*	*3rd Division* *Maj. Gen. Abner Doubleday*
1st Brigade *Brig. Gen. Solomon Meredith* 19th Indiana 24th Michigan 2nd Wisconsin 6th Wisconsin 7th Wisconsin	*1st Brigade* *Brig. Gen. Gabriel Paul* 16th Maine 13th Massachusetts 94th New York 104th New York 107th Pennsylvania	*1st Brigade* *Col. Chapman Biddle* 20th New York State Militia 121st Pennsylvania 142nd Pennsylvania 151st Pennsylvania
2nd Brigade *Brig. Gen. Lysander Cutler* 7th Indiana 76th New York 14th Brooklyn 95th New York 147th New York 56th Pennsylvania	*2nd Brigade* *Brig. Gen. Henry Baxter* 12th Massachusetts 83rd New York 97th New York 11th Pennsylvania 88th Pennsylvania	*2nd Brigade* *Col. Roy Stone* 143rd Pennsylvania 149th Pennsylvania 150th Pennsylvania
Artillery Brigade *Col. Charles Wainwright* 2nd Maine Light 5th Maine Light 1st NY Light, Batteries L-E 1st Pennsylvania Light, Battery B 4th U.S. Battery B		*3rd Brigade* *Brig. Gen. George J. Stannard* 12th Vermont 13th Vermont 14th Vermont 15th Vermont 16th Vermont

Source: Official Records, Vol. 27, I, 155–57.

The five Green Mountain State units were the 12th, 13th, 14th, 15th, and 16th Regiments. Stannard's boys would be called into service from the Washington defenses for a late-month march north to Pennsylvania. Stannard had been the first citizen of his state to volunteer in 1861. A colonel in the militia, Stannard was an officer in the 2nd Vermont Infantry early in the war, then he led the 9th Vermont. He would be captured when Harpers Ferry surrendered in September 1862.[8]

The campaign adding Stannard's Brigade to the First Corps began on June 12. The six brigades moved away from their camps near Fredericksburg to pursue Lee. The 12th marked the beginning of the three most intense days of marching the First Corps would experience, with the opening day being especially arduous. To not show themselves to any remaining Confederates, the corps marched northeast toward Stoneman's Switch, then west to Deep Run, a creek that flows into the Rappahannock about 3 miles north of U.S. Ford. The corps covered more than 20 miles that day.

"The march was very trying on account of the intense heat, the dust, and want of water," a man in the 150th Pennsylvania wrote. With Stone on leave, Langhorne Wister of the 150th commanded the Second Brigade. The 9th New York State Militia remembered the day as "one of the hottest the men had ever experienced," while walking on "dusty roads through the devastated country."[9]

In addition to a fatiguing march, the execution of a deserter occurred on June 12. Hooker approved the death sentence, then ordered all of Wadsworth's Division to witness the event. After starting to march early in the morning, the men were halted near noon. Twelve soldiers were detailed from various regiments to serve in the firing squad for John P. Wood, 19th Indiana. Wood had deserted multiple times, then the Hoosier apparently served in a Confederate regiment. Even with the circumstances of Wood's cowardice and treason, the 24th Michigan's historian wrote, "It was a most melancholy experience for all who saw it and one that none could desire to see again." Lyman Holford of the 6th Wisconsin observed how Wood "seated himself on his coffin and received his doom without flinching."[10]

The 150th Pennsylvania stayed busy during the long trek of June 13. Having the last position in the line of march, the new Bucktails had "plenty to do" in their role of gathering stragglers. Fourteen difficult miles brought the men to Bealton Station after covering ground mainly in a northerly direction. Of the early part of the campaign, Rufus Dawes informed his future wife, "You can hardly imagine what our poor loaded soldiers suffer on such marches."[11]

Headquarters noted the "crime of straggling" in General Orders 62, issued on June 12. Any straggling soldier could be arrested, with the price of resistance to authority being death.[12] Regardless of how important the pursuit of Lee was, however, men enduring difficult conditions for days could be expected to sometimes fall behind. Unlike the needed alacrity on one day in early May to get to Chancellorsville, there was time for halts and some rest during the course of the opening three days of the Gettysburg campaign. Still, thousands of men could not keep up.

The First Corps commander had immense responsibility from the start of the campaign. Trusting Reynolds greatly, Hooker placed him in charge of the entire western wing of the army. In addition to cavalry, Reynolds directed the First, Third, Fifth, and 11th Corps. Generals Slocum and Sedgwick were the only major generals subordinate to Hooker who topped Reynolds in seniority.

Reynolds performed excellent service during the early days of the

Maj. Gen. John Reynolds did an excellent job moving the First Corps and other elements of the Army of the Potomac toward Gettysburg through most of June 1863. He would be killed in action on July 1, leading the Iron Brigade into battle near Herbst Woods. LIBRARY OF CONGRESS

campaign. On June 13, headquarters informed the First Corps leader, "It is probable that a movement is on foot to turn our right or go into Maryland." The key, Reynolds read, was an ability for the army to "concentrate at once." The order included discretion for Reynolds to direct movements as circumstances dictated.[13]

On the 13th, the First Corps was ordered to reach Manassas the next day through "forced marches," then push on a few miles to Centreville. "The day was hot and the dust was at times almost suffocating," Lyman Holford remembered. After a trek through the night and into the next afternoon, one wonders how any men had energy left. Exhausted on the 15th, Rufus Dawes wrote home, "Here we are again on our annual visit to Bull Run. I think, however, we shall miss our annual drubbing." Dawes said the men were "tired, sore, sleepy, hungry, dusty and dirty as pigs," but the veterans of the 6th Wisconsin "have come through without a murmur." Charles Wainwright described the difficulty and length of the march with humor generally absent from the officer's memoirs. Writing from Centreville on the 15th, the colonel remarked, "It would be hard to divide our march to this place from Bealton into days, as yesterday's march did not end until three o'clock this morning." In another surprise, Wainwright praised the good marching of the First Corps' volunteer soldiers.[14]

Accounting for tough marching and the unknown nature of the enemy's plans, the First Corps made excellent time in reaching Centreville. In under eighty hours, the command had covered 70 miles in very hot weather. "We are here well and hearty," George McFarland informed his wife, although the experience since June 12 "has exhausted all very much." As the Second, Sixth, and 12th Corps began arriving close by, six of the army's seven corps were in an east-west line from Fairfax Court House to Groveton. Reynolds accomplished Hooker's key goal: concentration while keeping Lee from swinging east to cut off the army from Washington.[15]

Worthy of a break, the men remained ready to face the enemy. A Wisconsin man was unafraid to fight, even around the historically depressing fields of Manassas. Referring to his fellow soldiers, he suggested, "No multiplicity of defeats, no fear of fate or dread of destiny would have prompted them to avoid a battle at Bull Run more than any other field." The soldier admitted that General Lee's decisions about where he would take the Confederate army controlled how the Army of the Potomac would respond.[16]

Just like the previous September, Lee did not have the Union army or Washington, DC, as his target. Richard Ewell's Second Corps was well to the northwest. Pennsylvania was within easy reach. Lee's second campaign to occupy Northern territory could not have been a surprise to anyone. As the First Corps and most of Hooker's army rested on June 16, Robert Rodes, now one of nine division commanders under Lee, had reached the Potomac across from Williamsport, Maryland. The Pennsylvania border was about 15 miles away.[17]

BACK IN MARYLAND

After not even a full day of rest, men from Massachusetts hoped for a quiet June 17 to celebrate the anniversary of the battle of Bunker Hill. The 1775 engagement north of central Boston solidified the American vision of the patriotic citizen soldier. Along with their First Corps comrades and many others in the army, June 17, 1863, would be anything but easy for the 12th and 13th Massachusetts Regiments. "Reveille at one A.M.; marched at four A.M.," was how the historian of the 12th remembered the day. The temperature reached 100 degrees during the march. "Sixty men in the corps were sunstruck," Charles Davis recorded of the movement toward Guilford Station.[18]

Both the First and 11th Corps started the day around Centreville, with headquarters and Reynolds confusing each other on the routes the two corps were taking. Orders were set on the evening of the 16th for all four of the corps Reynolds oversaw to be ready to march at 3:00 A.M. the next day. The goal was Goose Creek near Leesburg by the end of June 17. Although not as long as previous days of the campaign, the 17th was remembered as a time when, "The heat was intolerable, the dust an enveloping fog."[19]

Six days of relative rest awaited the army while still south of the Potomac. Toilsome, hot marches gave way to searches for water and provisions. Since departing White Oak Church east of Fredericksburg, the men were forced to fill canteens "from the muddy brooks and sluggish runs of Virginia," a Maine man recorded. The 9th New York State Militia only covered four miles on the 20th, with roads muddy after two days of heavy rain. At Guilford Station, the regiment found little water, including a meager amount available from wells across the depressing countryside. Details to guard supply trains or find necessities were part of these days of rest. Charles Wainwright enjoyed days of "perfect quietness, and a good deal of comfort." Much of the army reposed near Edward's Ferry. After the extended break, the spot would become the crossing point for the army as the pursuit of Lee renewed.[20]

George McFarland was not too worried about the obvious designs Lee's army had for his native state. He remained confident in the Union's ultimate triumph. The more Confederates making a dash for Pennsylvania, the better, McFarland suggested on June 18, "because but few would ever get out again." Besides, "The men are rejoiced to get away from the Rappahannock," he continued, adding, "The country here is so much like Penna that it has a *home* appearance about it that pleases them."

During the prolonged respite, mail became a source of joy for many in the First Corps. Delivery of letters and packages became uncertain while armies marched, especially when covering 20 or more miles in a day. By the 20th, the postal wagons caught up to Wadsworth's Division. Resting warriors busily scrawled missives, with Meredith's men sending 2,041 letters from camps just south of the Potomac.[21]

Returns for June 20 show the First Corps well below the numbers of just ten days before. The trying marching during a hot late spring meant the entire army had more than 2,000 fewer men present and equipped. The First Corps accounted for this loss in men available for the firing line; the rest of the army was nearly equal to the reported June 10 strength. Men on detached duty were a reason for some of the reduction, but the First Corps' straggling problems played a role. Only 8,967 of Reynolds's troops were present and equipped while resting around Guilford Station, a reduction of 20 percent in ten days. Only the 11th Corps had fewer men.[22]

With some rearrangement of troops over the period of relative repose, orders from headquarters made June 25 the day when Hooker's forces started moving into Maryland. Reynolds was informed of a change to his wing command. In addition to the First Corps, Reynolds controlled only the Third Corps under Daniel Sickles and the 11th Corps. "They are all under orders to cross the river to-day," Hooker wrote. The goal was to quickly seize Crampton and Turner's Gaps. "The movements must be rapid," Reynolds was informed. The First Corps commander was also given cavalry to scout "in the direction of Frederick and Gettysburg." The mounted troops were directed to "drive from that country every rebel in it."[23]

The tough talk sounded like Hooker was thinking solely of offensive movements. However, Fighting Joe knew his bosses were still concerned about Washington's security. Seizing the South Mountain gaps offered obvious defensive advantages if Lee moved southeast to threaten Washington.[24] At the same time, Hooker knew Pennsylvania was Lee's current area of operations, so continuing the move north kept all options open. Either way, the First Corps was the vanguard of the army.

Most troops were returning to Maryland for the first time since the end of October. After so much anguish in Virginia, the men looked forward to treading on friendlier soil. Yet, there were the unfortunate soldiers who had never left Maryland. Charles Hayden, 97th New York, suffered through a series of hospitals in the Old Line State since his September wound. Due to yet another invasion by Lee's army, Hayden and many casualties in Frederick hospitals were evacuated 50 miles east to Baltimore. Based on a June 22 letter, Hayden witnessed work to improve defenses in Baltimore. More than nine months after being shot in Miller's Cornfield, Hayden was still not well enough to assist.[25]

With the need for swift movements, Reynolds wrote headquarters in the late morning of June 25. He reported the 11th Corps still crossing at Edward's Ferry. Hooker was informed Howard led the only one of Reynolds's three corps able to stretch toward the South Mountain gaps on the first day north of the Potomac. By the late evening, the First Corps was in the vicinity of Barnesville, Maryland. Rain fell yet again, and the men grumbled over their soggy fate once more.[26]

After Barnesville, some familiar towns were seen by Reynolds's command, including bivouacs in Middletown and Frederick by the evening of the 28th. Confirmed information of the Confederates covering large swaths of territory in south central Pennsylvania made Hooker realize the need for bolder movements. Unfortunately for Fighting Joe, he would not witness the end of the campaign. General-in-Chief Halleck had waged a war of his own against Hooker, and the dispute over who controlled forces at Harpers Ferry was used as a chance to accept the resignation Hooker offered. In the midst of a great crisis, the former First Corps commander handed army command to another general with service in the corps, George Meade.[27]

Men in the ranks did not seem as interested in the change of commanders this time. Perhaps they were simply too focused on the difficult, humid weather. Like the year before, soldiers absorbed unforgettable natural beauty. Around Middletown on June 28, Uberto Burnham wrote of "the finest country I ever saw," made more special because the First Corps could "walk again on loyal soil." He continued, "The army is in good spirits and will give a good account of itself." Having pondered grand strategy with his letters, Burnham was torn on what would result from the latest Confederate invasion. Confident enough to predict a strong showing for the army, Burnham still doubted whether Lee could be defeated.[28]

With the return to Maryland, Benjamin Cook looked back on the two-year history of the 12th Massachusetts. On June 27, the day the First Corps reached Middletown, he noted the total of 1,476 miles marched during the regiment's period of service.[29] To meet destiny in the campaign, the regiment and the rest of the First Corps had plenty more miles to go.

"Was There Any War?"

In the last two days of his command, Hooker pushed the Army of the Potomac in a northeastern direction. Lee responded by seeing the imperative to unite his scattered forces. Even as General Ewell positioned his three divisions to lay siege to Harrisburg, Lee ordered a reunification of his army. Although frustrating for Ewell, the moves were necessary. The Army of the Potomac was in an excellent position to concentrate quickly. One key element of the Union's advantage was the placement of two cavalry brigades under Brig. Gen. John Buford as the guardian of the army's left flank at Gettysburg.[30]

The plan for June 29 was for the First and 11th Corps to reach Emmitsburg after another long march. Reynolds was to ensure the two corps took parallel roads to decrease traffic jams. The Third and 12th Corps were ordered to Taneytown, southeast of Emmitsburg. The long march was set to begin at 4:00 A.M., with "strong exertions" expected to prevent straggling. Even with a difficult day, a 9th New York State Militia soldier wrote, "The men had got their marching legs in order by this time, and the twenty-five-mile tramp was accomplished with little difficulty."[31]

The First Corps slightly exceeded its goal. Most regiments bivouacked on the evening of June 29 a mile north of Emmitsburg. A long day's march may not have been inherently enjoyable, but men recorded many positive aspects of the day. The 11th Pennsylvania's historian noted "demonstrations of delight" from Maryland's residents, as "a prolonged cheer rose from the moving ranks."

Even with some rain, another man in Robinson's Division greatly enjoyed the items Maryland's Unionist citizens presented. "Bread, milk, cheese, and other eatables" kept the men moving along. "To be the recipients of such kindness from the people had a great effect in enlivening the spirits of the boys," he added.[32]

Soldiers in Wadsworth's Division recalled a great day, albeit with so many miles to tread. When reaching Mechanicstown (now Thurmont), a 24th Michigan man found the locality "overflowing with patriotism and hospitality." Rufus Dawes wrote, "We have marched through some beautiful country." He much preferred "the land of thrift and plenty" in Maryland to Virginia's desolation.[33]

The Third Division found much happiness on the 29th as well. Rainy weather did not dull the Pennsylvanians' optimism as their native state grew closer with each step. The historian of the 150th recalled, "The troops gave less evidence of fatigue than on any of the previous marches." Later in the day, Emmitsburg's residents came through for the men. A soldier in the 121st Pennsylvania recorded how the citizenry "handed cakes and bread to soldiers as they went by." The slow commissary wagons made the food much appreciated, as the men were famished after another long day. With the First Brigade on the division's left, Col. Chapman Biddle's regiments guarded the left flank of Reynolds's infantry. Morale seemed excellent, with "the men all in fine spirits and anxious to go forward." The bucolic scenery and orderly farms made one man wonder, "Was there any war?"[34]

Stannard's Vermonters had been moving north since June 25. At first about 50 miles behind the rest of the First Corps, the Green Mountain State troops crossed the Potomac, then made excellent time, arriving in Emmitsburg only a day behind the rest of the command. Having started the trek, "in the warmest time of the Virginia summer," Henry Willey of the 16th Vermont recalled, "We would occasionally stop a few minutes to rest, probably not more than five, when the comrades would drop on the ground and make the most of it."

Some men discarded items, including ammunition, to make the hurried pace easier. A lieutenant in the 13th Vermont said the oppressive days assisted in getting the brigade ready for hard service. But fatigue was becoming a problem for men more familiar with easy duty in Washington's fortifications.[35]

"Beeves were shot and dressed last night," a Vermonter recorded on the morning of the 29th, "so we have fresh meat with hard tack for breakfast." At least the new beef was able to contrast the normally appalling quality of the government-issued hard cracker. "We in the ranks actually know nothing at all where we are going," he added. Ninety of Stannard's men were left in Frederick, with horribly blistered feet or utter exhaustion leading to their hospitalization.[36]

BETWEEN PIPE CREEK AND DESTINY

At 3:15 P.M. on the 29th, Reynolds informed headquarters of his arrival in Emmitsburg. He still had incomplete information on the enemy's location but was determined to press forward. Reynolds learned Meade "is entirely satisfied with the progress you have made, and only wishes you to get over as much ground as you can without fatiguing your men." Fifteen minutes later, Dan Sickles, whose Third Corps was part of Reynolds's wing, was chided for not moving fast enough. Slow Third Corps supply trains were impairing the movement of other troops, Sickles was informed.[37]

Thus far, Reynolds retained command of his own corps while also overseeing additional troops on the army's western flank. As contact with the Confederates grew imminent, Meade formally elevated Reynolds to wing command, leading the First, Third, and 11th Corps. The order forming the three-corps wing illustrates the great confidence Meade held in Reynolds, formerly the army commander's superior when both were in the First Corps. Reynolds was to "make such dispositions and give such orders as circumstances may require, and report from time to time to the commanding general."[38]

Contentment with Reynolds's work and the grant of discretionary authority to the wing commander does not mean Meade was recklessly walking into a fight. On the morning of the 30th, Meade informed Reynolds, "In case of an advance in force either against you or Howard at Emmitsburg, you must fall back to that place," where reinforcements would be available.[39]

Reynolds had already found good defensive ground on the north side of Emmitsburg, which explains why the First Corps marched through town before camping on the night of June 29. The general wished to protect the road coming from Fairfield, to the west, due to rumors of enemy troops in the vicinity. Doubleday, corps commander after Reynolds's elevation to wing command, recalled how the Emmitsburg bivouac site "had been carefully selected by General Reynolds as a defensive line."[40]

Reynolds clearly aimed for a brawl. Doubleday knew his wing commander meant business, writing "Reynolds had the true spirit of a soldier." He was "inflamed at seeing the devastation of his native state" and "most desirous of getting at the enemy as soon as possible." Earlier in the campaign, Doubleday said Reynolds wanted to swiftly engage the Confederates to prevent continued plundering of Pennsylvania. Reynolds was "determined to advance and hold Gettysburg."[41]

Orders granting Reynolds the ability to make choices about where to fight also noted the importance of defensive action if attacked. The dichotomy was further outlined in the strategy Meade crafted on the 30th, known to history as the Pipe Creek Circular. His idea was to create a defensive position along the northern part of Parr Ridge to cover Baltimore and Washington. In a line of more than 20 miles southeast of Taneytown—from Middleburg to Manchester—the First Corps was slated to join other elements of Reynolds's wing on the left of the Pipe Creek line, if Meade found circumstances dictated. Three more corps to the right under Slocum were to complete the Pipe

Creek line, with the Second Corps in reserve. Meade no longer intended "to assume the offensive until the enemy's movements or position should render such an operation certain of success." He added, "The time for falling back can only be developed by circumstances."

Meant to be issued during the evening of June 30, the circular was not distributed until July 1, likely in the late morning.[42] The timing was too tardy to erase Reynolds's drive to prevent Confederate control of Gettysburg.

The Pipe Creek Circular would not be implemented without a Rebel attack. Meade wrote, "This order is communicated, that a general plan, perfectly understood by all, may be had for receiving attack, if made in strong force, upon any portion of our present position." And, leaving open the possibility of his own army's attack, the circular read, "Developments may cause the commanding general to assume the offensive from his present positions."[43]

Decisiveness and diffidence existed simultaneously in Meade, which is not as contradictory as the literal words appear. Some historians latched on to Meade's creation of a fallback position as a sign the commanding general lacked the will to engage Lee's army in Pennsylvania.[44] The die was already cast, however, by letting Reynolds decide whether to commence battle at Gettysburg.

Battle was all but inevitable, based on Buford's reports to Reynolds. On the evening of June 30, the cavalry general reported, "I am satisfied that A. P. Hill's corps is massed just back of Cashtown," less than 10 miles west of Gettysburg. With his cavalry scouts combing a wide swath of country, Buford also learned Ewell's Corps "is crossing the mountains from Carlisle," north of Gettysburg, while Longstreet was behind Hill. This showed the bulk of Lee's force of about 73,000 men was moving toward Gettysburg. Buford even reported rumors of enemy troops approaching from the east. The only federal troops in Gettysburg, a town where roads from the surrounding localities came together, were two of Buford's three brigades, less than 3,000 men.[45]

Marching orders for July 1 had the First Corps move to Gettysburg, with the 11th Corps required to reach the town or supporting distance.[46] Reynolds knew the two corps could field about 20,000 infantry to support Buford. When given the choice between forming a defensive posture either in Emmitsburg or along the left flank of the Pipe Creek line, or fighting Confederates in Pennsylvania, Reynolds chose aggression.

The extensive amount of confidence Meade had for Reynolds was obvious in a dispatch on July 1. Intelligence showed the Confederates were close to reuniting, likely in the line between Chambersburg and York, with Gettysburg in the middle. "The commanding general cannot decide whether it is his best policy to move to attack until he learns something more definite of the point at which the enemy is concentrating," the missive declared. Meade lacked knowledge of the ground's ability to support attack or defense, so Reynolds's views were requested. The message informed Reynolds that the order sending the First Corps to Gettysburg was received prior to knowledge of the disturbing intelligence of the Confederate advance. Nonetheless, Reynolds was not ordered to retreat to either Emmitsburg or Pipe Creek. Meade no longer seemed interested in the June 30 policy instructing Reynolds to fall back if Lee simply advanced in force.[47]

The most important reason why Meade did not order Reynolds to emphasize defense rests in a very simple fact: The army commander held great faith in Reynolds's judgment. Obviously concerned about the possibility of battle sooner than he wished, Meade rested firmly on his understanding of and friendship with Reynolds. If John Reynolds felt aggression was the best policy on July 1, Meade was not going to override that determination. As Fishel points out so well, Meade probably made the conscious choice to let Reynolds decide if a major battle would occur at Gettysburg. Meade was ceding the decision about opening a fight to a man he trusted greatly.[48]

Doubt exists about whether Reynolds even received the Pipe Creek Circular or the later July 1 message.[49] Neither would have mattered, because Reynolds was already acting under discretionary orders allowing a battle at Gettysburg. Meade's fallback strategy—moving to the excellent defensive ground running diagonally below Taneytown—could not have been viable for long. Lee would likely have not attacked such a strong position when given the option of remaining untouched in Pennsylvania and occupying the state's capital. Or, Lee could have forced Meade out of the Pipe Creek line by maneuvering around the Union left. More importantly, Lincoln and Halleck would not have allowed the sacking of Harrisburg while their army remained safe and sound filling canteens from Pipe Creek. Meade was right to envision a strong contingency position focused on defensive warfare. But giving Reynolds the choice to fight at Gettysburg was the best decision the army commander could have made.[50]

The aggressive impulse meant the First Corps was in for a very tough day on July 1. In returns for June 30, the command had gained strength. There were 8,716 infantrymen and 687 officers present and equipped. The total of 9,403 reflected an increase of nearly 5 percent in ten days. Every man was about to be needed more than at any other point in the history of the corps. The men who had survived Sharpsburg the previous September likely never imagined the corps could lose more than twice as many men in one day. But such are the fates of war.

DID BUFORD MEET REYNOLDS AT MORITZ TAVERN ON JULY 1?

Making his headquarters just across the state line in Pennsylvania, Reynolds fell asleep at Moritz Tavern at around midnight on July 1. He still did not have orders for the morning, but his penchant for a fight drove the two armies to a fateful collision. Much was to be done, but Reynolds needed rest just like his troops, although the First Corps had only marched about 5 miles on June 30.[51]

Maj. William Riddle, one of Reynolds's staff members, did not have the luxury of even the slightest rest. He was ordered to make a round trip to Taneytown, where orders from Meade were obtained. By 4:00 A.M., Riddle arrived at Moritz Tavern. Hints of daylight were already evident, with sunrise slated for thirty-five minutes later. Looking at Meade's orders for an advance to Gettysburg, Riddle woke Reynolds, read the order multiple times, and then assisted the general with the task of preparing the army's left wing for action. A farmer and his family cooked breakfast for Reynolds and his staff early in the morning.

One possible incident around this time has been widely ignored by historians: Buford arriving at Moritz Tavern, about 5 miles from the cavalry's position west of Gettysburg, to confer with Reynolds. The primary recorder of the meeting was First Corps artilleryman James Hall, commander of the Second Maine Battery, posted near the tavern.[52]

Most historians covering either the first day's fight at Gettysburg or the entire battle do not say the meeting never happened. Rather, the very idea of the meeting is completely ignored. In a review of contemporary and modern sources, Hall's credibility is not questioned, so his account should not be dismissed on its face.

One reason to reject the possibility of the tavern parley between the two generals is the dearth of reporting on the event from those who would have known. Buford's report on the Gettysburg campaign does not mention such a meeting. The same lack of confirmation exists in reports from Doubleday and Wadsworth. In several postwar writings on Gettysburg, Doubleday's silence continued. Interestingly, Hall's report of Gettysburg fails to say he saw Buford and Reynolds talk, and no other First Corps officer reported on the meeting.

Hall may simply have been one of the few officers near where the meeting took place. Senior commanders may have subsequently ignored the Buford-Reynolds meeting on July 1 because later events made a short exchange between the two generals fade into irrelevance. Few days for any of the participants were more significant than July 1, 1863, and logging every meeting in the early morning could not be expected.

Hall's reporting of the event gains credibility because of the details he recorded. Based on the circumstances Buford's men encountered west of Gettysburg, the cavalryman could be expected to focus on the danger posed by Confederate pickets east of Cashtown, barely 5 miles from Gettysburg's town square. In the newspaper article Hall wrote about the meeting, he claimed Buford showed up with a few other troopers early in the morning, perhaps as Reynolds was enjoying breakfast. The cavalry general then requested Reynolds's advance with the First Corps to probe the Confederate regiments closest to town.

In addition to his interest in confronting the invaders of his home state, Reynolds may very well have used an early morning in-person report from Buford to see the inevitability of a battle. Hall claimed the request from Buford for the First Corps to probe Confederate positions led Reynolds to dictate a letter to Meade. As discussed in a speech where Hall was quoted, Chapman Biddle, acting commander of the First Brigade, Third Division, noted how Reynolds informed Meade,

> *Buford just now reports that he finds a small force of the enemy's infantry in a point of woods near Gettysburg, which he is unable to dislodge; and while I am aware that it is not your desire to force an engagement at that point, still from the scope of instructions I have all the time had from you since commanding this wing of the army, I feel at liberty to advance to Gettysburg and develop the strength of the enemy at that point.*[53]

Neither historians nor Hollywood screenwriters could come up with better words for Reynolds to use in defense of his decision to fight for Gettysburg.

Maybe history should be silent on any Buford-Reynolds meeting at Moritz Tavern. No dispatch exists to corroborate Hall's words quoting Reynolds's missive to Meade. Yet, Hall did not need to write of the meeting to make a hero of Reynolds, whose death in action later in the morning led to his elevated status as a bold and intrepid commander.

If the story of a Buford-Reynolds meeting at Moritz Tavern seems unlikely, why do virtually all historians of the battle not mention the falsity of Hall's account? If Hall told such a tall tale, why has no historian informed the world about a young officer's farcical yarn of a meeting that never took place? Clearly, no one should rule out the possibility of the two generals holding a short discussion at Moritz Tavern before the First Corps started marching on July 1.

REYNOLDS'S LAST MISTAKE

On his final morning of life, John Reynolds could rightfully look back at the last three weeks with pride. He was key to the Union's generally good position on July 1. He used the choices given him to see the value of confronting Lee in the Keystone State. He knew the 11th Corps was close behind the First. Sickles's Third Corps could also be on hand later in the day. Coming from the other side of town, Slocum's 12th Corps would reach the field on July 1. With immense faith in his troops—and possibly due to an urgent in-person request from Buford early in the morning—Reynolds would be bold.

Unfortunately, the period of his best service during the war ended with a terrible decision: a late start to the First Corps' march on July 1. His men would not arrive on the field until approximately 10:00 A.M., a moment when Buford's two brigades were close to being overwhelmed. Although pressing for a fight, Reynolds failed to get the six brigades of the First Corps on the road in a timely way. The late start nearly proved fatal to Union fortunes.

Preparing paperwork for his artillery brigade during the morning, Colonel Charles Wainwright had input directly from Reynolds about expectations for July 1. The men were up early, Wainwright noted, "but it rather promised then to be a quiet day for us." In a conversation with Reynolds, Wainwright learned of the wing commander's belief of battle being unlikely; the move to Gettysburg was intended merely to support Buford. Shortly after the discussion, Reynolds then moved forward to join Wadsworth's Division. He would ride with the initial infantry advance of the First Corps, undoubtedly in an effort to get quicker updates from Buford.[54]

Several historians believe there existed no need for a rapid advance from camps along Marsh Creek. Martin's detailed review of the first day's battle suggests Reynolds and the First Corps had no need for haste. Defending a leisurely advance, Pfanz's book on July 1 concludes Reynolds was unaware of the advance of Heth's Confederate division, starting about 5:00 A.M. With the troops needing rest and battle unexpected, these eminent historians suggest, a slow advance was defensible.[55]

However, Reynolds had the primary responsibility of supporting Buford and figuring out where, if anywhere, the army should make a stand. Even if no significant battle began on July 1, the wing commander had an obligation to visualize for Meade the best steps to take. Getting the First Corps to town earlier in the morning was the only credible way for Reynolds to keep Meade in the know, defend Gettysburg, and avoid sending a portion of the army to defeat.[56]

As those critical of Reynolds must avoid hindsight, so should historians who excuse the wing commander's lack of alacrity on July 1. Just because the battle of Gettysburg became a major Union victory does not mean the general bringing on the fight made no significant errors. The relative lethargy of Reynolds's advance may very well have spelled great disaster. Pfanz gives Reynolds a pass for not knowing of the Confederate advance early in the morning, but no great general would assume Lee's men were not moving to Gettysburg. Intelligence from the day and night before made such a move completely predictable. Reynolds either should have moved the First Corps to Gettysburg sooner or ordered Buford to abandon the town subsequent to Heth's early advance. After waiting until 8:00 A.M. to get going, a slow start was not conducive to the best outcome for the Union at Gettysburg.

"Our Pace Was Considerably Quickened"

The men in the two brigades of Wadsworth's Division led the advance on the 30th, which usually meant they would bring up the rear of the corps the following day. Reynolds wanted to get the lines moving faster, so Wadsworth, with about 3,500 men, was to lead the army's infantry again. Hall's Battery, on detached duty from Wainwright's artillery brigade, went along with Wadsworth's men. Cutler was in the advance, with Hall's six guns behind, followed by Meredith's five regiments.[57]

Colonel Fowler of the 14th Brooklyn received marching orders at about 7:00 A.M. Bugles quickly sounded, prompting Cutler's Brigade to prepare for the renewal of the march. With heat and humidity increasing, and the sounds of battle growing louder, the men at least had the solace of beautiful countryside. "Upon reaching a point about two miles from Gettysburg," a soldier recalled, the men "suddenly beheld a panorama of the hills and valleys lying at the foot of the Blue Ridge."[58]

The 19th Indiana served on picket during the night. Although usually an undesirable chore, the short distance covered on the 30th made the detail bearable. Lt. Col. William Dudley recalled the regiment monitored a significant amount of territory during the evening. The 19th's men marched more than 2 miles north of the division, then spread out a total of nearly 3 miles, with their skirmish line on either side of the Emmitsburg Road.[59] Thus, some Hoosiers spent the night not far from Buford's camp at Gettysburg.

With some early morning precipitation, the Hoosiers donned rain ponchos, perhaps even feeling a bit of an early summer overnight chill. The low temperature in the 60s undoubtedly provided some relief. Later in the morning, Col. Sam Williams had 288 men and officers in his Indiana regiment as the 19th melded into the line of the advancing Iron Brigade.[60]

Wadsworth reported how the division moved out "under the immediate direction" of Reynolds. Regardless of the slow start, the wing commander wished to arrive sooner than later as the day progressed. The men did not immediately face heat and humidity; weather was fair to start the day, with another light rain shower arriving around 6:00 A.M. The sun reappeared about the time Cutler's Brigade started their 8:00 A.M. march, with Buford's troopers only 5 miles away. Before the First Division reached town, high humidity would become noticeable.[61]

While still in Emmitsburg, Reynolds had decided to detach the 7th Indiana. These Hoosiers would not march to Gettysburg alongside Cutler's five other regiments. With the 76th New York in the lead, Cutler took his regiments north. The marching order continued with the 56th Pennsylvania, 147th New York, 95th New York, and the 14th Brooklyn bringing up the rear. The regimental historian of the 76th wrote of the strong desire throughout the ranks to expel Lee from Pennsylvania. "The men all felt that they were now called upon to fight, not merely for an abstract principle, but for their own hearth-stones," and "to preserve their homes from the desolations of war."[62]

At the beginning of the Iron Brigade's trek, they were about a mile behind Cutler's troops. The order of march put the 2nd Wisconsin in the lead, followed by the 7th Badger regiment, then the 19th Indiana, with the 24th Michigan and 6th Wisconsin behind. The Brigade Guard, a total of one hundred men taken from across the five regiments, was last in line.[63]

Soldiers recalled positive feelings and a lack of concern about the possibility of imminent battle. With 340 officers and men, the 6th Wisconsin under Lieutenant Colonel Dawes made their way north. "All were in the highest spirits," a Company A soldier recalled. Proud Americans of German ancestry increased the levity by singing songs in their native language. Other impromptu vocalists made the march to Gettysburg memorable for the brigade. Dawes ordered the drum corps to the front of his regiment, adding to the merriment of a seemingly routine day.[64]

Then, obvious signs of battle registered with the tough veterans. "All seemed merry until yonder booms and puffs of cannon smoke" signaled the need for alacrity. As Colonel Morrow of the 24th Michigan reported, "Our pace was considerably quickened." Doubleday correctly described Buford's cavalrymen as being in a "perilous condition" since the previous day, due to the advance of separate wings of Lee's army. The Confederates were essentially moving toward Gettysburg in a pincer movement, capable of crushing Union forces moving to defend the town. Holding the advanced picket posts gallantly, then keeping Heth's Division confused and in check, Buford was performing immortal work, but he desperately needed help.[65]

"As Solid As a Stone Wall"

Buford sent two staff officers south in an effort to find Reynolds and expedite arrival of the First Corps. The plea was delivered about 3 miles south of town. The wing commander swiftly went ahead of his infantry to confer with Buford in Gettysburg.

The meeting location has been subject to some debate. Reynolds potentially found Buford scanning to the west from the cupola of a building on the grounds of the Lutheran Theological Seminary. "What is the matter John?" was the query Reynolds was said to lob at Buford. "The devil's to pay," the tired brigadier replied. Moving forward for a quick review of how the two cavalry brigades were fairing, Reynolds announced the imminent arrival of infantry support. A signal officer suggested Buford was close to pulling his men back to Cemetery Hill on the other side of Gettysburg at the time Reynolds reached the field.[66]

After a keen albeit quick review of the ground closer to the action, Reynolds saw the virtue of getting a shortcut created for Wadsworth's two brigades. After the removal of fencing, the infantrymen left the Emmitsburg Road about a mile-and-a-half south of Buford's position for more direct access to the battlefield. With every second counting, the virtue of the move to save some steps for Cutler and Meredith's men cannot be denied.

Buford's signal officer recalled the imposing sight of Wadsworth's soldiers as they raced among the chaos to relieve the Union troopers. The infantry "moved up on a run, wheeled into line apparently without command, as solid as a stone wall, and were in action instantly."[67] The ability of soldiers to take such vital actions while rushing ahead and under great stress testifies to their training and the leadership of officers who insisted on regular drill.

The initial First Corps troops on the scene found themselves in a very tight spot against a partially hidden, numerically superior force. Cutler's stone wall had a difficult start on the battlefield. Reynolds was in the midst of these opening moments. He personally posted Hall's Second Maine Battery just north of the Chambersburg Pike. Because of the slopes in the ground and the existence of a railroad cut near Hall's position, the Second Brigade could not form a connected, single line. Difficulties mounted quickly for infantrymen and cannoneers alike.

The 147th New York—untested in battle—was the regiment closest to Hall's guns. Cutler oversaw two other regiments on the right, the 56th Pennsylvania and the 76th New York, with the Empire State soldiers manning the army's northern flank. Meanwhile, Colonel Fowler led the 14th Brooklyn and 95th New York south of the Chambersburg Pike.

Hall knew the tenuous nature of his position, more than 1,000 feet west of Seminary Hill. Reynolds ordered Wadsworth to ensure adequate infantry support for Hall, while the cannoneer was to target Rebel artillery. The nature of the ground and the advanced stage of Confederate deployments made Reynolds's impromptu vision far more difficult to execute than to conceive. Yet, the necessity of the moment required a strong show from the initial First Corps troops on the field. To the west stood a Confederate battery ready to give the Maine men a greeting, as Heth's infantry division advanced after reorganizing in the wake of the battle with Buford.[68]

Accurate battery fire from Hall's men forced the Confederate guns to redeploy before much time elapsed. Six shots were all the Maine men fired before the enemy moved two guns "under the cover behind a barn," the McPherson barn, which would play a prominent role in the battle's first day. Perhaps twenty minutes after his guns' effective work, Hall reported the advance of enemy infantry, which were less than 200 feet from the battery's northernmost cannon. The Confederates were under the command of Brig. Gen. Joe Davis, the nephew of the Confederate president. Undoubtedly barking orders in an animated fashion, Hall had the right guns blast canister at Davis's men while the left artillery section kept targeting Confederate cannons.[69]

Hall's fire did not keep the Confederates from inflicting great loss on the trio of Cutler's regiments north of the pike. The 2nd and 42nd Mississippi, with the 55th North Carolina had approximately 1,700 men on their battle line, outnumbering Cutler's three regiments nearly two to one.

Using the ground and a thick crop of wheat, the Confederates confused the 76th New York and 56th Pennsylvania as the Union troops were arriving north of the pike, attempting to form a line of battle. The Keystone Staters, although second in line, formed themselves slightly faster than the 76th. Col. J. William Hofmann, commanding the 56th, asked Cutler to scan the ground to the west with his field glasses. After the general confirmed the men were Confederates, Hofmann ordered what was almost certainly the first volley Union infantry unleashed at Gettysburg.[70]

"ALL WILL REGRET HIS LOSS VERY MUCH"

The Confederates did not take kindly to having their plan of occupying Gettysburg interrupted. A "shower of bullets" was the reply Unionists received after the first volley. The Confederate fire wounded dozens of the Second Brigade's men, as well as three staff horses, including Cutler's mount. Then, "the battle raged furiously for twenty minutes."[71]

Those twenty minutes were some of the most difficult any First Corps men would face in the war. Neither the 56th Pennsylvania nor the 76th New York had participated in much combat in recent campaigns. The two regiments, then under Doubleday, came to the aid of Gibbon's men as they grappled with Stonewall Jackson at Brawner Farm. The men were about to make up for their reserve positions at Antietam, Fredericksburg, and Chancellorsville.

In addition to surprise and Davis's manpower advantage, the Confederate attack gained immense leverage with the flanking action of the 55th North Carolina, the left of the brigade line. Moving to the northeast, then turning south, the Tar Heels were able to overlap the right of the 76th New York. In response, Maj. Andrew Jackson Grover skillfully attempted to turn his regiment north to meet the threat. There was only so much mortal men could do against the excellent tactics Col. John Connally employed against Grover's regiment. The North Carolinian made a less brilliant decision when he hoisted the regimental colors to lead on his men. Connally quickly suffered a wound, costing him an arm.[72]

The 56th Pennsylvania's rough time did include their wounding of a future governor of Mississippi. Col. John Marshall Stone had to get over a fence with his men to advance against Hofmann's pressed but determined line. Leaving his horse while the Pennsylvanians engaged his 2nd Mississippi, Stone was wounded as he climbed over the fence.[73]

The Confederate tide could not be resisted for long. Capt. John Cook of the 76th said the regiment endured "a galling cross-fire" from the 55th North Carolina as Stone's Mississippians made progress against Hofmann's men. Cutler was undoubtedly correct when he praised his regiments. The units north of the pike "fought as only brave men can fight, and held their ground until ordered to fall back." Wadsworth credited Cutler and his regiments with waging "a resolute contest" prior to their retreat to Seminary Ridge.[74]

Brig. Gen. Lysander Cutler led Wadsworth's Second Brigade into the opening infantry fight at Gettysburg. He would pen a deeply emotional letter to the widow of Maj. Andrew Grover, who died while commanding the 76th New York north of the Chambersburg Pike. LIBRARY OF CONGRESS

The losses among the engaged regiments were extensive. The respected leader of the 76th New York was killed in action. Andrew Grover, who was thirty-two years old, enjoyed strong support from his superiors and the rank and file. Grover had earned an honorable discharge after suffering wounds at Brawner Farm, but on gaining the rank of major, he decided to return to the field. Cutler referred to Grover as "a brave and efficient officer."

Uberto Burnham, who recorded so many of his thoughts during the war, noted Grover was "very popular." The day after the battle's opening fight, Burnham added to his praise of Grover by lamenting, "All will regret his loss very much." A memorial published in the regimental history expanded the tributes, suggesting Grover was "a man of high integrity," with "most courteous manners," and "a keen sense of honor."

Mrs. Grover received letters in which she learned how deeply revered her husband had become. General Cutler wrote:

He was among the bravest of the brave, and fell lamented by all who knew him. His regiment behaved worthy of their leader, and although losing more than half their number, fought on through the three bloody days, and are still ready to avenge their fallen leader and comrades, and to restore the Government of the Union. Allow me to offer you my sincere condolence for your great loss, and to assure you that he died in a glorious cause, and without a fear or murmur.

Col. William Wainwright, who left the regiment shortly before Gettysburg, knew Grover as well as any other person could have in the army. In an August letter, he added to the laudatory words Mrs. Grover had been reading.

As commanding officer of the Seventy-sixth, I had learned to esteem and value very highly your lamented husband, for his distinguished courage on the field, and for his knowledge of his duties, as well as his unflinching determination in performing them. As a man and a soldier, Major Grover always appeared to me a model, and in the management of his Company when Captain, in the gallant manner in which he led our skirmishers at Gainesville, or more recently as commander of the Regiment at Gettysburg, he has given every reason for those who knew him to lament his loss.[75]

Major Grover was known to staff at a New York newspaper that received a telegram about his death. The tragic news was delivered "to the bereaved wife and mother in as gentle a manner as possible, but it proved none the less heart-rending." The editor subsequently added, "May God and the good angels extend their especial care and kindness over her as her fatherless children!"

Many other men from the 76th were lost in the short engagement. Franklin Pratt missed the fighting but was on the field shortly after the battle. He informed his parents of the death of cousin Charles, who was only twenty-three years old. Pratt wrote, "Our company suffered severely. One of

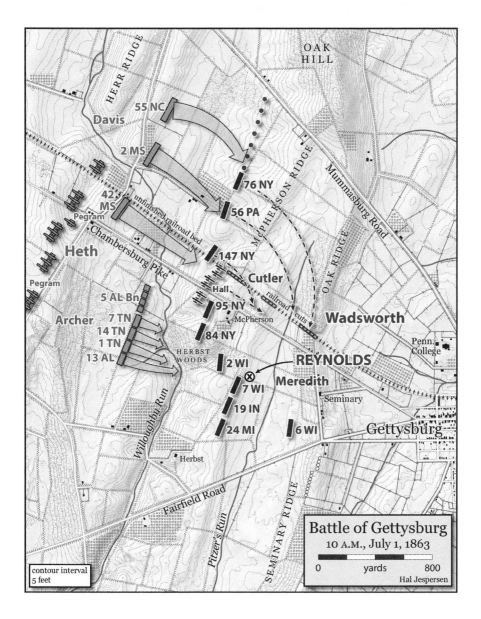

OAK
HILL

HERR RIDGE

55 NC

Davis

2 MS

76 NY

42
MS

Pegram

unfinished railroad bed

56 PA

McPHERSON RIDGE

Mummasburg Road

Chambersburg Pike

147 NY

Heth

Cutler

OAK RIDGE

Pegram

Hall

railroad

5 AL Bn

95 NY

cuts

Wadsworth

Archer

7 TN

McPherson

Penn.
College

14 TN

84 NY

1 TN

REYNOLDS

13 AL

HERBST
WOODS

2 WI

Meredith

Seminary

7 WI

19 IN

SEMINARY RIDGE

Willoughby Run

24 MI

6 WI

Gettysburg

Herbst

Fairfield Road

Pitzer's Run

Battle of Gettysburg
10 A.M., July 1, 1863

contour interval
5 feet

0   yards   800

Hal Jespersen

the boys stated that out of thirty men in our company, but six remained." He concluded, "The whole Regiment was almost annihilated."[76]

"IT COULD ONLY HAVE BEEN A KIND PROVIDENCE"

Other Mississippians battled the 147th New York and Hall's guns closer to the Chambersburg Pike, southwest of Cutler's two regiments. The intensity of this engagement was fierce, providing a disastrous baptism for the men from Oswego County.

Because of the difficult, unknown ground, the 147th did not stay connected to the 76th New York and 56th Pennsylvania. Originally moving out south of the Chambersburg Pike, the Oswego County boys moved to the right and crossed a shallow part of the Railroad Cut to better support Hall's six cannons. The 147th's main competition would be the 42nd Mississippi, which Hall had earlier seen so close to the cannon on his right flank. Quickly, the situation became unbearable for the regiment and battery deployed in such an exposed position.

Both regiments in this fight were tasting combat for the first time, and under a man named Miller. Although many could rightfully question the competence of General Davis, the rookie 42nd Mississippi benefited from a strong military leader, Col. Hugh Reid Miller. Active in politics and extremely devoted to the Southern cause, Miller was the captain of a company in the 2nd Mississippi as early as First Bull Run. He pushed the 42nd hard against the 147th and Hall's guns.[77]

Fighting close to Hall's cannons, members of the 147th New York experienced sheer horror. One soldier recalled how he and his comrades

could see nothing and did not know where the rebels were till they fired a volley into our ranks, and could only tell then by the way the wheat was mowed in front of us by their bullets. On the first fire while we were advancing, Hiram Stowel and Celestine Berkley were killed instantly for I saw them fall. Then Fred. Rife, one of the finest men I ever saw, both in personal appearance and gentlemanly conduct—and as a soldier he had no superior in the ranks; in fact, I have not a man but I can give a good name, for they have all won my respect by their good conduct and soldierly qualities.[78]

"The storm of iron and lead was terrific," a newspaper wrote after receiving information from officers in the 147th. A wounded soldier would inform his parents of the fight. He spelled out the enormity of the 147th's ordeal by detailing the sad fate of several in the regiment.

Becker is shot in the knee, and broke one bone, but will get it set and be well before many months; Al. Bartly shot dead Chauncey Miller is not hurt; Wm. Flanery prisoner; Peter Perry, prisoner; C. Backus, prisoner; Denney Connely, wounded; Lieut. Schenck, wounded, dangerously;—Lieut. Van Dusen is killed; Joe Disten, killed; Joe Eldred, killed; Ed. Yoping shot in thumb; John Smith and Dan Chitman are not hurt; Pat Brown is also safe; Bristol and Hubbard are all safe, with a slight wound in Hubbard's head; Miles Baker is shot in the face; Orderly King wounded in the arm, slightly.

Lt. Col. Francis Miller, who took 380 men into the fight, tried to protect the 147th with an order for the men to lie down. The prone position meant concealment in the high wheat but also downgraded the regiment's offensive power. The 147th remained under intense pressure, so Wadsworth ordered the regiment back to the line of woods near the Seminary. A serious wound Miller received meant the order was never transmitted to his men; new commander Maj. George Harney was not aware of Wadsworth's order. The Confederates were then able to imperil the entire regiment.[79]

Color sergeant John Hinchcliff was killed as the order to retreat finally reached the 147th. Sgt. William Wybourn, still in his early twenties, earned great approbation for going back to retrieve the colors while under a severe fire. Although wounded by a shot in the back, Wybourn won a lieutenant's commission for the brave deed. By November 1864, he would be a captain.[80]

Hall discovered the Confederates' attempt to cut off his guns as well as the 147th. Losing men and horses rapidly, he "ordered the battery to retire by sections, although having no orders to do so." Hoping a new position for one section would provide cover for other guns to escape, Hall was disappointed. Enemy troops continued to flank the guns and infantry, with the chance to escape less likely each second. All horses of one retreating gun were killed, and the piece had to be left on the field. Summing up his morning, Hall remembered, "It was *hellish*."[81]

Several retreating soldiers tried to find shelter in the Railroad Cut. The indentation of ground could only shield the New Yorkers for a short time, as the Confederates surrounded the cut, firing down the line or from above. As one very lucky Oswego boy wrote, "How any of us escaped out of that trap alive, I cannot tell. It could only have been a kind Providence that shielded me through this fight, for I have had hair-breath escapes without number, still I have not the least scratch, neither has my clothes a single rent." Somehow, the remnant of the 147th joined Cutler's other two retreating units closer to town. More than half of the 147th were already casualties.

Elmina Spencer was on the field to help the Oswego regiment. The wife of a soldier, Spencer worked tirelessly throughout the war to assist the unit. Known to ride 40 or more miles a day, Spencer's efforts at Gettysburg included working with surgeon Algernon Coe. Her tireless efforts led to great admiration for Spencer among veterans of the war.[82]

The lack of direct connection between the 147th New York and any other regiment was the central problem with Cutler's position. Colonel Hofmann reported being unaware of the 147th's location; he could not see the Oswego Countians during the battle.[83] Even if the three regiments had been able to link up, there was no way for Cutler to stop the charge of Davis's Brigade, especially after the 55th North Carolina flanked the 76th New York. Help was needed to stem the tide. The Union cause could rejoice as the Iron Brigade swung into action. Undoubtedly, the gallant stand of Cutler and Hall's men bought precious time for soldiers in one of the most revered brigades in American history to make their first mark at Gettysburg.

BRILLIANT COUNTERSTROKE FROM THE IRON BRIGADE

Meredith's Western warriors quickly took charge of their tactical situation. The Iron Brigade would create considerable woe for Gen. James Archer, leading his four regiments toward what he thought was an easy conquest of untrained militia. Instead, Archer's 1st, 7th, and 14th Tennessee and 13th Alabama ran into the boys in the tall black hats.

The morning's second brawl between two brigades did not start well for the Unionists. The 2nd Wisconsin, filing a bit to the right from the line of march, formed a battle line of about 300 men.

> *The field officers, Colonel Fairchild, Lieutenant-Colonel Stevens, and Maj. John Mansfield, immediately dismounted, and, taking their proper places in line, advanced the regiment up a gentle slope, and when on its crest, we received a volley of musketry from the enemy's line, from which many officers and men fell, among them Lieutenant-Colonel Stevens.*

This devastating first fire from Archer's troops hit about one hundred men in the 2nd Wisconsin. Stevens suffered hits to the left side and bowels. He lingered for a few days, then succumbed to the severe injuries. He rests with other immortals at Gettysburg National Cemetery.[84]

Revenge belonged to the Iron Brigade. A flanking maneuver would devastate the nascent Confederate charge. As three more of Meredith's regiments lined up south of the 2nd Wisconsin, Archer's preliminary advantage withered. The 2nd Wisconsin continued to advance into the woodlot to the west. With a sudden drive against the Confederates, Mansfield observed, "the line of the enemy in our immediate front yielded," with many of Archer's troops looking to completely flee or hide. As the Iron Brigade dominated his front and encircled his right flank, Archer knew he was in trouble. "I ordered a charge upon this last

As tough as any of his indomitable veterans in the 2nd Wisconsin, Col. Lucius Fairchild lost an arm while leading the Badger warriors into the morning fight at Gettysburg.
LIBRARY OF CONGRESS

position of the enemy," Mansfield declared, "which was gallantly made at the double-quick." The Iron Brigade captured hundreds, including Archer, the first Army of Northern Virginia general taken prisoner in battle.[85]

"It was a victory indeed, but at the cost of precious lives," concluded the historian of the 24th Michigan. In such a short time, the victorious Iron Brigade lost immensely. With the shattering of his left elbow, Lucius Fairchild wanted to go back into action after a heavy dose of morphine. The tough colonel unfortunately could not save his arm. On learning of the amputation, Fairchild thanked God for his remaining single arm.[86]

General Reynolds's life ended as Meredith's men charged. The senior Union commander on the field was shot near the base of his skull, likely when he was looking back among the 2nd Wisconsin to see the continued advance of the Iron Brigade. A shot from Tennesseans under Archer seems the most likely source of the fatal bullet. The possibility of a soldier from Davis's Brigade hitting Reynolds from the area of the Railroad Cut cannot be discounted. Doubleday now was in charge of the battle until the arrival of Major General Howard.[87]

In what would be a very deadly day for the 24th Michigan, Sgt. Abel Peck lost his life in the initial action against Archer. Morrow deeply felt the death of such a resolute man. Considered "a brave and faithful soldier," Peck stood as the first color-bearer in the 24th to fall at Gettysburg. He was "a man greatly admired for his almost saintly character."[88]

Doubleday extolled the conduct of the Iron Brigade in defeating Archer. He was especially pleased with the ground the four regiments now possessed. Known as Herbst Woods, the eastern side of the trees was notably higher than the ground to the west. "These woods possessed all the advantages of a redoubt, strengthening the center of our line," Doubleday wrote.[89]

"With the Ferocity of Wild Cats"

Another monumental aspect of the Iron Brigade's service at Gettysburg occurred farther to the north as the rout of Archer unfolded. The 6th Wisconsin and Iron Brigade Guard were held in reserve as the other four regiments charged Herbst Woods. As Davis pushed the 147th New York back, the possibility existed for a counterattack against Meredith from the north. Instead, Doubleday called for Dawes to go after the victorious yet confused line Davis could not fully manage along the Railroad Cut. Cutler's two regiments south of the Chambersburg Pike, the 14th Brooklyn and 95th New York, also saw the opportunity. The three regiments were about to give President Davis's nephew a big piece of humble pie.[90]

The duo of Cutler's regiments under Fowler had already been harassed by Archer's skirmishers. Thanks to the Iron Brigade's valiant charge into Herbst Woods, Archer soon faced way more than his men could handle. Fowler saw how his services were needed north of the pike. He started to move the 14th Brooklyn and 95th New York in the direction of the cut to assist the 147th New York and Hall's cannons. Although he would take more credit for the entire action at the Railroad Cut than he deserved, Fowler was a vital piece of the puzzle leading to the important victory against Davis.[91]

Dawes divided the Brigade Guard in half shortly before the advance. Lt. Loyd Harris, leading one half of the Guard, thought his fifty men might prefer being with their original regiments. No dishonor was attached to men in the Brigade Guard, but Harris spoke to his men, wanting them to know he was there for them and willing to stand with the Guard as they moved toward harm. Per an order from Dawes, Harris placed his small command to the left of the 6th Wisconsin. The other wing of the Brigade Guard, under Lt. Levi Showalter of the 2nd Wisconsin, formed on Dawes's right.[92]

Dawes may have been wondering if his men were ever going to get into the fight. During a short time after reaching the field, the 6th was ordered to move elsewhere twice, with both commands being quickly rescinded. Finally, as the crisis of the morning boiled over along the Railroad Cut, Doubleday got the First Division's only infantry reserve moving north. The acting corps commander reported how the 6th Wisconsin was "a gallant body of men, whom I knew could be relied upon." Orders from division staff also reached Dawes, with one adjutant imploring, "Go like hell!"[93]

Dawes was about to affirm Doubleday's confidence in the 6th Wisconsin. Mounted at first, Dawes ordered his troops to quickly make their way north. As Davis's Brigade tried to counter the Union units moving toward them, several Confederates sought security in the Railroad Cut. Many soon learned of their mistake, for the cut was 10 or more feet deep in the area known as the Middle Cut, the part of the line Dawes's men were approaching.

The trapped Confederates did not simply surrender. Across two paragraphs in his Gettysburg report, Dawes referred to the Confederate fire as "very galling," "murderous," and "terribly destructive." He estimated 160 men in the 6th Wisconsin fell during the charge.[94]

Near the Chambersburg Pike, the mare carrying Dawes suffered a wound. Dawes somehow dismounted without injury as his horse "fell heavily on her haunches." Looking back after standing, Dawes saw the equine hobbling away from the fight. She would live many years with a Confederate bullet 17 inches deep in her breast.[95]

The intrepid Badgers had to climb two fences on the north side of the pike. More men became casualties while dealing with the obstacles. Company K's Capt. John Ticknor was killed during this part of the fight. In his report, Dawes recalled Ticknor's promotion to captain after leading skirmishers at South Mountain. "Distinguished for bravery upon every battle-field of the regiment," the captain remained to the end "a good officer, a brave man, a genial, whole-souled companion" and "always a dashing leader."[96]

Lyman Holford's field service in the First Corps ended as a result of the destructive Confederate musketry. The wounded soldier wrote, "I had fired three shots when I was struck just above the knee." He would not lose the limb but spent the next several months in multiple hospitals. By April 1864, Holford's convalescence had him performing guard duty in Washington as part of the 22nd Corps.[97]

The force of the charge had a telling effect on the ability of Davis's command to resist. Another aspect of the important First Corps victory in the area was the quick thinking of adjutant Edward Brooks, another man Dawes praised in his report. Surveying the field, Brooks saw how the east end of the cut offered a means for Confederates to escape their self-made trap. With twenty men assisting, Brooks moved to seal off the right flank of the position. The small command delivered some lead down the cut to the west, further pressuring the Confederates trapped by the high grade of earth.[98]

Fowler reported his order led to the final push against the cut, but Dawes clearly moved forward on his own initiative. The centrality of the Wisconsin regiment to the attack was noted by John Kellogg, the same staff officer who sided with the 56th Pennsylvania in the debate over which First Corps troops initiated the infantry battle at Gettysburg. Kellogg said Fowler's two regiments reached the Railroad Cut about three minutes after Dawes.[99]

Nonetheless, the 14th Brooklyn and 95th New York, to the left of Dawes, had plenty of courage to contribute. Resistance was very strong along the whole line. Approaching a slight rise, the 14th's historian wrote, the two regiments "met with a murderous hail of musket bullets." The intensity of the Confederate fire "came so thick and fast that the whirring noise they made sounded like the steady rhythm of machinery." There was some wavering of Fowler's attack, but "with another cheer, louder and more determined, the men rushed on." Still, the remnants of Davis's command fought in close quarters "with the ferocity of wild cats."[100]

Several Wisconsin men decided to make a dash for the regimental flag of the 2nd Mississippi, which was posted on the south side of the cut. Multiple waves of Badger warriors were shot down in the attempt, but flag bearer W. B. Murphy could not resist the force of Francis Wallar, who was supported by his brother Sam. Stealing the Confederate colors earned Wallar the Medal of Honor.[101]

Due to the confusion on the field, the capture of the 2nd Mississippi's flag and several additions to the casualty lists occurred after Maj. John Blair surrendered his troops to Dawes. Many Confederates were able to escape, especially members of the two other regiments in Davis's Brigade. Early initial success at Gettysburg turned into bitter disappointment for Southern hopes. Dawes was informed 232 Confederates were captured due to the charge against the Railroad Cut.[102]

ARRIVAL OF ADDITIONAL FIRST CORPS TROOPS

With only Wadsworth's Division and one battery, the First Corps performed a masterful deed during the morning of July 1. Cutler endured difficult moments north of the Railroad Cut, but nearly 600 Confederates in two brigades were prisoners only about an hour after Wadsworth's troops reached the field. The Union men had suffered heavy losses already, but Henry Heth walked into a meat grinder west of town, disrupting Lee's plan to avoid a general engagement until his nine divisions were closer together.[103]

The Confederates could still concentrate more quickly than Meade's army. Heth would soon have two fresh brigades. Moreover, Ewell's Corps was nearing Gettysburg from the north, and Dorsey Pender's Division in Hill's Corps was starting to arrive. The First Corps' morning victory could quickly turn into afternoon disaster.[104]

The severe gaffe in Confederate tactics during the morning guaranteed a wider engagement. Doubleday embraced Reynolds's determination to hold Gettysburg while the rest of the army moved to his assistance. As the senior officer present after the death of Reynolds, Doubleday wrote how he was "determined to hold on to the position until ordered to leave it." Taking inspiration from Reynolds, Doubleday suggested "great sacrifices" were needed to defend Gettysburg.[105]

Doubleday was also thinking of the honor of the First Corps, which he had been affiliated with across several bloody fields. Although he knew Confederates were massing forces around Gettysburg, a swift retreat without orders "might have inflicted lasting disgrace upon the corps, and as General Reynolds, who was high in the confidence of General Meade, had formed his lines to resist the entrance of the enemy into Gettysburg, I naturally supposed that it was the intention to defend the place."[106]

Four additional First Corps brigades started to arrive as the rout of Heth's two overwhelmed brigades was wrapping up. Along with four batteries, the infantry under Robinson and Rowley would be vital to afternoon resistance against growing enemy numbers.

Robinson's men started the morning near Marsh Creek. They would take the same route as Wadsworth's Division. One member of Paul's Brigade

Although he would lose command of the First Corps on July 2, 1863, Abner Doubleday, pictured with his wife, Mary, competently managed the defense of Gettysburg on July 1, a day when the soldiers of the First Corps suffered nearly 6,000 casualties. LIBRARY OF CONGRESS

noted how the troops departing later than Cutler and Meredith were "under no pressure of haste" at the beginning of the march. Doubleday's report reiterated how the high command's lack of concern for hasty marching kept Robinson and Rowley's troops from being hurried in the wake of Wadsworth. The acting corps commander noted, "Owing to the intervals between the divisions and the necessity of calling in the pickets, from an hour and a half to two hours elapsed before the remaining troops were *en route*."[107]

Like the 19th Indiana, the 88th Pennsylvania in Baxter's Brigade started the new month on picket duty. After the 88th returned to camp, the brigade moved out around 9:00 A.M. Marching conditions were quite bad. "An impalpable powder" from the thick dust likely made men wish more rain had fallen the night before. Uncomfortable heat and humidity created "ploughed furrows" of streaming, dusty sweat on each soldier. Audible sounds of battle became evident as Robinson's band of 2,500 neared the town.[108]

A Pennsylvanian in Baxter's Brigade suggested men from the Keystone State felt a special mission, knowing their home had been invaded. "As they neared the battle-field," the historian of the 11th Regiment wrote, "a firmer and a steadier step struck the ground." A New Yorker in the brigade also felt the drive to get to Gettysburg faster. Discharges of artillery grew more frequent, "and the familiar sound served to quicken the steps of the men," the historian of the 9th New York State Militia recalled.[109]

Rowley's two brigades began their day west of other troops in the First Corps. Lt. Col. Alexander Biddle, older cousin of acting First Brigade commander Chapman Biddle, had his 121st Pennsylvania on picket overnight. The center of the picket line was at Ross White's house about 2 miles west of Marsh Creek. White's farm served as the bivouac for Stone's Brigade. The western extension of the corps line was due to Reynolds's concern about reports of Confederate troops near Fairfield, southwest of Gettysburg. Cooper's Battery of four 3-inch guns joined Rowley's men.[110]

By late morning, two brigades of the Third Division would reach Gettysburg on different roads. Stone took the more easterly Millerstown Road, which intersected the Emmitsburg Road south of Gettysburg. As with other members of the First Corps, plans for a leisurely day eroded as Stone's marching warriors heard sounds of battle. Covering about 5 total miles, Stone moved his men along at quick time or double quick to expedite their arrival.

Like other elements of the First Corps, the Third Division felt the withering effects of summer weather. The historian of the 150th Pennsylvania noted the "intensely sultry" air. He added, "the men quickly felt the weight of their campaigning outfit, and perspired as they had rarely perspired before."[111]

Doubleday had time to place the new troops and reposition the First Division, taking advantage of a lull in the Confederate advance while Heth reorganized his forces. Engaging the enemy farther away from town made sense, but the First Corps lacked sufficient troops and artillery to hold back Hill's Corps for long. Doubleday knew maintaining the position until most of the army arrived would require immense casualties. When given the choice between the lives of his men and preserving a defensive position at a strategically important town, Doubleday made the only choice possible.

The First Corps commander was no longer the highest-ranking officer on the field. Oliver Howard of the 11th Corps was senior to Doubleday. Howard agreed with the need to hold the area west of town until forced back. In his autobiography, Howard remembered, "I returned to my headquarters feeling exceedingly anxious about the left flank." He continued with forebodings about "Doubleday's weak left" being "overlapped and pressed back."[112]

Making the Most of the Situation

Arrival of the 11th Corps provided additional troops to defend Gettysburg. Like the First Corps, the 11th was undermanned and heavily outnumbered as two divisions moved north of town to counter Ewell. Howard had hoped some elements of his corps could create a link with Doubleday's line, but Robert Rodes and his division of about 8,000 men were already occupying the space, known as Oak Hill. Even with the disadvantages of their position, Howard and Doubleday determined to stand as long as possible, with the final fallback position being Cemetery Hill, an exceptional defensive spot to the southeast.

On reaching the Seminary, Robinson first held his entire command in reserve. Paul's men were soon directed to build earthworks. Whatever defenses the men could create offered the chance for some protection for those making a final stand later on Seminary Ridge, something Doubleday envisioned the First Corps doing. Paul's regiments proceeded with their task using "vigor and haste" according to Charles Davis of the 13th Massachusetts.[113]

As Paul's laborers worked around the Seminary, Baxter went north, adding troops to Cutler's right flank. The 11th Pennsylvania and 97th New York initially moved toward the Railroad Cut. The two units then marched farther north, approaching Mummasburg Road. Some casualties occurred, including one killed from the 97th New York's Company F, part of Baxter's skirmish line. Then, as Baxter wrote, "The remaining four regiments were ordered forward in a very few moments, and formed on the right of the two already sent forward."[114]

Not all of the remaining four regiments in the brigade arrived along Mummasburg Road at the same time. The 12th Massachusetts was on the scene first. The entire brigade eventually formed an inverted "V" pointing toward Confederate units on Oak Hill, with the Mummasburg Road on their right. The 12th Massachusetts manned the point of the position, with the 90th Pennsylvania, 9th New York State Militia, and 88th Pennsylvania on the right along the road. The 11th Pennsylvania and 97th New York formed the left of the "V" position, facing northwest. Baxter was essentially alone; his men had no contact with the 11th Corps' left, and a gap existed between Baxter's left and Cutler's right.[115]

Baxter did not have the luxury of keeping any of his regiments in reserve. With so little time—and visible signs of Rodes's five brigades taking position on Oak Hill—having all six regiments on a firing line facing multiple directions was undoubtedly the best Baxter could do. Serious work was about to begin on the right flank of the First Corps.

Although not directly connected, Baxter's Brigade received help from some in the 11th Corps as Rodes was preparing his forces. For the early part of the afternoon, a highly accurate cannoneer and some infantry from the 11th Corps, now under the command of Carl Schurz, protected Baxter's isolated command. The infantry units were from the brigade of Col. George von Amsberg. Excellent shooting was unleashed from Hubert Dilger's Ohio battery. One shot was seen striking a Confederate gun directly in the opening of the barrel.[116]

To the south, Doubleday worried about his position west of town. The Chambersburg Pike offered the Confederates a good road to advance. As Doubleday recalled, "I was very desirous to hold this road, as it was in the centre of the enemy's line." Additionally, by marching up the Fairfield Road to the south, Hill could possess a direct route around Doubleday's left flank.[117]

Herr Ridge to the west of the McPherson Farm and Herbst Woods gave Hill a great place to launch infantry or pound the First Corps with artillery. Stone's Brigade quickly learned of the danger after being posted south of the Chambersburg Pike among McPherson's house and buildings. Midday cannon fire was damaging to the 149th Pennsylvania and unnerving to other troops. Heth's morning repulse did not knock the fight out of the Confederates.[118]

Commanding the brigade most at risk from Confederate artillery, Stone would reposition his regiments in an effort to garner some protection from roaring shells flying in from multiple directions. Arriving at the McPherson property before noon, the three regiments first formed a line facing west. A company from each regiment moved closer to the Confederates on skirmish duty, a task admirably performed, according to Col. Langhorne Wister of the 150th. The trio of companies "fought splendidly." Col. Walton Dwight, 149th Pennsylvania, praised the conduct of Capt. John Johnson and his Company K while posted to probe Hill's line to the west. "The skirmishing of Johnson was lively," Dwight reported, adding, "Loss, severe; conduct, excellent."[119]

With casualties from artillery fire mounting, multiple alignment changes occurred for Stone's three regiments. The troops would meet Confederate attacks with the 150th Pennsylvania as the only one of Stone's regiments still peering toward Herr Ridge. Forming a right angle with the 150th, the 149th and 143rd gazed north along the pike, still subject to artillery fire. The original line of three skirmish companies remained in place.[120]

None of the three brigades south of the pike were connected with another. Closest to Stone, the Iron Brigade solidified its hold on Herbst Woods east of Willoughby Run. The 19th Indiana had switched places with the 24th Michigan. The Hoosiers now manned the left flank of the Iron Brigade.

On the left flank of the First Corps, Chapman Biddle's Brigade lined up to the left rear of the Iron Brigade. The rookie 151st Pennsylvania went forward at first with the other three regiments but then backtracked to the Seminary as a reserve. Like Stone, Biddle's command had to change positions on several occasions to minimize danger from Confederate artillery. A 121st Pennsylvania man suggested Confederate cannoneers "seemed to particularly favor" shooting at the "conspicuous target" Biddle's line offered. After some time, the men were ordered to lie down to await what was the inevitable Confederate assault.[121]

Alexander Biddle likely agreed with his cousin's realignment of the brigade. Nonetheless, the unknowns of the afternoon and the lack of flank protection impacted morale. As the commander of the 121st Pennsylvania reported, "The constant changes of position which the regiment was ordered to make, and the seeming uncertainty of which way we were to expect an attack, or what position we were to defend, was exceedingly trying to the discipline of the regiment."[122]

Two More Confederate Brigades Humbled

The three bullet wounds Henry Baxter suffered in 1862 did not knock the fight out of him. With six solid regiments in his inverted "V" formation and assistance from the 11th Corps several hundred feet to his right, Baxter's first major engagement as a brigade commander would demonstrate his mettle once again. The pluck of Baxter's men and disjointed attacks from two brigades under Rodes made the early afternoon a period of great success for Meade's army. With their strong showing along the Mummasburg Road, Baxter's men displayed why they were second to none in the First Corps.

Rodes grew concerned about the arrival of the 11th Corps and movements of First Corps troops to the south. Then, Baxter's first two regiments appeared, heading toward Oak Hill. The Unionist skirmishers, simply by marching toward Rodes, did much to ruffle the feathers of the Confederate general. Alarmed, Rodes decided to attack as quickly as possible, because he felt "threatened from two directions." This was not really the case. Rodes had to know the rest of Ewell's Corps was approaching to keep the 11th Corps quite busy north of Gettysburg.

Because Baxter "was rash enough to come out from the woods to attack me," Rodes reported, "I determined to meet him when he got to the foot of the hill I occupied." He had no reason to hastily attack the unknown position. Rodes's decision generally receives a pass from historians who criticize less respected men like Edward O'Neal and Alfred Iverson, brigade commanders who performed poorly on July 1. Thirty minutes of further study would have served Rodes well. An officer in the 12th North Carolina, on Iverson's right, summed up Rodes's misreading of Baxter's moves perfectly: "He mistook the process of formation for defense for an advance upon him."[123]

With O'Neal moving first and starting much closer to Baxter than Iverson, the Confederates fell victim to teamwork between two Union corps. Continuing to harass Rodes's troops as they moved forward, 11th Corps cannons and infantry contributed to stopping O'Neal. With Baxter's determined units also pouring lead into the charging Southerners, O'Neal had no hope. For reasons never fully explained, only three of O'Neal's five regiments took part in the attack.[124]

O'Neal reported his fight with Baxter lasting thirty minutes. One Confederate officer cut the duration in half. Either way, O'Neal's men found Baxter "strongly posted and in heavy force." After receiving a First Corps bullet in the hip, an officer in the 12th Alabama recalled, "It was wonder, a miracle, I was not afterwards shot a half dozen times." He added, "After long exposure to heavy fire from a superior force of the enemy, we were ordered to fall back."[125]

The disaster was only just beginning. The inept work of Iverson would doom his career and culminate in the outright slaughter of his men. Nearly all of Baxter's six-regiment front shifted to directly face Iverson's sweeping diagonal line, which started on the Forney farm. Baxter's right rested along the Mummasburg Road, where part of the 90th Pennsylvania faced north. Otherwise, the regiments gazed primarily west and slightly north, finding cover from the lay of the land and a stone fence hiding the Union soldiers from Iverson's advance. To the left of the 90th Pennsylvania, the brigade included the 12th Massachusetts, its right on the road, followed by the 88th Pennsylvania, 9th New York State Militia, 97th New York, and the left flank manned by the 11th Pennsylvania.[126]

Some artillery fire harassed Iverson's formation, a member of the 23rd North Carolina recalled. In the right-center regiment moving against Baxter, this Tar Heel saw how the lack of a guiding hand from Iverson contributed to the catastrophe. "Our alignment soon became false," the Confederate lamented. Seeing the long rocky shield Baxter's men made use of, the North Carolinian added, "There seems to have been utter ignorance of the force crouching behind the stone wall." The 12th North Carolina, farthest from Baxter's men, escaped serious damage, but most in the attacking column were "at the mercy of the enemy."[127]

The withering opening fire against the Tar Heels may be considered one of the finest moments in the history of the First Corps. The 9th New York State Militia's historian summed up the thundering desolation from a thousand muskets by noting, "Rarely has such a destructive volley been fired on any field of battle." Sources suggest 500 Confederates dropped from Baxter's opening fire. The surprise from the overwhelming sheet of flame about 200 feet away withered Iverson's line, "and sent them streaming back toward the left in defenseless confusion," a Pennsylvanian wrote. Leading his 11th Pennsylvania, "Fighting Dick" Coulter suggested the North Carolinians experienced "a galling and effective fire," with Baxter himself reporting how his brigade's aim forced the Confederates "to recoil and give way."[128]

Lt. Oliver Williams of the 20th North Carolina, the regiment second from the left of Iverson's line, would not dispute the words First Corps men used to describe the impact of Baxter's volleys. "I was wounded early in the fight. I believe every man who stood up was either killed or wounded," Williams wrote.[129] Hugging the ground was the best hope to save oneself during those horrible few moments south of the Mummasburg Road.

Forney's field offered no cover for the remnants of Iverson's brigade. A gulley in the rear was the closest thing to protection the men could find, and that provided nothing of relative value in the vain effort against Baxter's zealous infantry. Soon after the hopelessness of their position was apparent, signs of surrender arose, with some of Baxter's officers concerned about the possibility of a trap. The time for good leadership was obvious, and Henry Baxter never showed fear at such moments. Although the exact impulse for a charge was not consistently reported, the historian of the 88th Pennsylvania recalled how the debate over the Confederates setting a trap was broken when Baxter "advised an application of cold steel."[130]

Lt. Col. John Spofford of the 97th New York, mounted and on the left of the regiment, also saw the benefits of charging. Spofford was not in command of the 97th but called on the men to leap the wall and go after the enemy. Admitting later that his order, if creating disaster, likely meant dismissal from the army, Spofford rightly suggested, "The moment was critical." During the westward assault against Iverson, Spofford came close to losing his life. As a newspaper reported, "nearly one half of his hat was carried away by a piece of shell during this charge; his horse was hit in the head; but he escaped uninjured."[131]

Col. Charles Wheelock did not interfere with Spofford's action. Instead, the regiment's commander went forward with his exuberant troops. In his report, Wheelock noted Spofford "acted most bravely" during the battle. The 11th Pennsylvania joined the 97th in the charge.[132]

Sgt. Edward Gilligan, Company E, 88th Pennsylvania, had to work harder than he likely desired after firing at and then charging Iverson's line. His company commander, Capt. Joseph Richard, was ensnared in a hand-to-hand fight with the color-bearer of the 23rd North Carolina. Gilligan quickly laid down the law by clubbing the unfortunate Confederate. In addition to capturing the flag while earning the gratitude of his superior officer, Gilligan's action won him a Medal of Honor.[133]

Although Baxter's opening volley was devastating, one member of the brigade wrote, "it was the charge immediately ordered by General Baxter that produced the greatest demoralization" among Iverson's survivors. Various regiments in the brigade brought in several hundred prisoners and some battle flags to mark the impressive and rapid demise of another Confederate brigade at the hands of the First Corps.[134]

Obliterating Iverson did not mean Baxter's men were safe. The troops found themselves as helpless as the doomed North Carolinians, at least for a moment. A Pennsylvanian recalled, "a galling fire in front and flank rendered the place too hot to hold," prompting a retrograde back to the stone wall, with the Confederate prisoners coming along.[135]

Rodes still had plenty of troops left. Fire from the other side of Mummasburg Road continued to damage the Union brigade. Col. James Bates of the 12th Massachusetts was hit in the neck. The brave Bay State officer received aid from a member of the regiment, who tied a handkerchief around the colonel's neck because the wound was very bloody. When a lieutenant offered to take Bates to the rear, the colonel refused the help, saying all available officers must be on the firing line. Only after receiving a second wound did Bates leave the field.[136]

Other men saw the necessity of protecting the brigade's right. Thinking fast, Maj. Alfred Sellers of the 90th Pennsylvania, who was only twenty-seven years old, would win a Medal of Honor for his heroics. The valiant officer "led the regiment under a withering fire to a position from which the enemy was repulsed."[137]

Most accounts of men from Cutler's Brigade do not detail much of their battle against the North Carolinians. Near the left of the 11th Pennsylvania, Cutler's five regiments lined up to the south. Dawes and the 6th Wisconsin were close by, providing battery support. Clearly, Baxter inflicted the most damage on Iverson. Nonetheless, Cutler's troops fired a large number of rounds during the contest.[138]

No one but Rodes had the responsibility for placing the division's two worst brigade commanders at the apex of the attack. He should have done more to align the two attacking brigades while ensuring a simultaneous attack. Moreover, where was Rodes and what was the division commander doing as Iverson's regiments were being so easily captured in Forney Field? Baxter's men were fired on from the hill to the north, but the time offered a brilliant chance for Rodes to sweep Baxter from the field and perhaps change the course of the war. This seems to be another area where Rodes escapes unscathed from most historians.[139]

Stalwart work from Baxter's Brigade went along with unimaginative Confederate leadership to doom two more Southern brigades on July 1 at Gettysburg. Robert Rodes needed more time to get revenge against the First Corps for South Mountain. After shaking off the embarrassment of his first attacks at Gettysburg, the Southern warrior would not have long to wait.

"Any Unusual Danger"

The rest of the First Corps line would soon be pressed. No new Union soldiers arrived after the 11th Corps lined up north of town. Conversely, Lee's army had masses of fresh troops arriving to the west, near the First Corps' three brigades south of the Chambersburg Pike. The Confederates held a major manpower advantage against Stone, Meredith, and Biddle.

Lined up on Herr Ridge against the three First Corps brigades south of the pike were Heth's other two brigades. Johnston Pettigrew commanded what to many of the Union soldiers appeared as a division. The four North Carolina regiments had about 2,500 men, stretched out against both Biddle and Meredith. The two Unionist brigades had slightly fewer soldiers combined than the men they were facing. Pettigrew's largest regiment, the 26th North Carolina, was also the largest in Lee's army.[140]

In the early afternoon, Doubleday requested more troops from Howard, who was holding an 11th Corps division in reserve on Cemetery Hill. Perhaps Doubleday would have preferred to withdraw the First Corps prior to an afternoon Confederate attack. Howard's idea was for Doubleday to wait for a retreat until after renewed Confederate pressure reached a breaking point. This likely made the First Corps commander acknowledge a fate he seemingly accepted anyway. "Final success in this war can only be attained by desperate fighting, and the infliction of heavy loss upon the enemy," Doubleday wrote. Besides, Howard had a better view of the field from Cemetery Hill. As Doubleday reported, Howard "could overlook all the enemy's movements as well as our own, and I therefore relied much upon his superior facilities for observation to give me timely warning of any unusual danger."[141]

The imperative to stand on McPherson Ridge raised concerns among Doubleday's regimental leaders. Skirmishers along Willoughby Run stayed busy, adding to the signs of impending enemy advance. Colonels Morrow and Robinson, of the 24th Michigan and 7th Wisconsin respectively, requested redeployment to a better location. As Morrow was told, "The position was ordered to be held, and must be held at all hazards." Colonel Williams of the 19th Indiana, on the left of the brigade line in an area with fewer trees, informed his men, "Boys, we must hold our colors on this line, or lie here under them."[142]

To the south, Rowley's First Brigade faced grim reality without the benefit of the trees protecting the Iron Brigade. One Confederate described the area in front of Biddle as offering "no other obstruction than the nearly ripe wheat." Rowley could see the impossibility of prolonged resistance, "The disparity between the contending forces was too great to render it possible for our line to hold its position."[143]

Chapman Biddle and his four regiments faced a great deal of unknowns by early afternoon. The brigade commander must have felt an eerie unease, especially after the 151st Pennsylvania returned to the Seminary as the only reserve south of the Chambersburg Pike. With no new troops to call on, Biddle, with perhaps 800 muskets across three regiments, stood as the most isolated First Corps brigade.

Being the unsupported left flank of the corps must have been unnerving enough. Lack of a competent division commander also rankled. Biddle's annoyance with an absent Rowley undoubtedly rose after receiving Confederate fire from near the Harman Farm, west of Willoughby Run. Theodore Gates, leading the 20th New York State Militia, found James Wadsworth south of the Chambersburg Pike, essentially acting as Third Division commander. Wadsworth endorsed the idea to go after the bothersome Confederates.

Gates called on "a most capable and courageous officer," Capt. Ambrose Baldwin, Company K of the 20th, to push the Confederates out of the Harman buildings. Baldwin took his forty men to the west. After some initial success, a counterattack from Tar Heels in Heth's Division prompted the call for more support. Biddle obliged by having Gates send Capt. William Cunningham's Company G to assist.[144]

By taking control of the farm buildings, Gates's two companies solidified the area to the west of the First Corps' left flank, bringing some pause to the renewal of the Confederate attack. The 52nd North Carolina, near the Harman Farm, grew "greatly annoyed" by the fire from men under Baldwin and Cunningham.[145] Doubleday, Wadsworth, and all their troops south of the pike could use the time the two companies bought.

The first sign of serious trouble for the First Corps south of the pike was Confederate pressure from the north, not Herr Ridge. Junius Daniel's excellent brigade of North Carolinians, part of Rodes's Division, were rapidly sweeping to the south, about to hit Stone's line.[146]

TENACITY WRITTEN IN STONE

Junius Daniel had the misfortune of commanding the brigade in line behind Alfred Iverson prior to the first Confederate attacks from Oak Hill. Daniel seemed perplexed by Iverson's decision to swing sharply to the left as the assault began. With four regiments and one battalion from North Carolina, Daniel gave some support to Iverson. This left only the 2nd Battalion and 45th Regiment initially moving south toward Stone.[147]

Stone witnessed the disorganized beginnings of the Confederate advance. He even reported some of his Pennsylvanians firing at long range. They likely did not impact Daniel from such a distance. As Stone prepared to receive the attack, several pieces of First Corps artillery found a tremendous opportunity to deal out damage from Seminary Ridge. Among Stewart's gunners, double rounds of canister were used against Daniel, whether the North Carolinians were advancing toward the western side of the Railroad Cut against Stone or supporting Iverson.[148]

The young Pennsylvania brigade commander made two excellent decisions prior to Daniel's arrival near the Chambersburg Pike. First, Stone ordered the colors of the 149th Pennsylvania to the northwest, in a successful effort to draw enemy fire to the flags as a means to protect infantry. Then, Stone ordered Lt. Col. Walton Dwight of the 149th to take his regiment north of the pike to occupy the Railroad Cut. This advanced infantry planted a firm line of muskets in ambush against Daniel. Marching from lower ground, the Confederates could not see Dwight's line.[149]

Dwight suggested his advanced colors, to the left of the regiment as the men awaited Daniel's first wave, attracted a good deal of fire from the Confederates. As Daniel's men stood behind a rail fence only twenty-two paces north of the cut, the 149th began firing. "Its effects on the enemy were terrible," the regimental commander reported. Shortly after reforming his lines, Daniel tried again, with Dwight noting his opponent's "most desperate effort." During Daniel's second attack, Dwight's men lost heavily. But the brave stand at the cut left "the enemy's dead and wounded completely covering the ground in our front."[150]

Like American warriors earlier in the day, men from both sides learned the advantages and disadvantages of the Railroad Cut. Stewart's section of guns in particular helped Dwight defend the area, but Confederate guns could also do their worst. With artillery to the west pointing down the cut, Dwight saw the potential for the slaughter of his regiment. With the cut being very deep in some places, soldiers in the 149th had to scramble quickly to escape canister fire from the left or Daniel's men from above. Members of the regiment farther to the west had the most trouble getting out after Dwight called for a retreat. A soldier from the 150th suggested men in his sister regiment returned to the position south of the pike in "a very scattering order," including the loss of perhaps thirty prisoners.[151]

Daniel was held in high regard by his command, and he was a much better brigade commander than Iverson or O'Neal. Daniel proved his tactical acumen while rallying his forces for a renewed offensive against Stone. Part of his commanding presence was a voice capable of being heard above the din at great distances. Determined soldiers from two armies became locked in a horribly lethal brawl.

The 143rd Pennsylvania contributed to the protection of the 149th, then the two regiments worked in tandem as Daniel pressed his attack. A Confederate gave credit where due as he recalled the bloody afternoon. The Southern veteran wrote, "These regiments were from the lumber region of Pennsylvania and were expert riflemen." Their volleys, he continued, "were said by the Confederate officers to have been the most destructive they ever witnessed."[152]

Daniel was capable of returning fire in droves. The enemy's pressure had a devastating impact on men across Stone's three regiments. The historian of Pennsylvania units accurately summed up the impact of the Daniel-Stone battle lines as "fearful slaughter."[153]

The 32nd North Carolina joined the fray on Daniel's right, with the potential to flank the 150th, then the entire Pennsylvania line. The 32nd grew tentative in the early part of the fight due to the unexpected presence of the Railroad Cut, but the men pressed on. Gaining an initial advantage, the Tar Heels felt strong volleys from the determined defense of the McPherson Farm and Unionist artillery. As the colonel of the 32nd reported, the cannons "thoroughly commanded" the area of his regiment's flank attack, creating "a terrific fire."[154]

The 150th Pennsylvania had to be skillfully led to meet the dangers from two directions. Soldiers moved to the pike and beyond for a short time, as part of the regiment faced north. Then, the men formed a right angle to confront the threat from the 32nd, as well as a few men from Davis's Brigade in reserve to the west. Sgt. William Ramsey recalled the chaos. The seesaw moments of the regiment concluded with a return to face west again when Maj. Thomas Chamberlin received a serious wound. Lt. Col. Henry Huidekoper had some volunteers move Chamberlin out of immediate danger. Ramsey thought Chamberlin was mortally wounded as the officer was placed in the McPherson house. Thankful for the help, Chamberlin, who would live well into the twentieth century and write the regiment's history, implored the men for some water—then ordered their return to the battle.[155]

During charge and counter charge across the Chambersburg Pike and McPherson parcel, fearful losses occurred among the high command of Stone's Brigade. Stone went down with a hip wound, elevating Colonel Wister of the 150th to brigade command. Wister also suffered a wound, giving Edmund Dana of the 143rd leadership of the brigade, a title he certainly could not have coveted during the carnage. Wister's mouth injury was rather bloody and prohibited him from talking. Lieutenant Colonel Dwight was inspired to see several injured officers still on the field "cheering their men on to noble deeds by their actions." Dana reported, "The contest soon became severe and close."[156]

One of the captains lost was Alfred Sofield, leader of Company A, 149th Pennsylvania. The captain's demise occurred during a charge toward the Railroad Cut, a counterattack against Daniel's bloodied but determined men. "As a gentleman and man possessed of true courage and coolness, he had no superior," Dwight wrote of Sofield. The same shell tearing the brave captain in half killed two other men in the regiment. Sofield rests at Gettysburg National Cemetery.[157]

Huidekoper took the reins of the 150th after Wister's elevation. Huideko-per suffered a wound that would cost him an arm. He must have been one of the men Dwight saw with the fortitude to remain on the field while injured. For his intrepid leadership, Huidekoper would win the Medal of Honor. His citation reads, "While engaged in repelling an attack of the enemy, received a severe wound of the right arm, but instead of retiring remained at the front in command of the regiment." Capt. Cornelius Widdis—only twenty-three years old—became the third commander of the 150th within a few minutes.[158] The maelstrom continued; the God of Battles cares not how many a youthful countenance appears on those leading at the front.

Extreme pressure against the First Corps line south of the Chambersburg Pike was about to begin. The renewed advance from Heth portended disaster. The bitter denouement Doubleday and so many others saw began to unfold.

"YELLING LIKE DEMONS"

As Pennsylvanians struggled mightily against Daniel, Iron Brigade soldiers began their fierce resistance immediately to the south in Herbst Woods. Pettigrew's Brigade assaulted the area with Colonel Burgywn's 26th North Carolina and the 11th North Carolina targeting Meredith's men, while the 47th and 52nd North Carolina confronted Biddle on the Confederate right. Additionally, Brockenbrough's Brigade moved out to the north of Pettigrew. The brigade of Virginians eventually pressured Stone's men as well as the 2nd and 7th Wisconsin on the northern part of the Iron Brigade's line.

"It was a hotly contested field," a North Carolinian recalled, where the "stubborn resistance of the 'Iron Brigade' was met with more than equal determination on the part of Pettigrew's Brigade." Against the impressive line of the largest Confederate brigade on the field, a Tar Heel wrote, Union troops "fought as they had never done before." Witnessing the persistent attack of his own men and the resolute determination of the First Corps, the North Carolinian concluded, "I have taken part in many hotly contested fights, but this I think, was the deadliest of them all."[159]

Firing from the Union troops began while Pettigrew's large force was still west of Willoughby Run. Morrow and his Michigan boys wanted to make sure every shot counted. He therefore ordered his men to withhold fire until the Confederates grew closer. "This was done," Morrow reported, "but the nature of the ground was such that I am inclined to think we inflicted but little injury." This conclusion gains corroboration in Confederate sources. Although some Tar Heels fell before reaching the creek, the Iron Brigade's "aim was too high to be very effective," the assistant surgeon of the 26th North Carolina wrote. Much to Morrow's chagrin, the Confederate attack "was not checked, and they came on with rapid strides, yelling like demons."[160]

Further to the left, Company B, 19th Indiana served as skirmishers. With experience in the important role of observing and slowing an enemy, Company B, even when reinforced by others in the regiment, simply could not effectively screen Pettigrew's large and unwavering force. Although fearless Sgt. Maj. Asa Blanchard courageously moved forward to bring several of the company back to the regiment's line, some members of Company B were wounded or captured early in the engagement. Seeing some of their comrades swept up by enemy skirmishers cast another disturbing pall over the Hoosiers manning the left flank of the Iron Brigade.[161]

Multiple reasons explain the especial peril the 19th Indiana faced. The Hoosiers were still in Herbst Woods, but the cover was considerably less than on the immediate right, the line of the 24th Michigan. The Wisconsin men farther north held the best part of the brigade's line, thanks to the considerable amount of tree cover. Also, the unsupported nature of the flank position was obvious. Biddle's men were lined up several hundred feet away, so the 19th Indiana's left dangled in the summer heat.[162] Perhaps the 6th Wisconsin should have returned to the Iron Brigade before Heth's afternoon attack.

The disparity in numbers presented the most pressing danger to the Hoosiers. As Carolinians and Westerners blazed away at each other along the line, the 11th North Carolina—with twice as many men as the 19th Indiana—moved to exploit the Hoosier's unsupported flank.

After returning to the regiment, Company B had another impossible task: placement on the brigade's left flank. Skilled skirmishers, the men knew to drop to the ground as they saw enemy troops about to fire. This

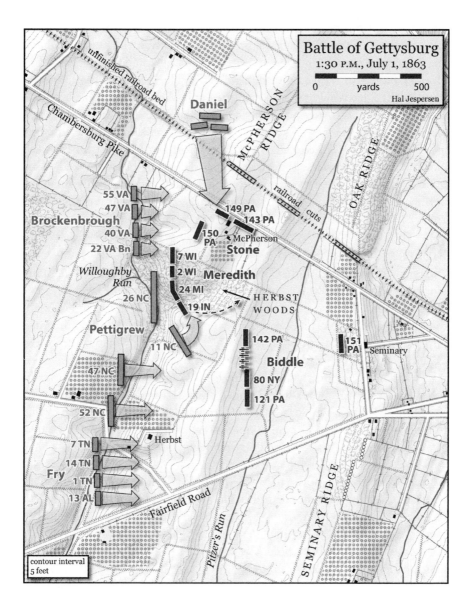

Battle of Gettysburg
1:30 P.M., July 1, 1863

0   yards   500

Hal Jespersen

unfinished railroad bed

Chambersburg Pike

McPHERSON RIDGE

OAK RIDGE

Daniel

railroad cuts

55 VA

47 VA

Brockenbrough

40 VA

22 VA Bn

149 PA

143 PA

150 PA

McPherson

Stone

7 WI

2 WI

Meredith

24 MI

19 IN

HERBST WOODS

Willoughby Run

26 NC

Pettigrew

11 NC

142 PA

Biddle

80 NY

121 PA

151 PA

Seminary

47 NC

52 NC

7 TN

Herbst

14 TN

Fry

1 TN

13 AL

Fairfield Road

Pitzer's Run

SEMINARY RIDGE

contour interval
5 feet

saved lives. The small company faced south to brace for the flanking Confederates as fire decimated the 19th Indiana. Still, the Hoosiers maintained their original position for a time, buying precious minutes before the regiment's retreat to a new line.

The stand of the 19th Indiana proved very costly, with twenty dead and one hundred wounded in a few minutes. Casualties were being inflicted by Hoosier bullets in return, with dozens of Tar Heels falling. The immortal stand of the 24th Michigan also exhibited epic Western grit. One Confederate wrote of the steady progress against Meredith's line requiring "great sacrifice of life." As the Westerners formed a second line up the hill, one of the few officers well enough to write the post-battle report for the 26th North Carolina witnessed heartbreaking slaughter. He remarked, "The fighting was terrible—our men advancing, the enemy stubbornly resisting, until the two lines were pouring volleys into each other at a distance not greater than 20 paces."[163]

BIDDLE'S DOOMED STAND

Chapman Biddle was another officer in the First Corps who had flanking North Carolinians to worry about. With cannon fire from Oak Hill a key concern, Biddle's men were facing north as Pettigrew began the attack. With the 47th and 52nd North Carolina moving forward, Biddle placed his men into the western-facing position from which the brigade would confront the assault. The Unionists had perhaps 300 fewer men than the duo of Tar Heel regiments moving directly toward the First Corps' southernmost brigade. From left to right, Biddle's line included the 121st Pennsylvania, 20th New York State Militia, Reynolds's Battery (commanded by Lt. George Breck due to a previous injury to the senior cannoneer), and the 142nd Pennsylvania. The 151st Pennsylvania remained on Seminary Ridge.[164]

Like their Confederate comrades to the north, soldiers in the 47th and 52nd North Carolina moved forward in grand style and with a sense of their imminent victory. "The morale of the men was splendid," a man in the 47th recorded. He suggested Pettigrew's command moved forward "with the feelings of conquerors." As inevitable as seizing Gettysburg appeared, the outmanned Unionists had the firepower to lessen the enemy's bravado. A First Corps cannon blast killed three men on the right side of the 47th's advance, "and exploding in the line of file closers, by the concussion, felled to the earth every one of them."[165]

Colonel Gates of the 20th New York State Militia was impressed with the artillery support Biddle received. "A torrent of death-dealing missiles leaped from the guns," he declared, and "Terrible rents were made; but closing up, they came on undaunted." The appreciative New Yorker concluded, "Never were guns better served; and though the ground was strewn with the slain, their line seemed instantly to grow together." The intensity of the Northern resistance led Alexander Biddle, 121st Pennsylvania, to proclaim, "The immediate attack on our front was destroyed by our first fire."[166] Still, the Southerners pressed ahead.

Confederate soldiers had a reputation of being ragged, dirty, and donning garb of various colors, not the stereotypical gray. John D. S. Cook, a company commander in the 20th New York State Militia, did not brag about his men beating the enemy in a fashion and cleanliness contest. Instead, Cook recalled, the Confederates "could shoot all right, and as they stood out there in line in the open field and poured in a rapid fire of musketry they gave us no time to criticise their appearance." With several men prone along Biddle's line, Cook added, "Our men sprang to their feet, returned their fire, and the battle was on."[167]

From the start of the engagement, Biddle's Brigade and the North Carolinians battled with resolute intensity. "The musketry rattle and artillery fire kept up such a constant roar as would bewilder men under any other circumstances," according to the regimental history of the 121st Pennsylvania. A "leaden storm" fired into each battle line caused immense suffering, with skilled and stubborn battlefield commanders doing their utmost to keep men to their task. Chapman Biddle received great credit for leading his regiments at the vortex of carnage. Considering Biddle's example "remarkable," men in the left flank regiment of the First Corps benefited as their brigade commander rode along the line "cheering his men and urging them through that fiery ordeal." Called "a modest, unassuming gentleman," Biddle gained tremendous respect from the soldiers in his regiments.[168]

Pettigrew's ability to flank Biddle's left dictated the outcome on the field, regardless of the valor the First Corps brigade commander and his men exhibited. As the 121st began to break under fire from multiple directions, a North Carolinian noted, "The earth just seemed to open and take in that line which five minutes ago was so perfect." Gates wrote of the "terrible fire" the North Carolinians were able to pour "into our front and left flank."[169]

As if Captain Cook did not have enough trouble countering the Confederates, he was charged with keeping two men of shaky courage on the battle line. Cook remembered:

In the thick of the firing one of the men I was watching turned to run. I stopped him by presenting my revolver and turned him back into the line. As he turned he fell mortally wounded by a shot from the enemy and the next moment he had me clasped by the legs and begged piteously for help. Of course I could do nothing then to relieve him and he sank down in death.[170]

With his line starting to give way, Biddle's strong leadership continued. An amazed North Carolinian wrote, "Just then a Federal officer came in view and rode rapidly forward bearing a large Federal flag." Even with regiments losing ground, Biddle's men "swarmed around him as bees cover their queen." Enthralled by how Biddle ignored all danger to provide inspiration to his men, the enemy soldier concluded, "It was with genuine and openly expressed pleasure our men heard he was not killed." Biddle did sustain a minor head wound but quickly returned to rally his regiments while Breck removed his four cannons.[171]

The example Biddle set contributed to his soldiers' determination to delay the Confederate advance, even after the collapse of the brigade's initial line. Recalling the moment in his history of the 20th New York State Militia, Gates noted, "The parting volley on the ridge was very destructive, and while it checked the advance for a few minutes it taught the enemy caution. We damaged the enemy quite as much in our retreat as he did us."[172]

However doomed and short-lived, a counter charge from the 142nd Pennsylvania also let Confederates know plenty of life still existed in the Keystone Staters fighting on their own soil. Muskets had become so hot men along the line "were compelled to drop them, when they would take the one nearest the ground, rendered useless because the owner of it was dead," an officer of the 142nd noted. Col. Robert Cummins was one of the regiment's seriously wounded during this portion of the fight. Destined to die the following day, Cummins was "loyal and much-beloved." Biddle considered Cummins, originally a captain in the 10th Pennsylvania Reserves, "a brave and efficient officer," whose loss "has occasioned feelings of regret throughout the command."[173]

Dozens fell as Biddle worked to stabilize his men during the eastward ret-rograde to the higher ground along Seminary Ridge. While falling back, Gates said the brigade was "fighting so obstinately as they moved off that the enemy's pursuit was cautious and tardy." Finding a new position closer to the Seminary, regiments held their ground longer. James Balsley of the 142nd Pennsylvania thought the new position was about 50 yards east of the original line. He was probably incorrect in the duration of the relatively short resistance, which Balsley recalled being thirty minutes. He had already been hit twice while along the first line of his regiment. A third wound during the retreat may have been from friendly fire. Balsley was knocked down by the blast, but still alive. Balsley, who was only seventeen years old, perhaps wondered what his fate would be as an injured prisoner of war. He would live for more than sixty years.[174]

"LET THEM FLANK AND BE DAMNED"

Asa Blanchard likely figured he had moments to live while standing with remnants of the 19th Indiana. The determined soldier was only twenty years old. His life was less important to him than an unshakeable sense of duty, which required protection of the regiment's national standard. With other color-bearers already down in the southern part of Herbst Woods, Lt. Col. William Dudley, barely older than Blanchard, reached the fallen colors dur-ing the height of Pettigrew's attack. Dudley received a bullet in the right leg, which would cost him the limb. Blanchard told his injured friend he could never forgive himself knowing the colonel was hurt holding the flag. After others tried to pick up Old Glory, Blanchard begged Colonel Williams for the right to carry the colors. Shortly after winning the dispute, Blanchard received a wound to his groin, destroying an artery. He lived for only a few seconds.[175]

The flag Blanchard protected, stained with his blood, was in his sis-ter's possession for several years. In the 1880s, Dudley requested the flag be donated to the State of Indiana. Blanchard's sister agreed. Of the noble ser-geant, Dudley wrote, "No braver man fell that day in all the Union lines."[176]

Further Tar Heel trouble rippled up the Iron Brigade's line. The 24th Michigan was sorely victimized by the continued pressure of the 11th and 26th North Carolina. The death of Capt. William Speed—acting major for the regiment suffering so many casualties—was one of hundreds of tragic moments as the McPherson Ridge line gave way. A bullet to the heart quickly ended Speed's life. Remembering such a devoted officer, Morrow wrote, "Captain Speed's death was a severe loss to the service and an almost irreparable one to his regiment." Another officer, Maj. Edwin Wight, would lose an eye not far from where Speed fell. Knocked to the ground, Wight was able to continue the retreat with the remnants of the 24th.[177]

By the time the northern flank of Heth's attack got going, the 150th Pennsylvania had returned to a line fully facing west. If Brockenbrough acted with dash, his Virginians could have contributed more to the Union's retreat. Like so much of the First Corps' afternoon, the tide sweeping McPherson Ridge could not be resisted for long. As the regimental history of the 150th noted, "The enemy drew closer and closer, firing and loading as he advanced, but was met by a resistance which time and again staggered him, though it could not shake him off."[178]

On higher ground with more trees, the 2nd and 7th Wisconsin tried to hold on. Lt. Col. John Callis, who performed excellent service at South Mountain, became worried about the danger from Confederate flanking efforts. He communicated the concern to Capt. Henry Young. Of the fellow officer's retort, Callis wrote, "He replied in his peculiar way, 'let them flank and be damned, we are giving them hell in front.'"[179]

Young's lack of concern about the brigade's flanks proved he was an obstinate Unionist patriot, but his reply to Callis would not be enough to prevent a retreat. After all, the fire Badger warriors were doling out seemed less effective than Young's boast. Colonel Robinson reported, "The Second and Seventh were keeping up a rapid fire upon the enemy in front," but "without doing him much injury, as he was protected by the hill and timber." As the doomed stand of the Wisconsin men continued, Robinson received an order to begin retiring to Seminary Ridge.[180]

While hellfire overtook them, the Iron Brigade lost the services of General Meredith. Both the general and his horse were knocked to the ground. Meredith received a slight head wound from a shell. The more serious effects came when he could not escape the weight of his wounded horse. Meredith sustained serious leg and chest injuries, including painful damage to his ribs. He would be out of action until November.[181]

THE CHARGE OF THE 151ST PENNSYLVANIA

As the McPherson Ridge line faced imminent peril, the bold action of the 151st Pennsylvania bought additional time for the retreating First Corps. Rowley gave the in-person order to Col. George McFarland to plug the gap between elements of Meredith and Biddle's brigades. Hopping over the breastworks Paul's men had created earlier in the day, McFarland led forward more than 400 men.[182] Stopping the Confederate advance with his small force could not happen, but the untested regiment had a chance to make a difference. Like many other units on both sides of the day's battle, the 151st Pennsylvania earned a distinguished place in history—at an appalling price.[183]

Approaching Biddle's right flank, McFarland's men were hit hard before they had a chance to form a firing line. A commander with foresight, McFarland had already "cautioned the men against excitement and firing at random." Every shot finding a mark meant more time for the First Corps, so McFarland said the regiment was not instructed to unleash a coordinated volley. Rather, a soldier was "to fire as he saw an enemy on which to take a steady aim." The men obeyed the order, which added to the efficiency of the relatively limited firepower one regiment could unleash.

As Company C man Alva Adams wrote, "The material of this regiment was excellent, being composed of splendid marksmen and hardy men." They had the difficult goal of implementing McFarland's order while being hard-pressed themselves during the effort to fill in the dangerous space between two brigades. The tactical situation was as desperate as any First Corps troops faced in the war. Adams recalled, "There was a gap between the brigades of Biddle and Meredith, which was threatening fatality to the left wing."[184]

Immense harm was inflicted across McFarland's regiment. Company E would sustain forty-two casualties at Gettysburg, with one family mourning two men killed. First Lt. Aaron Seaman, the leader of the company, died instantly after a bullet to the head. William, his younger brother and a corporal, was also a fatality. Lt. Charles Potts, Company I, recalled the scene nearly half a century after the battle. He noted, "I could see we could not hold our position long, as the rebel reinforcements were being thrown on to our left flank, and our men gradually giving way."[185]

The Strause Family contributed greatly to the muster roll of the 151st. Across companies G and H, seven men from the family fought on July 1, including two sets of brothers. Six of the seven would be wounded. Adam and William W. Strause were injured in Company G, with William T. Strause killed in Company H, while John, Soloman, and William S. Strause received wounds serving in the latter company.[186]

Captain Lafayette "Lafe" Westbrook, commanding Company B on the left of the 151st Pennsylvania, ordered his men to scatter somewhat, essentially trying to form a belated skirmish line. The idea saved some lives, one member of the company suggested, by not presenting as connected a mass of men as a traditional battle line. Westbrook had a good approach, if judged by the casualty list. Company B suffered the second lowest number of losses in the regiment. Still, twenty-six men in Westbrook's command fell.[187]

Pvt. Michael Link, in hard-hit Company E, was another brave man trying to assist retreating units by giving pause to the pursuing North Carolinians. While on the firing line, the musician received a wound costing him both eyes.[188]

Surveying the dreadful scene, McFarland realized his regiment was the victim of another flank attack, the bane of First Corps units this day. Showing great pride in his regiment, McFarland recalled, "I know not how men could have fought more desperately." Battling with a "determined courage," McFarland witnessed how "gallant officers and men fell thick and fast."

Only the 24th Michigan, struggling slightly to the north of McFarland's regiment, would suffer more Union casualties at Gettysburg than the 151st Pennsylvania's 337. Casualties by company for the 151st are listed in Table 3.2.

By the time the Keystone Staters created a "considerable distance" between attacking Confederates and the retreating elements from Biddle and Meredith's brigades, McFarland knew his time to return to the Seminary had arrived. Finding his men "in danger of being surrounded," the brave officer ordered "the regiment to fall back, which it did in good order."[189]

Table 3.2: Casualties by Company in the 151st Pennsylvania at Gettysburg

Company	Killed	Wounded	Captured/Missing	Total
A	7	16	8	31
B	9	7	10	26
C	1	6	2	9
D	12	11	6	29
E	11	25	6	42
F	7	26	8	41
G	6	24	10	40
H	7	20	4	31
I	9	21	17	47
K	12	22	4	38
Total	81	178	75	334

Source: To the total casualties of 334 across the ten companies must be added three staff casualties, including commanding officer Lt. Col. George McFarland. This data was extracted from the list of individual casualties for the regiment in Dreese, *The 151st Pennsylvania Volunteers at Gettysburg: Like Ripe Apples in a Storm*, 157–60.

A certain degree of competition prevailed in Biddle's Brigade. The 20th New York State Militia was outnumbered three to one by Pennsylvania regiments. Concern existed among some Empire State soldiers about the fighting quality of their brigade comrades. This was especially true of the rookie 151st, which had never seen combat before. Witnessing the powerful charge from McFarland's men, Captain Cook said, "I can testify for them that they behaved as gallantly as veterans."[190]

ROBINSON'S RESISTANCE AND RETREAT

Robinson's Division faced the same general problem the First Corps south of the Chambersburg Pike was grappling to overcome: too few troops against a much larger number of Confederates. As Baxter's men were running out of ammunition, Paul's five regiments began to form on both sides of the line. With the continued need for protection from the north, the 13th Massachusetts and 104th New York faced that direction on the south side of the Mummasburg Road. The 104th was on the left of the 13th. Col. Gilbert Prey's New Yorkers formed a right angle with Baxter's line, still facing west. Paul's other three regiments were on Baxter's left, with the 107th Pennsylvania, 16th Maine, and 94th New York confronting Iverson's remnants and other elements of Rodes's Division.

Regardless of the poor leadership from some senior officers under Rodes, Robinson's men were in dire straits. The Second Division had little more than 2,000 men facing more than twice that number, even after O'Neal and Iverson's failed assaults. Robinson also had no artillery. Defending the line would be futile after Rodes figured out what to do.[191]

Paul's two north-facing regiments had plenty of work. The 13th Massachusetts was engaged before the rest of Paul's line formed to the left. The space was an initial concern of Lt. Col. N. Walter Batchelder of the 13th, who led the regiment after the early wounding of Colonel Leonard. The Bay Staters performed quite well as the right flank of the corps, even though the 13th's line did not directly connect with other regiments. Steady firing continued for a prolonged period (Batchelder wrote of an hour elapsing, but that was likely an overstatement). "Seriously annoyed" with enemy fire, the 13th Massachusetts charged across the road, with one Unionist declaring, "Give it to 'em for Fredericksburg!" Batchelder proudly saw his men "driving the enemy from their position, leaving in our hands 132 prisoners," including seven officers.[192]

Early success also occurred on the front of the 104th New York. Col. Gilbert Prey found Confederates "posted behind a stone wall covered with underbrush." This prompted Prey to send his "three left companies to gain the wall and dislodge the enemy," leading to another haul of prisoners, perhaps fifty.[193]

During the fight, the 107th Pennsylvania received direct help from General Robinson. The division commander, "finding many of the soldiers running out of cartridges, engaged in supplying them from the cartridge boxes of the dead and the wounded soldiers." One youngster on the firing line reportedly "received three cartridges from the general's own hand." Officers and color-bearers in the 107th were falling during the intense combat, so Robinson clearly had no problems entering dangerous spots on a contested field.[194] Such are the actions of generals exhibiting great leadership when their outnumbered men need all available help.

Growing Confederate pressure made Paul's strong start look less like victory. Leonard was not the brigade's most senior officer to fall. "While gallantly directing and encouraging his command," Gabriel Paul suffered a horrendous shot to the head. The bullet entered his right temple and exited his left eye. By some miracle, he would live for more than twenty years, albeit completely blind, with impaired senses, and suffering terrible seizures.[195]

Rodes's men may have been a confused morass lacking necessary leadership, but they had the numbers to push the undermanned First Corps division back, especially after the withdrawal of Baxter's troops, which occurred at about 3:00 P.M. Then, the good posting and tactics of Stephen Ramseur's brigade finally pressed Robinson's First Brigade back.

Ramseur was a shining star in the Confederate army. Only twenty-six years old, he led four North Carolina regiments down Oak Hill to near the spot where O'Neal started his feeble attack earlier in the afternoon. Ramseur saw the value of swinging around Robinson's right, placing the dwindling ranks of the Union regiments in a vice against a charge of other Confederates from the west. Ramseur was aided by the remnants of O'Neal's Brigade, who found the third time was the charm in their attack against Robinson. Ramseur rightfully receives great credit from history for his efforts, which provided the necessary vitality against the northern flank of the First Corps.[196]

Despite not having artillery or infantry support, the First Brigade did not collapse immediately. "Soon we were exposed to a severe fire," recalled an officer in the 4th North Carolina, Ramseur's left flank regiment. Nonetheless, men defending the area south of Mummasburg Road knew the impossibility of prolonged resistance. As the 13th Massachusetts historian wrote, "An officer in our rear was shouting for us to hold on as long as we could," but "our line looked ridiculously small." Ramseur's men knew they were fighting skilled Northerners under strong leaders. As Col. Francis Parker of the 30th North Carolina noted, "The fighting was of a desperate character, and our losses were heavy." Nonetheless, compared to First Corps brigades at Gettysburg, Ramseur's men essentially vacationed. Casualties were under 180 men across the four North Carolina regiments.[197]

Falling back became imperative for Robinson to save his men, with Adrian Root of the 94th New York acting as brigade commander, the third of the day. "We remained at the front until we were nearly surrounded," Maj. Sam Moffatt wrote shortly after the battle. He took command of the 94th when Root moved up to brigade leadership. Root was another man along the line wounded during the fight. Men from the brigade attempted to rally somewhat, with Robinson saying his men "retired fighting."[198]

Desperation ruled the crumbling line. As one historian wrote, "Already the First Corps had prolonged its gallant resistance beyond the limit of prudence; and it could be saved from destruction only by heroic sacrifices." The effort to avert disaster gave the 16th Maine a shot at immortality. Colonel Tilden received an order first from a staff officer to head back north in an attempt to stem the tide as close to the Mummasburg Road as possible. Lt. Col. Augustus Farnham said Robinson soon appeared to repeat the order "to take possession of a hill which commanded the road, and hold the same as long as there was a man left."

Moving forward on his impossible mission, Tilden formed the regiment in a reversed "V" in an effort to direct fire at Confederates charging from multiple directions. After a short time, Tilden had his men retreat, with many doomed to capture. More than one hundred Maine men were taken prisoner by some of Daniel's men and others near the eastern Railroad Cut. Barely 20 percent of the regiment escaped being a casualty on July 1. In a last act of defiance, several members of the regiment ripped up their flags, spreading the sacrosanct shards among them, with some keeping pieces of cloth through Confederate captivity. As Maine's adjutant general was informed on July 17, "The colors were torn to pieces to prevent capture."[199]

Dozens of men in the brigade's other regiments became prisoners during efforts to escape the Confederate swarm. Sgt. Sam Fuller, 94th New York—destined to die of wounds later in the month—wrote to a hometown newspaper shortly after the battle. Fuller had been "cornered up along with Capt.

McMahon, and ordered to surrender. Poor Jack! I never shall forget the look he gave me as he smashed his sword over a log."[200]

Jerome Fisher, a captain in the 104th New York, wrote a short letter on July 2 as a prisoner of war. This was Fisher's second stint as a captured man. The men of the regiment "were in the thickest of the fight, and are badly cut up. I am again a prisoner, with numerous others," Fisher reported. In mid-July another man in the 104th showed how weak many First Corps units were after Gettysburg: "Col. Prey, Major Strang, Dr. Rugg, and Lieut. McConnely are the only officers with the Regiment, which contains but 40 privates."

Some seriously wounded men in the 104th would survive. Lt. Col. Henry Tuthill was hit in the bowels. His condition seemed hopeless, but Tuthill survived days in a Gettysburg hospital, then convalescence at home in Corning. He would never take the field again, but had many years left. The brave officer lived until 1914.[201]

Root's return to brigade command was brief. After being wounded, he became a prisoner. Later in the day, with the 11th Pennsylvania detached from Baxter to join the First Brigade, "Fighting Dick" Coulter became the fifth commander of Paul's regiments on July 1.[202]

BLOODIED CONFEDERATES CONQUER THE FIELD
While Robinson struggled so hard to the north, First Corps soldiers to the south realized their own hopeless situation. Through all the chaotic maelstrom of wounds and death around them near the Chambersburg Pike, six members of the 149th Pennsylvania remained with their colors, still floating north of the road and south of the Railroad Cut.

With battle raging, the flags had ended up forgotten. Colonel Dwight saw his regiment under intense pressure from Daniel and Confederate artillery while the 149th was posted along the Railroad Cut. He did not have time to order the retreat of the small group guarding the detached colors. Dwight's command faced "certain surrender or destruction," so, "I saved the regiment and lost the colors."[203]

Sgt. Henry Brehm adamantly refused to leave his post near the fencing used to prop up the two flags, even after some men in the small band requested a return to the regiment. Because the flags had not moved in a while, Confederates to the west were drawn to the possibility of capturing what appeared as unprotected Unionist emblems. Some men from Davis's

Brigade decided to move forward at about the time Stone's men were starting to retreat. After giving a war whoop near the flags, the Confederates were startled when the six Pennsylvanians guarding the colors stood to protect their sacred banners.

During the melee, Brehm was able to wrestle an enemy soldier for the national colors, while seventeen-year-old Henry Spayd tried to escape with the regiment's state flag. Neither were standing long enough to reach friendly lines, which were now farther east due to the brigade's withdrawal. Brehm suffered a mortal wound from a shell, while four other members of the determined band sustained less serious injuries. Pvt. Frederick Hoffman was the only unscathed member of the brave group of six who went forward with the colors. He had previously been sent back to the regiment to seek orders for the flags' withdrawal but was unable to return to Brehm's group.

Franklin Lehman, 149th Pennsylvania, was one of the many dozens of young men in Stone's Brigade who fought brilliantly on July 1, 1863.
LIBRARY OF CONGRESS

Dwight received the blame from John Bassler, commander of the 149th's color company, for the wounds to five of his men and the loss of the regiment's two flags. Bassler alleged Dwight was drunk during the battle.[204] Perhaps blame does not belong to anyone. The decision to move the flags early in the battle drew Confederate artillery and musketry fire, undoubtedly saving lives. The sacrifice endured by the six men who took the flags forward epitomized courage at the battle of Gettysburg, where such a virtue was so readily in abundance.

Sgt. James Rutter, 143rd Pennsylvania, was another man showing great bravery during the retreat toward the Seminary. North of Chambersburg Pike, Rutter became aware of wounds to Capt. George Reichard, a well-liked leader of Company C. Dodging Confederate bullets, Rutter made his way to assist his injured superior. Although the brave deed was not mentioned in the regiment's report, others learned of the sergeant's act of valor. Rutter's Medal of Honor citation reads, "At great risk of his life went to the assistance of a wounded comrade, and while under fire removed him to a place of safety."[205]

Confederate general A. P. Hill witnessed the spirited act of another member of the 143rd Pennsylvania. Sgt. Ben Crippen wished the Confederates to know Keystone Staters were not pleased to yield ground at Gettysburg. Perhaps in an effort to caution Lee's army for what could be in store for them later in the battle, Crippen shook a raised fist at the advancing line of the enemy as he clutched a regimental flag on his retrograde toward the Seminary. His act gained immortality when the 143rd unveiled its regimental monument, which stands along Chambersburg Pike. Crippen's stone likeness shows him with raised fist, looking toward the west. Crippen's courage, based on the comments of a foreign observer, led Hill to feel "quite sorry when he had seen this gallant Yankee meet his doom."[206]

One member of the Iron Brigade would win a Medal of Honor while suffering a ghastly wound during the retreat. Like Mike Link and Gabriel Paul, Jefferson Coates would lose both eyes on July 1. One source describes how the wounded Coates had a Confederate benefactor.

> *A noble hearted Georgian carried him to a compassionate shade tree and sat him up against its scarred and bracing trunk, and brought him a canteen of water for which Mr. C. gave the Georgian half his coffee. There he sat, wrapped in darkness, in the enemy's lines, hungry, bleeding, friendless, day and night, till victory perched upon the Union banners, when his comrades found him and carried him into the city.*[207]

Through the horrible conflagration between the 24th Michigan and the 26th North Carolina starting in Herbst Woods, a total of twenty-three flag bearers were killed or wounded, including Colonel Morrow, who would become a prisoner. Greatly diminished, the Iron Brigade would quickly reform along Seminary Ridge.

Stalwarts until the end, the three regiments in Stone's Brigade fought incredibly well on the afternoon of July 1. Like other members of the First Corps south of the Chambersburg Pike, the three Pennsylvania regiments retreated to their final defensive line, near the Iron Brigade. Unlike initial positions earlier in the day, the last stand of the First Corps around the Seminary was well supported by nearby artillery. The Confederates had yet to win the field, and the First Corps was not ready to quit.

Confederate exhaustion was a primary factor in the orderly retreat of the three brigades south of the Chambersburg Pike. Heth's Division was not in a condition to press their advantage. Dorsey Pender sent units from his division to augment the attack, but the delay gave the First Corps time to improve defenses near the Seminary. A Confederate in Col. Abner Perrin's Brigade described the grisly ground over which he advanced from Herr Ridge: "The field was thick with wounded hurrying to the rear, and the ground was grey with dead and wounded."[208]

Doubleday and artillery commander Charles Wainwright spent time during the infantry's delaying action to assemble an impressive array of cannons. A heavy concentration of twelve guns stood near the Seminary, "massed at this point so closely that they were hardly five yards apart," according to Greenleaf Stevens of the 5th Maine Battery. Additionally, Stewart's dependable Battery B, 4th U.S. remained on either side of the Railroad Cut. Four guns first posted to assist Biddle were still near the southern portion of what would be the infantry's final line. Cannons assisted retreating infantry, "retarding the enemy by their fire," according to Doubleday.[209]

Excellent planning under the pressure of the afternoon allowed the First Corps to inflict massive losses on two of Pender's brigades prior to the day's final retreat to Cemetery Hill. Brig. Gen. Alfred Scales led his North Carolinians against the right of the First Corps' defensive line, posted on both sides of the Chambersburg Pike. In addition to artillery, Cutler's command, the Iron Brigade, and Stone's men were in the area. Perrin moved forward with five regiments from South Carolina against the left flank of the Union position manned by Biddle's regiments, Lieutenant Breck's battery, and some cavalry.[210]

Intense waves of fire were the main memory for Confederates writing about the charge against Seminary Ridge. Like Heth's earlier assault, Pender's men were in numbers sufficient to prevail, but Lee's army had to sacrifice greatly to take the position. Because Pender did not survive the battle, an adjutant wrote the division's report. Of the opening of the First Corps' defensive fire, the officer recalled how Scales "was met by a furious storm of musketry and shell from infantry posted behind temporary breastworks and artillery from batteries to the left of the road near Gettysburg." Meanwhile, Perrin's brigade "received a most withering and destructive fire, but continued to charge without returning the fire of the enemy until reaching the edge of the grove which crowns the crest of the ridge."[211]

The thinned Confederate ranks pressed on. An officer in Perrin's 12th South Carolina, directly across from Biddle's Brigade, recalled how the First Corps "opened on us with grape and canister to our left, while the infantry poured leaden hail in front; I received a grape shot in my right leg below the knee, which shattered the bone into splinters." Near the left of Pender's advance, the 13th North Carolina only had 30 of 180 men left after the harsh treatment from Stewart's guns and supporting infantry. "As so many had been shot down in the advance we did not have men enough for the final charge," the regimental adjutant wrote. On the left flank of Scales's line, the 38th North Carolina suffered intensely, with the First Corps launching "a most terrific fire," where "every discharge made sad loss in the line."[212]

On such a horrible killing ground, the Confederates pressed on, knowing the need to suffer further before being able to overtake the Unionist resistance. A member of Company K, 14th South Carolina, on Perrin's left, penned a vivid impression. He wrote of being close enough to hear First Corps officers giving orders and "distinctly encouraging their men to hold their fire, until the command to fire was given. They obeyed their command implicitly, and rose to their feet and took as deliberate aim as if they were on dress parade, and to show you how accurate their aim was, 34 out of our 39 men fell at the first fire of the enemy."[213]

First Corps batteries were firing dozens of canister rounds over a few short minutes, each shot adding hundreds of shards of metal to the desperate afternoon work. Sometimes the artillerists placed two rounds of canister in the barrel prior to firing. Stevens noted how his guns were turned to the right later in the attack as a means to hit Scales's men. The battery commander estimated his guns alone fired fifty-seven rounds of canister in the roughly twenty minutes from the beginning of the attack to the First Corps' retreat.[214]

As he stood admiring the work of Stewart's gunners, Rufus Dawes was happy to see the mass of Iron Brigade men and Stone's Pennsylvanians awaiting the order to fire. Reviewing "the splendid lines" of the enemy, Dawes added, "Their bearing was magnificent." Even as the Confederates sustained great losses, they also took down infantrymen in blue, as well as Stewart's cannoneers and horses.[215]

The impressive rates of fire into Scales's line left the North Carolinians unable to break through the defenses. Perrin's strong leadership proved decisive. With the 12th and 13th South Carolina engaging cavalry to his right, Perrin himself led the 1st South Carolina into the gap between Buford's horsemen and Biddle's left. Although the resistance from Doubleday's men remained notable, Biddle's flank unraveled, dooming the rest of the line.[216]

TO CEMETERY HILL

The day's fighting so far had proven the mettle of the First Corps. They had perhaps the hardest job in their history starting at about 4:20 P.M. on July 1: to extricate the command while under intense pressure on Seminary Ridge. General Howard's headquarters, at Cemetery Hill on the other side of town, was the beacon for whatever remaining First Corps troops could rally there. The only question was how many—or how few—men could make the journey safely. The task proved more difficult because the 11th Corps was retreating from the north with the same goal.

Colonel Williams of the 19th Indiana had enough to worry about just getting away from Seminary Ridge. With so many infantry units disorganized from the intense afternoon, Williams recalled, "I found it impossible to form my command and we retired, each to care for himself, through the town."[217]

With Robinson's Division and the Seminary Ridge line reeling under pressure, Lieutenant Stewart felt heartbreak with the necessity of retreat. In a speech years later, he remembered, "I did realize what the horrors of war meant. As I gave the command to limber to the rear, I could not bring my wounded with me, and the beseeching looks that these men gave me quite unnerved me, and I was sorry indeed to leave them to their fate."[218]

Through the horror, only one cannon was lost. Breck's great service this day could not keep the Confederates at bay long enough to save the gun after the loss of battery horses. A determined South Carolinian wrote, "The brigade set its heart upon the artillery that had so severely tried it." Wainwright reported a loss of eighty-three men and about eighty horses on July 1.[219] Strong leadership from artillerymen and officers, in addition to good support from nearby infantry, explains why nineteen of the twenty guns along Seminary Ridge were saved.

Horrible injuries were the fate of many men during the retreat. Colonel McFarland of the 151st Pennsylvania wrote poignantly of his terrible wound. As he was ordering his decimated regiment to Cemetery Hill,

> *I was hit by a flank fire in both legs at the same instant, which caused the amputation of my right leg, and so shattered my left that it is now, at the end of eight and a half months, still unhealed and unservice-able. I was carried into the seminary by Private Lyman D. Wilson, Company F, the only man near me, and who narrowly escaped, a ball carrying away the middle button of my coat-sleeve while my arm was around his neck.*[220]

Trying minutes awaited those who were left in the First Corps as the spent and famished troops escaped to the east and south. Much debate would arise about how well the 11th Corps had fought that day, which troops from which corps fled first, or ran the fastest to Cemetery Hill. Far more heat than light has been generated as a result of this unfortunate competition. This book will not dwell on the matter. Certainly, the 11th Corps had major leadership problems, starting at the top with Oliver Howard, but even he would prove excellent during the late afternoon crisis while organizing the defense on Cemetery Hill. The 11th Corps should not receive harsh criticism for its performance on July 1, and neither should the First Corps. Retreat was inevitable for both commands, and the two units inflicted significant losses on the Confederates. James Pula makes this case very well in his recent history of the 11th Corps.[221]

Capt. Charles M. Conyngham, Company A, 143rd Pennsylvania was one of so many who experienced an exceedingly trying day. Leading the regiment's skirmishers on McPherson Ridge, Conyngham received his first wound but remained at his post. He also stood with the regiment on Seminary Ridge. While nearing Cemetery Hill, Conyngham received help from Lieutenant Colonel Musser. The regimental commander recalled, "I saw him, after we had passed through town, seemingly exhausted, and ordered my horse back to help him up the hill, but, just as he was mounting, he was again shot in the hip." Unable to assist further, Musser did not see Conyngham after his second wound. Two months later, less than a week shy of his twenty-third birthday, Conyngham would be promoted to major.[222]

"HE BEING DEAD, YET SPEAKETH"

One officer added to the casualty rolls was not imploring men into battle or making difficult tactical moves under fire, yet he did heroic and vital work. Rev. Horatio Howell, chaplain of the 90th Pennsylvania, found himself at Christ Lutheran Church on Chambersburg Pike during the afternoon chaos. Howell was the only chaplain killed at Gettysburg, and only one of the eleven chaplains who died in action during the entire war.[223]

As Baxter's men moved toward the Seminary from Emmitsburg Road in the morning, Howell likely accompanied the regimental surgeon to find a spot for a hospital. They selected Christ Lutheran Church, then began to set up facilities to efficiently treat the inevitable wounded. These were typical kinds of activities for a chaplain at the start of a battle. Howell would assist with a variety of tasks at the hospital, which served more than one hundred men at a time for weeks after the fighting.[224]

With mounting Confederate pressure against the First Corps followed by the retreat through town, hospital staff had to continue their work. Hearing noise from the street, Howell informed the surgeon of his interest in learning details of the commotion. Apparently, Howell was asked to surrender by a Confederate pursuing the fleeing Unionists. After a conversation, with details forever unknown to history, Howell—wearing an officer's uniform—was shot on the steps of the church, receiving a fatal head wound.[225]

On September 1, 1889, survivors of the regiment dedicated a monument to their departed adviser and friend. The monument on the church steps states Howell was "cruelly shot dead." Regardless of his role as a noncombatant, the chaplain was subject to being taken prisoner. Perhaps if Howell immediately complied with a demand to surrender, the Confederate may have spared his life. This would have been the best option, because Howell was likely helping treat some wounded Southern soldiers. Shooting a hospital assistant, even an enemy officer, brought nothing but more death to a town overflowing with tragedy.

Howell had performed a variety of duties for the regiment, such as delivering and sending mail, taking care of money soldiers wished to send home, and providing guidance and confidence to the rank and file. He was respected by the soldiers of the 90th, who labeled themselves "personal friends of the lamented chaplain" on his Gettysburg memorial. The monument includes two biblical verses. First, from the 18th Psalm: "He delivereth me from mine enemies; yea, thou liftest me up above those that rise up against me." The second verse, from Hebrews 11:4, "He being dead, yet speaketh."[226]

"THE SHORTNESS OF LIFE AND THE NOTHINGNESS OF FAME"

The few thousand men of the First Corps finding defensive positions on Cemetery Hill were further bolstered by rallying elements of the 11th Corps and other parts of the arriving Unionist horde. Slocum's 12th Corps was filing into nearby positions, and two of Sickles's divisions were arriving. Second Corps commander Winfield Scott Hancock, who Meade selected to take charge on the field while the army commander issued orders and got troops moving from Taneytown, provided solid leadership on Cemetery Hill. Howard felt slighted, but Meade—after the loss of Reynolds—sent someone he deeply trusted to provide advice about the viability of continuing the battle at Gettysburg.[227]

Doubleday spoke with Hancock during the late afternoon. Seeing the need to protect the army's right flank, the generals discussed the necessity of occupying part of Culp's Hill, east of Cemetery Hill. The Army of the Potomac simply could not be secure without firm control of both heights. Acknowledging the wrecked state of the First Corps, Hancock sensed the high level of the emergency. The Iron Brigade, after suffering nearly 65 percent casualties since 10:00 A.M., went to Culp's Hill, extending the army's line at a vital time.[228]

Big guns provided an excellent boost to the security of the army's position. Wainwright worked with his batteries and the head of artillery in the 11th Corps to take advantage of the topography. For the rest of the battle, Cemetery Hill would be a bulwark of cannons. Thanks to 11th Corps ammunition trains, First Corps batteries were prepared to repel an attack, with guns generally pointing northeast on East Cemetery Hill. After an order from Hancock, Stevens's 5th Maine Battery deployed to the southeast—closer to Culp's Hill—and facing north. Although concerned about a night attack, Wainwright noted, "I felt quite comfortable."[229]

The arrival of the 7th Indiana gave the First Corps another chance to augment the defensive position of Meade's army. A part of Cutler's Brigade, Col. Ira Grover and his men had remained in Emmitsburg to guard supplies. The Hoosiers began to grow impatient as the morning of July 1 progressed. Without authority, Grover left his assigned position to march north, reaching Cemetery Hill during the period when the army's retreat transitioned into a more orderly defensive posture. Later in the afternoon, Grover was sent to Culp's Hill. While on the right of the Iron Brigade, some members of the 7th Indiana, nothing more than a few pickets on the east side of the hill, scared off Confederates probing the area. In history, the 7th Indiana receives credit for keeping Lee's army off of Culp's Hill. Later, Henry Slocum's 12th Corps occupied the area.

The important work of the 7th Indiana in securing Culp's Hill would not stop court-martial proceedings against Grover. History has not been silent on Grover's court-martial, but many writers about the incident state the facts incorrectly. Most historians erroneously claim Grover's court-martial was due to his decision to leave his post to march to Gettysburg on July 1. In reality, Grover was put on trial for late marching on separate mornings in June and July.[230]

Soldiers of the First Corps had certainly done enough work for one day. Additional service from the hungry and tired band augmented the army's safety. Rufus Dawes, on the right of the Iron Brigade's line on the western side of Culp's Hill, noticed a number of spades in wagons sent with the redeployed Westerners. The utterly exhausted colonel recalled how his men quickly sprang to action when ordered to construct breastworks. "The men worked with great energy" to improve their defenses, an act "plainly dictated by necessity," Dawes asserted.[231]

Col. Ira Grover took his 7th Indiana to the battlefield at Gettysburg on his own initiative after his Hoosiers spent part of the morning of July 1 guarding supplies south of town. The regiment would play a vital role later in the day by protecting Culp's Hill. Grover would be court-martialed for incidents unrelated to his decision to march without orders to Gettysburg. LIBRARY OF CONGRESS

To the southwest, not far below Cemetery Hill, skeleton commands in the Second and Third Divisions also worked to improve the ground. The small group ready for duty in Robinson's command—barely 1,000 men—were slightly farther to the south than Doubleday's Division, which was closer to the base of Cemetery Hill. "The men lost no time in throwing up temporary breastworks," the 9th New York State Militia historian wrote.

Many later drifted off to sleep after finding a safe spot. In the 13th Massachusetts, the 99 men left—after 284 went into the fight earlier in the day—were able to get some imperative rest, "insensible to the tramp and clatter of an approaching army" intent on kicking Lee's men out of Pennsylvania. As his men slumbered, Doubleday noted the symbolism of a greatly fatigued group of American warriors finding solace and sleep among the tombstones. The resting place for the dead and the living, Doubleday suggested, could remind sinful man "of the shortness of life and the nothingness of fame."[232]

With so much immortal bravery on display in the First Corps on July 1, Thomas Rowley ended the day completely disgraced. Many men wondered about his questionable behavior during the afternoon, with several concluding Rowley was drunk. Although some came to his defense at a subsequent court-martial, Rowley's career was in ruins. His last act as a First Corps general was submitting to arrest by a junior officer. First Lt. Clayton Rogers, on the First Division staff, acting on his own responsibility, detained Rowley on Cemetery Hill.[233]

A modern book does a solid job trying to redeem Rowley's reputation. John Krumwiede's review of Rowley's generalship, health problems, and July 1 actions deserves close study, especially due to the excellent analysis the book gives to Rowley's court-martial proceedings, which occurred in the spring of 1864. Although found guilty on three of four charges, Rowley received a reprieve from Secretary of War Stanton, who noted the contradictory testimony leading to the guilty verdicts against the division commander.[234]

"Good God, Kenfield, Where Did You Come From?"

By early evening on July 1, all seven brigades of the First Corps were at Gettysburg. Stannard's Vermonters started filing into position to the south of Cemetery Hill near sundown. They missed the first day of battle but were now on hand, even in their dog-tired condition. Their arrival delighted the exhausted Abner Doubleday, who referred to the three Vermont regiments, about 1,800 men, as "a very welcome reinforcement."[235]

Thirty-six hours earlier, some Vermonters were left behind, unable to keep up on the trek north from Frederick. As the day's target of Emmitsburg grew closer, "not a man can hardly drag one blistered, bleeding foot under the other," a soldier wrote. Another exhausted man declared, "It seems as though the General meant to kill the whole of us." As the Green Mountain boys reached their bivouac at about 6:00 P.M. on the 30th, they had covered 120 miles in six days, great time in high heat from troops who spent the last eight months in light duty around Washington. The impressive marching placed Stannard's troops within 5 miles of the other six brigades of the First Corps. Sensing the likelihood of an engagement with Lee's army, a member of the 14th Vermont noted, "A collision must soon take place."[236]

During the morning of July 1, Stannard lost the services of two regiments. Per the order of Reynolds, the 12th and 15th Vermont were left near Emmitsburg. The 13th, 14th, and 16th Regiments began the march north after 9:00 A.M. By mid-afternoon, sounds of battle were evident to Stannard's soldiers, who were still several miles from the battlefield. Henry Willey wrote, "We were all sober, but none showed fear. It was what we were there for." Numbing fatigue did not keep the determined Unionists from their duty, although Willey viewed the brigade "as weary a lot of boys as could be found."[237]

All the Vermonters had experienced privations on the march from Virginia. Frank Kenfield, a first lieutenant for only two weeks, endured difficult health problems keeping him from starting with his Company E, 13th Vermont, as they left Virginia. July 25, Kenfield wrote, "was an extremely warm day and through some unknown cause my face had become so swollen and puffed up that I could hardly see, and it was with difficulty that I could march." Later in the day, he arrived at a hospital in Alexandria, south of Washington. Recovering sufficiently to march on the 27th, Kenfield began a lonely quest to seek his place in Company E once again. He was already well behind the 13th Vermont but determined to do his duty.

Kenfield found the regiment on July 1. Making an inquiry of Third Corps commander Dan Sickles, Kenfield was informed Stannard's Brigade was only about 3 miles behind. Seeing the men come up the Emmitsburg Road, Kenfield recalled, the 13th "never looked so good to me." On meeting Col. Francis Randall, the healed but weary lieutenant retained a vivid picture of what his commanding officer said to him, "Good God, Kenfield, where did you come from?" The men of Company E provided hefty cheers on Kenfield's return to duty. They had figured their esteemed officer was still in a Virginia hospital.[238]

As Stannard's men started forming on the south side of Cemetery Hill during the evening of July 1, the three Vermont units represented perhaps 40 percent of the First Corps' present manpower. Other men in the corps took notice of how the Vermonters looked compared to the six brigades engaged during the day. "A mere handful of men" in the 13th Massachusetts enjoyed the "delighted vision" of Stannard's regiments, which together "seemed like a great army."[239]

"We ate our supper in silence and in the dark," Henry Willey remembered. Groups of Vermonters went out to fill canteens. They had not suffered like others in the First Corps during the day, but Stannard's Brigade performed spectacular service by reaching the field so fast.[240] Their centrality to the Gettysburg story was only just beginning.

A Most Meaningful Seven Hours

Scott Hartwig has earned great praise as a Civil War historian. His analytical prowess and cogent study of the war's Eastern Theater have shined through for more than a third of a century. Few comments he has made are more correct than his review of Doubleday's defense of Gettysburg on July 1, 1863: "The job of the 1st Corps was to buy time and inflict losses." They did both remarkably well. The brigades of Davis and Archer were non-factors after their separate morning debacles. Rodes failed to take advantage of his numbers and position, wasting hundreds of casualties and hours against Robinson's Division. The 11th and 26th North Carolina suffered 800 casualties against Meredith, and Daniel lost about 500 pushing Stone back. Pender's Division then suffered more than 1,100 fallen men while hammering the First Corps' final stand on Seminary Ridge. What did Lee get for all these casualties? A tactical victory but strategic defeat. The bulk of Meade's army was waiting for him on the hills around Gettysburg.[241]

Not all historians are as correct as Hartwig. Trudeau is totally wrong in his view that the fighting—and, therefore, the losses—on the first day "pale" in comparison to the following two days at Gettysburg. Much battle remained, but the casualties of July 1 were mind-boggling when considering the relatively small number of men engaged. Two federal corps grappled with three Confederate divisions, with both sides combining for 15,000 men killed, wounded, captured, or missing.

The seven infantry brigades and five artillery batteries in the First Corps sustained more than 6,000 casualties at Gettysburg, 38 percent higher than the Second Corps, which placed second on the list of corps casualties for the first three days of July. Even when comparing casualties each day at Gettysburg, Trudeau is wrong. Trudeau's numbers make one wonder how the author could say the horrendous fight of July 1 could "pale" against the other two days. Trudeau lists 15,000 total casualties for both armies on July 1, with his total for July 2 approaching 17,000. Interestingly, he admits that far more men were engaged on July 2. Additionally, Trudeau's own data shows the losses of July 1 surpassing July 3.[242]

There were fifty-one Union infantry brigades at Gettysburg. Only three of those units suffered at least 1,000 casualties during the battle, all of which were in the First Corps. Cutler, Meredith, and Paul combined for nearly 3,200 total casualties, or 14 percent of the Army of the Potomac's loss across three days at Gettysburg. Perhaps 95 percent of those three brigades' loss was on July 1. The losses in the forty-eight other brigades did not "pale" when compared to the trio from the First Corps topping the army's casualty list. But to say so would be more accurate than Trudeau's inanity.

Trudeau's comment diminishing the significance of July 1 at Gettysburg stands as the most vicious calumny issued against the First Corps since the war. Oliver Howard uttered a potentially more impactful falsehood. On Cemetery Hill during the afternoon of July 1, Howard's overriding goal was to protect the 11th Corps' fragile reputation by vilifying Doubleday's men. In a message to Meade at 5:25 P.M., Hancock wrote, "Howard says that Doubleday's command gave way."[243]

If Howard had remained silent about the First Corps at Gettysburg, Doubleday still may not have been given permanent corps command. Meade named John Newton the new First Corps commander late in the day on July 1.[244] Doubleday deserved to command the First Corps, especially after leading such a staunch defense west of Gettysburg. He returned to command the Third Division.

Company E, 20th New York State Militia, provides an example of the First Corps' difficult afternoon. Under the command of George Washington Brankstone, a glass blower by trade who had been wounded at Fredericksburg, the company took twenty-three men into the fight at Gettysburg. After stalwart work defending the town, Brankstone was dead with a bullet in the brain. He had yet to reach his twenty-third year. Only four men would be present for duty in the company by the end of the battle.[245]

General Meredith saw an immense amount of sacrifice while leading the Iron Brigade on July 1. Later in July, Meredith wrote a very heartfelt letter to Edward Salomon, governor of Wisconsin. Meredith's pride in his association with the brigade from the very beginning shines through his marvelous words. He suggested the brigade "beat back the foe and fought as only intelligent and patriotic freemen can fight, when defending our priceless institutions."

Meredith named the commanders of each Wisconsin regiment, first stating how Rufus Dawes and the 6th "fully sustained the honor of your State." Colonel Robinson and the entire 7th Regiment "were the admiration of all." Salomon also read of the immense casualties in the 2nd Wisconsin, including Colonel Fairchild. "The decimated ranks" of the regiment "speak their bravery in more emphatic terms than any words I could use," Meredith added. After tributes to his staff members, the general concluded,

> *While I take great pleasure in acknowledging the distinguished gallantry of your troops, yet it is attended with deep sorrow at the great loss of life which attended this brilliant engagement. Those who fell died as American citizens should when their crisis demands the sacrifice—their faces to the foe, defending the rich and glorious inheritance which God has signally bestowed upon our people.*[246]

As Meredith and so many others knew—and some historians cannot seem to echo—the First Corps at Gettysburg did not "pale" to troops on any other day in American history.

"THE YOUTHFUL MARTYR TO LIBERTY SLEEPS QUIETLY"

Even during the successful initial hours for the First Corps at Gettysburg, the town's defense proved very costly. Men young and old wearing a red, white, or blue disc on their cap fell across the entire front nearly every minute from the time Cutler's three regiments lined up north of the Chambersburg Pike through the retreat to Cemetery Hill. Hamilton College in New York gave another young lieutenant to the country's cause. Rush Cady, who enlisted in 1861 at the age of twenty, followed in the footsteps of William Bacon, the student who had left the school early only to die at Fredericksburg.

Cady, a member of Company K in the 97th New York, was a highly revered officer when he joined Baxter's other men in the effort to beat back the Confederates. Names of those in the regiment who were killed or wounded started showing up in newspapers around Utica less than a week after the battle. In a letter from the field on July 12, a New York editor was informed, "Lieut. Rush P. Cady is wounded in the arm and side,—case doubtful."

The wounded youngster clung to life. On July 20, a friend telegraphed Cady's parents with Rush's request for their presence. By the time Mrs. Cady reached Gettysburg, there was limited hope her son could recover. The devastated mother tried to persevere through the pain, but her son soon died. At Cady's memorial service, a friend praised the departed.

> *He combined personal characteristics which endeared him to those with whom he came in contact: strictly methodical in everything which pertained to business, and, at the same time, combining that energy and perseverance which is requisite to success, our youthful fancy had marked out for him a prosperous future, but time, the disposer of events, has set at nought our predictions, and to-day, our community mourns another hero.*[247]

After Cady's burial in his hometown of Rome, a newspaper marked the solemn occasion. Cady's body was "consigned to its final resting place, and amid the scenes of his boy-hood, the youthful martyr to liberty sleeps quietly."[248]

When the regiment returned home in 1865, Cady was remembered by name in speeches to honor those who fell during their war service. Roscoe Conkling, then serving in the U.S. House of Representatives, listed some names of those who had died in the war, including the young lieutenant at Gettysburg. Conkling declared, "We mourn your absence on this joyful day; but there is victory in dying well for freedom, and you have not died in vain!"[249]

RELATIVE REPRIEVE ON JULY 2

"Our loss was fearful," Uberto Burnham accurately wrote home on July 2. Other men busied themselves with notifying kin about the great battle of the day before. Archibald Penny, 9th New York State Militia, informed his parents, "Yesterday we fought a hard battle. Your son came off safe. Thank God." Seeing divine favor as the only reason he could have survived, Penny later added, "God has spared me." Similar sentiments likely filled the minds of many other First Corps soldiers on July 2. One man in the 6th Wisconsin summed up July 1 by declaring, "so fierce and hard was the battle that the first corps was practically annihilated."[250]

Comparative quiet ruled the hills and fields around Gettysburg for much of the day. By mid-afternoon, Confederates were attacking positions all across Meade's defenses. The Union army held excellent topographical positions in what has historically been called a "fish hook." Meade possessed the curving ground on Culp's Hill, down Cemetery Ridge to the great duo of heights south of town, known as Big Round Top and Little Round Top. Lee's intense attacks hammered several portions of the Army of the Potomac, but the high ground remained Meade's.

Wadsworth's Division, posted near the 12th Corps brigade of George Sears Greene, took part in successful efforts to push Ewell's attacks away from the main height on Culp's Hill. Greene's New Yorkers made a resolute stand. When other elements of the 12th Corps were called to reinforce Cemetery Ridge, works to Greene's right were emptied. Confederates occupied some of this area in the evening darkness.

When called, the 14th Brooklyn and 6th Wisconsin ran into elements of Brig. Gen. George Steuart's regiments south of Greene's command. "This remarkable encounter did not last a minute," Rufus Dawes wrote. The engagement was not very costly—two killed in Dawes's regiment, while the Brooklyn men reported none killed—but Steuart was given a shock. This was enough for the Confederates to give up seizing the Union army's right flank. Confederates would never again get so close, even after intense assaults the next morning.[251]

To the west, First Corps artillery played a role in repulsing another intense fight, a Confederate attack against East Cemetery Hill. Wainwright's guns were active earlier in the day, but the greatest threat to the position began with an evening infantry assault. Cooper's Battery had to be pulled out of the line, replaced by guns from the Artillery Reserve, but other First Corps cannoneers found plenty to shoot at. As Wainwright recalled, "About an hour after sundown, the moon shining brightly, the enemy made a push for our position."[252]

Earlier in the day, Greenleaf Stevens had been "shot through both legs" by an enemy sharpshooter. Lt. Edward Whittier, who turned twenty-three years old the day before, took command of the 5th Maine Battery. The Pine Tree State gunners had a much better position than two months before at Chancellorsville. Facing north, with 11th Corps infantry support on their left, the battery would be able to punish the left flank of the Confederate attack. Artillery on East Cemetery Hill itself were disadvantaged at short range due to the steepness and the presence of supporting infantry down the slope. As Whittier noted, the Maine battery's better spot meant the fields to the north "could be swept clean of any troops assailing the front" of East Cemetery Hill "by an enfilading fire of double canister."[253]

The attack from two Confederate brigades showed promise. Nonetheless, after some breakthroughs against 11th Corps infantry, the "Louisiana Tigers" could not keep East Cemetery Hill. Closer to the 5th Maine Battery, three North Carolina regiments attacked the southern part of the hill. They would lose their brigade commander and hundreds of men. Wainwright gave insufficient credit to the 11th Corps infantry, reporting falsely how the attack "was almost entirely repelled by the artillery." Lieutenant Breck knew better. In his report, the First Corps battery commander noted, "This charge was most repelled by the infantry in support, whose presence in front prevented the use of canister."[254]

Whittier reported firing forty-six rounds of canister to engage the North Carolinians sweeping from right to left of the battery's field of view. He was thankful for active musketry from his right, fired by the Iron Brigade. Also, the 33rd Massachusetts from the 11th Corps, "rendered loyal service." Later in the evening, the Maine battery left the line to refill ammunition but quickly returned before the end of July 2.[255]

Most First Corps infantry had escaped danger during the day. Parts of Robinson's Division were kept busy rushing to support different sections of the army's line, including the collapsed Third Corps to the south. Troops from other corps stemmed the rout. By the time Robinson's regiments returned, heavy fighting had ended on Cemetery Hill. "So far as exposure to danger is concerned," the historian of the 13th Massachusetts concluded, "our division may be said to have had very good luck." Knowing the entire army was on hand, a man in the 11th Pennsylvania happily thought, "our men were not contending against the fearful odds of the first day's battle."[256]

John Newton expressed delight in his men when reporting on his first day as commander of the First Corps. He witnessed the quick action of Robinson and Doubleday's Divisions to assist other troops. Although only in a support- ing role, "I was deeply gratified at the promptitude with which these divisions moved at this crucial period," Newton wrote. Five companies of the 13th Ver- mont had charged west from the southern part of Cemetery Ridge, reclaim- ing four Unionist cannons previously captured, taking two cannons from the enemy, and seizing eighty prisoners on July 2. The action led to a Medal of Honor for Capt. John Lonergan.[257] After ferocious fighting all along the Army of the Potomac's line, Meade remained in a solid defensive position.

Defeating Pickett

The First Corps was not yet done at Gettysburg. Stannard's three Vermont regiments would play a vital role in the repulse of the most famous charge in the history of American soldiers, Pickett's Charge along Cemetery Ridge. Thus, while the First Corps became immortal on July 1, elements of the corps thwarted the final major infantry engagement on July 3.

After two days of some gains, Robert E. Lee's options were quite limited, especially since supplying his army from immediately around Gettysburg could not continue indefinitely. With no hope of Confederate reinforcements, Lee redoubled his faith in his undaunted army. Bringing battle to Meade for a third consecutive day likely was Lee's best option.[258]

Meade had an overwhelming advantage of position, as well as "interior lines." Unlike the Army of the Potomac, the wings of Lee's army could not assist each other. Conversely, Meade's fishhook placed the two flanks of his army within easy supporting distance. The sacrifice of the First Corps on July 1 bore fruit in the army's retention of exceptional ground offering quick reinforcement to any point in the line.

To the south, a horrendous barrage of cannon fire preceded the attack Lee planned along Cemetery Ridge. Between the two armies, more than 200 big guns blazed away, with Lee's goal being to soften the position of Hancock's Second Corps, the focal point of the attack. As a Virginian in Kemper's Brigade remembered, "Thunder answered thunder, and the very ground appeared to tremble." The duration of the firing cannot be pinpointed with exactness. Some eyewitnesses suggested the barrages continued for two hours.[259]

Stannard's regiments and some others of the First Corps were on Hancock's left. The Vermonters had some protection from the artillery fire thanks to trees and "the tumbled down stone wall in our front." Nearby, Col. Theodore Gates, leading both his own 20th New York State Militia and the 151st Pennsylvania, had men work on defensive improvements. Gates reported how a rail fence was "converted into a barricade," providing "especial service" during the artillery barrage.[260]

The intense noise must have been extremely unnerving. Doubleday, apparently not brooding about his demotion back to division command, witnessed the big guns in action. "The batteries on both sides suffered severely," Doubleday wrote. "Not less than eleven caissons were blown up and destroyed," he continued, "one quite near me." Confederates cheered the sound of such explosions in the Union lines, while a good shot in reply from the Northern gunners brought shouts of joy all along Cemetery Ridge.[261]

The deafening blasts from so many cannons were a time for officers to set an example. Hancock has received praise across generations for his lack of concern about the danger to his person as he rode down the entire defensive line. Stannard also inspired. "His eagle eye saw every movement within his range," a Vermonter wrote of his general, as Stannard "quickly comprehended the strategic point of contact and advantage."[262]

Confederate cannons did not inflict excessive punishment on Cemetery Ridge before 13,000 men would charge about a mile to the Union stronghold. Pickett's entire division, fifteen regiments of Virginians, started marching from the southern portion of the battle line. Other parts of the attack included soldiers from two of A. P. Hill's divisions, exhausted men who had engaged the First Corps two days before.[263]

At first, Pickett's Division marched nearly straight at Stannard's Vermonters. The Virginians were moving east for several hundred feet before swinging to the northeast near the Codori Farm along the Emmitsburg Road. The moves to the left were necessary to attempt to retain linkage with Hill's troops. Although the attack included a significant amount of Lee's infantry strength south of Gettysburg, too few men took part. The nearby brigades of Lang and Wilcox did not support Pickett in a timely fashion, so the Virginians must have felt alone.

Not all of Pickett's brigades were in the front line. Lewis Armistead started out in support behind his fellow Virginians, Richard Garnett and James Kemper. Pickett was compelled to turn in a way exposing his right flank to Stannard's Brigade. The Vermonters were more than willing to take advantage of the Confederate errors in planning and supporting the attack.[264]

Stannard ordered the 13th and 16th Vermont to move forward and attack the right of Kemper's Brigade. Nearby, the 14th Vermont had an important role to play in repelling the attack, as well. The effort to pummel Kemper's flank did not go unnoticed by all of the Virginians. Some of the Confederate infantry started shooting at Stannard's men, who performed quite well under the pressure. The 16th Vermont, under Col. Wheelock Veazey, formed on the left of Colonel Randall's regiment. The effects of the Vermonters' fire would be severely felt on Kemper's flank. As a member of Stannard's command noted, "The charge of the enemy was met with a warm reception by the Vermont boys." Stannard reported how his regiments "opened a destructive fire at close range."[265]

Colonel Randall of the 13th Vermont had a front-row seat at the slaughter. He suggested Pickett's Division "passed directly in review before us." The proud colonel then noted how his regiment was "pouring one of the most withering fires I had ever beheld into their exposed flank." Randall happily reported, "I do not know how many prisoners my regiment captured, but I had apparently more than there were men in my regiment."[266]

The movement against Kemper took place under trying circumstances for the rookie soldiers. As one member of the brigade recalled, the effort to flank the Virginians put the Vermonters "in a terrific storm of shell, grape and musketry." For his own strong leadership bringing the 16th Regiment into the fight, Veazey would win the Medal of Honor. The citation states Veazey, "Rapidly assembled his regiment and charged the enemy's flank; charged front under heavy fire, and charged and destroyed a Confederate brigade, all this with new troops in their first battle." Of his regimental commander, Henry Willey suggested, "no better officer mounted a horse or drew a sabre."[267]

Gates led his two regiments into the fight. The 20th New York State Militia and 151st Pennsylvania would move a bit north as the attack continued, adding to the devastation the Virginians endured. While contributing to such an impressive victory, Gates lost men, including Capt. Ambrose Baldwin. Two days before, Baldwin bought time for Biddle's Brigade with his impressive performance in an advanced position at the Harman Farm. The captain was killed by an artillery shell. Only twenty-four years old, Baldwin would be buried in Jewett, New York.[268]

Hundreds of Virginians were slain, maimed, or taken prisoner as a result of the First Corps' effort against Pickett. Each of Pickett's three brigade commanders would fall, with Kemper the only one to survive. More than twenty years after the battle, Kemper referred to the field of his advance as "a *cul-de-sac* of death," due to the division's lack of support. Of the 4,500 men in Pickett's attacking column, only 900 were present for duty the next morning. One Vermonter remembered the scene as he looked across the field after the battle. Of Pickett's men, he wrote, "Their path was marked by a windrow of corpses."[269]

Through the chaos, Stannard received excellent staff support from 2nd Lt. George Benedict, originally with the 12th Vermont. For his bravery in delivering orders and working with the three beleaguered regiments, Benedict would be the third member of Stannard's Brigade to win the Medal of Honor at Gettysburg.[270]

The precision of the Vermonters' hard work showed how well-trained troops could stand by their country, even though they were a month away from going home. The cost was high. Stannard lost 40 killed, 248 wounded, and 58 missing during the battle. The 14th Vermont recorded 17 of the killed, the most across the three regiments, while the 13th and 16th Regiments each suffered 119 casualties.[271]

After his rapid march to join the 13th Vermont at Gettysburg, company commander Frank Kenfield was injured as Pickett's defeat was near. Kenfield's chest wound was considered serious, but he was not mortally injured. Praised as "a man of courage," Kenfield's "coat sleeve was covered with the blood and brains of Sergeant Major H[enry]. H. Smith, who had just been instantly killed by a piece of shell." Receiving some medical treatment on the field from drummer Gilman Foster, Kenfield would be confined to a hospital for a time, unable to rejoin the regiment until they mustered out back in Vermont.[272]

Second Corps troops and dozens of Union artillery batteries performed nobly and contributed to the repulse of the entire attack across Cemetery Ridge. However, the actions of a small part of the First Corps were a key factor in the defeat of Pickett's Charge. Confederates who took part in the doomed effort paid respects to Stannard's men. "I have been in many battles and was never beaten before," a captured officer in Pickett's Division commented shortly after the charge. "I was never more confident of victory," the proud Confederate added. Yet, "when I saw that Damn Vermont Colonel on foot, hat off, sword swinging in air in front of his men and cheering them on upon our flank, I knew we were doomed."[273]

THOUGHTS FROM THE WRETCHED FIELD

A great sense of relief pervaded the lines of the Army of the Potomac on July 4. The day was special for Rufus Dawes, and not just because he had survived another brutally intense battlefield. Dawes, sharing a birthday with his country, turned twenty-five years old on the 4th. At noon, he noted, "The fighting has been the most desperate I ever saw. On July 1st, our corps was thrown in front, unsupported and almost annihilated." Six hours later, Dawes wrote, "No fighting to-day. Both armies need rest from the exhaustion of the desperate struggle. My boys until just now had nothing to eat since yesterday morning. No regiment in this army or in any other army in the world ever did better service than ours."[274]

Some men had an even more dangerous few days than Dawes. An especially valiant officer from the 97th New York boldly escaped from Confederate captivity. Capt. Rouse Eggleston successfully risked escape on July 5. He needed nearly a week to find his regiment. On the way back to friendly lines, he gained help from two other Union soldiers. Together they captured eleven Confederate prisoners. Summing up his motivation to escape, Eggleston wrote, "I would like to go to Richmond but didn't just like the style of being taken there."[275]

Another officer of the 97th New York found himself in trouble with brigade commander Baxter on July 4. Dedicated to exactness and discipline, Baxter reported unacceptable conduct from Maj. Charles Northrup, commanding the regiment after the battle's first day, when he failed to keep his picket line in the proper position. Without orders, Northrup moved his line back nearly 50 feet by daylight. Baxter reported, "I refused to relieve him until he re-established his line, which was done, but not without some work."[276]

After very long days of marching and battle for his five batteries, Charles Wainwright rose early on the victorious Independence Day. Soon he was hearing evidence of a Confederate withdrawal around Cemetery Hill. Along with Lieutenant Stewart of Battery B, 4th U.S. and an orderly, Wainwright cautiously moved into town. They came up to a house where some wounded artillerists were being housed. Wainwright saw Captain Reynolds there, who had to give up command of his battery to Lieutenant Breck on July 1. Reynolds's "right eye is completely gone," Wainwright noted. Farther to the west, the artillerists discovered three of Battery B's abandoned caissons still on the field, undamaged three days after the First Corps left Seminary Ridge.

"I have no fondness for looking at dead men," Wainwright continued, "and less for seeing those who are suffering from wounds." He must have found some comfort back at Cemetery Hill. Moving farther south along the ridge, Wainwright began to see considerably more evidence of a horrific fight. Returning to his cannoneers, the colonel needed to lay down the law a bit. "It was hard work keeping the battery men in their places; all wanted to go around and see the sights," the tired officer concluded.[277]

Picket details had plenty to witness and hear. The 9th New York State Militia had so few men present, the entire regiment went out to scout the ground in front of northern Cemetery Ridge. By the evening of the 4th, most of the wounded had been removed to hospitals, or whatever care the unfortunate scores of American warriors could encounter. Firing from some Confederates continued into the wee hours of July 5, so First Corps men were still not completely safe.[278]

An officer in the 13th Massachusetts nearly lost his life on Independence Day. With occasional shots coming from whatever remained from the Confederates, Union men had to be careful. The Bay State officer, in a wooded spot, must have expected no problem due to the cover. As he lifted a ladle to pour some coffee, a bullet hit the utensil. Uninjured, the relieved officer poured what remained from the ladle.[279]

Regardless of the close calls with death on July 4, joy filled the hearts of men across Union lines. "There was a complacent smile on the face of every Federal soldier," the 11th Pennsylvania's historian remembered. When a Confederate officer busy taking the names of First Corps prisoners suddenly departed, with news of other enemy troops moving away from Gettysburg, the exultation continued. One Michigan man who lost an arm on July 1 did not seem to mourn his missing limb. Rather, he held up his remaining arm, saying for victory he gladly would have lost it, as well.[280]

CLOSING OUT THE CAMPAIGN

The First Corps was everywhere the Union needed its soldiers at the battle of Gettysburg. Although July 1 would be the corps' worst day of losses across the entire war, noble service was rendered on the following two days. From helping to protect Culp's Hill, the artillery's defense of East Cemetery Hill, and withering Pickett's right flank on July 3, soldiers in the First Corps performed magnificently during the first three days of July 1863. The victory at Gettysburg did not end the campaign. What would Meade do as the Confederates limped back to Virginia? What role would the battered First Corps play for the rest of July?

Newton learned early in the post-battle period of Meade's wish to not push the Confederates with a risky level of haste. The First Corps commander was informed Meade "only desires to know where the enemy are, and not by any means to bring on an action." As a senior officer in the First Corps, and then the commander of the Fifth Corps, Meade proved he was not afraid to fight. The previous three days also showed Meade would not cower before the legendary brilliance of Robert E. Lee. Yet, his caution took control after the victory in Pennsylvania. Meade could not stay in Gettysburg indefinitely, but he felt the exhaustion of his army meant a measured pursuit of the Confederates. A counsel of war with his senior officers, where a slower pursuit against Lee's retreat was supported, likely did not set Meade's course. Rather, his generals merely pointed out what Meade preferred to do.[281]

Without a doubt, supply problems plagued the Army of the Potomac after the battle. Stores were concentrated in Maryland, and many men needed shoes, to say nothing about more reliable supplies of food. But like McClellan in Maryland, Meade faced an enemy army strapped by even worse conditions. Lee had to pull his army away from Gettysburg while Confederate divisions were spread across more than 5 miles. Simply extracting his army safely from north and west of town after the bitter defeat would be a major accomplishment. Lee's retreat began in earnest on July 5. Like so many other times during the war, the Confederates worked miracles.[282]

The First Corps would not begin to march out of Gettysburg until July 6. Most of Meade's army would not follow Lee's westerly move. The Confederates soon reached South Mountain's Monterey Pass in Pennsylvania. Except for the Sixth Corps and cavalry, which was sent west to keep an eye on Lee's retreat, Meade turned south. Originally seen as support for Sedgwick's Sixth Corps, Newton was later ordered to head to Emmitsburg.[283]

In addition to the supply and exhaustion problems both armies faced, Lee and Meade's men also had to contend with the weather. Rain was a problem, with Charles Davis of the 13th Massachusetts noting, "it rained in torrents" for a large part of the march on July 7. Nonetheless, the two armies covered much ground. Lee's force started arriving in Hagerstown on the evening of July 6. Although Meade's questions about Lee's intentions and concerns about supply limitations meant a slower start for the Army of the Potomac, advanced elements of Meade's force reached Frederick on July 7. The First Corps was not the vanguard of the army this time, ending the 7th in the Catoctin Mountains north of Frederick. The day's march topped 20 miles. Downpours continued.[284]

The next few days brought more marching south, then west through South Mountain. Lee's wagons and troops were stuck in Williamsport, Maryland, unable to cross the Potomac due to high water. With a strong defensive position, Lee gave pause to Meade while the Confederates worked to get out of danger.

Men in the First Corps had an opportunity to reflect on the immensity of their service since the start of July. On the 9th, Archibald Penny suggested, "The rebels are used up." Quick to thank protection from above once again, Penny hoped his mom would not worry. "He who has been my shield will be with me," the soldier wrote.[285]

From the small size of many units, evidence of July's sacrifices was on display across Newton's regiments. On July 8, Company H of the 12th Massachusetts rejoined the regiment after a day of duty guarding wagons. During the company's absence, the veteran regiment included only seventy men across nine companies.[286]

Supply problems still plagued the worn-out army, with thousands of soldiers without shoes. Near Boonsboro on the 9th, Rufus Dawes hoped the victorious army could win the war in a few days. "If we can end this war right here, I will cheerfully abide the terrible risk of another battle, and personal discomforts are small comparatively," Dawes wearily noted. He added, "I feel very hopeful now, and prouder than I can tell you that the old army has vindicated itself."[287]

The army's July 10 returns pointed to the severe trial of battle at Gettysburg. The aggregate number of men present in the First Corps was slightly above 6,000. Of those, only 3,881 men and officers were present for duty and equipped, compared to 9,403 on June 30, a drop of nearly 60 percent in under two weeks.[288]

Meade's men drew closer to Lee's lines, but the moves could not force a decisive conflict. Moving to Funkstown and crossing Antietam Creek, Meade did not press any advantage in a timely manner due to the strength of Lee's lines. By July 13, the 97th New York reported the completion of its own breastworks in the First Corps lines. The next morning, pickets discovered Lee's army was gone—escaping to Virginia across a temporary bridge at Falling Waters, south of Williamsport. As the historian of the 97th lamented, "Lee was able to render his position virtually impregnable until he could perfect his arrangements for a safe retreat." Later in the day, the First Corps was ordered to move toward Williamsport.[289]

Newton's men would make their way to the Potomac in Berlin on July 16, with some receiving a deserved day of rest in a spot along the river. The previous October, Berlin served as the staging area for crossing the Potomac weeks after the battle of Antietam.

Elements of the First Corps had crossed the river the day before. Archibald Penny wrote a letter home from Waterford, Virginia, on July 17. He expressed regret about the inability to confront the Confederates in Maryland. "The boys are sick of Meade since he let Lee make his escape," Penny complained. Other First Corps members understood the difficulty Meade faced in "bagging" the entire Confederate army. The historian of the 97th New York lauded Meade for the strong leadership he had provided. The army commander "exhibited the true qualities of a prudent and thorough general," since taking command. A Vermonter also supported Meade, considering criticism of his performance "very unjust."[290]

Notable changes to the First Corps were starting to play out. With Special Orders 316, dated July 17, the resignation of First Division commander

James Wadsworth was accepted, with army headquarters stating the general was beginning a leave of absence. Wadsworth grew quite distraught after Lee's army escaped into Virginia. In his letter of resignation, he couched his anger in measured terms, suggesting the army had too many generals, justifying his own departure. Deeply respected for his bravery and concern for his men, Wadsworth's service showed a profound well of patriotism. Perhaps he was not placed on earth to be a great general, but Wadsworth showed a tremendous amount of compassion for his volunteer soldiers.[291]

The next several days saw what a Wisconsin man termed a "leisurely" march to Warrenton and Warrenton Junction, which the First Corps started reaching on July 23. The corps was ordered to wait in the area for the arrival of the Sixth Corps. Rufus Dawes noted the desolate landscape. "The water is undrinkable, and wood is very scarce," the Badger warrior wrote on the 25th.[292] The army would make the area home for several weeks. At the end of the month, orders were issued for the First Corps to assist Buford's cavalry along the Rappahannock, offering a chance to vacate the insalubrious surroundings around Warrenton.

July had seen the corps' most desperate battle, followed by another round of major organizational changes, beyond the departure of Wadsworth. Newton still commanded three divisions with seven brigades, but the regiments included in the First Corps changed dramatically. Fresh troops at least increased the number of men in Newton's command. On July 31, the First Corps had more than 9,000 men present, with 6,600 equipped.[293] Both numbers were still considerably lower than the month before, but the immense losses of July showed signs of healing, in numbers at least.

Lysander Cutler commanded the First Division at the end of the month. The Iron Brigade included soldiers from outside the Western states for the first time, with the addition of the 167th Pennsylvania. William Robinson led the brigade, while Edward Fowler, 14th Brooklyn, commanded Cutler's old outfit. The Second Brigade's regiments were the same, but each had a new commander.

The Second Division showed the least amount of change since the morning of July 1. John Robinson still led the two veteran brigades, with Peter Lyle and Henry Baxter each in command of six regiments. Several short-term regiments joined the division after Gettysburg, but most mustered out before the end of July. The 39th Massachusetts, under Col. Phineas Davis, added new manpower to the First Brigade. After moving from Paul's to Baxter's command on the afternoon of July 1, the 11th Pennsylvania remained part of the Second Brigade.

With Doubleday on leave due to a wound at Gettysburg, John Kenly led the Third Division. Chapman Biddle only had his cousin's 121st Pennsylvania and the 142nd Pennsylvania in the First Brigade. The 20th New York State Militia had returned to Patrick's provost marshal headquarters, while the 151st Pennsylvania mustered out at the end of the month. Edmund Dana of the 143rd Pennsylvania commanded the Second Brigade, which included the same three regiments. The Third Brigade changed completely, with Stannard's brave Vermonters heading home. The new Third Brigade included the 1st, 4th, 7th, and 8th Maryland regiments.[294]

Kenly, an active Unionist from generally secessionist Baltimore, would command the Third Division through the dissolution of the First Corps. Like many generals in the 1860s, Kenly gained experience fighting in Mexico. He was an officer in Maryland and District of Columbia units in that war, then raised and commanded the 1st Maryland Volunteer Infantry for the Union in 1861. Wounded and taken prisoner at Front Royal, Virginia, in 1862, Kenly was exchanged over the summer, while also earning his general's star. His Maryland Brigade served in various commands before joining the First Corps.[295]

Conclusion: The Fate of Heroes

Relative safety prevailed during the last months of the First Corps. From the rebirth of the command through the Gettysburg campaign—less than one year—the corps suffered 13,000 battle casualties, while the final eight months included almost no fighting.

Lack of intense marching and battles suited Uberto Burnham. From Bealton Station on August 7, he noted the First Corps' work guarding bridges and keeping an eye on the Rappahannock River. "It is hot all the time," he wrote of the Virginia summer. "It would be a mistake to attempt to move forward," he added four days later. For the entire army, "Time is needed to strengthen and reorganize."[1]

On August 10, the First Corps reported 6,276 officers and men present and equipped, out of 8,552 present. Both numbers ranked second to last out of the seven corps in the army. Only the 11th Corps, also devastated on July 1, had fewer men.[2]

With camps close to the Rappahannock, refreshing water offered relief from summer's torment. Chaplain John Ferguson, 97th New York, said staying cool took up much of the soldiers' time. In an August 25 letter, he recorded, "We have a fine chance to keep clean & enjoy bathing & hundreds are in the river daily."[3]

The bureaucracy stocked regiments with new soldiers. Many of these men were not volunteers, but part of the country's first ever military draft. Such recruits were sometimes unwelcomed by soldiers who had joined the army during the patriotic fervor of 1861 or 1862.[4]

Few organizational changes impacted the First Corps as summer turned to autumn. The Pennsylvania regiment was gone from the Iron Brigade, with four companies of New York sharpshooters replacing the Keystone Staters. Minor leadership changes took place in other infantry and artillery units.[5]

As weeks passed, some marching portended a strike at Confederates. By late October, the First Corps was as far north as Thoroughfare Gap, near

Haymarket, a few miles west of Manassas. Movements north had been made earlier in the month, due to a concern Lee was attempting to circle around Meade's northern flank.

Confederate cavalry surprised some men from the First Division's Second Brigade at the gap. Maryland soldiers in the First Corps were involved in the fracas. They made a good showing for the Old Line State. The engagement created fifty total First Corps casualties, including the loss of fifteen prisoners.[6]

An officer in the 14th Brooklyn found himself before a court-martial for alleged misconduct while leading a picket detail near Haymarket. Newton ordered the prosecution against Lt. Col. Robert Jordon. Rufus Dawes was judge advocate, contrary to his wishes. Cutler refused Dawes's request to be excused from the duty. Dawes simply did not feel up to the required task, advising the panel of officers overseeing what the Badger warrior called "one of the most important cases ever tried in our division." Although found guilty, Jordon was restored to his rank on recommendation of Dawes and all officers involved in the case. Jordon received mercy due to "his good character and gallant service."[7]

The Haymarket engagement did not lead to a wider conflagration. On the 22nd, Uberto Burnham recorded, "We are following up Lee not very fast, but still moving every day." After a few days around the gap, troops headed east again. Later in the month, Isaac Hall, at Bristoe Station, between Thoroughfare Gap and Manassas, wrote, "Everything is quiet here now, but we are constantly on alert and I have hardly time to attend to the business affairs of my company." By mid-November, surgeon Henry Burr, 97th New York, added, "The 1st Corps is distributed along the road from Bristow to the Rappahannock River doing guard duty and repairing the road as fast as possible to the river." On the same day, Hall suggested he liked staying busy. "It is better to wear out than to rust out," he claimed.[8]

After brief time away from Thoroughfare Gap, Newton's men returned west before the month closed. On October 31, Rufus Dawes sent "My Best Girl" a letter from the gap. Dawes seemed upset that the regiment's dinner the night before was interrupted by marching orders. The men finished their 5 miles around midnight to once again reach Thoroughfare Gap. Darkness and fatigue could have presented problems for the 6th Wisconsin during the march. Fortunately, the regiment had a trusty equine guide. "I often fall asleep on my horse," the future Mrs. Dawes read, "but whenever the troops ahead start, she starts, and she is in no more danger of losing our regiment than a hound is of losing a fox."[9]

Mine Run

Returns for the end of October showed major changes to the Army of the Potomac. Only five infantry corps were present, with the 11th and 12th sent to the Western Theater. The First Corps slightly exceeded 12,000 men present for duty, with the entire army at just under 80,000. If sick soldiers and those not equipped were counted, Meade's force increased to 95,455.[10]

After Halleck vetoed Meade's plan to seize Fredericksburg, early November included a promising start for a new plan. Although ending as inconclusively as the movements west of Manassas in October, the month concluded with what nearly became a major battle along Mine Run, west of Chancellorsville.[11]

On November 5, Newton was ordered to get the First Corps to Catlett's Station, then have two divisions ready for further marching. The First and Second Divisions went forward as Kenly's men drew the task of guarding supplies and the railroad between Manassas and Warrenton Junction, a distance of about 10 miles.

The southern movement of Meade's force was ordered for November 7, with the two First Corps divisions in the army's left wing with the Second and Third Corps. "The pleasant fall weather was favorable for a campaign," a New Yorker in the First Corps wrote.[12]

Stalemate followed. Lee used the fine defensive terrain around Mine Run to stymie the Union's plans. Meade soon learned about the building of Confederate entrenchments. While dealing with rainy days, Meade's men were prepared for battle.[13]

After four days back in Ohio thanks to a short leave of absence, Rufus Dawes returned to the 6th Wisconsin in time to see the indecisive denouement. "We are lying in the mud and water in hourly expectation of moving forward," Dawes wrote from south of the Rapidan on November 28. The following day was equally distressing. The Confederates "worked like beavers" to create strong defenses, making Dawes wish he was "again on the hill tops of Ohio."[14]

Even without an attack, danger lurked along Mine Run, especially as the troops moved closer to Lee's works. An example includes the skirmish duty of companies G and I, 147th New York. Capt. James A. McKinley, Company

I, was so sick he should not have been on duty, but he was with his men. Later in December, an appreciative member of the 147th recalled how McKinley "could not be induced to remain in hospital while there was any fighting going on." McKinley was suffering enough to need medical attention in Washington, and his return was keenly hoped for by his men, because "he is as good a soldier as ever drew a sword in the service of the United States. An army of such men could not be beat."[15]

"Chilling wind that swept through the leafless trees" created additional miseries as American soldiers pondered their fate while awaiting an order to charge. The area the two armies occupied along Mine Run included a large opening in the otherwise thick woods and brambles south of the Rapidan. "Our batteries were planted in a good position on a hill to the front of the right of Baxter's brigade," wrote the historian of the 97th New York. Cannon blasts and active skirmishing pointed to the likelihood of a major engagement. Yet, attempts to deal with the cold constituted some of the most significant movements during the tense few days. As the 97th's historian continued, "The cold was intense, but no fires were allowed, and to keep from freezing the troops marched—in the woods—in a circle instead of standing."[16]

On the evening of November 30, Newton reported, "I regard any attempt to storm as hopeless, unless the troops can be massed near the point of attack without the knowledge of the enemy, and unless strongly supported on both right and left." Cutler had previously articulated his view, suggesting the works in front of the First Corps could be carried only after preliminary assault farther from the left. Cutler still saw how only "a great sacrifice" could bring a successful outcome. After more concern from other corps, Meade decided to give up attacking Lee along Mine Run.[17]

The First Corps suffered ninety-three casualties during the campaign, with most of the losses taken prisoner and only three killed in action. The strong impressions Confederate defensive preparations made on the men led many to be thankful for the canceled attack. A First Corps veteran recorded, "We had been out on the skirmish line, and knew too well what the strength of the enemy was to doubt the result of such a charge."[18]

Kenly's Division reunited with First Corps comrades in early December. Although orders on the 5th required all corps commanders to prepare their men for marching, nothing meaningful resulted. Near Kelly's Ford, Rufus Dawes noted, "We do not feel sure that we will stay here for the winter, but we hope to." Men of the 6th Wisconsin, who had Col. Edward Bragg back in command, assembled log cabins as a way to get comfortable. Enjoying the soldiers' ingenuity, Dawes recorded, "With no tool but the little hatchet, they house themselves snugly and comfortably, and provide all the necessary furniture." By December 10th, Dawes sent a drawing of his log home to M.B.G.[19]

The landscape presented scenes of wretched sadness. A member of the 147th New York, in a letter home on the 17th, noted, "The few houses that are left standing are well marked with shot and shell which passed through them." The writer added, "The hills in the vicinity of the Ford are also well marked with field works" and other desolating changes warfare brings. "The country around is dotted with the graves of the brave men of both armies, who died gallantly fighting for the cause each loved best," the soldier wrote.[20]

Weather forced sacrifices on the living. On December 14, Rufus Dawes penned, "The rain is pouring down in floods," leading to "mud unfathomable." Men could still be kept busy with sundry tasks. William Ray, 7th Wisconsin, wrote of the prize a housemate found. A pane of glass brought back on December 15 made for a luxury few men could boast: a window in their new hut.[21]

An esteemed leader departed the First Corps in December. Chapman Biddle decided he was done. During a formal ceremony on the 12th, men in Biddle's Brigade—especially those from the 121st Pennsylvania—felt an acute sense of loss. The regiment's historian noted how the colonel possessed "a discipline that was a model of exactness" and a feeling that each soldier must "fulfill the law." Nonetheless, "behind the outward appearance of a rigid disciplinarian," Biddle "cherished for his men a fondness that was almost paternal."[22]

Messages between army headquarters and Washington led to the development of a policy impacting many soldiers. Meade requested clarification on his authority to expand the granting of leave to a wider pool of the army. Halleck said the army could offer furloughs to veterans with less than one year left to serve who elected to reenlist. This led to Special Orders 329 on December 21. Men reenlisting as "veteran volunteers" would receive thirty-five days of leave. If 75 percent of a regiment's men agreed to reenlist, they could "go home in a body," taking their arms and equipment with them.[23]

Lieutenant Colonel Huidekoper, commanding the 150th Pennsylvania, wrote of the humor created when men sought furloughs. "I am thronged with worthy applicants," Huidekoper wrote, adding, "As a rule, I give preference to the married men, and the boys laughingly ask permission to go home *to get married*."

The one-armed colonel found comedy as a means to instill better discipline in his men. After a supply of stockings arrived, Huidekoper used soldiers' incessant desire for warmer feet to improve their respect for his rank. Huidekoper noted, "The man who saluted me worst yesterday, and who was evidently the most needy, had a pair promised him as soon as he should learn to salute properly, which he soon did."[24]

As relative quiet prevailed around Kelly's Ford, Special Orders 331, issued on December 22, sent the men to Culpepper. The First Corps had the duty of assisting cavalry pickets while on the way. Additionally, headquarters commanded, "A special guard around the town of Culpepper will be maintained by the First Corps." On the 30th, Robinson's Division was ordered to Cedar Mountain, south of town. Newton reported a delay in the move due to the weather.[25] Once again, Mother Nature wished great armies to know who truly was in charge.

THE LAST NEW YEAR

"The soldier seldom knows the day of the month and often cannot tell even the day of the week," Uberto Burnham wrote at the start of his 1864 diary.[26] His January 1 entry set the tone for the bland existence many men of the First Corps experienced around Culpepper.

Like Burnham, Lewis Plass of the 9th New York State Militia started an 1864 diary on January 1. He recorded "a rather hard day" in his initial entry. Although the men marched less than 2 miles, conditions were very muddy. Plass was a newer member of the regiment, having enlisted after Gettysburg. He quickly discovered what veterans across the entire army knew: Virginia's winters made mud a very bitter enemy.[27]

The army had 81,000 troops present, with Newton's command including 11,600. The First Corps began 1864 with organizational symmetry unknown since the rebirth of the command more than a year before. Three divisions with two brigades each now prevailed. Gone were divisions of three or four brigades as in previous campaigns.

In the Third Division, the departure of Chapman Biddle gave Col. Langhorne Wister command of the First Brigade, with the 143rd, 149th, and 150th Pennsylvania joining 121st and 142nd Keystone State regiments. The four Maryland regiments constituted the Second Brigade.[28]

Several units went home, based on the 75 percent reenlistment rule. The Iron Brigade benefited greatly from the policy. By January 11, the 6th and

7th Wisconsin, as well as the 19th Indiana, were temporarily gone from the army. The excellent soldiers experienced the welcome home in grand style, with waves of cheers in Milwaukee greeting the 6th Wisconsin. On January 17, William Ray celebrated his first Sabbath home in some time. He deeply enjoyed seeing family and friends. The tremendous regiments would return to the army by late February. Due to the manpower reduction, the 76th New York was temporarily transferred from the Second Brigade to the First.[29]

Strong administrative leadership gave soldiers necessities across the cold months of general inactivity. Although Meade could be a cruel curmudgeon, he understood how supplying the wants and needs of the men must be the center of his priorities. He became an excellent overseer of the army's welfare. Support for the troops from organizations such as the Christian Commission and the Sanitary Commission also proved vital to soldiers' higher morale.[30]

Thanks to all the work building winter homes from the plentiful logs around Culpepper, Uberto Burnham reported, "We have comfortable living quarters" in a January 13 letter. Two days later, the mundane winter did not keep Burnham down. "I am very pleasantly situated," the First Division soldier added, with "a good room and a good stove and what is better, good company."[31]

During the limited time in the First Brigade, troops in the 76th New York enjoyed a great diversion thanks to the creation of a regimental theatrical troupe. The performances were imperfect in the large log cabin, but soldiers deeply relished the diversion, which started on January 23. "Never was the drama or the comedy enacted to a more appreciative auditory than that assembled on these cracker-box seats," the regiment's historian wrote.[32]

Soldiers in the 14th Brooklyn also yearned for cultural festivities to conquer seasonal doldrums. After receiving approval from First Corps headquarters, men in the 14th moved forward to create an opera company. By early February, the endeavor first hit the stage. According to the regiment's historian, "The Culpepper Academy of Music was crowded to the window sills on the night of the troupe's premier." The high expectations were met, because, "Without a dissenting word the critics adjudged the show to be the success of the season." Attendees at the debut included generals Newton and Robinson.[33]

On the same day as the first opera performance, men in the Second Division received a highly unwelcome order from Robinson. The command noted, "Gambling within the limits of this division is prohibited. The attention of brigade and regimental commanders is called to the suppression of this evil." Charles Davis, 13th Massachusetts, regretted how the order "was too plain to be misunderstood, except by a person whose mind was as opaque as a billiard-ball." As he so often did, Davis used humor to conquer the vagaries of army life. Although the men had strong respect for Robinson, they assumed he crafted the order in response to his own gambling losses.[34]

Grand cultural entertainment and poking fun at a general's orders could not erase war's grip over lives. On February 6, the First Corps headed toward Raccoon Ford on the Rapidan River, about 12 miles south of Culpepper. The action was part of a general advance of the army. Newton's soldiers were not heavily engaged. Three hundred First Corps men taken from several regiments moved to the ford in order to burn a village, suffering no loss. The next day, three First Corps batteries moved to Raccoon Ford, firing dozens of rounds. An order to return to camp was received at dark on February 7. In the end, no military benefit accrued, with the Second Corps engaged the most, yet suffering well under 300 casualties.[35]

Men were miserable during the return trip. "The violent rain made the road a sea of mud, through which we floundered till nightfall," a 12th Massachusetts man lamented. After the operation, "The roads were frightful" due to the rainy weather. With the infernal mud, artillerists needed assistance from infantrymen to pull cannons through the quagmire.[36]

Busy Maine men kept warm by constructing a brigade chapel, with work completed on February 26. A justifiably proud member of the state's 16th Regiment wrote how the fine log building "does credit to the mechanical skill of Maine men." Chaplains dedicated the structure on the following day. "The interior was tastefully decorated with evergreens, which were festooned," then "hung in crosses, anchors, and circles, upon the walls." Words from Scripture were added to liven up the interior.[37] Once again, enthusiastic men of the First Corps put their mind to a task, worked hard, and improved their lives during what continued to be a rainy and unpleasant February.

Over the winter, several men injured at Gettysburg mended their broken bodies. Roy Stone returned in late February. Word of Stone's successful convalescence contributed to the resignation of Colonel Wister, who still commanded Kenly's reorganized First Brigade. Stone had certainly earned respect from his men, but Wister's departure prompted feelings of great sadness. Perhaps lingering wounds led to Wister's resignation; his request early in the winter to leave the army had been rejected. With Stone's return, Wister's effort to depart finally gained the approbation of his superiors.[38]

Abram Duryée paid a visit to the 97th New York on March 8. "Colonel Wheelock introduced our distinguished visitor," Isaac Hall wrote, with the men providing "three rousing cheers" for "the late gallant commander of our Brigade." Hall added, "He taught us how to fight." Deeply respectful of Duryée, Hall said the former brigade leader "despised a sculking coward," yet "he evinced a true appreciation of merit and was ever ready to bestow praise upon the deserving." After a "brief but touching speech," Duryée chatted with several of the regiment's officers.[39]

END OF A COMMAND

While men in the ranks endured the rest of winter, the bureaucracy made decisions culminating in the end of the First Corps. In a March 4 dispatch to Washington, Meade proposed "to reduce the number of corps, now five, to three." He specifically asked to keep the Second, Fifth, and Sixth Corps. Merging of Third Corps divisions would precede transfer of that command to the Fifth Corps. Meade added, "I propose to consolidate the First Corps into a division." Newton's men would then join the Second Corps.[40]

Meade's original plan was altered in a key way. First Corps soldiers would join Gouverneur Warren's Fifth Corps, not the Second. Reducing the number of corps made sense. By definition, a corps was designed to subsist in isolation for a time until other parts of the army could arrive. With sometimes less than 10,000 men fit for duty, some of the Army of the Potomac's largest units did not meet a reasonable threshold of strength. Meade's corps were roughly half the size of Lee's. Noting "the reduced strength of nearly all the regiments serving in the army," Meade defended the elimination of the First and Third Corps as "a measure imperatively demanded by the best interests of the service."

Meade stressed the expected temporary nature of the order and the right of units to keep their distinctive corps badges. Although the dissolution ended up being permanent, the retention of the old First Corps badges no doubt led some men to accept the army's consolidation. With months of hard service in the First Corps, Meade undoubtedly did not willfully mislead the troops. He explained how the organizational changes were "in no respect founded upon any supposed inferiority of those corps to the other corps in this army."[41]

James Wadsworth, who had been spending time in Washington writing reports and testifying before Congress, leaned toward a return to the field, rather than his New York farm. On March 15, the War Department ordered Wadsworth to report to Meade. Then, the dedicated general was assigned the Fourth Division under Warren. Uberto Burnham likely spoke for thousands when he wrote on March 28, "We are glad that the brave old man is to be with us again."[42]

Three First Corps generals lost their jobs in the reorganization. On the same day the army's consolidation was announced, Newton was ordered to Cincinnati, John Kenly to Baltimore, and Solomon Meredith to Illinois. Newton's banishment appears to have been a priority for Meade. The army commander did not approve of Newton's politicking. Meade bristled after hearing of Newton's criticism about the lack of a decisive victory at Mine Run.[43]

The First Corps would be divided between two of Warren's divisions. The Second Division held the same number in the Fifth Corps while keeping John Robinson as commander. His two former brigades were part of the division, as were the Maryland troops Kenly had led. Wadsworth's Division included the two brigades from his former First Division, as well as Stone's Pennsylvanians.[44]

The First Corps meant a great deal to many soldiers still wearing the red, white, or blue disc, yet they knew their duty was to save their country and accept orders. After all, the First Corps retained a strong claim to the nation's gratitude. A soldier from the 6th Wisconsin spoke emotionally and truthfully of the First Corps when he declared, "its record of achievements can never be destroyed; that will last as long as history."[45]

New general-in-chief Lt. Gen. Ulysses S. Grant made his headquarters with the Army of the Potomac, which Meade still commanded. The awkward arrangement all but marginalized Meade while still making him the senior major general in the army. Grant was uninterested in replacing Meade with a general from the Western Theater. Knowing the failure of Western generals like John Pope after higher command in Virginia, Grant made a sound decision to keep Meade, who had offered his resignation.[46]

REGIMENTS BECOME MEMORIES

The Lincoln Administration expected intense offensive action from Grant. Washington did not need to wait long. Grant's first move against Lee culminated in the battle of the Wilderness, fought between Chancellorsville and Mine Run on May 5 and 6, 1864. After the battle of Spotsylvania Court House a week later, Grant's direct oversight of operations in the Eastern

Theater created extensive losses in both armies, but the Unionists kept pressing south, toward the Confederate capital. The horrendous carnage had an immense impact on those who had served in the First Corps.

Newton's former command suffered 2,800 casualties at the battle of the Wilderness, more than 70 percent of which were in Wadsworth's Division. To the great sadness of his men, Wadsworth was killed on May 6. His penchant to lead from the front proved deadly in the tangled undergrowth south of the Rapidan. Lysander Cutler took command of Warren's Fourth Division, as massive bloodletting continued.[47]

Some First Corps regiments were out of the army even as fighting raged in Virginia. The 14th Brooklyn returned home in May after the conclusion of three years of service. Looking back on the previous thirty-six months a veteran recorded, "There was hardly one who did not present in some manner an evidence of the terrible service they had seen." By the afternoon of May 24, the veterans boarded railcars in Washington. On arrival in Brooklyn, "the city seemed to shake itself and blaze up in a mighty roar" to express appreciation.[48]

The 12th Massachusetts began the journey home on June 27. Those who still had months to serve transferred to the 39th Massachusetts. On the way back to Boston, a reunion occurred between the 12th Massachusetts and some men from the 9th New York State Militia. "An exhibition drill by Company H of the Twelfth was greeted with hearty applause," a Bay Stater recorded. The New York boys had departed the army earlier in June. Colonel Moesch lost his life in the Wilderness, and dozens of the regiment's men suffered death or wounds in the month preceding their return home.[49]

On June 30, the Massachusetts adjutant general received a telegram: "Twelfth Mass., one seventy one strong, leave for Boston by New Haven RR eight o'clock this evening." The soldiers were mustered out in early July on Boston Common.[50] The regiment suffering the Union's highest percentage loss at Antietam then existed only in memory.

THE DESTINIES OF TWENTY FIRST CORPS MEN

This book cannot be complete without touching on the later lives of some of the soldiers mentioned in the preceding pages.

Curtis Abbott was wounded in May 1864, then he earned promotion to first lieutenant. He finished military service in the Fourth Vermont Infantry. Mustering out in 1865, Abbott subsequently graduated from Harvard Law School. While enduring the travails of Civil War life, Abbott likely would have been amazed at the number of years he would live. On November 25, 1935, ninety-four years old, he died in Massachusetts.[51] The sharpshooter from Vermont was one of the last surviving members of the First Corps.

Griffen Baldwin kept serving in the Pennsylvania Reserves after the distinguished outfit departed the First Corps. He married after the war, then raised a son and daughter. He proudly taught his son "that in no event must he fail in his duty to the Old Flag, even to the giving of his life." A widower in 1885, Baldwin remarried eight years later. His second wife, Sallie de Jarnette, was the daughter of a man who had served both the United States and the Confederate States. Baldwin noted how his late father-in-law "plotted treason and rebellion" while a U.S. representative, then served the government Baldwin fought so hard to defeat. He added, "I call a spade, a spade; and treason, treason. But the war is over. The bloody chasms should be bridged, and there is no way so effectual as through matrimony."[52]

Griffen Baldwin, seated second from left, took part in a reunion of the 7th Pennsylvania Reserves in 1906. LIBRARY OF CONGRESS

Unfortunately, the union was not a happy one. Baldwin sued for divorce in 1901, after his wife apparently abandoned him and returned to Virginia. He died on September 13, 1909, at the age of seventy-two.[53]

Henry Baxter survived his fourth wound of the war, a shot to the leg in the Wilderness. He was absent from his men for a short time but returned to brigade command in June. For conduct during actions late in the war, Baxter would receive brevet promotion to major general. He mustered out of the army in August 1865, then worked as a lumberman in Michigan. Service to his country did not end with his excellent military career. After an appointment from President Grant, Baxter spent three years as U.S. minister to Honduras. He died in Jonesville, Michigan, on December 30, 1873, only fifty-two years old.[54]

The extensive writings of ***Uberto Burnham*** are a national treasure. He observed much and wrote so well. Burnham very likely was the last surviving member of his regiment. A 1928 newspaper article noted how Burnham walked a mile to register to vote in the upcoming election. Then in his early nineties, Burnham had been blind for several years. He employed school children to read newspapers to him. He died on July 3, 1930, in Duluth, Minnesota.[55]

After heroic efforts at Chancellorsville leading to a Medal of Honor, ***John Chase*** remained in the Fifth Maine Battery. At Gettysburg, he lost his right arm and left eye while serving the guns positioned near East Cemetery Hill. Presumed dead, Chase was nearly buried on the field. Still just twenty years old, he had plenty of life left. After spending time in several hospitals, he returned to his home in Augusta. Moving to Florida in the 1890s, Chase became a valuable member of the community of Gulfport. He died in 1914.[56]

Richard Coulter earned the brevet rank of major general before his military career ended. A leader of the 11th Pennsylvania through the war, Coulter returned home with the regiment after the hard-earned peace of 1865. "Its best friend would hardly have recognized the old Eleventh," the regiment's historian wrote at muster out, "had not General Coulter and one or two of the original staff officers remained to prove its identity." Much life was in store for "Fighting Dick." He died in the autumn of 1908, with burial in his hometown of Greensburg.[57]

Rufus Dawes chronicled an extensive number of highly meaningful stories throughout his war service. Somehow, he would not be wounded in action. Worn out later in 1864, Dawes returned to M.B.G., his new wife, Mary.

Dawes had two sons who won elective office for the United States. Charles Dawes would become vice president, while his brother Beman served

At the Fiftieth Anniversary of the battle of Gettysburg in 1913, members of the 90th Pennsylvania posed during the ceremonies honoring Union and Confederate veterans. LIBRARY OF CONGRESS

two terms in the House of Representatives. Rufus won a term in the House, as well, representing southeast Ohio in the early 1880s. He worked in the lumber business before and after his congressional term. In December 1881, he visited Arlington National Cemetery to honor the graves of twenty-four soldiers of the 6th Wisconsin who died under his command.

With a memoir considered one of the best written by a Civil War soldier, Dawes greatly honored his comrades. He offered words about the meaning of what they did during the war to those remaining veterans. "You have lived to see spring up as the result of your suffering, toil, and victory," Dawes declared, "the most powerful nation of history and the most beneficent government ever established. While you are in the sear and yellow leaf your country is in the spring-time of the new life your victory gave it. This is your abundant and sufficient reward."[58]

Dawes died on August 1, 1899, less than a month after his sixty-first birthday. More than two decades later his devoted wife, Mary, would be placed by her husband's side at Oak Grove Cemetery, Marietta, Ohio.[59]

John Delaney, a fourteen-year-old wounded at Antietam, served with the 107th Pennsylvania through the rest of the war. For the battle of Hatcher's Run, Virginia, in February 1865, Delaney was awarded a Medal of Honor. His citation noted how the heroic teenager "sprang between the lines and brought out a wounded comrade about to be burned in the brush."[60]

While providing an employment reference for Delaney after the war, Colonel McCoy of the 107th praised the boy warrior: "I cannot recall one who excelled him in personal courage in the charge of battle, or for admirable soldierly qualities on the march or in camp." Delaney died in Washington on April 4, 1915. He rests in Arlington National Cemetery.[61]

Samuel Dick continued showing strong leadership for the rest of his life. Although lingering effects from an 1861 wound led him to resign in early 1863, he joined Pennsylvania's militia during the Gettysburg campaign. Dick organized troops and led the 5th Militia Regiment during the emergency, with the men spending some time in West Virginia. In the 1870s, Dick served as mayor of his hometown of Meadville and then a single term in the U.S. House of Representatives, choosing not to seek reelection in 1880. Leadership of a railroad and an iron works occupied later years. Dick died in Meadville on May 10, 1907, aged seventy.[62]

Horace Hanks was discharged from the army in the summer of 1863, along with the 30th New York. Remaining in the medical field, Hanks wrote a variety of articles about gynecology, a specialty in which he is considered a pioneer. Sadly, "Mattie," who became Hanks's wife in 1864, died before the decade ended. The couple lived in Massachusetts, then moved to New York City. Hanks remarried and raised three children while continuing to practice medicine. He held several prestigious medical posts, dying in New York City in 1900 at the age of sixty-three.[63]

John Hatch remained in the army after his serious wound on South Mountain. Returning to duty months later, he expressed optimism about taking the field again. From Washington in February 1863, Hatch felt "considerably better," and, "I expect to throw away my crutches in a day or two." One of his first assignments during convalescence was "to try some rebels charged with being spies. It is considered a very important court, being the first of the kind during the war." Never able to return to field command, Hatch still led the draft rendezvous in Philadelphia. He then found several administrative positions. At the end of the war, Hatch led the District of Charleston. He left volunteer service in early 1866, receiving a major general brevet the year before. Later army service included years in

Texas before and after being superintendent of the Mounted Recruiting Service in Pennsylvania. He retired with the permanent rank of colonel in 1886. Hatch died in New York City in 1901, with Arlington National Cemetery as his resting place.[64]

Frank Kenfield did not end his military service when Stannard's men went home shortly after Gettysburg. He organized a company of what became the 17th Vermont, later attached to the Ninth Corps. Colonel Randall of the 13th Regiment commanded the new unit. Promoted to captain, Kenfield was wounded at the Wilderness, then given a furlough to convalesce back home. After returning to the army, Kenfield was captured in Virginia, then not released until after the war. Working as a merchant and then a farmer, Kenfield spent years in the state legislature. His active postwar life included time as president of the Vermont Maple Sugar Makers' Association and years in the Grand Army of the Republic and other fraternal organizations. Kenfield was widowed, then remarried in 1874. He died in 1914. He was born, raised, and buried in Lamoille County.[65]

Mike Link, like many other Civil War veterans, showed how someone suffering horrible wounds could still find purpose in life. The loss of his eyes at Gettysburg often led to intense headaches, as well as swelling in eye sockets and discharges of pus for weeks at times. A resident of Reading, Pennsylvania, with great motivation and a full pension, Link learned a variety of skills, including the manufacturing of chairs. He continued his interest in music, playing several instruments and becoming quite an entertainer and teacher. Active in remembrance ceremonies, a high point for Link was attending the reunion of the 151st Pennsylvania in 1888. Not yet sixty years old, Link died on July 12, 1899. The men who had carried him off the field at Gettysburg served as pallbearers. Link rests at Charles Evans Cemetery in Reading.[66]

George McFarland suffered terribly due to his wound at Gettysburg. He had a prolonged stay at the Seminary hospital, then spent most of a year in bed after returning home. A friend noted, "The shattered leg was for many years an open, running sore," shedding pieces of bone. The difficult healing process and protracted pain were borne with great fortitude from the leader of the 151st Pennsylvania. His friend added of McFarland, "He was a man of wonderful energy and will-power, and worked to maintain his family, hobbling about on crutches and his wooden leg."

McFarland led efforts to educate the children of soldiers, gaining a position supervising the thirty-seven orphans' schools in the state. The job led the McFarland family to Harrisburg. The busy man found time to serve the cause of veterans, including as secretary for the Society of the First Corps. McFarland wrote several letters on behalf of former soldiers.[67]

McFarland also became president of the 151st's survivors' association. At the unit's monument dedication at Gettysburg on July 1, 1888, he thanked the state for crafting the monument at the spot "so sacred to us all." He died on a trip to Georgia in 1891, aged fifty-seven. He rests in Harrisburg.[68]

Archibald Penny, 9th New York State Militia, wrote of the difficulties preparing for Grant's 1864 campaign. In an April 28 letter, Penny complained, "Drill 4 hrs/day with knapsack. I think that rather hard on old soldiers." He must have known major action was pending, because, "We have target practice twice per week." Penny often had reminded his parents of the divine protection he felt. Unfortunately, his safety would not last. The twenty-two-year-old was killed in the Wilderness on May 6. Penny rests at Maple Avenue Cemetery, Patterson, New York.[69]

After the loss of his leg at Chancellorsville, *Napoleon Perkins* still enjoyed much about life—including five children—while living in different towns in New Hampshire and Vermont. Perkins stayed busy in fraternal and veteran organizations, as well as in elective office. Among the numerous positions held, Perkins served in the New Hampshire legislature and at the state's 1903 constitutional convention. He died at the age of seventy on December 28, 1913, in St. Johnsbury, Vermont. Perkins was buried across the Connecticut River in Northumberland, a town he had lived in for several years. Perkins's wife, Mary, lived until 1943.[70]

John Robinson led a strong attack at Laurel Hill, two days after the battle of the Wilderness. Losing a leg, Robinson's bravery culminated in a Medal of Honor. The citation notes how the general was at "the head of the leading brigade in a charge upon the enemy's breastworks." Remaining in the military, Robinson held several administrative posts, retiring as a major general in 1869. He spent two years in the 1870s as lieutenant governor of New York, then took a leading role in the fraternal Grand Army of the Republic. Blind in his later years, Robinson died on February 18, 1897, in Binghamton.[71]

Truman Seymour kept fighting after Antietam. Assigned to the Department of the South, he served in several positions, including chief of staff. He was injured during the attack on Battery Wagner in Charleston, South Carolina, which cost him three months of convalescence. After a less than solid performance at the battle of Olustee in Florida, Seymour returned to the Army of the Potomac. He was captured at the Wilderness, then exchanged in August. Seymour ended the war as a Sixth Corps division commander. He remained in the army with the Fifth Artillery, retiring with the permanent rank of major in 1876. He spent his final years in Europe, greatly enjoying his skill as a painter. Seymour died in Florence on October 30, 1891, perhaps the only First Corps veteran buried in Italy.[72]

Roy Stone performed court-martial duty for several months after his Gettysburg wound. His hardy Pennsylvanians confronted intense Confederate pressure along Wadsworth's line in the Wilderness. Like Henry Baxter, Stone would be wounded there. He served in the army through early 1865, then spent years as an engineer and inventor. A staff officer in Puerto Rico during the Spanish-American War, Stone remained on the island to assist in development efforts as part of a long fascination with transportation engineering. Stone died in New Jersey in 1905, with burial at Arlington National Cemetery.[73]

Charles Tilden was confined to Richmond's infamous Libby Prison after being captured at Gettysburg. He was one of the Unionists to make a daring escape via tunnel in February 1864. Back in the army, he rejoined the 16th Maine at the First Corps' dissolution. Captured again by Confederates in August, Tilden's time as a prisoner lasted only one day before he escaped again and returned to his Pine Tree Staters. Becoming a brigade commander, Tilden earned a star through brevet in March 1865. Leaving the army in June, he returned to his hometown of Castine, Maine. He worked multiple jobs, including secretary and treasurer at the Hallowell Granite Company. Tilden died at the age of eighty-one in 1914. He was buried in Castine Cemetery.[74]

Each member of the First Corps would be worthy of his own biography. Their important lives deserve a spotlight to inspire later generations. Yet, if each veteran wrote daily letters and long, surviving diaries for four years, coverage of every soldier would not be possible in the lifetimes of a thousand historians. Rufus Dawes, who lived through so much death around him, made the same point in his memoir. The eminent officer noted, "It is a matter of sincere regret that many noble deeds and some brave men are overlooked."[75] Despite the inherent limitations on completeness, perhaps this book contributes to a deeper appreciation for the sacrifice of a devoted band of American warriors. Certainly, the deeds of those in the First Corps spoke mightily enough.

NOTES

Preface

1 U.S. War Department, *The War of the Rebellion: A Compilation of the Official Records of the Union and Confederate Armies* (Washington, DC: GPO, 1880–1901), Vol. 33, 735. Henceforth cited as *OR*.

2 Noah Andre Trudeau, *Gettysburg: A Testing of Courage* (New York: Harper Collins, 2001), 272.

3 Lawrence A. Kreiser Jr., *Defeating Lee: A History of the Second Corps, Army of the Potomac* (Bloomington: Indiana University Press, 2011), x.

Introduction

1 Robert Goetz, *1805: Austerlitz, Napoleon and the Destruction of the Third Coalition* (Mechanicsburg, PA: Stackpole Books, 2005), 48; Marion V. Armstrong Jr., *Unfurl Those Colors!: McClellan, Sumner, and the Second Army Corps in the Antietam Campaign* (Tuscaloosa: University of Alabama Press, 2008), 29–32.

2 www.civilwarhome.com/armyorganization.htm.

3 John C. Waugh, *Lincoln and McClellan: The Troubled Partnership Between a President and His General* (New York: Palgrave Macmillan, 2010), 38–40.

4 *OR*, Vol. 5, 587–89; Stephen W. Sears, ed., *The Civil War Papers of George B. McClellan, Selected Correspondence 1860–1865* (Cambridge, MA: Da Capo Press, 1992), 95–97.

5 Carl Sandburg, *Abraham Lincoln: The War Years* (New York: Harcourt, Brace & Company, 1939), 467–68.

6 George B. McClellan, "The Peninsular Campaign," in *Hearts Touched By Fire: The Best of Battles and Leaders of the Civil War* (New York: Modern Library, 2011), 342; George B. McClellan, *McClellan's Own Story* (New York: Charles L. Webster & Company, 1887), 222.

7 Roy P. Basler, ed., *The Collected Works of Abraham Lincoln* (New Brunswick, NJ: Rutgers University Press, 1953), Vol. V, 149–51; William Swinton, *Campaigns of the Army of the Potomac* (Secaucus, NJ: Blue & Grey Press, 1988), 64; Russel H. Beatie, *Army of the Potomac, Volume III: McClellan's First Campaign, March–May 1862* (New York: Savas Beatie, 2007), 249.

8 George G. Meade, *Life and Letters of George Gordon Meade, Major-General United States Army*, George Gordon Meade Jr., ed., Vol. 1 (New York: Charles Scribner's Sons, 1913), 241–42.

9 McClellan, *Own Story*, 222.

10 Stephen W. Sears, *George B. McClellan: The Young Napoleon* (Cambridge, MA: Da Capo Press, 1999), 159.

11 Jeffry D. Wert, *The Sword of Lincoln: The Army of the Potomac* (New York: Simon & Schuster, 2005), 62–63; Donald Stoker, *The Grand Design: Strategy and the U.S. Civil War* (New York: Oxford University Press, 2010), 140; Sears, *Young Napoleon*, 163–65; Rufus R. Dawes, *A Full Blown Yankee of the Iron Brigade: Service with the Sixth Wisconsin Volunteers* (Lincoln: University of Nebraska Press, 1999), 36.

12 Sears, ed., *Papers of McClellan*, 230.

13 Sears, *Young Napoleon*, 173–81; Waugh, *Lincoln and McClellan*, 86–89.

14 The brief overview of the Peninsula Campaign presented here was aided by Sears, *Young Napoleon*, 168–222, and *To the Gates of Richmond: The Peninsula Campaign* (New York: Ticknor and Fields, 1992). For a more supportive treatment of McClellan, see, Ethan Rafuse, *McClellan's War: The Failure of Moderation in the Struggle for the Union* (Bloomington: Indiana University Press, 2005).

15 Rafuse, *McClellan's War*, 253–72.

16 Ezra Warner, *Generals in Blue: Lives of the Union Commanders* (Baton Rouge: Louisiana State University Press, 1992), 159–60.

17 Reynolds Family Letters, Eleanor Reynolds Scrapbook, https://digital.fandm.edu/collections/eleanor-reynolds-scrapbook.

18 Warner, *Generals in Blue*, 396–97.

19 Ethan Rafuse, *George Gordon Meade and the War in the East* (Abilene, TX: McWhiney Foundation Press, 2003), 17–21.

20 Evan Morrison Woodward, *Our Campaigns: Marches, Bivouacs, Battles, Incidents of Camp Life and History of Our Regiment During Its Three Years Term of Service* (Philadelphia: John E. Potter and Company, 1865), 39–44.

21 Warner, *Generals in Blue*, 269–70.

22 Wayne Mahood, *General Wadsworth: The Life and Times of Brevet Major General James S. Wadsworth* (Cambridge, MA: Da Capo Press, 2003).

23 John J. Hennessy, *Return to Bull Run: The Campaign and Battle of Second Manassas* (New York: Simon and Schuster, 1993), 168–88; Alan D. Gaff, *Brave Men's Tears: The Battle of Brawner Farm* (Dayton, OH: Morningside Bookshop, 1985).

24 William F. Fox, *Regimental Losses in the American Civil War, 1861–1865* (Albany, NY: Brandow Printing Company, 1889), 66.

25 The Antietam Collection, Dartmouth College, Folder 2-68.

Part One: Defending Maryland

1 Stephen W. Sears, *Landscape Turned Red: The Battle of Antietam* (Boston: Houghton Mifflin, 1983), 12–18; Joseph Pierro, ed., *The Maryland Campaign of September 1862: Ezra Carman's Definitive Study of the Union and Confederate Armies at Antietam* (New York: Routledge, 2008), 65; John W. Schildt, *Roads to Antietam* (Shippensburg, PA: Burd Street Press, 1997), 4–6, 8–9; Perry D. Jamieson, *Death in September: The Antietam Campaign* (Fort Worth, TX: Ryan Place Publishers, 1995), 19–26; D. Scott Hartwig, *To Antietam Creek: The Maryland Campaign of September 1862* (Baltimore: John Hopkins University Press, 2012), 41; *OR*, Vol. 12, II, 80 and, III, 807; Robert Taggart Papers, MG 124, Pennsylvania State Archives (PSA), Harrisburg.

2 *OR*, Vol. 12, III, 808.

3 *OR*, Vol. 12, III, 805; Rafuse, *McClellan's War*, 273–74; Sears, *Young Napoleon*, 261–62; Reel 30, George Brinton McClellan Papers, Manuscript Division, Library of Congress, Washington, DC. The McClellan Papers were fully digitized in April 2019. See, https://www.loc.gov/collections/george-brinton-mcclellan-papers/about-this-collection.

4 Penny Family Papers, Folder 14, New York State Library (NYSL), Albany.

5 Uberto Burnham Papers, NYSL.

6 George A. Hussey and William Todd, *History of the Ninth Regiment N.Y.S.M., N.G.S.N.Y. Eighty-Third N.Y. Volunteers, 1845–1888* (New York: Press of J.B. Ogilvie, 1889), 180.

7 *OR*, Vol. 12, I, 331–32; Warner, *Generals in Blue*, 298–99.

8 *OR*, Vol. 19, II, 188; Sears, ed., *Papers of McClellan*, 437–40.

9 *OR*, Vol. 19, II, 188–91.

10 Warner, *Generals in Blue*, 233–34; Walter H. Hebert, *Fighting Joe Hooker* (Lincoln: University of Nebraska Press, 1999), 17–129; Rafuse, *George Gordon Meade*, 40.

11 Wert, *Sword of Lincoln*, 144.

12 George W. Cullom, *Biographical Register of the Officers and Graduates of the United States Military Academy at West Point, New York, Since Its Establishment in 1802*, Vol. II (Boston: Houghton, Mifflin, and Company, 1891), 537–40.

13 John H. Eicher and David J. Eicher, *Civil War High Commands* (Stanford, CA: Stanford University Press, 2001), 287; Warner, *Generals in Blue*, 216–17; John Porter Hatch Papers, Library of Congress.

14 Charles A. Stevens, *Berdan's United States Sharpshooters in the Army of the Potomac, 1861–1865* (St. Paul, MN: Price-McGill Company, 1892), 2.

15 *The Third Vermont Company of the United States Sharpshooters: A History by Curtis Abbott*, microfilm reel F-02846, Vermont State Archives, Middlesex. Quotes are from page 4.

16 Company D Regimental Correspondence, Folder 4, Maine State Archives, Augusta.

17 Warner, *Generals in Blue*, 129–30.

18 Cullom, *Biographical Register*, 622–23; Antietam Collection, Dartmouth College, Folder 2-13.

19 Lance J. Herdegen, *The Men Stood Like Iron: How the Iron Brigade Won Its Name* (Bloomington: Indiana University Press, 1997), 67–68; Lance J. Herdegen, *The Iron Brigade in Civil War and Memory* (El Dorado Hills, CA: Savas Beatie, 2012), 117–18; Warner, *Generals in Blue*, 171–72.

20 Eicher and Eicher, *High Commands*, 453; Warner, *Generals in Blue*, 403–4.

21 Franklin B. Hough, *History of Duryee's Brigade During the Campaign in Virginia Under Gen. Pope, and in Maryland Under Gen. McClellan in the Summer and Autumn of 1862* (Albany, NY: J. Munsell, 1864), 10–11; Warner, *Generals in Blue*, 133.

22 Hennessy, *Return to Bull Run*, 394–404; Warner, *Generals in Blue*, 510–11.

23 Cullom, *Biographical Register*, 484–90.

24 William Henry Locke, *The Story of the Regiment* (Philadelphia: J. B. Lippincott and Company, 1868).

25 Meade, *Life and Letters*, 297, 307–8.

26 John C. Waugh, *The Class of 1846: From West Point to Appomattox: Stonewall Jackson, George McClellan and Their Brothers* (New York: Ballantine Books, 1994), 183–84; Warner, *Generals in Blue*, 432–33.

27 O. R. Howard Thomson and William H. Rauch, *History of the "Bucktails," Kane Rifle Regiment of the Pennsylvania Reserve Corps (13th Pennsylvania Reserves, 42nd of the Line)* (Philadelphia: Electric Printing Company, 1906), 201.

28 Letters of Henry H. Glasier, MG 7, Military Manuscripts Collection, Pennsylvania State Archives, Harrisburg.

29 Meade, *Life and Letters*, 308.

30 Gibbs, Joseph, *Three Years in the Bloody Eleventh: The Campaigns of a Pennsylvania Reserves Regiment* (University City: Pennsylvania State University Press, 2002), 25–26.

31 Compare March 31 strength numbers at *OR*, Vol. 11, 53 to the early September numbers at *OR*, Vol. 19, II, 196.

32 Locke, *Story of the Regiment*, 117; George F. Noyes, *The Bivouac and the Battlefield* (New York: Harper & Brothers, 1863), 151.

33 William P. Maxson, *Camp Fires of the Twenty-Third* (New York: Davies & Kent, 1863), 96–97.

34 Glasier Letters, PSA, Harrisburg.

35 Theodore B. Gates, *The "Ulster Guard" and the War of the Rebellion* (New York: Benjamin H. Tyrrel, 1879), 287; Hartwig, *To Antietam Creek*, 168–70.

36 Hugh W. McNeil Collection, MG-87, Pennsylvania State Archives, Harrisburg.

37 Reel 31, McClellan Papers, LOC; *OR*, Vol. 19, II, 213.

38 Richard Slotkin, *The Long Road to Antietam: How the Civil War Became a Revolution* (New York: Liveright Publishing Company, 2012), 171.

39 Abbott, *Third Vermont Company*, 46.

40 E. B. Quiner, *E. B. Quiner Papers: Correspondence of the Wisconsin Volunteers, 1861–1865* (Madison, WI: State Historical Society of Wisconsin), Vol. 2, 300.

41 Edward L. Barnes, "The 95th New York: Sketch of Its Service in the Campaigns of 1862," *National Tribune*, January 7, 1886.

42 McNeil Collection, PSA, Harrisburg; Dawes, *Full Blown Yankee*, 76; J. Harrison Mills, *Chronicles of the Twenty-First Regiment, New York State Volunteers* (Buffalo: Gies and Company, 1887), 276–77.

43 Hough, *History of Duryee's Brigade*, 108.

44 Lyman C. Holford Papers, Library of Congress.

45 John D. Vautier, *History of the 88th Pennsylvania Volunteers in the War for the Union, 1861–1865* (Philadelphia: J. B. Lippincott, 1894), 69; Charles E. Davis Jr., *Three Years in the Army: The Story of the Thirteenth Massachusetts Volunteers from July 16, 1861 to August 1, 1864* (Boston: Estes and Lauriat, 1894), 128–29.

46 Locke, *Story of the Regiment*, 118–19; Benjamin F. Cook, *History of the Twelfth Massachusetts Volunteers, Webster Regiment* (Boston: Twelfth [Webster] Regiment Association, 1882), 66.

47 A. R. Small, *The Sixteenth Maine Regiment in the War of the Rebellion, 1861–1865* (Portland, ME: B. Thurston & Company, 1886), 9–33.

48 Reel 63, McClellan Papers, LOC; Sears, ed., *Papers of McClellan*, 450.

49 "Names and Records of All the Members Who Served in the First New Hampshire Battery Light Artillery During the Late Rebellion from September 26, 1861 to June 15, 1865" (Manchester, NH: Budget Job Print, 1891), 20.

50 *OR*, Vol. 19, 252–53; Reel 31, McClellan Papers, LOC.

51 *OR*, Vol. 19, II, 273–74; Hebert, *Fighting Joe*, 132–33.

52 Meade, *Life and Letters*, 310.

53 Robert Taggart Papers, PSA; Dawes, *Full Blown Yankee*, 79; Herdegen, *Iron Brigade*, 218.

54 Hussey and Todd, *History of the Ninth*, 188.

55 Maxson, *Camp Fires of the Twenty-Third*, 98.

56 Joseph L. Harsh, *Taken at the Flood: Robert E. Lee and Confederate Strategy in the Maryland Campaign of 1862* (Kent, OH: Kent State University Press, 1999), 145–46.

57 J. H. Stine, *History of the Army of the Potomac*, 2nd ed. (Washington, DC: Gibson Bros., 1893), 160.

58 Sears, ed., *Papers of McClellan*, 456–57; Hartwig, *To Antietam Creek*, 288–90.

59 Abbott, *Third Vermont Company*, 47.

60 Woodward, *Our Campaigns*, 173.

61 OR, Vol. 19, I, 214.

62 D. H. Hill, "The Battle of South Mountain, or Boonsboro: Fighting for Time at Turner's and Fox's Gaps," in *Battles and Leaders of the Civil War*, Vol. 2 (New York: Century Company, 1888), 564–65; Hal Bridges, *Lee's Maverick General: Daniel Harvey Hill* (Lincoln: University of Nebraska Press, 1991), 107.

63 OR, Vol. 19, I, 214.

64 OR, Vol. 19, I, 422–23; Hartwig, *To Antietam Creek*, 375.

65 OR, Vol. 19, I, 417; Brian M. Jordan, *Unholy Sabbath: The Battle of South Mountain in History and Memory* (New York: Savas Beatie, 2012), 200–202.

66 William Marvel, "The Making of a Myth: Ambrose E. Burnside and the Union High Command at Fredericksburg," in *The Fredericksburg Campaign: Decision on the Rappahannock*, Gary W. Gallagher, ed. (Chapel Hill: University of North Carolina Press, 1995), 20.

67 Hebert, *Fighting Joe*, 135.

68 Hill, "South Mountain," 580.

69 Thomson and Rauch, *History of the "Bucktails,"* 204.

70 Francis Winthrop Palfrey, *The Antietam and Fredericksburg*, Campaigns of the Civil War—V, (New York: Scribner's and Sons, 1882), 33; James K. Swisher, *Warrior in Grey: General Robert Rodes of Lee's Army* (Shippensburg, PA: White Mane Books, 2000), 59.

71 McNeil Collection, PSA, Harrisburg.

72 Samuel Bates, *History of Pennsylvania Volunteers, 1861–1865*, Vol. I (Harrisburg, PA: B. Singerly, 1869), 698, 702, 704.

73 Stine, *History*, 167; OR, Vol. 51, I, 142.

74 John David Hoptak, *The Battle of South Mountain* (Charleston, SC: History Press, 2011), 100–101.

75 M. D. Hardin, *History of the Twelfth Regiment Pennsylvania Reserve Volunteer Corps* (New York: self-published, 1890), 117.

76 Hartwig, *To Antietam Creek*, 379, 385, 388; James B. Casey, ed., "The Ordeal of Adoniram Judson Warner: His Minutes of South Mountain and Antietam," *Civil War History*, Vol. 28, #3, September 1982, 217–18.

77 Hartwig, *To Antietam Creek*, 388; OR, Vol. 51, 149.

78 Gibbs, *Three Years*, 176, 178; https://www.findagrave.com/memorial/103944384/nathaniel-nesbit.

79 OR, Vol. 51, 149; and, Vol. 19, I, 1093.

80 John Michael Priest, *Before Antietam: The Battle for South Mountain* (Shippensburg, PA: White Mane Publishing Company, 1992), 240–43, 324.

81 J. R. Sypher, *History of the Pennsylvania Reserve Corps* (Lancaster, PA: Elias Barr & Co., 1865), 369–70.

82 *OR*, Vol. 51, 155.

83 *OR*, Vol. 19, I, 268.

84 John Bryson, *History of the 30th New York Volunteers*, 70–71, unpublished manuscript, NYSL.

85 Hartwig, *To Antietam Creek*, 396–97.

86 Thomas P. Lowry, *Tarnished Eagles: The Courts-Martial of Fifty Union Colonels and Lieutenant Colonels* (Mechanicsburg, PA: Stackpole Books, 1997), 40–43.

87 Mills, *Chronicles of the Twenty-First*, 280–81.

88 Abbott, *Third Vermont Company*, 48.

89 Mills, *Chronicles of the Twenty-First*, 282.

90 Letter of Henry Cranford, South Mountain vertical file, Western Maryland Room, Washington County Free Library, Hagerstown, MD.

91 *OR*, Vol. 19, I, 232.

92 Gates, *"Ulster Guard,"* 297.

93 Abram Smith, *History of the Seventy-Sixth Regiment New York Volunteers* (Cortland, NY: Truair, Smith, and Miles, 1867), 153.

94 Barnes, "The 95th New York," 2.

95 Maxson, *Camp Fires of the Twenty-Third*, 99–100.

96 C. V. Tevis and D. R. Marquis, *The History of the Fighting Fourteenth* (New York: Brooklyn Eagle Press, 1911), 45.

97 Silas Felton, "The Iron Brigade Battery: An Irregular Regular Battery," in *Giants in Their Tall Black Hats: Essays on the Iron Brigade*, Alan T. Nolan and Sharon Eggleston Vipond, eds. (Bloomington: Indiana University Press, 1998), 146.

98 Hartwig, *To Antietam Creek*, 419–20; Quiner, *Quiner Papers*, Vol. 2, 237.

99 Quiner, *Quiner Papers*, Vol. 2, 303; *OR*, Vol. 19, I, 253.

100 *OR*, Vol. 19, I, 250; Alan D. Gaff, *On Many a Bloody Field: Four Years in the Iron Brigade* (Bloomington: Indiana University Press, 1996), 181.

101 *OR*, Vol. 19, I, 256–57.

102 Holford Papers, LOC.

103 *OR*, Vol. 19, I, 253–54.

104 *OR*, Vol. 19, I, 256–57; Hartwig, *To Antietam Creek*, 422–26; Priest, *Before Antietam*, 265–71.

105 State of Wisconsin, *Roster of Wisconsin Volunteers*, Vol. I (Madison, WI: Democrat Printing Company, 1886), 540, 544, 548, 559.

106 Philip Cheek and Mair Pointon, *History of the Sauk County Riflemen* (self-published, 1909), 49.

107 *OR*, Vol. 19, I, 52.

108 Slotkin, *Long Road*, 205–6.

109 Hartwig, *To Antietam Creek*, 681–82.

110 Quiner, *Quiner Papers*, Vol. 4, 16.

111 *OR*, Vol. 51, 831; *OR*, Vol. 19, I, 215.

112 Dawes, *Full Blown Yankee*, 84.

113 Harsh, *Taken at the Flood*, 287–302.

114 Davis, *Three Years*, 134.

115 *OR*, Vol. 51, 837.

116 Jacob Dolson Cox, *Military Reminiscences of the Civil War, Volume I, April 1861–November 1863* (New York: Charles Scribner's Sons, 1900), 383; *OR*, Vol. 19, I, 216.

117 Davis, *Three Years*, 135; Hussey and Todd, *History of the Ninth*, 190; Cook, *History of the Twelfth*, 67.

118 Antietam Collection, Dartmouth College, Folder 1-63; Augustus D. Ayling, *Revised Register of the Soldiers and Sailors of New Hampshire in the War of the Rebellion, 1861–1866* (Concord, NH: Ira C. Evans, 1895), 979.

119 Smith, *History of the Seventy-Sixth*, 163–64; Stine, *History*, 174–75.

120 Sears, ed., *Papers of McClellan*, 462–63.

121 Gates, *"Ulster Guard,"* 307.

122 Basler, ed., *Collected Works*, Vol. V, 426.

123 Vautier, *History of the 88th*, 71.

124 Antietam Collection, Dartmouth College, Folder 2-74; John W. Jaques, *Three Years' Campaign of the Ninth N.Y.S.M. During the Southern Rebellion* (New York: Hilton and Co., 1865), 112.

125 *OR*, Vol. 19, I, 217; Reel 31, McClellan Papers, LOC.

126 Pierro, ed., *Maryland Campaign*, 183–84.

127 Sears, *Landscape*, 160–61; Hartwig, *To Antietam Creek*, 509–17; Slotkin, *Long Road*, 216–22.

128 *OR*, Vol. 19, I, 268; Casey, ed., "Ordeal," 219; Locke, *Story of the Regiment*, 124; Antietam Collection, Dartmouth College, Folder 2-80.

129 McClellan, *Own Story*, 588.

130 Sears, ed., *Papers of McClellan*, 465.

131 Hartwig, *To Antietam Creek*, 598; Edwin Fishel, *The Secret War for the Union: The Untold Story of Military Intelligence in the Civil War* (Boston: Houghton Mifflin Company, 1996), 234–35.

132 Adjutant General rosters of the 26th New York and 84th New York, http://dmna.ny.gov/historic/reghist/civil/rosters/rostersinfantry.htm.

133 George B. McClellan, *Report on the Organization and Campaigns of the Army of the Potomac in Virginia and Maryland* (New York: Sheldon and Company, 1864), 375; McClellan, *Own Story*, 588–89; Rafuse, *McClellan's War*, 308; Harsh, *Taken at the Flood*, 335; http://emergingcivilwar.com/2016/09/16/the-fog-of-war-when-modern-weather-gives-us-a-history-lesson.

134 Pierro, ed., *Maryland Campaign*, 205; Slotkin, *Long Road*, 222–28.

135 Hartwig, *To Antietam Creek*, 505–17, 582–96 and Pierro, ed., *Maryland Campaign*, 177–86, 204–11.

136 *OR*, Vol. 19, I, 29, 55.

137 Rafuse, *McClellan's War*, 304–14.

138 Armstrong Jr., *Unfurl Those Colors*, 159.

139 Slotkin, *Long Road*, 243–51; Hartwig, *To Antietam Creek*, 638–40; *OR*, Vol. 51, I, 839.

140 John Michael Priest, *Antietam: The Soldiers' Battle* (New York: Oxford University Press, 1989), 11–28.

141 Thomson and Rauch, *History of the "Bucktails,"* 209–10; *OR*, Vol. 19, I, 268–69.

142 McNeil Collection, PSA, Harrisburg; Thomson and Rauch, *History of the "Buck-tails,"* 210.
143 Woodward, *Our Campaigns,* 205; https://www.findagrave.com/memorial/21778/augustus-t.-cross.
144 Antietam Collection, Dartmouth College, Folder 2-83.
145 Antietam Collection, Dartmouth College, Folders 2-53 and 4-13; Hartwig, *To Antietam Creek,* 646–47.
146 *OR,* Vol. 19, I, 144.
147 *OR,* Vol. 19, I, 223.
148 M. Shuler Diary, Library of Congress.
149 *OR,* Vol. 19, I, 259; Davis, *Three Years,* 185; Hough, *History of Duryee's Brigade,* 117; Locke, *Story of the Regiment,* 125–26.
150 Antietam Collection, Dartmouth College, Folders 2-14 and 2-16.
151 Antietam Collection, Dartmouth College, Folder 2-20; Vautier, *History of the 88th,* 74.
152 Uberto Burnham Papers, NYSL.
153 Louis M. Starr, *Bohemian Brigade: Civil War Newsmen in Action* (New York: Alfred A. Knopf, 1954), 140.
154 Bradley M. Gottfried, *The Maps of Antietam: An Atlas of the Antietam (Sharpsburg) Campaign, Including the Battle of South Mountain, September 2–20, 1862* (New York: Savas Beatie, 2013), 125–29.
155 Antietam Collection, Dartmouth College, Folder 2-49.
156 Antietam Collection, Dartmouth College, Folder 2-66.
157 Letter from unidentified soldier, 5th Alabama Regimental File, Antietam National Battlefield Library.
158 Antietam Collection, Dartmouth College, Folder 2-76.
159 *OR,* Vol. 19, I, 976; Sears, *Landscape,* 184–85; Pierro, ed., *Maryland Campaign,* 216; Gottfried, *Maps of Antietam,* 130–31.
160 *OR,* Vol. 51, I, 147.
161 Reel 31, McClellan Papers, LOC.
162 *OR,* Vol. 19, I, 259.
163 Antietam Collection, Dartmouth College, Folder 2-7.
164 Franklin Hough Papers, Box 34, NYSL.
165 Antietam Collection, Dartmouth College, Folders 2-11 and 2-4; https://www.findagrave.com/memorial/7734592/howard-carroll.
166 James Adsit Papers, NYSL.
167 Antietam Collection, Dartmouth College, Folder 2-2.
168 *OR,* Vol. 19, I, 233; https://www.findagrave.com/memorial/68455520/david-knoxnoyes; Dawes, *Full Blown Yankee,* 87; Holford Papers, LOC. The literature on Gibbon's Brigade is vast. The following paragraphs rely on several excellent works about the Iron Brigade at Antietam. See, Alan T. Nolan, *The Iron Brigade: A Military History* (Bloomington: Indiana University Press, 1994), 136–48; Herdegen, *Iron Brigade,* 249–78; Herdegen, *Men Stood Like Iron,* 160–84; Gaff, *On Many a Bloody Field,* 184–93; D. Scott Hartwig, "'I Dread the Thought of the Place': The Iron Brigade at Antietam," in *Giants in Their Tall Black Hats,* Nolan and Vipond, eds. 30–52.

169 *OR*, Vol. 19, I, 224, 233; Antietam Collection, Dartmouth College, Folder 1-63; https://www.findagrave.com/memorial/151839666/silas-wright-howard; Abbott, *Third Vermont Company*, 49; Second U.S. Sharpshooters Regimental File, Antietam National Battlefield.

170 M. Shuler Diary, Library of Congress.

171 *OR*, Vol. 51, I, 140.

172 Antietam Collection, Dartmouth College, Folder 2-28.

173 Antietam Collection, Dartmouth College, Folder 2-41.

174 Arthur A. Kent, ed., *Three Years with Company K: Sergt. Austin C. Stearns, Company K, 13th Mass. Infantry* (Rutherford, NJ: Fairleigh Dickinson University Press, 1976), 126–30.

175 William Prince letter, September 22, 1862, NYSL.

176 Priest, *Antietam: The Soldiers' Battle*, 333.

177 Vautier, *History of the 88th*, 74.

178 Antietam Collection, Dartmouth College, Folder 2-13.

179 Paul Taylor, *Glory Was Not Their Companion: The Twenty-Sixth New York Volunteer Infantry in the Civil War* (Jefferson, NC: McFarland and Company, Inc., 2005), 84–85; Sears, *Landscape*, 187–88.

180 *OR*, Vol. 19, I, 976–77.

181 Vautier, *History of the 88th*, 76; Antietam Collection, Dartmouth College, Folder 2-20.

182 John Bell Hood, *Advance and Retreat: Personal Experiences in the United States and Confederate States Armies* (New York: Da Capo Press, 1993), 43.

183 Gates, "Ulster Guard," 317–18; E. W. Shepard, *The Campaign in Virginia and Maryland: June 26th to Sept 20th, 1862* (London: George Allen and Comp., 1911), 249–50.

184 Antietam Collection, Dartmouth College, Folder 1-71.

185 Priest, *Antietam: The Soldiers' Battle*, 62–65; www.cmohs.org/recipient-detail/288/cook-john.php; www.cmohs.org/recipient-detail/630/hogarty-william-p.php; www.cmohs.org/recipient-detail/706/johnson-john.php.

186 Pierro, ed., *Maryland Campaign*, 225–28; Antietam Collection, Dartmouth College, Folder 2-24.

187 Priest, *Antietam: The Soldiers' Battle*, 333.

188 www.cmohs.org/recipient-detail/1037/paul-william-h.php; www.cmohs.org/recipient-detail/96/beyer-hillary.php.

189 Antietam Collection, Dartmouth College, Folder 2-65.

190 *OR*, Vol. 19, I, 269; Gottfried, *Maps of Antietam*, 146–47.

191 E. M. Woodward, *History of the Third Pennsylvania Reserve: Being a Complete Record of the Regiment, with Incidents of the Camp, Marches, Bivouacs, Skirmishes and Battles; Together with the Personal Record of Every Officer and Man During His Term of Service* (Trenton, NJ: MacCrellish & Quigley, 1883), 183.

192 Antietam Collection, Dartmouth College, Folder 2-71; Richard E. Eberly Jr., *Bouquets from the Cannon's Mouth: Soldiering with the Eighth Regiment of the Pennsylvania Reserves* (Shippensburg, PA: White Mane Books, 2005), 131–35.

193 *OR*, Vol. 51, I, 148; Antietam Collection, Dartmouth College, Folder 2-68.

194 Antietam Collection, Dartmouth College, Folder 2-80; Gibbs, *Three Years*, 184; *OR*, Vol. 51, I, 151, 154; 9th Pennsylvania Reserves Regimental File, Antietam National Battlefield.

195 www.cmohs.org/recipient-detail/709/johnson-samuel.php; https://www.findagrave
.com/memorial/10280180/samuel-johnson; Reel 32, McClellan Papers, LOC.
196 Gaff, *On Many a Bloody Field*, 186–87.
197 Hood, *Advance and Retreat*, 44; George E. Otott, "Clash in the Cornfield: The 1st Texas
Volunteer Infantry in the Maryland Campaign," *Civil War Regiments*, Vol. V, No. 3 (El
Dorado, CA: Savas Publishing Company, 1997), 73–123; Richard M. McMurry, *John Bell
Hood and the War for Southern Independence* (Lincoln: University of Nebraska Press, 1992),
58–59.
198 Antietam Collection, Dartmouth College, Folder 2-41.
199 Hebert, *Fighting Joe*, 142–43; George O. Otis and D. L. Huntington, *The Medical and
Surgical History of the War of the Rebellion*, Part III, Vol. II, Surgical History (Washington,
DC: GPO, 1883), 60.
200 Sears, *Landscape*, 216–20; Rafuse, *McClellan's War*, 315–17; Slotkin, *Long Road*, 279–81.
201 *OR*, Vol. 19, I, 225.
202 *OR*, Vol. 19, I, 245.
203 Jacob Cox, "The Battle of Antietam," in *Battles and Leaders of the Civil War*, Vol. 2, (New
York: Century Company, 1888) 641–42; Pierro, ed., *Maryland Campaign*, 251.
204 Sears, ed., *Papers of McClellan,* 474; *OR*, Vol. 19, I, 219.
205 *OR*, Vol. 19, II, 349.
206 Meade, *Life and Letters*, 310–11, 314.
207 http://paemergencymen.blogspot.com/2011/08/pennsylvania-reserve-corps-part-ii.html.
208 Noyes, *Bivouac*, 215.
209 Quiner, *Quiner Papers*, Vol. 2, 307.
210 Herdegen, *Iron Brigade*, 278–81.
211 Uberto Burnham Papers, NYSL; Second U.S. Sharpshooters Regimental File, Antietam National Battlefield.
212 Antietam Collection, Dartmouth College, Folders 2-2 and 2-54; William Prince letter,
NYSL.
213 James Adsit Papers, NYSL.
214 7th Pennsylvania Reserves Regimental File, Antietam National Battlefield; https://
www.findagrave.com/memorial/26040393/james-smith-colwell.
215 www.pa-roots.com/pacw/reserves/11thres/deathoftsmooresep231861.htm.
216 *OR*, Vol. 19, II, 305–6; William DeLoss Love, *Wisconsin in the War of the Rebellion*
(Chicago: Church and Goodman, 1866), 337; Herdegen, *Iron Brigade*, 289.
217 McNeil Collection, PSA, Harrisburg; https://www.findagrave.com/memorial/
23020133/hugh-watson-mcneil.
218 13th Pennsylvania Reserves Records, MG 234, PSA, Harrisburg.
219 Glasier Letters, PSA, Harrisburg.
220 Vautier, *History of the 88th*, 78.
221 Maxson, *Camp Fires of the Twenty-Third*, 103.
222 Locke, *Story of the Regiment*, 135.
223 Antietam Collection, Dartmouth College, Folder 2-13.
224 Hebert, *Fighting Joe*, 146–52, Wert, *Sword of Lincoln*, 178.
225 http://library.fandm.edu/archives/Reynolds/JFR/transcriptions/s88.htm.

226 Meade, *Life and Letters*, 315–16.

227 Warner, *Generals in Blue*, 495–96.

228 Warner, *Generals in Blue*, 363–64.

229 Gaff, *On Many a Bloody Field*, 193.

230 16th Maine Regimental Correspondence, Folder 5, Maine State Archives, Augusta.

231 *OR*, Vol. 19, II, 368–69, 374.

232 http://library.fandm.edu/archives/Reynolds/JFR/Files/scrapbook-1240.jpg.

233 O. B. Curtis, *History of the Twenty-Fourth Michigan of the Iron Brigade* (Gaithersburg, MD: Olde Soldier Books, reprinted 1988), 65–66; Donald L. Smith, *The Twenty-Fourth Michigan of the Iron Brigade* (Harrisburg, PA: Stackpole Company, 1962), 40–43; Herdegen, *Iron Brigade*, 292–96; Gaff, *On Many a Bloody Field*, 193–94.

234 Meade, *Life and Letters*, 317–18; *OR*, Vol. 19, II, 348.

235 Bryson, *History of the 30th*, 74.

236 Franklin Hough Papers, Box 35, NYSL.

237 Uberto Burnham Papers, NYSL.

238 Abbott, *Third Vermont Company*, 50.

239 Holford Papers, LOC.

240 Brooks D. Simpson, "General McClellan's Bodyguard: The Army of the Potomac After Antietam," in *The Antietam Campaign*, Gary W. Gallagher, ed. (Chapel Hill: University of North Carolina Press, 1999), 55–58.

241 Abbott, *Third Vermont Company*, 50; Marlen C. Bumbera, ed., *The Civil War Letters of Cpl John H. Strathern: Eighth Pennsylvania Reserve Volunteer Corps* (Apollo, PA: Closson Press, 1994), 86; Eberly Jr., *Bouquets*, 140; Holford Papers, LOC.

242 Dawes, *Full Blown Yankee*, 100.

243 Antietam Collection, Dartmouth College, Folder 2-11; Uberto Burnham Papers, NYSL.

244 Hussey and Todd, *History of the Ninth*, 202.

245 Davis, *Three Years*, 142, 146.

246 McClellan, *Own Story*, 618.

247 Vautier, *History of the 88th*, 83; Herdegen, *Men Stood Like Iron*, 196–97.

248 Meade, *Life and Letters*, 319.

249 *OR*, Vol. 19, I, 72.

250 *OR*, Vol. 19, II, 454.

251 *OR*, Vol. 19, II, 466.

252 Dawes, *Full Blown Yankee*, 104.

253 *OR*, Vol. 19, I, 81 and Vol. 19, II, 464.

254 Kent, ed., *Three Years*, 138; Penny Family Papers, Folder 15, NYSL; Taylor, *Glory Was Not*, 89.

Part Two: Virginia Blues

1 Allan Nevins, ed., *A Diary of Battle: The Personal Journals of Colonel Charles S. Wainwright* (Boston: Da Capo Press, 1998), 119–20.

2 Cook, *History of the Twelfth*, 75; Carl A. Morrel, *Seymour Dexter, Union Army: Journal and Letters of Civil War Service in Company K, 23rd N.Y. Volunteer Regiment of Elmira, with Illustrations* (Jefferson, NC: McFarland and Company, 1996), 109–10.

3 John Gibbon, *Personal Recollections of the Civil War* (New York: G. P. Putnam's Sons, 1928), 92; Maxson, *Camp Fires of the Twenty-Third*, 109.

4 "Names and Records," 22.

5 Smith, *History of the Seventy-Sixth*, 178; Uberto Burnham Papers, NYSL; Stine, *History*, 235–36.

6 Woodward, *Third Reserve*, 196; Hardin, *History of the Twelfth*, 129; Rafuse, *McClellan's War*, 373.

7 Tevis and Marquis, *History of the Fighting Fourteenth*, 54.

8 Horace Hanks Papers, NYSL.

9 Curtis, *History of the Twenty-Fourth*, 75–77.

10 Robert Taggart Papers, PSA.

11 Nevins, ed., *Diary of Battle*, 124–25.

12 Locke, *Story of the Regiment*, 155.

13 Abbott, *Third Vermont Company*, 51.

14 Lewis A. Benedict Papers, NYSL.

15 Hussey and Todd, *History of the Ninth*, 214; Cook, *History of the Twelfth*, 76–77; Eberly Jr., *Bouquets*, 142–43.

16 Meade, *Life and Letters*, 325–26; Rafuse, *McClellan's War*, 377.

17 Robert Taggart Papers, PSA.

18 Dawes, *Full Blown Yankee*, 105.

19 Rogan H. Moore, ed., *The Civil War Memoirs of Sergeant George W. Darby, 1861–1865* (Bowie, MD: Heritage Books, 1999), 49–50; Davis, *Three Years*, 156.

20 Locke, *Story of the Regiment*, 154; Charles McClenthen, *Narrative of the Fall & Winter Campaign, by a Private Soldier of the 2nd Div. 1st Army Corps* (Syracuse, NY: Masters & Lee, 1863), 23–24.

21 Cheek and Pointon, *Sauk County Riflemen*, 54.

22 Survivors' Association, *History of the 121st Regiment Pennsylvania Volunteers* (Philadelphia: Catholic Standards and Times, 1906), 25–26.

23 Eicher and Eicher, *High Commands*, 461.

24 Cullom, *Biographical Register*, 686–87.

25 Bates, *History of Pennsylvania Volunteers*, Vol. I, 784–87.

26 Abbott, *Third Vermont Company*, 51.

27 *OR*, Vol. 19, II, 569, 583.

28 Fishel, *Secret War*, 256–57, 259–60; *OR*, Vol. 19, II, 552–54. Two histories of the campaign have been published in the twenty-first century. See, Francis Augustin O'Reilly, *The Fredericksburg Campaign: Winter War on the Rappahannock* (Baton Rouge: Louisiana State University Press, 2003) and George C. Rable, *Fredericksburg! Fredericksburg!* (Chapel Hill: University of North Carolina Press, 2002).

29 Davis, *Three Years*, 158; Hussey and Todd, *History of the Ninth*, 218.

30 Dawes, *Full Blown Yankee*, 106.

31 Uberto Burnham Papers, NYSL; 5th Maine Battery Regimental Correspondence, Folder 21, Maine State Archives, Augusta.

32 Meade, *Life and Letters*, 330.

33 Holford Papers, LOC.

34 Nolan, *Iron Brigade*, 171–73; Herdegen, *Iron Brigade*, 313–14; *OR*, Vol. 51, I, 951.

35 Eicher and Eicher, *High Commands*, 387; Gaff, *Brave Men's Tears*, 31; Gaff, *On Many a Bloody Field*, 19–22.

36 Curtis, *History of the Twenty-Fourth*, 83; Hussey and Todd, *History of the Ninth*, 219; Cook, *History of the Twelfth*, 79.

37 Robert Taggart Papers, PSA.

38 Maxson, *Camp Fires of the Twenty-Third*, 113.

39 Woodward, *Third Reserve*, 200.

40 *OR*, Vol. 51, I, 953; Cook, *History of the Twelfth*, 79; Dawes, *Full Blown Yankee*, 108; McClenthen, *Narrative*, 31–32.

41 *OR*, Vol. 51, I, 955; Davis Jr., *Three Years*, 161.

42 *OR*, Vol. 51, I, 956.

43 House of Representatives, 37th Congress, 3rd Session, *Report of the Joint Committee on the Conduct of the War*, Part I (Washington, DC: GPO, 1863), 702.

44 Jaques, *Three Years' Campaign*, 127–28; McClenthen, *Narrative*, 34.

45 Horace Hanks Papers, NYSL.

46 Survivors' Association, *History of the 121st Regiment*, 28.

47 Dawes, *Full Blown Yankee*, 108.

48 Robert Taggart Papers, PSA.

49 Abbott, *Third Vermont Company*, 51, 53–54.

50 *OR*, Vol. 21, 448–49.

51 Fishel, *Secret War*, 250–74.

52 Frank A. O'Reilly, *"Stonewall" Jackson at Fredericksburg: The Battle of Prospect Hill, December 13, 1862* (Lynchburg, VA: H. E. Howard, Inc., 1993), 32–34; Rable, *Fredericksburg!*, 184–85, 190–91.

53 *OR*, Vol. 21, 71.

54 Marvel, "Making of a Myth," 12–15, 21–24.

55 *OR*, Vol. 21, 450. Marvel's article generally supportive of Burnside counters contemporaries of Franklin who defended the grand division commander. For such a view, see Jacob L. Greene, *Gen. William B. Franklin and the Operations of the Left Wing at the Battle of Fredericksburg, December 13, 1862* (Hartford, CT: Belknap and Warfield, 1900).

56 O'Reilly, *"Stonewall" Jackson at Fredericksburg*, 202; Meade, *Life and Letters*, 336–37.

57 James I. Robertson Jr., *Stonewall Jackson: The Man, The Soldier, The Legend* (New York: Macmillan Publishing, 1997), 654–55.

58 Isaac Hall, *History of the Ninety-Seventh Regiment New York Volunteers ("Conkling Rifles") in the War for the Union* (Utica, NY: L. C. Childs & Son, 1890), 110; Gibbon, *Personal Recollections*, 102–3; Survivors' Association, *History of the 121st*, 30; Herdegen, *Iron Brigade*, 316–18.

59 *OR*, Vol. 21, 645.

60 H. F. Christy, "The 'Reserves' at Fredericksburg," *National Tribune*, September 19, 1901, 6; Bates, *History of Pennsylvania Volunteers*, 852; Gibbs, *Three Years*, 201.

61 *OR*, Vol. 21, 645; O'Reilly, *"Stonewall" Jackson at Fredericksburg*, 35–45; Thomson and Rauch, *History of the "Bucktails,"* 232.

62 "Names and Records," 23–24; Peter J. Cooper, *Samuel's Story: A Journey from Yorkshire to New Hampshire through the American Civil War* (Victoria, BC: Friesen Press, 2013), 96–98; *OR*, Vol. 21, 466, 468.

63 Bryson, *History of the 30th*, 78–79.

64 Bradley M. Gottfried, *The Maps of Fredericksburg: An Atlas of the Fredericksburg Campaign, Including All Cavalry Operations, September 18, 1862–January 22, 1863* (El Dorado Hills, CA: Savas Beatie, 2018), 98–101.

65 James Fitz James Caldwell, *The History of a Brigade of South Carolinians* (Philadelphia: King & Baird, 1866), 58; George C. Rable, "It Is Well That War Is So Terrible: The Carnage of Fredericksburg," in *The Fredericksburg Campaign*, Gary W. Gallagher, ed. (Chapel Hill: University of North Carolina Press, 1995), 48–51.

66 O'Reilly, *Fredericksburg Campaign*, 167.

67 *OR*, Vol. 21, 518–19.

68 Rable, *Fredericksburg!*, 205–7; *OR*, Vol. 21, 661; Bumbera, ed., *Civil War Letters*, 86.

69 Gibbs, *Three Years*, 202–3; *OR*, Vol. 21, 512; https://www.findagrave.com/memorial/85578618/arthur-dehon.

70 Thomson and Rauch, *History of the "Bucktails,"* 234.

71 www.cmohs.org/recipient-detail/1520/woodward-evan-m.php; O'Reilly, *"Stonewall" Jackson at Fredericksburg*, 85–94.

72 *OR*, Vol. 21, 520–21.

73 Woodward, *Third Reserve*, 210; Sypher, *Pennsylvania Reserve Corps*, 415; John W. Urban, *My Experiences Mid Shot and Shell and in Rebel Den* (Lancaster, PA: Hubbard Brothers, 1882), 254; O'Reilly, *Fredericksburg Campaign*, 179–85; Warren Lee Goss, *Recollections of a Private: A Story of the Army of the Potomac* (New York: Thomas Y Crowell and Company, 1890), 126; Eberly Jr., *Bouquets*, 150–52; Gibbs, *Three Years*, 204.

74 O'Reilly, *Fredericksburg Campaign*, 140.

75 *OR*, Vol. 21, 512–13.

76 Robert Taggart Papers, PSA.

77 *OR*, Vol. 21, 484.

78 Davis, *Three Years*, 164–66.

79 *OR*, Vol. 21, 503, 508; Vautier, *History of the 88th*, 90.

80 *OR*, Vol. 21, 450, 454.

81 *OR*, Vol. 21, 506.

82 *OR*, Vol. 21, 484–85.

83 *OR*, Vol. 21, 654.

84 *OR*, Vol. 21, 480; Locke, *Story of the Regiment*, 165; Hussey and Todd, *History of the Ninth*, 224.

85 Jaques, *Three Years' Campaign*, 129; Adjutant General roster, 83rd New York, http://dmna.ny.gov/historic/reghist/civil/rosters/Infantry/83rd_Infantry_CW_Roster.pdf; *OR*, Vol. 21, 505.

86 *OR*, Vol. 21, 496, 500–501.

87 *OR*, Vol. 21, 502; www.cmohs.org/recipient-detail/1055/petty-philip.php.

88 *OR*, Vol. 21, 501.

89 www.cmohs.org/recipient-detail/866/maynard-george-h.php; O'Reilly, *"Stonewall" Jackson at Fredericksburg*, 98.

90 Small, *Sixteenth Maine*, 65; *OR*, Vol. 21, 486–87, 490–91.

91 *OR*, Vol. 21, 494.

92 12th Massachusetts correspondence folder, Massachusetts National Guard Archives-Museum, Concord, MA; *OR*, Vol. 21, 498.

93 *OR*, Vol. 21, 655; Stine, *History*, 274; McClenthen, *Narrative*, 39; O'Reilly, *"Stonewall" Jackson at Fredericksburg*, 105; O'Reilly, *Fredericksburg Campaign*, 193–94.

94 www.cmohs.org/recipient-detail/1234/shiel-john.php.

95 *OR*, Vol. 21, 490; Charles H. Nichols Papers, Library of Congress; 16th Maine Regimental Correspondence, Folder 8, Maine State Archives, Augusta.

96 William Johnson Bacon, *Memorial of William Kirkland Bacon, Late Adjutant of the Twenty-Sixth Regiment of New York State Volunteers, By His Father* (Utica, NY: Roberts, Printer, 1863), 39–40, 42.

97 http://dmna.ny.gov/historic/reghist/civil/infantry/26thInf/26thInfCWN.htm.

98 *OR*, Vol. 21, 463; Gaff, *On Many a Bloody Field*, 209; Herdegen, *Iron Brigade*, 320.

99 *OR*, Vol. 21, 464; Noyes, *Bivouac*, 314–15.

100 William Marvel, *The First New Hampshire Battery, 1861–1865* (Conway, NH: Minuteman Press, 1985), 28–29.

101 *OR*, Vol. 21, 470; Holford Papers, LOC.

102 Dawes, *Full Blown Yankee*, 113; Gaff, *On Many a Bloody Field*, 211–12; *OR*, Vol. 21, 464.

103 Davis, *Three Years*, 171.

104 Stevens, *Berdan's United States Sharpshooters*, 224.

105 *OR*, Vol. 21, 143–45; Bates, *History of Pennsylvania Volunteers*, Vol. I, 670; https://www.findagrave.com/memorial/43676404/franklin-zentmyer and https://www.findagrave.com/memorial/38015057/david-zentmyer.

106 Quiner, *Quiner Papers*, Vol. 4, 29.

107 Survivors' Association, *History of the 121st*, 33–34; *OR*, Vol. 21, 455.

108 *OR*, Vol. 21, 455–56.

109 23rd New York Regimental File, Antietam National Battlefield.

110 Marvel, *First New Hampshire Battery*, 25.

111 *OR*, Vol. 21, 513; Meade, *Life and Letters*, 338; 12th Massachusetts Regimental File, Gettysburg National Military Park.

112 Franklin Hough Papers, Box 22, NYSL.

113 16th Maine Regimental Correspondence, Folders 8 and 9, Maine State Archives, Augusta.

114 12th Massachusetts correspondence folder, Massachusetts National Guard Archives-Museum, Concord.

115 Gibbon, *Personal Recollections*, 105.

116 *OR*, Vol. 21, 454, 484; McClenthen, *Narrative*, 41.

117 http://library.fandm.edu/archives/Reynolds/JFR/transcriptions/s95.htm.

118 House of Representatives, *Report of the Joint Committee*, 691.

119 Palfrey, *Antietam and Fredericksburg*, 180–82.

120 Hussey and Todd, *History of the Ninth*, 227.

121 www.pa-roots.com/pacw/reserves/11thres/cobltrsporter&sutor.html.

122 Hall, *History of the Ninety-Seventh*, 115; Dawes, *Full Blown Yankee*, 115.

123 Horace Hanks Papers, NYSL; A. Wilson Greene, "Morale, Maneuver, and Mud: The Army of the Potomac, December 16, 1862–January 26, 1863," in *The Fredericksburg Campaign: Decision on the Rappahannock*, Gary W. Gallagher, ed. (Chapel Hill: University of North Carolina Press, 1995), 177–79.

124 Uberto Burnham Papers, NYSL.

125 Gottfried, *Maps of Fredericksburg*, 243; Greene, "Morale, Maneuver, and Mud," 180–87.

126 Eicher and Eicher, *High Commands*, 385.

127 *OR*, Vol. 21, 877–79; Gibbs, *Three Years*, 209–10.

128 *OR*, Vol. 21, 860, 876.

129 *OR*, Vol. 21, 898; Eicher and Eicher, *High Commands*, 457–58; Warner, *Generals in Blue*, 407–8; Gottfried, *Maps of Fredericksburg*, 134–37.

130 Stevens, *Berdan's United States Sharpshooters*, 229–30; Abbott, *Third Vermont Company*, 56.

131 https://www.findagrave.com/memorial/6038271/george-h.-biddle.

132 Sypher, *Pennsylvania Reserve Corps*, 433–34.

133 Lewis A. Benedict Papers, NYSL; William Woodruff, 1863 Diary, NYSL.

134 www.nysl.nysed.gov/scandocs/civilwar.htm.

135 Curtis, *History of the Twenty-Fourth*, 107.

136 Frederick Ranger Letters, NYSL.

137 Newton Church letter, NYSL; Adjutant General roster for the 22nd New York, http://dmna.ny.gov/historic/reghist/civil/rosters/Infantry/22nd_Infantry_CW_Roster.pdf.

138 William Woodruff, 1863 Diary, NYSL.

139 Hiram Hodgkins Letters, microfilm reel F-02845, Vermont State Archives, Middlesex.

140 Locke, *Story of the Regiment*, 177.

141 William Woodruff, 1863 Diary, NYSL.

142 *OR*, Vol. 21, 941–42, 944–45, 954.

143 Greene, "Morale, Maneuver, and Mud," 193–95; O'Reilly, *Fredericksburg Campaign*, 471–74.

144 Tevis and Marquis, *History of the Fighting Fourteenth*, 61–62.

145 Horace Hanks Papers, NYSL.

146 Nevins, ed., *Diary of Battle*, 157–58.

147 Horace Hanks Papers, NYSL.

148 Hussey and Todd, *History of the Ninth*, 236.

149 Gottfried, *Maps of Fredericksburg*, 246–47.

150 Hussey and Todd, *History of the Ninth*, 237–38; Locke, *Story of the Regiment*, 181.

151 Stine, *History*, 296–98.

152 Cook, *History of the Twelfth*, 86–87; Locke, *Story of the Regiment*, 181.

153 Curtis, *History of the Twenty-Fourth*, 112; Greene, "Morale, Maneuver, and Mud," 199–203.

154 Nevins, ed., *Diary of Battle*, 160; www.cmohs.org/recipient-detail/1475/whittier
-edward-n.php.

155 Vautier, *History of the 88th*, 94; Swinton, *Campaigns*, 260; Herdegen, *Iron Brigade*, 328–
29; Wert, *Sword of Lincoln*, 214.

156 Dawes, *Full Blown Yankee*, 117.

157 Curt Anders, *Henry Halleck's War: A Fresh Look at Lincoln's Controversial General-in-
Chief* (Carmel, IN: Guild Press, 2000), 372–74; Ernest B. Furgurson, *Chancellorsville, 1863:
Souls of the Brave* (New York: Vintage Books, 1992), 17–18; Stephen W. Sears, *Chancellors-
ville* (Boston: Houghton Mifflin, 1996), 20–25.

158 *OR*, Vol. 25, II, 53.

159 *OR*, Vol. 25, II, 10.

160 *OR*, Vol. 25, II, 69–70.

161 Warner, *Generals in Blue*, 413–14; Eicher and Eicher, *High Commands*, 463.

162 Thomson and Rauch, *History of the "Bucktails,"* 21–22; Eicher and Eicher, *High Commands*, 514.

163 Bates, *History of Pennsylvania Volunteers*, Vol. IV, 611–12; Richard E. Matthews, *The
149th Pennsylvania Volunteer Infantry Unit in the Civil War* (Jefferson, NC: McFarland and
Company, 1994), 1–36.

164 *OR*, Vol. 25, II, 51.

165 *OR*, Vol. 25, II, 5, 57–59, 152; Swinton, *Campaigns*, 268; Stine, *History*, 311–13; Wert,
Sword of Lincoln, 224–26; Hebert, *Fighting Joe*, 179–80, 183–84; Vautier, *History of the 88th*,
95–96.

166 Patrick Walker Letters, NYSL.

167 Lance Herdegen and Sherry Murphy, eds., *Four Years with the Iron Brigade: The Civil
War Journal of William Ray* (Cambridge, MA: Da Capo Press, 2002), 139, 163.

168 Cook, *History of the Twelfth*, 90; Hussey and Todd, *History of the Ninth*, 239–40; Herdegen and Murphy, eds., *Four Years*, 166, 172.

169 Uberto Burnham Papers, NYSL.

170 J. Horace McFarland Papers, MG 85, PSA, Harrisburg.

171 Holford Papers, LOC.

172 Morrow-Hittle Family Collection, MG 94, Pennsylvania State Archives, Harrisburg.

173 Tyrel Family Correspondence, NYSL.

174 Cheek and Pointon, *Sauk County Riflemen*, 61–62; Dawes, *Full Blown Yankee*, 134.

175 Davis, *Three Years*, 189, 193, 195.

176 Charles H. Nichols Papers, LOC.

177 Quiner, *Quiner Papers*, Vol. 8, 133.

178 Small, *Sixteenth Maine*, 99–100.

179 Horace Hanks Papers, NYSL.

180 Nevins, ed., *Diary of Battle*, 156.

181 Tevis and Marquis, *History of the Fighting Fourteenth*, 62–63.

182 Reuben Abel Papers, NYSL.

183 Dawes, *Full Blown Yankee*, 126, 128–29.

184 McFarland Papers, PSA, Harrisburg.

185 Locke, *Story of the Regiment*, 192–93.

186 *OR*, Vol. 25, II, 65–66, 320.

187 Abner Doubleday, *Chancellorsville and Gettysburg* (New York: Charles Scribner's Sons, 1882), 2–3; Charles H. Nichols Papers, LOC.

188 *OR*, Vol. 25, I, 262.

189 *OR*, Vol. 25, I, 257–58.

190 *OR*, Vol. 25, I, 267, 286.

191 Tevis and Marquis, *History of the Fighting Fourteenth*, 67–68; *OR*, Vol. 25, 173.

192 Chris Mackowski and Kristopher D. White, *Chancellorsville's Forgotten Front: The Battles of Second Fredericksburg and Salem Church, May 3, 1863* (El Dorado, CA: Savas Beatie, 2013), 72–77; Marc Storch and Beth Storch, "'Like So Many Devils': The Iron Brigade at Fitzhugh's Crossing," in Nolan and Vipond, eds., *Giants in Their Tall Black Hats*, 87–100.

193 Uberto Burnham Papers, NYSL.

194 *OR*, Vol. 25, I, 272.

195 Stine, *History*, 331; Mahood, *General Wadsworth*, 139–40; Quiner, *Quiner Papers*, Vol. 8, 370.

196 Davis, *Three Years*, 200–201; *OR*, Vol. 25, 173, 263.

197 *OR*, Vol. 25, I, 173.

198 *OR*, Vol. 25, II, 274

199 Bryson, *History of the 30th*, 83.

200 *OR*, Vol. 25, II, 335–36.

201 *OR*, Vol. 25, II, 340–43.

202 Furgurson, *Chancellorsville*, 147–71; Hebert, *Fighting Joe*, 192–208.

203 *OR*, Vol. 25, II, 351, 361; Sears, *Chancellorsville*, 228–30.

204 *OR*, Vol. 25, I, 254, 257, 288, 296; Vol. 25, II, 362.

205 James S. Pula, *Under the Crescent Moon with the XI Corps in the Civil War, Volume 1: From the Defenses of Washington to Chancellorsville, 1862–1863* (El Dorado Hills, CA: Savas Beatie, 2017), 199–200, 210–11.

206 *OR*, Vol. 51, I, 1034; Sears, *Chancellorsville*, 243–44.

207 *OR*, Vol. 25, I, 263.

208 *OR*, Vol. 25, I, 282; Small, *Sixteenth Maine*, 103; Tevis and Marquis, *History of the Fighting Fourteenth*, 71; Dawes, *Full Blown Yankee*, 137.

209 Thomas Chamberlin, *History of the One Hundred and Fiftieth Regiment Pennsylvania Volunteers, Second Regiment, Bucktail Brigade* (Philadelphia: F. McManus, Jr & Co., 1905), 87.

210 *OR*, Vol. 25, I, 279, 288.

211 *OR*, Vol. 25, I, 261, 268.

212 *OR*, Vol. 25, I, 279; Locke, *Story of the Regiment*, 196–97.

213 Warner, *Generals in Blue*, 25; Eicher and Eicher, *High Commands*, 122.

214 Hennessy, *Return to Bull Run*, 394–96; *Memoirs of N. P. Perkins, 5th Maine Battery*, microfilm reel F-02846, Vermont State Archives, Middlesex, 100; State of Maine, *Annual Report of the Adjutant General of the State of Maine for the Year Ending 1863* (Augusta, ME: Stevens & Sayward, 1864), 62.

215 https://www.findagrave.com/memorial/21827/george-francis-leppien.

216 *OR*, Vol. 25, I, 285.

217 *Memoirs of N. P. Perkins*, 46–47.

218 *OR*, Vol. 25, I, 314.

219 *OR*, Vol. 25, I, 285.

220 www.cmohs.org/recipient-detail/247/chase-john-f.php.

221 *Memoirs of N. P. Perkins*, 49-52; https://www.findagrave.com/memorial/142322663/napoleon-b.-perkins.

222 Greenleaf Stevens, *Letter to Members of the Fifth Maine Battery Association* (Augusta, ME: Charles E. Nash, 1890), 8–9.

223 *OR*, Vol. 25, I, 259–60.

224 5th Maine Battery correspondence, Folder 21, Maine State Archives, Augusta.

225 Doubleday, *Chancellorsville and Gettysburg*, 53–54.

226 Hebert, *Fighting Joe*, 212–15.

227 *OR*, Vol. 25, I, 279, 294.

228 *OR*, Vol. 25, I, 283, 298.

229 *OR*, Vol. 25, I, 296–97, 299.

230 12th Massachusetts correspondence folder, Massachusetts National Guard Archives-Museum, Concord.

231 *OR*, Vol. 25, I, 288, 293; Bates, *History of Pennsylvania Volunteers*, Vol. IV, 309–10.

232 Curtis, *History of the Twenty-Fourth*, 135.

233 *OR*, Vol. 25, I, 272.

234 Stine, *History*, 361; Davis, *Three Years*, 206; Locke, *Story of the Regiment*, 204.

235 Vautier, *History of the 88th*, 102; Davis, *Three Years*, 209; Matthews, *149th Pennsylvania*, 61.

236 *OR*, Vol. 25, II, 464.

237 Curtis, *History of the Twenty-Fourth*, 139; John W. Schildt, *Roads to Gettysburg* (Parsons, WV: McClain Printing Company, 2003), 7.

238 *OR*, Vol. 25, II, 532.

239 Photocopy of General Order 36, NYSL.

240 *OR*, Vol. 25, II, 574–76, 471–72.

241 Stephen Minot Weld, *War Diary and Letters of Stephen Minot Weld* (privately printed, 1912), 204–5.

242 Uberto Burnham Papers, NYSL.

243 Stephen W. Sears, *Gettysburg* (Boston: Houghton Mifflin Company, 2003), 6–17; Scott Bowden and Bill Ward, *Last Chance for Victory: Robert E. Lee and the Gettysburg Campaign* (El Dorado Hills, CA: Savas Publishing Company, 2001), 18–21, 31–36.

Part Three: Gettysburg: Death of a Corps

1 *OR*, Vol. 51, I, 1043; Edwin B. Coddington, *The Gettysburg Campaign: A Study in Command* (New York: Simon & Schuster, 1968), 37, 611–12; Sears, *Gettysburg*, 40-42.

2 Marcia Reid-Green, ed., *Letters Home: Henry Matrau of the Iron Brigade* (Lincoln, NE: Bison Books, 1998), 56–57.

3 Cook, *History of the Twelfth*, 96; Matthews, *149th Pennsylvania*, 67–68.

4 Vautier, *History of the 88th*, 102–3.

5 Dawes, *Full Blown Yankee*, 146–47.

6 Hussey and Todd, *History of the Ninth*, 257, 261; Jaques, *Three Years' Campaign*, 144.

7 *OR*, Vol. 27, I, 151.

8 George A. Maharay, *Vermont Hero: Major General George J. Stannard* (Shippensburg, PA: White Mane Books, 2001), 11–124; Eicher and Eicher, *High Commands*, 505.

9 Schildt, *Roads to Gettysburg*, 46; Chamberlin, *History of the One Hundred and Fiftieth*, 108; Hussey and Todd, *History of the Ninth*, 259; Matthews, *149th Pennsylvania*, 68–69.

10 James McLean, "The Execution of John Wood on the March to Gettysburg," *Gettysburg Magazine*, #45, July 2011, 7–22. Herdegen, *Iron Brigade*, 345–46; Tevis and Marquis, *History of the Fighting Fourteenth*, 76; Reid-Green, ed., *Letters Home*, 58; Curtis, *History of the Twenty-Fourth*, 144–47; Lance J. Herdegen and William J. K. Beaudot, *In the Bloody Railroad Cut at Gettysburg* (Dayton, OH: Morningside House, Inc., 1990), 141–43; Holford Papers, LOC.

11 Chamberlin, *History of the One Hundred and Fiftieth*, 108; Dawes, *Full Blown Yankee*, 151.

12 *OR*, Vol. 27, III, 78.

13 *OR*, Vol. 27, III, 81, 84.

14 *OR*, Vol. 27, III, 89; Holford Papers, LOC; Dawes, *Full Blown Yankee*, 151–52; Nevins, ed., *Diary of Battle*, 219.

15 McFarland Papers, PSA, Harrisburg; Bradley M. Gottfried, *The Maps of Gettysburg: An Atlas of the Gettysburg Campaign, June 3–July 13, 1863* (New York: Savas Beatie, 2008), 8–17; *OR*, Vol. 27, III, 87.

16 Quiner, *Quiner Papers*, Vol. 8, 378–79.

17 Bowden and Ward, *Last Chance*, 133–35.

18 Cook, *History of the Twelfth*, 97; Davis, *Three Years*, 215.

19 *OR*, Vol. 27, III, 149–50, 173–74; Henry Greenleaf Pearson, *James S. Wadsworth of Geneseo: Brevet Major-General of United States Volunteers* (New York: Charles Scribner's Sons, 1913), 197.

20 Small, *Sixteenth Maine*, 112; Jaques, *Three Years' Campaign*, 151; Nevins, ed., *Diary of Battle*, 223.

21 McFarland Papers, PSA, Harrisburg; Dawes, *Full Blown Yankee*, 153; Gaff, *On Many a Bloody Field*, 253–54.

22 *OR*, Vol. 27, I, 151.

23 *OR*, Vol. 27, III, 305–6, 313.

24 Doubleday, *Chancellorsville and Gettysburg*, 107–8.

25 https://dmna.ny.gov/historic/reghist/civil/infantry/97thInf/97thInf_Hayden/97thInf_Letters_Hayden09.htm.

26 *OR*, Vol. 27, III, 313; Survivors' Association, *History of the 121st*, 48; Cook, *History of the Twelfth*, 98.

27 Wert, *Sword of Lincoln*, 265–66; Doubleday, *Chancellorsville and Gettysburg*, 113–14; Swinton, *Campaigns*, 321–24; Sears, *Gettysburg*, 125–29.

28 Uberto Burnham Papers, NYSL.

29 Cook, *History of the Twelfth*, 98.

30 Eric J. Wittenberg, *"The Devil's to Pay": John Buford at Gettysburg, A History and Walking Tour* (El Dorado Hills, CA: Savas Beatie, 2015), 36–61; David G. Martin, *Gettysburg, July 1* (Conshohocken, PA: Combined Books, 1996), 36–48; Fishel, *Secret War*, 502.

31 *OR*, Vol. 27, III, 375–76; Hussey and Todd, *History of the Ninth*, 266.

32 Locke, *Story of the Regiment*, 221; Davis, *Three Years*, 221.

33 Curtis, *History of the Twenty-Fourth*, 152; Dawes, *Full Blown Yankee*, 158.

34 Chamberlin, *History of the One Hundred and Fiftieth*, 115; Survivors' Association, *History of the 121st Regiment*, 49–51; Matthews, *149th Pennsylvania*, 75.

35 Henry S. Willey Papers, Library of Congress; Maharay, *Vermont Hero*, 125–30.

36 Edwin F. Palmer, *The Second Brigade; or Camp Life* (Montpelier, VT: E. P. Walton, 1864), 167–74.

37 *OR*, Vol. 27, III, 399.

38 *OR*, Vol. 27, III, 414–15.

39 *OR*, Vol. 27, III, 419–20.

40 *OR*, Vol. 27, I, 243.

41 Doubleday, *Chancellorsville and Gettysburg*, 122.

42 Robert Himmer, "A Matter of Time: The Issuance of the Pipe Creek Circular," *Gettysburg Magazine*, #46, January 2012, 7–18.

43 *OR*, Vol. 27, III, 458–59; Rafuse, *George Gordon Meade*, 73–77.

44 Martin, *Gettysburg*, 55–57; Sears, *Gettysburg*, 150–51; Coddington, *Gettysburg*, 237–41; Doubleday, *Chancellorsville and Gettysburg*, 119–20.

45 *OR*, Vol. 27, I, 923–24; Wittenberg, *"The Devil's to Pay,"* 62–73; Eric J. Wittenberg, "John Buford and the Gettysburg Campaign," *Gettysburg Magazine*, #11, July 1994, 35–40.

46 *OR*, Vol. 27, III, 416.

47 *OR*, Vol. 27, III, 460–61; Warren W. Hassler, *Crisis at the Crossroads: The First Day at Gettysburg* (Gettysburg, PA: Stan Clark Military Books, 1991), 27–28.

48 Fishel, *Secret War*, 519–21.

49 Coddington, *Gettysburg*, 672; Martin, *Gettysburg*, 57.

50 A great article makes a contrary point, suggesting Reynolds took too much risk. See, L. Patrick Nelson, "Reynolds and the Decision to Fight," *Gettysburg Magazine*, #23, July 2000, 31–50.

51 Harry W. Pfanz, *Gettysburg: The First Day* (Chapel Hill: University of North Carolina Press, 2001), 48; Schildt, *Roads to Gettysburg*, 407–8; Coddington, *Gettysburg*, 261.

52 http://library.fandm.edu/archives/Reynolds/JFR/transcriptions/s135.htm; Sears, *Gettysburg*, 158; Richard S. Shue, *Morning at Willoughby Run: The Opening Battle at Gettysburg, July 1, 1863* (Gettysburg, PA: Thomas Publications, 1998), 50–52.

53 Chapman Biddle, *The First Day of the Battle of Gettysburg: An Address Delivered Before the Historical Society of Pennsylvania, on the 8th of March, 1880* (Philadelphia: J. B. Lippincott & Co., 1880), 24.

54 Nevins, ed., *Diary of Battle*, 232.

55 Martin, *Gettysburg*, 90; Pfanz, *Gettysburg: First Day*, 70.

56 Mahood, *General Wadsworth*, 158.

57 *OR*, Vol. 27, I, 255–56, 354, 359.

58 Tevis and Marquis, *History of the Fighting Fourteenth*, 81–82.

59 David L. Ladd and Audrey J. Ladd, eds., *The Bachelder Papers: Gettysburg in Their Own Words*, Vol. II (Dayton, OH: Morningside House, 1994), 939.

60 William Thomas Venner, *The 19th Indiana Infantry at Gettysburg: Hoosiers' Courage* (Shippensburg, PA: Burd Street Press, 1998), 45; Craig L. Dunn, *Iron Men, Iron Will: The Nineteenth Indiana Regiment of the Iron Brigade* (Indianapolis: Guild Press, 1995), 184.

61 *OR*, Vol. 27, I, 265; Thomas L. Elmore, "Torrid Heat and Blinding Rain: A Meteorological and Astronomical Chronology of the Gettysburg Campaign," *Gettysburg Magazine*, #13, July 1995, 10.

62 James L. McLean, *Cutler's Brigade at Gettysburg* (Baltimore: Butternut and Blue, 1994), 55; Smith, *History of the Seventy-Sixth*, 235.

63 Herdegen, *Iron Brigade*, 356–57.

64 Martin, *Gettysburg*, 94; Pfanz, *Gettysburg: First Day*, 72; Schildt, *Roads to Gettysburg*, 452–54; Venner, *The 19th Indiana*, 46; Jeffry Wert, *A Brotherhood of Valor: The Common Soldiers of the Stonewall Brigade, C.S.A., and the Iron Brigade, U.S.A.* (New York: Simon & Schuster, 1999), 248–49; Ladd and Ladd, eds., *Bachelder Papers*, Vol. I, 322–23.

65 Curtis, *History of the Twenty-Fourth*, 155; Cheek and Pointon, *Sauk County Riflemen*, 71; *OR*, Vol. 27, I, 267; Abner Doubleday, *Gettysburg Made Plain* (New York: Century Company, 1888), 25; Wittenberg, *"The Devil's to Pay,"* 75–117.

66 J. Watts dePuyster, *The Decisive Conflicts of the Late Civil War, or Slaveholders' Rebellion*, #3 (New York: MacDonald & Company, 1867), 152–53; Edward G. Longacre, *The Cavalry at Gettysburg: A Tactical Study of Mounted Operations During the Civil War's Pivotal Campaign, 9 June–14 July 1863* (Lincoln, NE: Bison Books, 1993), 187–88; Mitchell G. Klingenberg, "Of Cupolas and Sharpshooters: Major General John Fulton Reynolds and Popular Gettysburg Myths," *Gettysburg Magazine*, #59, July 2018, 50–56.

67 dePuyster, *Decisive Conflicts*, 153.

68 Ladd and Ladd, eds., *Bachelder Papers*, Vol. I, 306, 385–86; Coddington, *Gettysburg*, 268; Tom Huntington, *Maine Roads to Gettysburg: How Joshua Chamberlain, Oliver Howard, and 4,000 Men from the Pine Tree State Helped Win the Civil War's Bloodiest Battle* (Guilford, CT: Stackpole Books, 2018), 206–8.

69 *OR*, Vol. 27, I, 359.

70 Shue, *Morning at Willoughby Run*, 222–24 and Ladd and Ladd, eds., *Bachelder Papers*, Vol. I, 205; Lance J. Herdegen, "Old Soldiers and War Talk: The Controversy Over the Opening Infantry Fight at Gettysburg," *Gettysburg Magazine*, #2, January 1990, 15–24.

71 Bates, *History of Pennsylvania Volunteers*, Vol. II, 220.

72 Sears, *Gettysburg*, 173–74; Shue, *Morning at Willoughby Run*, 115–17.

73 Ladd and Ladd, eds., *Bachelder Papers*, Vol. III, 1699.

74 *OR*, Vol. 27, I, 266, 282, 285.

75 http://dmna.ny.gov/historic/reghist/civil/infantry/76thInf/76thInfCWN.htm; *OR*, Vol. 27, I, 282; Uberto Burnham Papers, NYSL; Smith, *History of the Seventy-Sixth*, 354; David L. Callihan, "Among the Bravest of the Brave: Maj. Andrew Jackson Grover of the 76th New York," *Gettysburg Magazine*, #32, January 2005, 49–51.

76 http://dmna.ny.gov/historic/reghist/civil/infantry/76thInf/76thInfCWN.htm.

77 Terrence J. Winschel, "Part I: Heavy Was Their Loss: Joe Davis' Brigade at Gettysburg," *Gettysburg Magazine*, #2, January 1990, 6–7, 10–11.

78 http://dmna.ny.gov/historic/reghist/civil/infantry/147thInf/147thInfCWN.htm.

79 Martin, *Gettysburg*, 110–19.

80 Ladd and Ladd, eds., *Bachelder Papers*, Vol. I, 332; Adjutant General roster for 147th New York, http://dmna.ny.gov/historic/reghist/civil/rosters/Infantry/147th_Infantry_CW_Roster.pdf.

81 *OR*, Vol. 27, I, 359; Pfanz, *Gettysburg: First Day*, 88–90; Ladd and Ladd, eds., *Bachelder Papers*, Vol. I, 387; Shue, *Morning at Willoughby Run*, 122–24; D. Scott Hartwig, "Guts and Good Leadership: The Action at the Railroad Cut, July 1, 1863," *Gettysburg Magazine*, #1, July 1989, 9–11.

82 E. F. Conklin, "Elmina Keeler Spencer: Matron, 147th New York," *Gettysburg Magazine*, #8, January 1993, 120–26.

83 Ladd and Ladd, eds., *Bachelder Papers*, Vol. III, 1565.

84 *OR*, Vol. 27, I, 273; Lance J. Herdegen, *Those Damned Black Hats!: The Iron Brigade in the Gettysburg Campaign* (New York: Savas Beatie, 2008), 90–94; https://www.findagrave.com/memorial/5903866/george-h_-stevens.

85 *OR*, Vol. 27, I, 274; Shue, *Morning at Willoughby Run*, 126–38; Marc Storch and Beth Storch, "'What a Deadly Trop We Were In': Archer's Brigade on July 1, 1863," *Gettysburg Magazine*, #6, January 1992, 22–27; Venner, *19th Indiana*, 53–58.

86 Sam Ross, *The Empty Sleeve: A Biography of Lucius Fairchild* (Stevens Point, WI: Worzalla Publishing, 1964), 48–51.

87 Curtis, *History of the Twenty-Fourth*, 157; Shue, *Morning at Willoughby Run*, 218–21; Steve Sanders, "Enduring Tales of Gettysburg: The Death of Reynolds," *Gettysburg Magazine*, #14, January 1996, 27–36; and Klingenberg, "Of Cupolas and Sharpshooters," 56–65.

88 *OR*, Vol. 27, I, 267; www.montcalmhistory.com/civilwar/civilwarbiopeckabel.html.

89 *OR*, Vol. 27, I, 244–45.

90 Herdegen and Beaudot, *In the Bloody Railroad Cut*, 175–213; Pfanz, *Gettysburg: First Day*, 102–14.

91 Martin, *Gettysburg*, 105, 128; *OR*, Vol. 27, I, 286–87.

92 *OR*, Vol. 27, I, 275; Lance J. Herdegen and William J. K. Beaudot, eds., "With the Iron Brigade Guard at Gettysburg," *Gettysburg Magazine*, #1, July 1989, 32.

93 *OR*, Vol. 27, I, 246; Martin, *Gettysburg*, 122.

94 *OR*, Vol. 27, I, 276.

95 Dawes, *Full Blown Yankee*, 166–67.

96 *OR*, Vol. 27, I, 277; Dawes, *Full Blown Yankee*, 167.

97 Holford Papers, LOC.

98 *OR*, Vol. 27, I, 276; Roger Long, "A Mississippian in the Railroad Cut," *Gettysburg Magazine*, #4, January 1991, 24; Hartwig, "Guts," 13.

99 Ladd and Ladd, eds., *Bachelder Papers*, Vol. I, 205.

100 Tevis and Marquis, *History of the Fighting Fourteenth*, 83–84.

101 Herdegen and Beaudot, *In the Bloody Railroad Cut*, 279–85; Alan T. Nolan, "Three Flags at Gettysburg," *Gettysburg Magazine*, #1, July 1989, 26; William J. K. Beaudot, "Francis Asbury Wallar: A Medal of Honor at Gettysburg," *Gettysburg Magazine*, #4, January 1991, 16–24; Terrence J. Winschel, "The Colors Are Shrouded in Mystery," *Gettysburg Magazine*, #6, January 1992, 76–86. Wallar's medal citation, as well as several sources, spell his name Waller. www.cmohs.org/recipient-detail/1430/waller-francis-a.php.

102 Hartwig, "Guts," 14; Winschel, "Part I," 11, 13.

103 Bowden and Ward, *Last Chance*, 159–62.

104 Martin, *Gettysburg*, 186–89.

105 Doubleday, *Chancellorsville and Gettysburg*, 134.

106 *OR*, Vol. 27, I, 246.

107 Davis, *Three Years*, 225; *OR*, Vol. 27, I, 244.

108 Vautier, *History of the 88th*, 105.

109 Locke, *Story of the Regiment*, 228; Hussey and Todd, *History of the Ninth*, 268.

110 *OR*, Vol. 27, I, 325, 354.

111 James J. Dougherty, *Stone's Brigade and the Fight for McPherson Farm: Battle of Gettysburg, July 1, 1863* (Boston: Da Capo, 2001), 33–37; Michael A. Dreese, *The 151st Pennsylvania Volunteers at Gettysburg: Like Ripe Apples in a Storm* (Jefferson, NC: McFarland & Company, Inc., 2000), 33–35; Matthews, *The 149th Pennsylvania*, 78–79; Chamberlin, *History of the One Hundred and Fiftieth*, 117.

112 Oliver Otis Howard, *The Autobiography of Oliver Otis Howard*, Vol. 1 (New York: Trow Press, 1907), 416.

113 *OR*, Vol. 27, I, 289; Davis, *Three Years*, 226.

114 Hall, *History of the Ninety-Seventh*, 135–36; Locke, *Story of the Regiment*, 228–29; *OR*, Vol. 27, I, 292, 307, 309.

115 Gottfried, *Maps of Gettysburg*, 76–77; Gary G. Lash, "Brig. Gen. Henry Baxter's Brigade at Gettysburg, July 1," *Gettysburg Magazine*, #10, July 1994, 6, 12–13.

116 James S. Pula, *Under the Crescent Moon with the XI Corps in the Civil War, Volume 2: From Gettysburg to Victory, 1863–1865* (El Dorado Hills, CA: Savas Beatie, 2018), 14–19.

117 Doubleday, *Chancellorsville and Gettysburg*, 135.

118 Martin, *Gettysburg*, 189–94; Dreese, *151st Pennsylvania*, 36.

119 *OR*, Vol. 27, I, 332, 341.

120 D. Scott Hartwig, "The Defense of McPherson Ridge," *Gettysburg Magazine*, #1, July 1989, 16–19; Matthews, *149th Pennsylvania*, 80–85; Dougherty, *Stone's Brigade*, 39–50.

121 Survivors' Association, *History of the 121st Regiment*, 52; Gottfried, *Maps of Gettysburg*, 94–95.

122 *OR*, Vol. 27, I, 315, 317, 324.

123 *OR*, Vol. 27, II, 552–53; Walter Clark, ed., *Histories of the Several Regiments and Battalions from North Carolina in the Great War, 1861–'65,* Vol. I (Goldsboro, NC: Nash Brothers, 1901), 634.

124 Pula, *Under the Crescent Moon*, Vol. 2, 22–23; Robert J. Wynstra, *The Rashness of That Hour: Politics, Gettysburg, and the Downfall of Confederate Brigadier General Alfred Iverson* (New York: Savas Beatie, 2010), 222–23; William Wheeler, *In Memoriam: Letters of William Wheeler of the Class of 1855, Yale College* (Cambridge, MA: H. O. Houghton and Company, 1875), 409; D. Massy Griffin, "Rodes on Oak Hill: A Study of Rodes' Division on the First Day at Gettysburg," *Gettysburg Magazine*, #4, January 1991, 38–40.

125 *OR*, Vol. 27, II, 592, 601; Robert Emory Park, *Sketch of the Twelfth Alabama Infantry of Battle's Brigade, Rodes' Division, Early's Corps of the Army of Northern Virginia* (Richmond, VA: William Ellis Jones, 1906), 54; Paul Clark Cooksey, "They Died As If on Dress Parade: The Annihilation of Iverson's Brigade at Gettysburg and the Battle of Oak Ridge," *Gettysburg Magazine*, #20, January 1999, 95–102.

126 Bates, *History of Pennsylvania Volunteers*, Vol. III, 154–55; Gottfried, *Maps of Gettysburg*, 80–85.

127 Clark, ed., *Histories of the Several Regiments*, Vol. II, 235–36.

128 Hussey and Todd, *History of the Ninth*, 270; Locke, *The Story of the Regiment*, 229–30; *OR*, Vol. 27, I, 292, 307; Wynstra, *Rashness of That Hour*, 226–46; Lash, "Brig. Gen. Henry Baxter's Brigade," 16–21; Martin, *Gettysburg*, 224–38.

129 Clark, ed., *Histories of the Several Regiments*, Vol. II, 119.

130 Vautier, *History of the 88th*, 107.

131 Hall, *History of the Ninety-Seventh*, 138; http://dmna.ny.gov/historic/reghist/civil/infantry/97thInf/97thInfCWN.htm.

132 *OR*, Vol. 27, I, 310; Locke, *Story of the Regiment*, 230.

133 www.cmohs.org/recipient-detail/498/gilligan-edward-l.php; Wynstra, *Rashness of That Hour*, 242.

134 Vautier, *History of the 88th*, 107; Hussey and Todd, *History of the Ninth*, 270–71; Cooksey, "They Died As If on Dress Parade," 102–7.

135 Vautier, *History of the 88th*, 107.

136 Ladd and Ladd, eds., *Bachelder Papers*, Vol. II, 990; *OR*, Vol. 27, I, 307.

137 www.cmohs.org/recipient-detail/1215/sellers-alfred-j.php; Martin, *Gettysburg*, 251.

138 Gottfried, *Maps of Gettysburg*, 80–81; Smith, *History of the Seventy-Sixth*, 240.

139 Robert K. Krick, "Three Confederate Disasters on Oak Ridge: Failures of Brigade Leadership on the First Day at Gettysburg," in *The First Day at Gettysburg: Essays on Confederate and Union Leadership*, Gary W. Gallagher, ed. (Kent, OH: Kent State University Press, 1992), 115, 120.

140 Rod Gragg, *Covered with Glory: The 26th North Carolina Infantry at the Battle of Gettysburg* (New York: HarperCollins, 2000), 106–10.

141 Doubleday, *Gettysburg Made Plain*, 29; Martin, *Gettysburg*, 344–45; *OR*, Vol. 27, I, 247; Hartwig, "Defense of McPherson Ridge," 17–19, 24.

142 *OR*, Vol. 27, I, 268, 274, 279; Ladd and Ladd, eds., *Bachelder Papers*, Vol. II, 941; Alan D. Gaff, "'Here Was Made Out Our Last and Hopeless Stand': The 'Lost' Gettysburg Reports of the Nineteenth Indiana," *Gettysburg Magazine*, #2, January 1990, 31.

143 Clark, ed., *Histories of the Several Regiments*, Vol. V, 119; *OR*, Vol. 27, I, 313.

144 Gates, *"Ulster Guard"*, 433; Mahood, *General Wadsworth*, 174; Martin, *Gettysburg*, 180–83; https://www.hrvh.org/cdm/compoundobject/collection/gcla/id/278/rec/1; *OR*, Vol. 27, I, 320.

145 Clark, ed., *Histories of the Several Regiments*, Vol. III, 236.

146 Martin, *Gettysburg*, 342–50.

147 *OR*, Vol. 27, II, 566.

148 *OR*, Vol. 27, I, 330; Silas Felton, "The Iron Brigade Battery at Gettysburg," *Gettysburg Magazine*, #11, July 1994, 60; Thomas L. Elmore, "The Effects of Artillery Fire on Infantry at Gettysburg," *Gettysburg Magazine*, #5, July 1991, 117.

149 *OR*, Vol. 27, I, 342; Matthews, *149th Pennsylvania*, 87; Dougherty, *Stone's Brigade*, 55–57; Gottfried, *Maps of Gettysburg*, 86–87.

150 *OR*, Vol. 27, I, 342.

151 Chamberlin, *History of the One Hundred and Fiftieth*, 124; Gottfried, *Maps of Gettysburg*, 88–89; Dougherty, *Stone's Brigade*, 59–62.

152 Clark, ed., *Histories of the Several Regiments*, Vol. IV, 256 and Vol. III, 41–42; Griffin, "Rodes on Oak Hill," 44–46.

153 Bates, *History of Pennsylvania Volunteers*, Vol. IV, 488.

154 *OR*, Vol. 27, II, 571–72.

155 Ladd and Ladd, eds., *Bachelder Papers*, Vol. II, 947–49, 953, and Vol. III, 1592–93.

156 *OR*, Vol. 27, I, 335, 343; Hartwig, "Defense of McPherson Ridge," 19–23.

157 *OR*, Vol. 27, I, 343; Matthews, *149th Pennsylvania*, 83; https://www.findagrave.com/memorial/7685153/alfred-j_-sofield.

158 Bates, *History of Pennsylvania Volunteers*, Vol. IV, 651; https://www.findagrave.com/memorial/7223535/henry-shippen-huidekoper; https://www.findagrave.com/memorial/19199/cornelius-c_-widdis.

159 Clark, ed., *Histories of the Several Regiments*, Vol. V, 119–20.

160 *OR*, Vol. 27, I, 268; Clark, ed., *Histories of the Several Regiments*, Vol. II, 351; Herdegen, *Iron Brigade*, 395–97.

161 Venner, *19th Indiana*, 67–68; Gaff, *On Many a Bloody Field*, 260.

162 Ladd and Ladd, eds., *Bachelder Papers*, Vol. II, 941; Gottfried, *Maps of Gettysburg*, 96–97.

163 Clark, ed., *Histories of the Several Regiments*, Vol. V, 120; *OR*, Vol. 27, II, 643.

164 *OR*, Vol. 27, I, 315; Kevin E. O'Brien, "'Give Them Another Volley, Boys': Biddle's Brigade Defends the Union Left on July 1, 1863," *Gettysburg Magazine*, #19, July 1998, 37–52.

165 Clark, ed., *Histories of the Several Regiments*, Vol. III, 89.

166 Gates, *"Ulster Guard,"* 441; *OR*, Vol. 27, I, 323.

167 John D. S. Cook, "Personal Reminiscences of Gettysburg," in *War Talks in Kansas: A Series of Papers Read Before the Kansas Commandery of the Military Order of the Loyal Legion of the United States* (Kansas City, MO: Franklin Hudson Publishing Company, 1906), 326.

168 Survivors' Association, *History of the 121st Regiment*, 53; *OR*, Vol. 27, I, 317.

169 Clark, ed., *Histories of the Several Regiments*, Vol. III, 89–90; *OR*, Vol. 27, I, 317.

170 Cook, "Personal Reminiscences," 327.

171 Clark, ed., *Histories of the Several Regiments*, Vol. III, 90; Survivors' Association, *History of the 121st Regiment*, 54; *OR*, Vol. 27, I, 321.

172 Gates, *"Ulster Guard,"* 442.

173 Horatio N. Warren, *The Declaration of Independence and War History: Bull Run to the Appomattox* (Buffalo: Courier Company, 1894), 30; Bates, *History of Pennsylvania Volunteers*, Vol. IV, 466; *OR*, Vol. 27, I, 316; Michael A. Dreese, "Ordeal in the Lutheran Theological Seminary: The Recollections of First Lt. Jeremiah Hoffman, 142nd Pennsylvania Volunteers," *Gettysburg Magazine*, #23, July 2000, 103–4, 107.

174 *OR*, Vol. 27, I, 321; J. R. Balsley, "A Gettysburg Reminiscence," *National Tribune*, May 19, 1898; www.findagrave.com/memorial/90001848/james-robinson-balsley.

175 Venner, *19th Indiana*, 76–79; Gregory A. Coco, *Killed in Action: Eyewitness Accounts of the Last Moments of 100 Union Soldiers Who Died at Gettysburg* (Gettysburg, PA: Thomas Publications, 1992), 13; Herdegen, *Those Damned Black Hats!*, 138–39; Nolan, "Three Flags," 26–27; 19th Indiana Regimental File, Gettysburg National Military Park.

176 Norma Fuller Hawkins, "Sergeant-Major Blanchard at Gettysburg," Vol. 34, No. 2 (June 1938), 212–16.

177 Curtis, *History of the Twenty-Fourth*, 160; *OR*, Vol. 27, I, 270; Wiley Sword, "An Iron Brigade Captain's Revolver in the Fight on McPherson's Ridge," *Gettysburg Magazine*, #7, July 1992, 6–12; R. Lee Hadden, "The Deadly Embrace: The Meeting of the Twenty-fourth Regiment, Michigan Infantry and the Twenty-sixth Regiment of North Carolina Troops at McPherson's Woods, Gettysburg, Pennsylvania, July 1, 1863," *Gettysburg Magazine*, #5, July 1991, 28–29.

178 Bradley M. Gottfried, "To Fail Twice: Brockenbrough's Brigade at Gettysburg," *Gettysburg Magazine*, #23, July 2000, 66–71; Chamberlin, *History of the One Hundred and Fiftieth*, 129.

179 Ladd and Ladd, eds., *Bachelder Papers*, Vol. I, 141.

180 *OR*, Vol. 27, I, 280.

181 Herdegen, *Those Damned Black Hats!*, 139; Herdegen, *Iron Brigade*, 400; Dunn, *Iron Men*, 191.

182 *OR*, Vol. 27, I, 327.

183 Michael A. Dreese, "The 151st Pennsylvania Volunteers at Gettysburg: July 1, 1863," *Gettysburg Magazine*, #23, July 2000, 60–62; Dreese, *151st Pennsylvania*, 41–53.

184 *OR*, Vol. 27, I, 327; Winifred Patrizio Collection of Letters of Alva Marion Adams, MG 7, Military Manuscripts Collection, Pennsylvania State Archives, Harrisburg.

185 Dreese, *151st Pennsylvania*, 48, 158; Charles P. Potts, "A First Defender in Rebel Prison Pens," *Publications of the Historical Society of Schuylkill County*, Vol. IV (Pottsville, PA: Daily Republican Print, 1914), 342.

186 Dreese, *151st Pennsylvania*, 159.

187 https://www.findagrave.com/memorial/19388852/lafayette-westbrook; Dreese, *151st Pennsylvania*, 47, 157; R. B. Sayre, "A Day at Gettysburg," *National Tribune*, April 13, 1899.

188 Dreese, *151st Pennsylvania*, 48.

189 *OR*, Vol. 27, I, 327–28.

190 Cook, "Personal Reminiscences," 322.

191 Martin, *Gettysburg*, 386–93.

192 *OR*, Vol. 27, I, 297–98; Davis, *Three Years*, 227.

193 *OR*, Vol. 27, I, 300; Cooksey, "They Died As If on Dress Parade," 107.

194 John P. Nicholson, ed., *Pennsylvania at Gettysburg: Ceremonies at the Dedication of the Monuments Erected by the Commonwealth of Pennsylvania*, Vol. II (Harrisburg, PA: E. K. Meyers, 1893) 559; Bates, *History of Pennsylvania Volunteers*, Vol. III, 860–61; Pfanz, *Gettysburg: First Day*, 186–89.

195 *OR*, Vol. 27, I, 290; Larry Tagg, *The Generals of Gettysburg: The Leaders of America's Greatest Battle* (Cambridge, MA: Da Capo Press, 1998), 22–23.

196 Cooksey, "They Died As If on Dress Parade," 109–11; Wynstra, *Rashness of That Hour*, 247–56.

197 Clark, ed., *Histories of the Several Regiments*, Vol. I, 254; Davis, *Three Years*, 227; Clark, ed., *Histories of the Several Regiments*, Vol. II, 502; *OR*, Vol. 27, II, 588.

198 http://dmna.ny.gov/historic/reghist/civil/infantry/94thInf/94thInfCWN.htm; *OR*, Vol. 27, I, 290.

199 *OR*, Vol. 27, I, 295; 16th Maine Regimental File, Gettysburg National Military Park; Richard A. Sauers, "The 16th Maine Volunteer Infantry at Gettysburg," *Gettysburg Magazine*, #13, July 1995, 38–41; Report of Maine Commissioners, *Maine at Gettysburg* (Portland, ME: Lakeside Press, 1898) 41–44; Griffin, "Rodes on Oak Hill," 46–47; Huntington, *Maine Roads to Gettysburg*, 222–24; 16th Maine Regimental Correspondence, Folder 15, Maine State Archives, Augusta.

200 http://dmna.ny.gov/historic/reghist/civil/infantry/94thInf/94thInfCWN.htm; http://dmna.ny.gov/historic/reghist/civil/rosters/Infantry/94th_Infantry_CW_Roster.pdf.

201 http://dmna.ny.gov/historic/reghist/civil/infantry/104thInf/104thInfCWN.htm; https://www.findagrave.com/memorial/126910143/henry-g-tuthill.

202 Eicher and Eicher, *High Commands*, 461.

203 *OR*, Vol. 27, I, 342.

204 J. H. Bassler, "The Color Episode of the One Hundred and Forty-ninth Regiment, Pennsylvania Volunteers at Gettysburg, July 1, 1863," *Southern Historical Society Papers*, Vol. 37 (1909), 266–301. Also, Pfanz, *Gettysburg: First Day*, 360–66; Ladd and Ladd, eds., *Bachelder Papers*, Vol. I, 524–27; Matthews, *149th Pennsylvania*, 93–95.

205 Dougherty, *Stone's Brigade*, 84–85; www.cmohs.org/recipient-detail/1173/rutter-james -m.php.

206 Bates, *History of Pennsylvania Volunteers*, Vol. IV, 488–89.

207 24th Michigan Regimental File, Gettysburg National Military Park.

208 Caldwell, *History of a Brigade*, 97.

209 Report of Maine Commissioners, *Maine at Gettysburg*, 84; Nevins, ed., *Diary of Battle*, 235; *OR*, Vol. 27, I, 251.

210 Gottfried, *Maps of Gettysburg*, 108–9; J. Michael Miller, "Perrin's Brigade on July 1, 1863," *Gettysburg Magazine*, #13, July 1995, 24–25.

211 *OR*, Vol. 27, II, 657.

212 J. R. Boyles, *Reminiscences of the Civil War* (Columbia, SC: Bryon Printing, 1890), 41; Clark, ed., *Histories of the Several Regiments*, Vol. I, 698 and Vol. II, 692.

213 Daniel Tompkins, *Company K, Fourteenth South Carolina Volunteers* (Charlotte, NC: Observer Printing, 1897), 19–20.

214 Report of Maine Commissioners, *Maine at Gettysburg*, 85.

215 Dawes, *Full Blown Yankee*, 175; Matthews, *149th Pennsylvania*, 95–96; Felton, "Iron Brigade Battery," 60–61; Sears, *Gettysburg*, 217–21.

216 Gottfried, *Maps of Gettysburg*, 114–15; Caldwell, *History of a Brigade*, 97–98, 55–56; Survivors' Association, *History of the 121st Regiment*, 55–56; John F. Krumwiede, *Disgrace at Gettysburg: The Arrest and Court-Martial of Brigadier General Thomas A. Rowley, USA*, (Jefferson, NC: McFarland & Company, 2006), 84–86; *OR*, Vol. 27, I, 323, 328.

217 Gaff, "'Here Was Made,'" 30.

218 James Stewart, "Battery B of the Fourth U.S. Artillery at Gettysburg," *Sketches of War History 1861-1865, Papers Read Before Ohio Commandery, Military Order of the Loyal Legion of the United States*, Vol. 4, 186–87; Felton, "Iron Brigade Battery," 63.

219 Caldwell, *History of a Brigade*, 98; *OR*, Vol. 27, I, 357.

220 *OR*, Vol. 27, I, 328; Dreese, *151st Pennsylvania*, 58–59.

221 Pula, *Under the Crescent Moon*, Vol. 2, 103–21, 185–209.

222 *OR*, Vol. 27, I, 339; Bates, *History of Pennsylvania Volunteers*, Vol. IV, 493.

223 Fox, *Regimental Losses*, 43–45; Bates, *History of Pennsylvania Volunteers*, Vol. III, 155; https://www.findagrave.com/memorial/22094722/horatio-stockton-howell. James Durkin, "Never Shirking a Duty or Betraying a Trust," *Gettysburg Magazine*, #14, January 1996, 37–45.

224 www.christgettysburg.org/story.

225 11th Pennsylvania Regimental File, Gettysburg National Military Park.

226 https://www.gettysburgdaily.com/gettysburgs-christ-lutheran-church-part-1.

227 David M. Jordan, *Winfield Scott Hancock: A Soldier's Life* (Bloomington: Indiana University Press, 1996), 82–86; Pfanz, *Gettysburg: First Day*, 333–36; Herdegen, *Iron Brigade*, 405–6; Huntington, *Maine Roads to Gettysburg*, 225–27; Pula, *Under the Crescent Moon*, Vol. 2, 111–12; Harry W. Pfanz, *Gettysburg: Culp's Hill and Cemetery Hill* (Chapel Hill: University of North Carolina Press, 1993), 55–56, 100–103.

228 Doubleday, *Chancellorsville and Gettysburg*, 151.

229 Martin, *Gettysburg*, 474–77; Nevins, ed., *Diary of Battle*, 238.

230 Martin, *Gettysburg*, 553–58; Pfanz, *Culp's Hill and Cemetery Hill*, 86; Jim Heenehen, "Correcting the Record: The Court-Martial and Acquittal of Col. Ira Grover, 7th Indiana Infantry," *Gettysburg Magazine*, #45, July 2011, 78.

231 Dawes, *Full Blown Yankee*, 179.

232 Hussey and Todd, *History of the Ninth*, 273; Davis, *Three Years in the Army*, 229.

233 Lance J. Herdegen, "The Lieutenant Who Arrested a General," *Gettysburg Magazine*, #4, January 1991, 29.

234 Krumwiede, *Disgrace at Gettysburg*, 108–51, covers the court-martial and Rowley's reaction; Herdegen, "The Lieutenant," 29–30.

235 Doubleday, *Chancellorsville and Gettysburg*, 153; Christopher C. Dickson, "The Flying Brigade: Brig. Gen. George Stannard and the Road to Gettysburg," *Gettysburg Magazine*, #16, January 1997, 6–26.

236 Palmer, *Second Brigade*, 175; J. C. Williams, *Life in Camp: A History of the Nine Months' Service of the Fourteenth Vermont Regiment, from October 21, 1862, When It Was Mustered into the U.S. Service, to July 21, 1863, Including the Battle of Gettysburg* (Claremont, NH: Claremont Manufacturing Company, 1864), 137.

237 Ladd and Ladd, eds., *Bachelder Papers*, Vol. I, 53; *OR*, Vol. 27, I, 349; Henry S. Willey Papers, LOC.

238 Ralph Orson Sturtevant and Carmi Lathrop Marsh, *Pictorial History of the Thirteenth Regiment Vermont Volunteers, War of 1861–1865* (privately published, 1910), 796–97.

239 Davis, *Three Years*, 229.

240 Henry S. Willey Papers, LOC; Williams, *Life in Camp*, 139–40; Maharay, *Vermont Hero*, 132–33.

241 Hartwig, "Defense of McPherson Ridge," 24.

242 *OR*, Vol. 27, I, 173–87; Trudeau, *Gettysburg*, 272, 421, 529.

243 *OR*, Vol. 27, I, 366.

244 *OR*, Vol. 51, I, 1066.

245 https://www.findagrave.com/memorial/44535565/george-washington-brankstone#view photo=24304535; https://dmna.ny.gov/historic/reghist/civil/rosters/Infantry/80th_Infantry_ CW_Roster.pdf.

246 Quiner, *Quiner Papers*, Vol. 8, 151–52.

247 "Rush Telegraph to His Parents, July 20, 1863," *Hamilton College Library Online Exhibits*, accessed January 12, 2019, http://ulib.hamilton.edu/omeka/items/show/74; "Mrs. Cady to Mr. Cady July 23, 1863 pg. 4," *Hamilton College Library Online Exhibits*, accessed January 12, 2019, http://ulib.hamilton.edu/omeka/items/show/78.

248 http://dmna.ny.gov/historic/reghist/civil/infantry/97thInf/97thInfCWN.htm.

249 Hall, *History of the Ninety-Seventh*, 278.

250 Uberto Burnham Papers and Penny Family Papers, NYSL; Cheek and Pointon, *Sauk County Riflemen*, 75; Herdegen, *Those Damned Black Hats!*, 182–86.

251 Dawes, *Full Blown Yankee*, 182; Tevis and Marquis, *History of the Fighting Fourteenth*, 94.

252 Nevins, ed., *Diary of Battle*, 245; *OR*, Vol. 27, I, 358.

253 5th Maine Battery correspondence, Folder 23, Maine State Archives, Augusta; *OR*, Vol. 27, I, 361; Edward N. Whittier, "The Left Attack (Ewell's) Gettysburg," in *Campaigns in Virginia, Maryland and Pennsylvania 1862–1863* (Boston: Griffith-Stillings Press, 1903), 328.

254 Pfanz, *Culp's Hill and Cemetery Hill*, 235–83; Scott L. Mingus Sr., *The Louisiana Tigers in the Gettysburg Campaign: June–July 1863* (Baton Rouge: Louisiana State University Press, 2009), 148–80; Gary Lash, *The Gibraltar Brigade on East Cemetery Hill* (Baltimore: Butternut and Blue, 1995), 63–74; *OR*, Vol. 27, I, 358, 363; James S. Pula, "'A Promiscuous Fight': The Defense of Cemetery Hill," *Gettysburg Magazine*, #59, July 2018, 15–29.

255 *OR*, Vol. 27, I, 361; Whittier, "The Left Attack," 332; Report of Maine Commissioners, *Maine at Gettysburg*, 95–98; 5th Maine Battery correspondence, Folder 23, Maine State Archives, Augusta.

256 Davis, *Three Years*, 234; Hussey and Todd, *History of the Ninth*, 274–75; Locke, *Story of the Regiment*, 235–36.

257 *OR*, Vol. 27, I, 261; Maharay, *Vermont Hero*, 137–44; Williams, *Life in Camp*, 141–42; Sturtevant and Marsh, *Pictorial History*, 267–73; www.cmohs.org/recipient-detail/812/ lonergan-john.php.

258 Earl J. Hess, *Pickett's Charge—The Last Attack at Gettysburg* (Chapel Hill: University of North Carolina Press, 2001), 4–23; Doubleday, *Chancellorsville and Gettysburg*, 186–89; Sears, *Gettysburg*, 357–71; Bowden and Ward, *Last Chance*, 423–46.

259 Charles T. Leohr, *War History of the Old First Virginia Infantry Regiment, Army of Northern Virginia* (Richmond, VA: William Ellis Jones, 1884), 36.

260 George H. Scott, "Vermont at Gettysburgh," *Proceedings of the Vermont Historical Society*, Vol. I, No. 2, (1930), 67–69; Jeffry D. Wert, *Gettysburg: Day Three* (New York: Simon & Schuster, 2002), 167–79; Gottfried, *Maps of Gettysburg*, 250–53; Sturtevant and Marsh, *Pictorial History*, 283; *OR*, Vol. 27, I, 318.

261 Doubleday, *Chancellorsville and Gettysburg*, 189; Eric Ward, ed., *Army Life in Virginia: The Civil War Letters of George G. Benedict* (Mechanicsburg, PA: Stackpole Books, 2002), 195.

262 Kreiser Jr., *Defeating Lee*, 117–18; Sturtevant and Marsh, *Pictorial History*, 285.

263 Wert, *Gettysburg*, 188–92; Hess, *Pickett's Charge*, 166–80.

264 Hess, *Pickett's Charge*, 174–77.

265 Tony Trimble, "Paper Collars: Stannard's Brigade at Gettysburg," *Gettysburg Magazine*, #2, January 1990, 74–79; Williams, *Life in Camp*, 145; *OR*, Vol. 27, I, 350; Maharay, *Vermont Hero*, 157–66; Wert, *Gettysburg*, 226–32; Doubleday, *Chancellorsville and Gettysburg*, 193–94.

266 *OR*, Vol. 27, I, 353.

267 Ward, ed., *Army Life in Virginia*, 195–96; Palmer, *Second Brigade*, 195–96; www.cmohs .org/recipient-detail/1418/veazey-wheelock-g.php; Henry S. Willey Papers, LOC.

268 Dreese, *151st Pennsylvania*, 74–78; Osborne, "Ambrose Noble Baldwin," https://www .findagrave.com/memorial/11762513/ambrose-noble-baldwin.

269 David E. Johnson, *Four Years a Soldier* (Princeton, WV: 1887), 259–61; Gottfried, *Maps of Gettysburg*, 256–61; Scott, "Vermont at Gettysburgh," 69; Ladd and Ladd, eds., *Bachelder Papers*, Vol. I, 55–57.

270 www.cmohs.org/recipient-detail/87/benedict-george-g.php.

271 Microfilm reel F-02846, Vermont State Archives, Middlesex.

272 Sturtevant and Marsh, *Pictorial History*, 475.

273 Scott, "Vermont at Gettysburgh," 72.

274 Dawes, *Full Blown Yankee*, 159–60.

275 http://dmna.ny.gov/historic/reghist/civil/infantry/97thInf/97thInfCWN.htm.

276 *OR*, Vol. 27, I, 309.

277 Nevins, ed., *Diary of Battle*, 250–53.

278 Hussey and Todd, *History of the Ninth*, 285–86.

279 Davis, *Three Years*, 243.

280 Locke, *Story of the Regiment*, 238–39.

281 *OR*, Vol. 27, III, 513; Thomas J. Ryan and Richard R. Schaus, "'Our Task Is Not Yet Accomplished': Meade's Decision Making After Victory at Gettysburg, July 4, 1863," *Gettysburg Magazine*, #59, July 2018, 34–36, 47–48.

282 Kent Masterson Brown, *Retreat from Gettysburg: Lee, Logistics, and the Pennsylvania Campaign* (Chapel Hill: University of North Carolina Press, 2005), 41–120.

283 Hall, *History of the Ninety-Seventh*, 146–47; *OR*, Vol. 27, III, 517, 540–41; Nevins, ed., *Diary of Battle*, 256; Gottfried, *Maps of Gettysburg*, 280–83.

284 Davis, *Three Years*, 250; Brown, *Retreat from Gettysburg*, 262–77; Gottfried, *Maps of Gettysburg*, 282–83; Nevins, ed., *Diary of Battle*, 257.

285 Penny Family Papers, NYSL.

286 Cook, *History of the Twelfth*, 103.

287 Dawes, *Full Blown Yankee*, 185.

288 *OR*, Vol. 27, I, 151–52.

289 Hall, *History of the Ninety-Seventh*, 147–48; Gottfried, *Maps of Gettysburg*, 286–89; *OR*, Vol. 27, III, 689.

290 Penny Family Papers, NYSL; Hall, *History of the Ninety-Seventh*, 148; Henry S. Willey Papers, LOC.

291 *OR*, Vol. 27, III, 717; Mahood, *General Wadsworth*, 191–96; Pearson, *James S. Wadsworth*, 236–38.

292 Cheek and Pointon, *Sauk County Riflemen*, 79; *OR*, Vol. 27, I, 297–99 and III, 765; Dawes, *Full Blown Yankee*, 191.

293 *OR*, Vol. 27, I, 152.

294 *OR*, Vol. 27, III, 795–96.

295 Warner, *Generals in Blue*, 261–62.

Conclusion: The Fate of Heroes

1 Uberto Burnham Papers, NYSL.

2 *OR*, Vol. 29, II, 21, 28.

3 http://dmna.ny.gov/historic/reghist/civil/infantry/97thInf/97thInfFergusonLetters.pdf.

4 Davis, *Three Years*, 263–64.

5 *OR*, Vol. 29, I, 217–18.

6 *OR*, Vol. 29, I, 231–34.

7 Dawes, *Full Blown Yankee*, 216–18.

8 Uberto Burnham Papers, NYSL; Franklin Hough Papers, Box 34, NYSL.

9 Dawes, *Full Blown Yankee*, 215.

10 *OR*, Vol. 29, II, 405.

11 *OR*, Vol. 29, II, 409–10, 412, 415.

12 Stine, *History*, 583; Hussey and Todd, *History of the Ninth*, 300; Locke, *Story of the Regiment*, 288–89; Dawes, *Full Blown Yankee*, 222; *OR*, Vol. 29, II, 417, 425.

13 Wert, *Sword of Lincoln*, 318–20; Stine, *History*, 587.

14 Dawes, *Full Blown Yankee*, 224–25.

15 http://dmna.ny.gov/historic/reghist/civil/infantry/147thInf/147thInfCWN.htm.

16 Vautier, *History of the 88th*, 166; Hall, *History of the Ninety-Seventh*, 168.

17 *OR*, Vol. 29, II, 520–21, 527–29; Cook, *History of the Twelfth*, 120; Curtis, *History of the Twenty-Fourth*, 212–13.

18 *OR*, Vol. 29, I, 678; Hussey and Todd, *History of the Ninth*, 305; Davis, *Three Years*, 286.

19 Matthews, *149th Pennsylvania*, 117–18; *OR*, Vol. 29, II, 543; Dawes, *Full Blown Yankee*, 229–30.

20 http://dmna.ny.gov/historic/reghist/civil/infantry/147thInf/147thInfCWN.htm.

21 Dawes, *Full Blown Yankee*, 232; Herdegen and Murphy, eds., *Four Years*, 242.

22 Survivors' Association, *History of the 121st Regiment*, 73–74.

23 *OR*, Vol. 29, II, 573–74.

24 Chamberlin, *History of the One Hundred and Fiftieth*, 189.

25 *OR*, Vol. 29, II, 575, 593.

26 1864 Diary, Uberto Burnham Papers, NYSL.

27 1864 Diary of Lewis Plass, NYSL.

28 *OR*, Vol. 29, II, 598–600.

29 *OR*, Vol. 33, 460; Nolan, *Iron Brigade*, 270–71; Herdegen, *Iron Brigade*, 464–69; Cheek and Pointon, *Sauk County Riflemen*, 86–89; Gaff, *On Many a Bloody Field*, 314–20; Herdegen and Murphy, *Four Years*, 251–57.

30 John J. Hennessy, "I Dread the Spring: The Army of the Potomac Prepares for the Overland Campaign," in *The Wilderness Campaign*, Gary W. Gallagher, ed. (Chapel Hill: University of North Carolina Press, 1997), 72–81.

31 1864 Diary, Uberto Burnham Papers, NYSL.

32 Smith, *History of the Seventy-Sixth*, 275–76.

33 Tevis and Marquis, *History of the Fighting Fourteenth*, 109–11; Uberto Burnham Papers, NYSL.

34 Davis, *Three Years*, 307.

35 *OR*, Vol. 33, 114; Hussey and Todd, *History of the Ninth*, 312–13; Curtis, *History of the 24th*, 218–19; Gordon C. Rhea, *The Battle of the Wilderness, May 5-6, 1864* (Baton Rouge: Louisiana State University Press, 1994), 1–6; Kreiser Jr., *Defeating Lee*, 143–44.

36 Chamberlin, *History of the One Hundred and Fiftieth*, 195–96; Cook, *History of the Twelfth*, 124.

37 Small, *Sixteenth Maine*, 166.

38 Matthews, *149th Pennsylvania*, 120; Chamberlin, *History of the One Hundred and Fiftieth*, 192–93, 198.

39 Franklin Hough Papers, Box 34, NYSL.

40 *OR*, Vol. 33, 638–39.

41 *OR*, Vol. 33, 722–23.

42 Mahood, *General Wadsworth*, 197–212; Uberto Burnham Papers, NYSL.

43 Hennessy, "I Dread the Spring," 82–83; Stine, *History*, 597–98.

44 *OR*, Vol. 36, I, 110–11.

45 Cheek and Pointon, *Sauk County Riflemen*, 89.

46 Stine, *History*, 596; Rhea, *Battle of the Wilderness*, 44; Hennessy, "I Dread the Spring," 94–95; Rafuse, *George Gordon Meade*, 114–15.

47 *OR*, Vol. 36, I, 123–25; Mahood, *General Wadsworth*, 237–57.

48 Tevis and Marquis, *History of the Fighting Fourteenth*, 126–28.

49 Cook, *History of the Twelfth*, 139; Hussey and Todd, *History of the Ninth*, 325–28.

50 Cook, *History of the Twelfth*, 139–41; 12th Massachusetts correspondence folder, Massachusetts National Guard Archives-Museum, Concord.

51 State of Vermont, *Revised Roster of Vermont Volunteers and Lists of Vermonters Who Served in the Army and Navy of the United States* (Montpelier, VT: Watchman Publishing, 1892), 620; https://www.findagrave.com/memorial/120765773/curtis-abbott.

52 Antietam Collection, Dartmouth College, Folder 2-68.

53 https://www.ancestry.com/search/?name=Sallie+Lewis_DeJarnette&birth=1848_Spring+Grove-Caroline-Viriginia&death=1907&types=p; https://www.findagrave.com/memorial/41292154/griffin-lewis-baldwin.

54 Eicher and Eicher, *High Commands*, 122; Rhea, *Battle of the Wilderness*, 306.

55 Uberto Burnham Papers, NYSL; https://www.findagrave.com/memorial/96076918/uberto-adelbert-burnham.

56 Walter F. Beyer and Oscar F. Keydel, eds., *Deeds of Valor: How America's Heroes Won the Medal of Honor*, Vol. I (Detroit: Perrien Keydel Company, 1901), 158–59; Huntington, *Maine Roads to Gettysburg*, 291–92, 319–20; https://www.findagrave.com/memorial/5988532.

57 Locke, *Story of the Regiment*, 400; https://www.findagrave.com/memorial/5949415/richard-coulter; Eicher and Eicher, *High Commands*, 187.

58 Dawes, *Full Blown Yankee*, 316–17.

59 https://www.findagrave.com/memorial/5848728/rufus-r_-dawes.

60 www.cmohs.org/recipient-detail/348/delaney-john-c.php.

61 Antietam Collection, Dartmouth College, Folder 2-11; https://www.findagrave.com/memorial/6172366/john-carroll-delaney.

62 http://bioguide.congress.gov/scripts/biodisplay.pl?index=D000305; https://www.findagrave.com/memorial/7445228/samuel-bernard-dick.

63 www.nysl.nysed.gov/msscfa/sc14009.htm.

64 Hatch Papers, Library of Congress; Cullom, *Biographical Register*, 226–27; Eicher and Eicher, *High Commands*, 287.

65 Sturtevant and Marsh, *Pictorial History*, 797–800; https://www.findagrave.com/memorial/14475045/frank-kenfield.

66 Dreese, *151st Pennsylvania*, 138–39; https://www.findagrave.com/memorial/14306377/michael-link.

67 McFarland Papers, PSA, Harrisburg.

68 Nicholson, ed., *Pennsylvania at Gettysburg*, Vol. II, 748; Dreese, *151st Pennsylvania*, 132–33; https://www.findagrave.com/memorial/15909351/george-fisher-mcfarland.

69 Penny Family Papers, NYSL; https://www.findagrave.com/memorial/66396262/archibald-penny.

70 *Memoirs of N. P. Perkins*, 40; https://www.findagrave.com/memorial/142322663/napoleon-b_-perkins.

71 Gordon C. Rhea, *The Battles for Spotsylvania Court House and the Road to Yellow Tavern, May 7–12, 1864* (Baton Rouge: Louisiana State University Press, 1997), 54–59; Eicher and Eicher, *High Commands*, 458; Warner, *Generals in Blue*, 408–9.

72 Waugh, *Class of 1846*, 527; Eicher and Eicher, *High Commands*, 479–80.

73 Rhea, *Battle of the Wilderness*, 157–66; Eicher and Eicher, *High Commands*, 514; https://www.findagrave.com/memorial/5909813/roy-stone.

74 Small, *Sixteenth Maine*, 228; Eicher and Eicher, *High Commands*, 531; Huntington, *Maine Roads to Gettysburg*, 321–22; https://www.mainememory.net/artifact/4295.

75 Dawes, *Full Blown Yankee*, 317.

Bibliography

Manuscripts
Antietam National Battlefield, Sharpsburg, MD
5th Alabama Regimental File
9th Pennsylvania Reserves Regimental File
7th Pennsylvania Reserves Regimental File
23rd New York Regimental File
2nd U.S. Sharpshooters Regimental File

Dartmouth College, Hanover, NH
The Antietam Collection

Gettysburg National Military Park, Gettysburg, PA
11th Pennsylvania Regimental File
19th Indiana Regimental File
16th Maine Regimental File
12th Massachusetts Regional File
24th Michigan Regimental File

Library of Congress, Washington, DC
John Porter Hatch Papers
Lyman C. Holford Papers
George Brinton McClellan Papers
Charles H. Nichols Papers
M. Shuler Diary
Henry S. Willey Papers

Maine State Archives, Augusta, ME
Company D, 2nd U.S. Sharpshooters, Regimental Correspondence
5th Maine Battery Correspondence
16th Maine Volunteer Infantry Regimental Correspondence

New York State Library, Albany, NY
Reuben Abel Papers
James Adsit Papers
Lewis A. Benedict Papers
John Bryson, *History of the 30th New York Volunteers*
Uberto Burnham Papers
Newton Church letter
Horace Hanks Papers

Franklin Hough Papers
Penny Family Papers
Lewis Plass, 1864 Diary
William Prince letter
Frederick Ranger Letters
Adrian Root's General Order 36 (photocopy)
Tyrel Family Correspondence
Patrick Walker Letters
William Woodruff, 1863 Diary

Office of Adjutant General Archives–Museum, Concord, MA
12th Massachusetts Records and Correspondence

Pennsylvania State Archives, Harrisburg, PA
Alva Marion Adams Letters, MG 7, Military Manuscripts Collection
Henry H. Glasier Letters, MG 7, Military Manuscripts Collection
J. Horace McFarland Papers, MG 85
Hugh W. McNeil Collection, MG 87
Morrow-Hittle Family Collection, MG 94
Robert Taggart Papers, MG 124
13th Pennsylvania Reserves Records, MG 234

Vermont State Archives, Middlesex, VT
Hiram Hodgkins Letters, microfilm reel F-02845
Memoirs of N. P. Perkins, 5th Maine Battery, microfilm reel F-02846
The Third Vermont Company of the United States Sharpshooters: A History by Curtis Abbott,
    microfilm reel F-02846

Western Maryland Room, Washington County Free Library, Hagerstown, MD
Letter of Henry Cranford, South Mountain vertical file

Government Publications
Annual Report of the Adjutant General of the State of Maine for the Year Ending 1863.
    Augusta, ME: Stevens & Sayward, 1864.
House of Representatives, 37th Congress, 3rd Session. *Report of the Joint Committee on
    the Conduct of the War.* Part I. Washington, DC: GPO, 1863.
"Names and Records of All the Members Who Served in the First New Hampshire
    Battery Light Artillery During the Late Rebellion from September 26, 1861 to
    June 15, 1865." Manchester, NH: Budget Job Print, 1891.
Otis, George O., and D. L. Huntington. *The Medical and Surgical History of the War of the
    Rebellion.* Part III, Vol. II, Surgical History. Washington, DC: GPO, 1883.
Roster of Wisconsin Volunteers. Vol. I. Madison, WI: Democrat Printing Company, 1886.

State of Vermont. *Revised Roster of Vermont Volunteers and Lists of Vermonters Who Served in the Army and Navy of the United States.* Montpelier, VT: Watchman Publishing, 1892.

U.S. War Department. *The War of the Rebellion: A Compilation of the Official Records of the Union and Confederate Armies.* 128 vols. Washington, DC: GPO, 1880–1901.

Websites

https://www.ancestry.com

http://bioguide.congress.gov

www.christgettysburg.org/story

www.civilwarhome.com/armyorganization.htm

www.cmohs.org

http://dmna.ny.gov/

http://emergingcivilwar.com

www.findagrave.com

http://generalmeadesociety.org/old-baldy

https://www.gettysburgdaily.com/gettysburgs-christ-lutheran-church-part-1

https://www.hrvh.org/cdm/compoundobject/collection/gcla/id/278/rec/1

http://library.fandm.edu/archives

https://www.mainememory.net/artifact/4295

www.montcalmhistory.com/civilwar/civilwarbiopeckabel.html

www.nysl.nysed.gov

http://paemergencymen.blogspot.com/2011/08/pennsylvania-reserve-corps-part-ii.html

www.pa-roots.com/pacw

http://ulib.hamilton.edu

Books and Articles

Anders, Curt. *Henry Halleck's War: A Fresh Look at Lincoln's Controversial General-in-Chief.* Carmel, IN: Guild Press, 2000.

Armstrong, Marion V., Jr. *Unfurl Those Colors!: McClellan, Sumner, and the Second Army Corps in the Antietam Campaign.* Tuscaloosa: University of Alabama Press, 2008.

Ayling, Augustus D. *Revised Register of the Soldiers and Sailors of New Hampshire in the War of the Rebellion, 1861–1866.* Concord, NH: Ira C. Evans, 1895.

Bacon, William Johnson. *Memorial of William Kirkland Bacon, Late Adjutant of the Twenty-Sixth Regiment of New York State Volunteers, By His Father.* Utica, NY: Roberts, Printer, 1863.

Balsley, J. R. "A Gettysburg Reminiscence." *National Tribune,* May 19, 1898.

Barnes, Edward L. "The 95th New York: Sketch of Its Service in the Campaigns of 1862." *National Tribune,* January 7, 1886.

Basler, Roy P., ed. *The Collected Works of Abraham Lincoln.* Vol. V. New Brunswick, NJ: Rutgers University Press, 1953.

Bassler, J. H. "The Color Episode of the One Hundred and Forty-ninth Regiment, Pennsylvania Volunteers at Gettysburg, July 1, 1863." *Southern Historical Society Papers*, Vol. 37 (1909).

Bates, Samuel. *History of Pennsylvania Volunteers, 1861–1865*. 5 Vols. Harrisburg, PA: B. Singerly, 1869.

Beatie, Russel H. *Army of the Potomac, Volume III: McClellan's First Campaign, March–May 1862*. New York: Savas Beatie, 2007.

Beaudot, William J. K. "Francis Asbury Wallar: A Medal of Honor at Gettysburg." *Gettysburg Magazine*, #4, January 1991, 16–24.

Beyer, Walter F., and Oscar F. Keydel, eds. *Deeds of Valor: How America's Heroes Won the Medal of Honor*. Vol. I. Detroit: Perrien Keydel Company, 1901.

Biddle, Chapman. *The First Day of the Battle of Gettysburg: An Address Delivered Before the Historical Society of Pennsylvania, on the 8th of March, 1880*. Philadelphia: J. B. Lippincott & Co., 1880.

Bowden, Scott, and Bill Ward. *Last Chance for Victory: Robert E. Lee and the Gettysburg Campaign*. El Dorado Hills, CA: Savas Publishing Company, 2001.

Boyles, J. R. *Reminiscences of the Civil War*. Columbia, SC: Bryon Printing, 1890.

Bridges, Hal. *Lee's Maverick General: Daniel Harvey Hill*. Lincoln: University of Nebraska Press, 1991.

Brown, Kent Masterson. *Retreat from Gettysburg: Lee, Logistics, and the Pennsylvania Campaign*. Chapel Hill: University of North Carolina Press, 2005.

Bumbera, Marlen C., ed. *The Civil War Letters of Cpl John H. Strathern: Eighth Pennsylvania Reserve Volunteer Corps*. Apollo, PA: Closson Press, 1994.

Caldwell, James Fitz James. *The History of a Brigade of South Carolinians*. Philadelphia: King & Baird, 1866.

Callihan, David L. "Among the Bravest of the Brave: Maj. Andrew Jackson Grover of the 76th New York." *Gettysburg Magazine*, #32, January 2005, 49–51.

Casey, James B., ed. "The Ordeal of Adoniram Judson Warner: His Minutes of South Mountain and Antietam." *Civil War History*, Vol. 28, #3, September 1982.

Chamberlin, Thomas. *History of the One Hundred and Fiftieth Regiment Pennsylvania Volunteers, Second Regiment, Bucktail Brigade*. Philadelphia: F. McManus, Jr & Co., 1905.

Cheek, Philip, and Mair Pointon. *History of the Sauk County Riflemen*. Self-published, 1909.

Christy, H. F. "The 'Reserves' at Fredericksburg." *National Tribune*, September 19, 1901.

Clark, Walter, ed. *Histories of the Several Regiments and Battalions from North Carolina in the Great War, 1861–'65*. 5 Vols. Goldsboro, NC: Nash Brothers, 1901.

Coco, Gregory A. *Killed in Action: Eyewitness Accounts of the Last Moments of 100 Union Soldiers Who Died at Gettysburg*. Gettysburg, PA: Thomas Publications, 1992.

Coddington, Edwin B. *The Gettysburg Campaign: A Study in Command*. New York: Simon & Schuster, 1968.

Conklin, E. F. "Elmina Keeler Spencer: Matron, 147th New York." *Gettysburg Magazine*, #8, January 1993, 120–26.

Cook, Benjamin F. *History of the Twelfth Massachusetts Volunteers, Webster Regiment*. Boston: Twelfth (Webster) Regiment Association, 1882.

Cook, John D. S. "Personal Reminiscences of Gettysburg," in *War Talks in Kansas: A Series of Papers Read before the Kansas Commandery of the Military Order of the Loyal Legion of the United States*. Kansas City, MO: Franklin Hudson Publishing Company, 1906.

Cooksey, Paul Clark. "They Died As If on Dress Parade: The Annihilation of Iverson's Brigade at Gettysburg and the Battle of Oak Ridge." *Gettysburg Magazine*, #20, January 1999, 89–112.

Cooper, Peter J. *Samuel's Story: A Journey from Yorkshire to New Hampshire through the American Civil War*. Victoria, BC: Friesen Press, 2013.

Cox, Jacob Dolson. "The Battle of Antietam," in *Battles and Leaders of the Civil War*, Vol. 2. New York: Century Company, 1888.

Cox, Jacob Dolson. *Military Reminiscences of the Civil War, Volume I, April 1861–November 1863*. New York: Charles Scribner's Sons, 1900.

Cullom, George W. *Biographical Register of the Officers and Graduates of the United States Military Academy at West Point, New York, Since Its Establishment in 1802*. Vol. II. Boston: Houghton, Mifflin, and Company, 1891.

Curtis, O. B. *History of the Twenty-Fourth Michigan of the Iron Brigade*. Gaithersburg, MD: Olde Soldier Books, reprinted 1988.

Davis, Charles E., Jr. *Three Years in the Army: The Story of the Thirteenth Massachusetts Volunteers from July 16, 1861 to August 1, 1864*. Boston: Estes and Lauriat, 1894.

Dawes, Rufus R. *A Full Blown Yankee of the Iron Brigade: Service with the Sixth Wisconsin Volunteers*. Lincoln: University of Nebraska Press, 1999.

dePuyster, J. Watts. *The Decisive Conflicts of the Late Civil War, or Slaveholders' Rebellion*, #3. New York: MacDonald & Company, 1867.

Dickson, Christopher C. "The Flying Brigade: Brig. Gen. George Stannard and the Road to Gettysburg." *Gettysburg Magazine*, #16, January 1997, 6–26.

Doubleday, Abner. *Chancellorsville and Gettysburg*. New York: Charles Scribner's Sons, 1882.

Doubleday, Abner. *Gettysburg Made Plain*. New York: Century Company, 1888.

Dougherty, James J. *Stone's Brigade and the Fight for McPherson Farm: Battle of Gettysburg, July 1, 1863*. Boston: Da Capo, 2001.

Dreese, Michael A. "The 151st Pennsylvania Volunteers at Gettysburg: July 1, 1863." *Gettysburg Magazine*, #23, July 2000, 51–65.

Dreese, Michael A. *The 151st Pennsylvania Volunteers at Gettysburg: Like Ripe Apples in a Storm*. Jefferson, NC: McFarland & Company, Inc., 2000.

Dreese, Michael A. "Ordeal in the Lutheran Theological Seminary: The Recollections of First Lt. Jeremiah Hoffman, 142nd Pennsylvania Volunteers." *Gettysburg Magazine*, #23, July 2000, 101–10.

Dunn, Craig L. *Iron Men, Iron Will: The Nineteenth Indiana Regiment of the Iron Brigade*. Indianapolis: Guild Press, 1995.

Durkin, James. "Never Shirking a Duty or Betraying a Trust." *Gettysburg Magazine*, #14, January 1996, 37–45.

Eberly, Richard E., Jr. *Bouquets from the Cannon's Mouth: Soldiering with the Eighth Regiment of the Pennsylvania Reserves*. Shippensburg, PA: White Mane Books, 2005.

Eicher, John H., and David J. Eicher. *Civil War High Commands*. Stanford, CA: Stanford University Press, 2001.

Elmore, Thomas L. "The Effects of Artillery Fire on Infantry at Gettysburg." *Gettysburg Magazine*, #5, July 1991, 117–22.

Elmore, Thomas L. "Torrid Heat and Blinding Rain: A Meteorological and Astronomical Chronology of the Gettysburg Campaign." *Gettysburg Magazine*, #13, July 1995, 7–21.

Felton, Silas. "The Iron Brigade Battery: An Irregular Regular Battery," in *Giants in Their Tall Black Hats: Essays on the Iron Brigade*, Alan T. Nolan and Sharon Eggleston Vipond, eds. Bloomington: Indiana University Press, 1998, 142–59.

Felton, Silas. "The Iron Brigade Battery at Gettysburg." *Gettysburg Magazine*, #11, July 1994, 56–65.

Fishel, Edwin. *The Secret War for the Union: The Untold Story of Military Intelligence in the Civil War*. Boston: Houghton Mifflin Company, 1996.

Fox, William F. *Regimental Losses in the American Civil War, 1861–1865*. Albany, NY: Brandow Printing Company, 1889.

Furgurson, Ernest B. *Chancellorsville, 1863: Souls of the Brave*. New York: Vintage Books, 1992.

Gaff, Alan D. *Brave Men's Tears: The Battle of Brawner Farm*. Dayton, OH: Morningside Bookshop, 1985.

Gaff, Alan D. "'Here Was Made Out Our Last and Hopeless Stand': The 'Lost' Gettysburg Reports of the Nineteenth Indiana." *Gettysburg Magazine*, #2, January 1990, 25–31.

Gaff, Alan D. *On Many a Bloody Field: Four Years in the Iron Brigade*. Bloomington: Indiana University Press, 1996.

Gates, Theodore B. *The "Ulster Guard" and the War of the Rebellion*. New York: Benjamin H. Tyrrel, 1879.

Gibbon, John. *Personal Recollections of the Civil War*. New York: G. P. Putnam's Sons, 1928.

Gibbs, Joseph. *Three Years in the Bloody Eleventh: The Campaigns of a Pennsylvania Reserves Regiment*. University City: Pennsylvania State University Press, 2002.

Goetz, Robert. *1805: Austerlitz, Napoleon and the Destruction of the Third Coalition*. Mechanicsburg, PA: Stackpole Books, 2005.

Goss, Warren Lee. *Recollections of a Private: A Story of the Army of the Potomac*. New York: Thomas Y Crowell and Company, 1890.

Gottfried, Bradley M. *The Maps of Antietam: An Atlas of the Antietam (Sharpsburg) Campaign, Including the Battle of South Mountain, September 2–20, 1862*. New York: Savas Beatie, 2013.

Gottfried, Bradley M. *The Maps of Fredericksburg: An Atlas of the Fredericksburg Campaign, Including All Cavalry Operations, September 18, 1862–January 22, 1863*. El Dorado Hills, CA: Savas Beatie, 2018.

Gottfried, Bradley M. *The Maps of Gettysburg: An Atlas of the Gettysburg Campaign, June 3–July 13, 1863.* New York: Savas Beatie, 2008.

Gottfried, Bradley M. "To Fail Twice: Brockenbrough's Brigade at Gettysburg." *Gettysburg Magazine*, #23, July 2000, 66–75.

Gragg, Rod. *Covered with Glory: The 26th North Carolina Infantry at the Battle of Gettysburg.* New York: HarperCollins, 2000.

Greene, A. Wilson. "Morale, Maneuver, and Mud: The Army of the Potomac, December 16, 1862–January 26, 1863," in *The Fredericksburg Campaign: Decision on the Rappahannock*, Gary W. Gallagher, ed. Chapel Hill: University of North Carolina Press, 1995, 171–227.

Greene, Jacob L. *Gen. William B. Franklin and the Operations of the Left Wing at the Battle of Fredericksburg, December 13, 1862.* Hartford, CT: Belknap and Warfield, 1900.

Griffin, D. Massy. "Rodes on Oak Hill: A Study of Rodes' Division on the First Day at Gettysburg." *Gettysburg Magazine*, #4, January 1991, 33–48.

Hadden, R. Lee. "The Deadly Embrace: The Meeting of the Twenty-fourth Regiment, Michigan Infantry and the Twenty-sixth Regiment of North Carolina Troops at McPherson's Woods, Gettysburg, Pennsylvania, July 1, 1863." *Gettysburg Magazine*, #5, July 1991, 19–33.

Hall, Isaac. *History of the Ninety-Seventh Regiment New York Volunteers ("Conkling Rifles") in the War for the Union.* Utica, NY: L. C. Childs & Son, 1890.

Hardin, M. D. *History of the Twelfth Regiment Pennsylvania Reserve Volunteer Corps.* New York: self-published, 1890.

Harsh, Joseph L. *Taken at the Flood: Robert E. Lee and Confederate Strategy in the Maryland Campaign of 1862.* Kent, OH: Kent State University Press, 1999.

Hartwig, D. Scott. "The Defense of McPherson Ridge." *Gettysburg Magazine*, #1, July 1989, 15–24.

Hartwig, D. Scott. "Guts and Good Leadership: The Action at the Railroad Cut, July 1, 1863." *Gettysburg Magazine*, #1, July 1989, 5–14.

Hartwig, D. Scott. "'I Dread the Thought of the Place': The Iron Brigade at Antietam," in *Giants in Their Tall Black Hats: Essays on the Iron Brigade*, Alan T. Nolan and Sharon Eggleston Vipond, eds. Bloomington: Indiana University Press, 1998, 30–52.

Hartwig, D. Scott. *To Antietam Creek: The Maryland Campaign of September 1862.* Baltimore: John Hopkins University Press, 2012.

Hassler, Warren W. *Crisis at the Crossroads: The First Day at Gettysburg.* Gettysburg, PA: Stan Clark Military Books, 1991.

Hawkins, Norma Fuller. "Sergeant-Major Blanchard at Gettysburg." Vol. 34, No. 2 (June 1938).

Hebert, Walter H. *Fighting Joe Hooker.* Lincoln: University of Nebraska Press, 1999.

Heenehen, Jim. "Correcting the Record: The Court-Martial and Acquittal of Col. Ira Grover, 7th Indiana Infantry." *Gettysburg Magazine*, #45, July 2011, 71–83.

Hennessy, John J. "I Dread the Spring: The Army of the Potomac Prepares for the Overland Campaign," in *The Wilderness Campaign*, Gary W. Gallagher, ed. Chapel Hill: University of North Carolina Press, 1997, 72–81.

Hennessy, John J. *Return to Bull Run: The Campaign and Battle of Second Manassas.* New York: Simon and Schuster, 1993.

Herdegen, Lance J. *The Iron Brigade in Civil War and Memory.* El Dorado Hills, CA: Savas Beatie, 2012.

Herdegen, Lance J. "The Lieutenant Who Arrested a General." *Gettysburg Magazine,* #4, January 1991, 25–32.

Herdegen, Lance J. *The Men Stood Like Iron: How the Iron Brigade Won Its Name.* Bloomington: Indiana University Press, 1997.

Herdegen, Lance J. "Old Soldiers and War Talk: The Controversy Over the Opening Infantry Fight at Gettysburg." *Gettysburg Magazine,* #2, January 1990, 15–24.

Herdegen, Lance J. *Those Damned Black Hats!: The Iron Brigade in the Gettysburg Campaign.* New York: Savas Beatie, 2008.

Herdegen, Lance J., and William J. K. Beaudot. *In the Bloody Railroad Cut at Gettysburg.* Dayton, OH: Morningside House, Inc., 1990.

Herdegen, Lance J., and William J. K. Beaudot, eds. "With the Iron Brigade Guard at Gettysburg." *Gettysburg Magazine,* #1, July 1989, 29–34.

Herdegen, Lance J., and Sherry Murphy, eds. *Four Years with the Iron Brigade: The Civil War Journal of William Ray.* Cambridge, MA: Da Capo Press, 2002.

Hess, Earl J. *Pickett's Charge—The Last Attack at Gettysburg.* Chapel Hill: University of North Carolina Press, 2001.

Hill, D. H. "The Battle of South Mountain, or Boonsboro: Fighting for Time at Turner's and Fox's Gaps," in *Battles and Leaders of the Civil War,* Vol. 2. New York: Century Company, 1888.

Himmer, Robert. "A Matter of Time: The Issuance of the Pipe Creek Circular." *Gettysburg Magazine,* #46, January 2012, 7–18.

Hood, John Bell. *Advance and Retreat: Personal Experiences in the United States and Confederate States Armies.* New York: Da Capo Press, 1993.

Hoptak, John David. *The Battle of South Mountain.* Charleston, SC: History Press, 2011.

Hough, Franklin B. *History of Duryee's Brigade During the Campaign in Virginia Under Gen. Pope, and in Maryland Under Gen. McClellan in the Summer and Autumn of 1862.* Albany, NY: J. Munsell, 1864.

Howard, Oliver Otis. *The Autobiography of Oliver Otis Howard.* Vol. 1. New York: Trow Press, 1907.

Huntington, Tom. *Maine Roads to Gettysburg: How Joshua Chamberlain, Oliver Howard, and 4,000 Men from the Pine Tree State Helped Win the Civil War's Bloodiest Battle.* Guilford, CT: Stackpole Books, 2018.

Hussey, George A., and William Todd. *History of the Ninth Regiment N.Y.S.M., N.G.S.N.Y. Eighty-Third N.Y. Volunteers, 1845–1888.* New York: Press of J. B. Ogilvie, 1889.

Jamieson, Perry D. *Death in September: The Antietam Campaign.* Fort Worth, TX: Ryan Place Publishers, 1995.

Jaques, John W. *Three Years' Campaign of the Ninth N.Y.S.M. During the Southern Rebellion.* New York: Hilton and Co., 1865.

Johnson, David E. *Four Years a Soldier.* Princeton, WV: 1887.

Jordan, Brian M. *Unholy Sabbath: The Battle of South Mountain in History and Memory.* New York: Savas Beatie, 2012.

Jordan, David M. *Winfield Scott Hancock: A Soldier's Life.* Bloomington: Indiana University Press, 1996.

Kent, Arthur A., ed. *Three Years with Company K: Sergt. Austin C. Stearns, Company K, 13th Mass. Infantry.* Rutherford, NJ: Fairleigh Dickinson University Press, 1976.

Klingenberg, Mitchell G. "Of Cupolas and Sharpshooters: Major General John Fulton Reynolds and Popular Gettysburg Myths." *Gettysburg Magazine,* #59, July 2018, 49–65.

Kreiser, Lawrence A., Jr. *Defeating Lee: A History of the Second Corps, Army of the Potomac.* Bloomington: Indiana University Press, 2011.

Krick, Robert K. "Three Confederate Disasters on Oak Ridge: Failures of Brigade Leadership on the First Day at Gettysburg," in *The First Day at Gettysburg: Essays on Confederate and Union Leadership,* Gary W. Gallagher, ed. Kent, OH: Kent State University Press, 1992, 92–139.

Krumwiede, John F. *Disgrace at Gettysburg: The Arrest and Court-Martial of Brigadier General Thomas A. Rowley, USA.* Jefferson, NC: McFarland & Company, 2006.

Ladd, David L., and Audrey J. Ladd, eds. *The Bachelder Papers: Gettysburg in Their Own Words.* 3 vols. Dayton, OH: Morningside House, 1994.

Lash, Gary G. "Brig. Gen. Henry Baxter's Brigade at Gettysburg, July 1." *Gettysburg Magazine,* #10, July 1994, 6–27.

Lash, Gary. *The Gibraltar Brigade on East Cemetery Hill.* Baltimore: Butternut and Blue, 1995.

Leohr, Charles T. *War History of the Old First Virginia Infantry Regiment, Army of Northern Virginia.* Richmond, VA: William Ellis Jones, 1884.

Locke, William Henry. *The Story of the Regiment.* Philadelphia: J. B. Lippincott and Company, 1868.

Long, Roger. "A Mississippian in the Railroad Cut." *Gettysburg Magazine,* #4, January 1991, 22–24.

Longacre, Edward G. *The Cavalry at Gettysburg: A Tactical Study of Mounted Operations During the Civil War's Pivotal Campaign, 9 June–14 July 1863.* Lincoln, NE: Bison Books, 1993.

Love, William DeLoss. *Wisconsin in the War of the Rebellion.* Chicago: Church and Goodman, 1866.

Lowry, Thomas P. *Tarnished Eagles: The Courts-Martial of Fifty Union Colonels and Lieutenant Colonels.* Mechanicsburg, PA: Stackpole Books, 1997.

Mackowski, Chris, and Kristopher D. White. *Chancellorsville's Forgotten Front: The Battles of Second Fredericksburg and Salem Church, May 3, 1863.* El Dorado, CA: Savas Beatie, 2013.

Maharay, George A. *Vermont Hero: Major General George J. Stannard.* Shippensburg, PA: White Mane Books, 2001.

Mahood, Wayne. *General Wadsworth: The Life and Times of Brevet Major General James S. Wadsworth.* Cambridge, MA: Da Capo Press, 2003.

Martin, David G. *Gettysburg, July 1.* Conshohocken, PA: Combined Books, 1996.

Marvel, William. *The First New Hampshire Battery, 1861–1865.* Conway, NH: Minuteman Press, 1985.

Marvel, William. "The Making of a Myth: Ambrose E. Burnside and the Union High Command at Fredericksburg," in *The Fredericksburg Campaign: Decision on the Rappahannock,* Gary W. Gallagher, ed. Chapel Hill: University of North Carolina Press, 1995, 1–25.

Matthews, Richard E. *The 149th Pennsylvania Volunteer Infantry Unit in the Civil War.* Jefferson, NC: McFarland and Company, 1994.

Maxson, William P. *Camp Fires of the Twenty-Third.* New York: Davies & Kent, 1863.

McClellan, George B. *McClellan's Own Story.* New York: Charles L. Webster & Company, 1887.

McClellan, George B. "The Peninsular Campaign," in *Hearts Touched By Fire: The Best of Battles and Leaders of the Civil War.* New York: Modern Library, 2011, 336–64.

McClellan, George B. *Report on the Organization and Campaigns of the Army of the Potomac in Virginia and Maryland.* New York: Sheldon and Company, 1864.

McClenthen, Charles. *Narrative of the Fall & Winter Campaign, by a Private Soldier of the 2nd Div. 1st Army Corps.* Syracuse, NY: Masters & Lee, 1863.

McLean, James L. *Cutler's Brigade at Gettysburg.* Baltimore: Butternut and Blue, 1994.

McLean, James. "The Execution of John Wood on the March to Gettysburg." *Gettysburg Magazine,* #45, July 2011, 7–22.

McMurry, Richard M. *John Bell Hood and the War for Southern Independence.* Lincoln: University of Nebraska Press, 1992.

Meade, George G. *Life and Letters of George Gordon Meade, Major-General United States Army.* George Gordon Meade Jr., ed., Vol. 1. New York: Charles Scribner's Sons, 1913.

Miller, J. Michael. "Perrin's Brigade on July 1, 1863." *Gettysburg Magazine,* #13, July 1995, 22–32.

Mills, J. Harrison. *Chronicles of the Twenty-First Regiment, New York State Volunteers.* Buffalo: Gies and Company, 1887.

Mingus, Scott L., Sr. *The Louisiana Tigers in the Gettysburg Campaign: June–July 1863.* Baton Rouge: Louisiana State University Press, 2009.

Moore, Rogan H., ed. *The Civil War Memoirs of Sergeant George W. Darby, 1861–1865.* Bowie, MD: Heritage Books, 1999.

Morrel, Carl A. *Seymour Dexter, Union Army: Journal and Letters of Civil War Service in Company K, 23rd N.Y. Volunteer Regiment of Elmira, with Illustrations.* Jefferson, NC: McFarland and Company, 1996.

Nelson, L. Patrick. "Reynolds and the Decision to Fight." *Gettysburg Magazine,* #23, July 2000, 31–50.

Nevins, Allan, ed. *A Diary of Battle: The Personal Journals of Colonel Charles S. Wainwright.* Boston: Da Capo Press, 1998.

Nicholson, John P., ed. *Pennsylvania at Gettysburg: Ceremonies at the Dedication of the Monuments Erected by the Commonwealth of Pennsylvania.* Vol. II. Harrisburg, PA: E. K. Meyers, 1893.

Nolan, Alan T. *The Iron Brigade: A Military History*. Bloomington: Indiana University Press, 1994.

Nolan, Alan T. "Three Flags at Gettysburg." *Gettysburg Magazine*, #1, July 1989, 25–28.

Noyes, George F. *The Bivouac and the Battlefield*. New York: Harper & Brothers, 1863.

O'Brien, Kevin E. "'Give Them Another Volley, Boys': Biddle's Brigade Defends the Union Left on July 1, 1863." *Gettysburg Magazine*, #19, July 1998, 37–52.

O'Reilly, Francis Augustin. *The Fredericksburg Campaign: Winter War on the Rappahannock*. Baton Rouge: Louisiana State University Press, 2003.

O'Reilly, Frank A. *"Stonewall" Jackson at Fredericksburg: The Battle of Prospect Hill, December 13, 1862*. Lynchburg, VA: H. E. Howard, Inc., 1993.

Otott, George E. "Clash in the Cornfield: The 1st Texas Volunteer Infantry in the Maryland Campaign." *Civil War Regiments*, Vol. V, No. 3. El Dorado, CA: Savas Publishing Company, 1997.

Palfrey, Francis Winthrop. *The Antietam and Fredericksburg*. Campaigns of the Civil War—V. New York: Scribner's and Sons, 1882.

Palmer, Edwin F. *The Second Brigade; or Camp Life*. Montpelier, VT: E. P. Walton, 1864.

Park, Robert Emory. *Sketch of the Twelfth Alabama Infantry of Battle's Brigade, Rodes' Division, Early's Corps of the Army of Northern Virginia*. Richmond, VA: William Ellis Jones, 1906.

Pearson, Henry Greenleaf. *James S. Wadsworth of Geneseo: Brevet Major-General of United States Volunteers*. New York: Charles Scribner's Sons, 1913.

Pfanz, Harry W. *Gettysburg: Culp's Hill and Cemetery Hill*. Chapel Hill: University of North Carolina Press, 1993.

Pfanz, Harry W. *Gettysburg: The First Day*. Chapel Hill: University of North Carolina Press, 2001.

Pierro, Joseph, ed. *The Maryland Campaign of September 1862: Ezra Carman's Definitive Study of the Union and Confederate Armies at Antietam*. New York: Routledge, 2008.

Potts, Charles P. "A First Defender in Rebel Prison Pens." *Publications of the Historical Society of Schuylkill County*. Vol. IV. Pottsville, PA: Daily Republican Print, 1914.

Priest, John Michael. *Antietam: The Soldiers' Battle*. New York: Oxford University Press, 1989.

Priest, John Michael. *Before Antietam: The Battle for South Mountain*. Shippensburg, PA: White Mane Publishing Company, 1992.

Pula, James S. "'A Promiscuous Fight': The Defense of Cemetery Hill." *Gettysburg Magazine*, #59, July 2018, 15–29.

Pula, James S. *Under the Crescent Moon with the XI Corps in the Civil War, Volume 1: From the Defenses of Washington to Chancellorsville, 1862–1863*. El Dorado Hills, CA: Savas Beatie, 2017.

Pula, James S. *Under the Crescent Moon with the XI Corps in the Civil War, Volume 2: From Gettysburg to Victory, 1863–1865*. El Dorado Hills, CA: Savas Beatie, 2018.

Quiner, E. B., *E. B. Quiner Papers: Correspondence of the Wisconsin Volunteers, 1861–1865*. Madison, WI: State Historical Society of Wisconsin.

Rable, George C. *Fredericksburg! Fredericksburg!* Chapel Hill: University of North Carolina Press, 2002.

Rable, George C. "It Is Well That War Is So Terrible: The Carnage of Fredericksburg," in *The Fredericksburg Campaign*, Gary W. Gallagher, ed. Chapel Hill: University of North Carolina Press, 1995, 48–79.

Rafuse, Ethan. *George Gordon Meade and the War in the East*. Abilene, TX: McWhiney Foundation Press, 2003.

Rafuse, Ethan. *McClellan's War: The Failure of Moderation in the Struggle for the Union*. Bloomington: Indiana University Press, 2005.

Reid-Green, Marcia, ed. *Letters Home: Henry Matrau of the Iron Brigade*. Lincoln, NE: Bison Books, 1998.

Report of Maine Commissioners. *Maine at Gettysburg*. Portland, ME: Lakeside Press, 1898.

Rhea, Gordon C. *The Battle of the Wilderness, May 5-6, 1864*. Baton Rouge: Louisiana State University Press, 1994.

Rhea, Gordon C. *The Battles for Spotsylvania Court House and the Road to Yellow Tavern, May 7–12, 1864*. Baton Rouge: Louisiana State University Press, 1997.

Robertson, James I., Jr. *Stonewall Jackson: The Man, The Soldier, The Legend*. New York: Macmillan Publishing, 1997.

Ross, Sam. *The Empty Sleeve: A Biography of Lucius Fairchild*. Stevens Point, WI: Worzalla Publishing, 1964.

Ryan, Thomas J., and Richard R. Schaus. "'Our Task Is Not Yet Accomplished': Meade's Decision Making After Victory at Gettysburg, July 4, 1863." *Gettysburg Magazine*, #59, July 2018, 30–48.

Sandburg, Carl. *Abraham Lincoln: The War Years*. New York: Harcourt, Brace & Company, 1939.

Sanders, Steve. "Enduring Tales of Gettysburg: The Death of Reynolds." *Gettysburg Magazine*, #14, January 1996, 27–36.

Sauers, Richard A. "The 16th Maine Volunteer Infantry at Gettysburg." *Gettysburg Magazine*, #13, July 1995, 33–42.

Sayre, R. B. "A Day at Gettysburg." *National Tribune*, April 13, 1899.

Schildt, John W. *Roads to Antietam*. Shippensburg, PA: Burd Street Press, 1997.

Schildt, John W. *Roads to Gettysburg*. Parsons, WV: McClain Printing Company, 2003.

Scott, George H. "Vermont at Gettysburgh." *Proceedings of the Vermont Historical Society*, Vol. I, No. 2 (1930).

Sears, Stephen W. *Chancellorsville*. Boston: Houghton Mifflin, 1996.

Sears, Stephen W. *George B. McClellan: The Young Napoleon*. Cambridge, MA: Da Capo Press, 1999.

Sears, Stephen W. *Gettysburg*. Boston: Houghton Mifflin Company, 2003.

Sears, Stephen W. *Landscape Turned Red: The Battle of Antietam*. Boston: Houghton Mifflin, 1983.

Sears, Stephen W. *To the Gates of Richmond: The Peninsula Campaign*. New York: Ticknor and Fields, 1992.

Sears, Stephen W., ed. *The Civil War Papers of George B. McClellan, Selected Correspondence 1860–1865*. Cambridge, MA: Da Capo Press, 1992.

Shepard, E. W. *The Campaign in Virginia and Maryland: June 26th to Sept 20th, 1862*. London: George Allen and Comp., 1911.

Shue, Richard S. *Morning at Willoughby Run: The Opening Battle at Gettysburg, July 1, 1863*. Gettysburg, PA: Thomas Publications, 1998.

Simpson, Brooks D. "General McClellan's Bodyguard: The Army of the Potomac After Antietam," in *The Antietam Campaign*, Gary W. Gallagher, ed. Chapel Hill: University of North Carolina Press, 1999, 44–73.

Slotkin, Richard. *The Long Road to Antietam: How the Civil War Became a Revolution*. New York: Liveright Publishing Company, 2012.

Small, A. R. *The Sixteenth Maine Regiment in the War of the Rebellion, 1861–1865*. Portland, ME: B. Thurston & Company, 1886.

Smith, Abram. *History of the Seventy-Sixth Regiment New York Volunteers*. Cortland, NY: Truair, Smith, and Miles, 1867.

Smith, Donald L. *The Twenty-Fourth Michigan of the Iron Brigade*. Harrisburg, PA: Stackpole Company, 1962.

Starr, Louis M. *Bohemian Brigade: Civil War Newsmen in Action*. New York: Alfred A. Knopf, 1954.

Stevens, Charles A. *Berdan's United States Sharpshooters in the Army of the Potomac, 1861–1865*. St. Paul, MN: Price-McGill Company, 1892.

Stevens, Greenleaf. *Letter to Members of the Fifth Maine Battery Association*. Augusta, ME: Charles E. Nash, 1890.

Stewart, James. "Battery B of the Fourth U.S. Artillery at Gettysburg." *Sketches of War History 1861–1865, Papers Read Before Ohio Commandery, Military Order of the Loyal Legion of the United States*. Vol. 4.

Stine, J. H. *History of the Army of the Potomac*, 2nd ed. Washington, DC: Gibson Bros., 1893.

Stoker, Donald. *The Grand Design: Strategy and the U.S. Civil War*. New York: Oxford University Press, 2010.

Storch, Marc, and Beth Storch. "'Like So Many Devils': The Iron Brigade at Fitzhugh's Crossing," in *Giants in Their Tall Black Hats*, Alan T. Nolan and Sharon Eggleston Vipond, eds. Bloomington: Indiana University Press, 1998, 86–100.

Storch, Marc, and Beth Storch. "'What a Deadly Trop We Were In': Archer's Brigade on July 1, 1863." *Gettysburg Magazine*, #6, January 1992, 13–27.

Sturtevant, Ralph Orson, and Carmi Lathrop Marsh. *Pictorial History of the Thirteenth Regiment Vermont Volunteers, War of 1861–1865*. Privately published, 1910.

Survivors' Association. *History of the 121st Regiment Pennsylvania Volunteers*. Philadelphia: Catholic Standards and Times, 1906.

Swinton, William. *Campaigns of the Army of the Potomac*. Secaucus, NJ: Blue & Grey Press, 1988.

Swisher, James K. *Warrior in Grey: General Robert Rodes of Lee's Army*. Shippensburg, PA: White Mane Books, 2000.

Sword, Wiley. "An Iron Brigade Captain's Revolver in the Fight on McPherson's Ridge." *Gettysburg Magazine*, #7, July 1992, 6–12.

Sypher, J. R. *History of the Pennsylvania Reserve Corps*. Lancaster, PA: Elias Barr & Co., 1865.

Tagg, Larry. *The Generals of Gettysburg: The Leaders of America's Greatest Battle*. Cambridge, MA: Da Capo Press, 1998.

Taylor, Paul. *Glory Was Not Their Companion: The Twenty-Sixth New York Volunteer Infantry in the Civil War*. Jefferson, NC: McFarland and Company, Inc., 2005.

Tevis, C. V., and D. R. Marquis. *The History of the Fighting Fourteenth*. New York: Brooklyn Eagle Press, 1911.

Thomson, O. R. Howard, and William H. Rauch. *History of the "Bucktails," Kane Rifle Regiment of the Pennsylvania Reserve Corps (13th Pennsylvania Reserves, 42nd of the Line)*. Philadelphia: Electric Printing Company, 1906.

Tompkins, Daniel. *Company K, Fourteenth South Carolina Volunteers*. Charlotte, NC: Observer Printing, 1897.

Trimble, Tony. "Paper Collars: Stannard's Brigade at Gettysburg." *Gettysburg Magazine*, #2, January 1990, 74–79.

Trudeau, Noah Andre. *Gettysburg: A Testing of Courage*. New York: Harper Collins, 2001.

Urban, John W. *My Experiences Mid Shot and Shell and in Rebel Den*. Lancaster, PA: Hubbard Brothers, 1882.

Vautier, John D. *History of the 88th Pennsylvania Volunteers in the War for the Union, 1861–1865*. Philadelphia: J. B. Lippincott, 1894.

Venner, William Thomas. *The 19th Indiana Infantry at Gettysburg: Hoosiers' Courage*. Shippensburg, PA: Burd Street Press, 1998.

Ward, Eric, ed. *Army Life in Virginia: The Civil War Letters of George G. Benedict*. Mechanicsburg, PA: Stackpole Books, 2002.

Warner, Ezra. *Generals in Blue: Lives of the Union Commanders*. Baton Rouge: Louisiana State University Press, 1992.

Warren, Horatio N. *The Declaration of Independence and War History: Bull Run to the Appomattox*. Buffalo: The Courier Company, 1894.

Waugh, John C. *The Class of 1846: From West Point to Appomattox: Stonewall Jackson, George McClellan and Their Brothers*. New York: Ballantine Books, 1994.

Waugh, John C. *Lincoln and McClellan: The Troubled Partnership Between a President and His General*. New York: Palgrave Macmillan, 2010.

Weld, Stephen Minot. *War Diary and Letters of Stephen Minot Weld*. Privately printed, 1912.

Wert, Jeffry D. *A Brotherhood of Valor: The Common Soldiers of the Stonewall Brigade, C.S.A., and the Iron Brigade, U.S.A*. New York: Simon & Schuster, 1999.

Wert, Jeffry D. *Gettysburg: Day Three*. New York: Simon & Schuster, 2002.

Wert, Jeffry D. *The Sword of Lincoln: The Army of the Potomac*. New York: Simon & Schuster, 2005.

Wheeler, William. *In Memoriam: Letters of William Wheeler of the Class of 1855, Yale College*. Cambridge, MA: H. O. Houghton and Company, 1875.

Whittier, Edward N. "The Left Attack (Ewell's) Gettysburg," in *Campaigns in Virginia, Maryland and Pennsylvania 1862–1863*. Boston: Griffith-Stillings, 1903, 315–50.

Williams, J. C. *Life in Camp: A History of the Nine Months' Service of the Fourteenth Vermont Regiment, from October 21, 1862, When It Was Mustered into the U.S. Service, to July 21, 1863, Including the Battle of Gettysburg.* Claremont, NH: Claremont Manufacturing Company, 1864.

Winschel, Terrence J. "The Colors Are Shrowded in Mystery." *Gettysburg Magazine*, #6, January 1992, 76–86.

Winschel, Terrence J. "Part I: Heavy Was Their Loss: Joe Davis' Brigade at Gettysburg." *Gettysburg Magazine*, #2, January 1990, 5–14.

Wittenberg, Eric J. *"The Devil's to Pay": John Buford at Gettysburg, A History and Walking Tour.* El Dorado Hills, CA: Savas Beatie, 2015.

Wittenberg, Eric J. "John Buford and the Gettysburg Campaign." *Gettysburg Magazine*, #11, July 1994, 19–55.

Woodward, Evan Morrison. *History of the Third Pennsylvania Reserve: Being a Complete Record of the Regiment, with Incidents of the Camp, Marches, Bivouacs, Skirmishes and Battles; Together with the Personal Record of Every Officer and Man During His Term of Service.* Trenton, NJ: MacCrellish & Quigley, 1883.

Woodward, Evan Morrison. *Our Campaigns: Marches, Bivouacs, Battles, Incidents of Camp Life and History of Our Regiment During Its Three Years Term of Service.* Philadelphia: John E. Potter and Company, 1865.

Wynstra, Robert J. *The Rashness of That Hour: Politics, Gettysburg, and the Downfall of Confederate Brigadier General Alfred Iverson.* New York: Savas Beatie, 2010.

Index

8- 13- 21